D1236231

Israel Undercover

Contemporary Issues in the Middle East

ISRAEL UNDERCOVER

*Secret Warfare and Hidden Diplomacy
in the Middle East*

STEVE POSNER

Syracuse University Press

Copyright © 1987 by Syracuse University Press
Syracuse, New York 13244-5160

All Rights Reserved

First published 1987

First Edition
92 91 90 89 88 87   5 4 3 2 1

Library of Congress Cataloging-in-Publication Data

Posner, Steve
  Israel undercover: secret warfare and hidden diplomacy in the
Middle East / Steve Posner—1st ed.
    p. cm.—(Contemporary issues in the Middle East)
  Bibliography: p.
  Includes index.
  ISBN 0-8156-0220-0
  1. Israel-Arab conflicts. 2. Espionage—Israel. 3. Israel.
Sherut ha-bitahon ha-kelali. 4. Fedayeen. I. Title. II. Series.
DS119.7.P68 1987
956'.04—dc19   87-18811
                                                                     CIP

Manufactured in the United States of America

To enemies everywhere, who with the help of God may one day grow strong enough to declare their right to peace rather than the righteousness of their cause.

And to my wife, Mona, who teaches love daily, and made my life complete.

Steve Posner has spent more than seven years researching material for *Israel Undercover*, conducting interviews in cities across the U.S., Europe, and the Middle East. A published author and screenwriter, he holds an M.A. in Professional Writing and has taught writing at the University of Southern California.

Contents

Contents

Preface

INTELLIGENCE agencies like the CIA and the KGB are often viewed as tools for carrying out "dirty tricks," covert operations that lead to government coups, illegal bombings, and political killings. But in the Middle East, undercover operatives are frequently called upon to serve a dual purpose: to wage clandestine warfare behind enemy lines and to help public officials carry out secret diplomatic moves that would be impossible if conducted under the glare of the world press.

Israel Undercover: Secret Warfare and Hidden Diplomacy in the Middle East focuses on the execution of paramilitary operations against Palestinian terrorists and on the behind-the-scenes negotiations carried out among Arab statesmen, Israeli leaders, and American officials.

The book is divided into four sections: (1) *Inside Beirut*—Israel's use of its intelligence network in Lebanon during the 1970s to conduct military reprisals and its impact on the Israeli-Egyptian peace process; (2) *Across the River Jordan*—the decades-old secret relationship between Israeli leaders and Jordan's King Hussein; (3) *American Dreams*—America's quiet support for the Christian Phalangist militia and Washington's back-door channel to the PLO; (4) *The Mysterious Middle East*—the region's special mix of conspiracy and animosity.

In order to provide an historical setting and a political context for the events described in the book, I have included footnoted material from published sources and have integrated it with information gathered from private informants, some of whom have chosen to remain anonymous. In certain instances, names, places, dates, and other related details had to be fictionalized in order to protect the identity of espionage operatives, the security of contributors, and the effectiveness of ongoing intelligence procedures.

Acknowledgments

MANY people throughout the United States, Europe, and the Middle East offered their kind assistance and candid insights on a subject that arouses passionate emotions for both participants and observers of a crisis that has eluded solution for generations. Many of them opened their homes, their offices, and their hearts to discuss topics that for them are not merely political or cultural curiosities, but instead involve issues that directly impact their lives, families, friends, careers, futures, and the very question of their survival as part of a free people. To them I extend my sincere appreciation.

Leo Nevas, Warren and Harriet Berman, and Andrew Dickerman, without whose initial help and encouragement this book could have not been written, have my deep gratitude.

Barry Praver, who generously gave his time and expertise, deserves special thanks. For their helpful and diverse contributions to this project thanks also go to Mitchell Posner, Jeff Lederman, Dr. Richard Fliegel, Leslie and Jack Charney, Stan and Marian Praver, Bill Borden, Sylvia Sensiper, Dorothy King, Dr. George Irani, Bernard Nevas, Dr. Melanie Brown, Joe Domanick, Tim Ferris and Bob Pirosh and their colleagues at the University of Southern California's Professional Writing Program, and my agent Jonathan Dolger.

My parents, Faye and Ted Posner, who gave invaluable support during the many years of research and helped in the completion of the final manuscript, deserve a special note of appreciation.

None of the people who assisted in the preparation of this book predicated their aid on anything but the production of an honest work, even if it be ideologically objectionable or flawed in any other respect, nor does their association with my research imply an endorsement of the end result. For that I must take sole responsiblity, both for its possible merits as well as its shortcomings.

Santa Monica
Spring 1987

Israel Undercover

Inside Beirut

And Joshua the son of Nun sent out of Shit'tim two men to spy secretly, saying, Go view the land ...

Joshua 2:1

1

The Merciless Sword

IN THE Middle East, there are those who believe that the land cannot support both victor and vanquished. The terrain is barren, the water scarce. It is as if an unspoken commandment echoes through the region: destroy your enemy or see him rise again to steal your well and cut your throat. The dust and the sand seem to have left little room for compromise. Victory in battle is not enough; one has to annihilate the enemy.

Lebanon provides us with a tragic example: during this past decade of internecine battles, the country's Christian and Moslem communities have gone beyond the purely military aspects of war, perpetrating massacres, indiscriminately slaughtering their adversaries, civilian and soldier alike.

On 18 January 1976, during the height of the 1975-76 fighting in Lebanon, Christian fighters attacked the slum quarter known as Karantina near the port in East Beirut, killing hundreds of Lebanese Kurds, Shiite Moslems, Palestinians, and Syrian migrant workers, many of them civilians. "Christian militiamen with outsize wooden crosses around their necks, high on hashish or cocaine, and some wearing Nazi surplus helmets, killed to their heart's content," wrote *Washington Post* reporter Jonathan Randall, who witnessed the brutal aftermath.[1] Nearly all of the survivors were expelled to West Beirut. When the Christian forces finished emptying the quarter, they bulldozed it to the ground.

Five days later, on 23 January 1976, 16,000 Moslem troops stormed the Christian village of Damour, killing civilians and leaving half a dozen scalps strewn on the roads. The attackers included Palestinian commandos of the Syrian-backed Saiqa faction of the Palestine Liberation Organization (PLO); regular Syrian forces; Libyan fighters; mercenaries recruited from Iran, Afghanistan, and Pakistan; and units of sixteen Moslem militias including the Maourabitoun, a faction of Lebanese adherents to pan-Arab Nasserism.

"It was an apocalypse," said Father Mansour Labaky, a Christian Maronite priest who survived the massacre at Damour. "They were coming, thousands and thousands, shouting 'Allahu Akbar! God is great! Let us attack them for the Arabs, let us offer a holocaust to Mohammad!' And they were slaughtering everyone in their path, men, women and children."[2]

The carnage in Lebanon during the 1975-76 civil war was labeled a "carnival of death" by journalist Jillian Becker. Becker wrote that during the outbreak of fighting in the autumn of 1975, "dead and mutilated bodies lay everywhere in public places: corpses of sexually violated women and children, and of men with their genitals cut off and stuffed into their mouths."[3]

The bloodletting resumed on 16 September 1982, when Lebanese Christian soldiers from the Phalangist militia crossed into Moslem West Beirut and entered the Palestinian refugee camps at Sabra and Shatilla. The killing went on for thirty-six hours. Assad Germanos, the Lebanese military prosecutor in charge of investigating the massacre, reported that 328 bodies were recovered from the camps, while 991 people were never accounted for. Israeli intelligence estimated that the deaths at Sabra and Shatilla numbered between 700 and 800.[4] Nearly all of the victims were unarmed civilians.

In May 1985, in what became known as the Battle of the Camps, which pitted Lebanese Shiite Moslems against Palestinian refugees in Beirut, atrocities on both sides further testified to the region's extremist approach to war.

An Associated Press reporter was told by a Lebanese gunman that members of the Shiite Amal militia stopped ambulances carrying wounded Palestinians and "beat them up," and a *New York Times* reporter was told by witnesses that twenty-five Palestinians were pulled from Gaza hospital and shot to death.[5] "Even the Israelis didn't do this to us," one Palestinian woman said. Her young daughter had been killed when a mortar round fired by Amal militiamen hit their cinderblock home. Another reporter wrote that the Shiite attack against the Bourj al-Barajneh refugee camp appeared to have wrought almost as much destruction as that caused by the Israeli siege in August 1982, when the camp sustained week-long bombings.[6]

The United Nations Relief and Works Agency for Palestine Refugees (UNRWA) issued its own report documenting the Arab drive against the Palestinians in Lebanon:

> The month-long siege of Beirut Palestine refugee camps and neighbor-hoods which began on May 19 resulted in the death of at least 625 people and the injury of 2,500. Hundreds of refugee homes were damaged or

destroyed and most UNRWA installations in Shatilla and Burj el-Barajneh camps were damaged.

Over 33,000 Palestine refugees fled from their homes in Beirut to safer areas of the city (17,600), to Sidon (9,700), Tyre (4,300), Tripoli (1,800) and Baalbeck (200). In Beirut, UNRWA provided food and household supplies to displaced refugees living in garages and basements in 50 locations and emergency rations were provided to those who fled to other areas of Lebanon. Mobile medical teams with the help of Australian and French health workers looked after the thousands of displaced in Beirut.

Refugees remaining in Shatila [*sic*] and Burj el-Barajneh were totally isolated for weeks. On 7 June, UNRWA tried to get a convoy of food, water, medical supplies and sanitation equipment into Burj el-Barajneh. In the attempt, UNRWA's Lebanon Director Robert Gallagher and Austrian Ambassador to Lebanon Georg Znidaric and other UNRWA staff were held at gunpoint for three hours.[7]

There were also reports that PLO commandos had committed atrocities against Shiite Moslem civilians. Amal claimed that Palestinians had slipped into a hospital near the refugee camps, killing twelve wounded Shiites with axes and clubs. On 28 May, Amal's politburo chief Akef Haidar accused PLO forces of drugging the tea served to a garrison of Shiite militiamen stationed in a seven-story nursing home in West Beirut. They then crept into the building around 3 A.M., murdering twenty soldiers as they slept. The Palestinians "cut their throats and slaughtered them like sheep," Haidar charged.[8]

A year after the Battle of the Camps, toward the end of 1986, fighting between Palestinians and Shiites again erupted. Palestinians overran the Christian hilltop village of Maghdushah in Southern Lebanon, and Shiites besieged the Palestinian refugee camps of Sabra, Shatilla, and Bourj al-Barajneh outside Beirut, Ain al-Hilweh near Sidon, and Rashidieyh on the outskirts of Tyre, pounding the camps for nearly fifty days, the fighting leaving over 300 dead and 600 wounded on both sides.[9]

By the winter of 1987, the death toll had reached 700 with 2,000 injured. The cruelty reached new heights inside the Bourj al-Barajneh camp, where 30,000 Palestinian refugees had to endure a months-long cut-off of food supplies. The Shiite Amal militiamen had thrown a blockade around the camp, sealing off the area, halting all relief convoys, barring supplies of food, medicine, and fuel. "With no food and little heating in the cold weather, people have very little resistance to illnesses," Dr. Pauline Cutting, a British surgeon working inside Bourj al-Barajneh, reported. "One of my fellow doctors recently fainted in the operating room because he had gone without food for quite some time." Amal leader Nabih Berri had declared that only if PLO fighters abandoned Maghdushah and other positions that had been captured from Shiite militiamen in Southern Lebanon would he order an end to the siege of the camp in Beirut. As Amal and the PLO fought to a standoff, the men, women, and children of Bourj al-Barajneh were reduced to eating cats, dogs, and rats. "I have eaten dogs myself," Cutting told reporters by radio. "A Dutch nurse has seen five children cooking a rat and eating it hungrily." Malnutrition killed off babies in the camp, others were stricken with bouts of vomiting and diarrhea. "One woman was shot while trying to pick some grass to feed her seven children," Cutting said. Camp residents issued an appeal to the Moslem authorities asking for a religious ruling that would allow them to eat human flesh in order to survive the siege.[10]

Lebanon was once held up as an example of pluralistic harmony, its government carefully constructed to balance the rights of its diverse ethnic communities: Druze, Shiite Moslem, Sunni Moslem, Maronite Christian, Armenian Christian, Greek Orthodox, Greek Catholic. But a decade of bloody civil war set a different, perhaps more traditional, example for Mideast minorities: ethnic allegiances had triumphed over national loyalties.

The Lebanese fighting had "distinct communal and religious dimensions," wrote the Israeli scholar Itamar Rabinovich. "Religious hatred and fanaticism manifested in the 'identity card killings': individuals were kidnapped or arrested at roadblocks and executed if the religion designated on their identity cards was not in accord with their captors'."[11]

Such confessional strife had its parallels around the globe—in the brutalities between Sikhs and Hindus in India, Protestants and Catholics in Northern Ireland, Bahais and Shiites in Iran—but the proximity of the Lebanese quagmire made it particularly ominous for the Jews of Israel. In the past they had benefitted from the communal impulses of the Lebanese, impulses that had made Israel's northern neighbor one of the least threatening of all of the Arab states.

Of course, the savagery of Middle East internecine warfare has not been limited to Lebanon. In Syria, President Hafez Assad frequently unleashed his troops against his own people. In 1981, he sent his army into the Syrian village of Hama to crush a dissident uprising. The result was a massacre of at least twenty thousand people and the near total destruction of the town.

And in the war with Israel, Syrian officials boasted of their soldiers brutality. *Washington Post* reporter Lawrence Meyer quoted the Syrian defense minister who, in a speech honoring a war hero, described how he had killed twenty-eight Israelis:

> He butchered three of them with an ax and decapitated them. In other
> words, instead of using a gun to kill them he took a hatchet to chop off

their heads. He struggled face to face with one of them, and throwing down the ax managed to break his neck and devour his flesh in front of his comrades. This is a special case. Need I single it out to award him the Medal of the Republic? I will grant this medal to any soldier who succeeds in killing twenty-eight Jews, and I will cover him with appreciation and honor for his bravery.[12]

Kamal Joumblatt, the leader of the mystical Druze sect who was assassinated on 16 March 1977, once commented on the forces which fueled much of the Middle East's extremist violence: "The ferocity which ravaged Lebanon carried echoes of the practices of some of the ancient Hebrews, when, guided by their God, Yahweh, they swept into Palestine, killing men, women, children, horses, mules and donkeys, burning the harvests, cutting down trees and razing their enemies' houses. Nothing was to be left standing before this barbarian wave, this Bedouin fury, this bandit raid."[13]

In Deuteronomy, the God of the Old Testament did indeed instruct the Israelites to annihilate the inhabitants of those cities that fell within the boundaries of the Promised Land. They were to "utterly destroy them" so "that they teach you not to do after all their abominations, which they have done unto their gods, so should ye sin against the Lord your God."[14]

Mercy could prevail only in those places that lay beyond Israel's borders: "thou shalt smite every male thereof with the edge of the sword: but the women, and the little ones, and the cattle, and all that is in the city, even all the spoil thereof, shalt thou take unto thyself; and thou shalt eat the spoil of thine enemies, which the Lord thy God hath given thee."[15]

The practice of utter destruction was carried out during the conquest of Canaanite cities such as Jericho, where Joshua, obeying the commandments of his Lord, instructed his army to surround the city as the seven priests blew the seven trumpets: "and it came to pass, when the people heard the sound of the trumpet, and the people shouted with a great shout, that the wall fell down flat, so that the people went up into the city, every man straight before him, and they took the city.

"And they utterly destroyed all that was in the city, both man and woman, young and old, and ox, and sheep, and ass, with the edge of the sword."[16]

Indeed, massacres of Arabs by the founders of modern Israel have occurred, such as the one that took place at Deir Yasseen during the 1948 War of Independence. Between 100 and 250 Arabs were killed by Menachem Begin's extremist Irgun Zvai Leumi and Yitzhak Shamir's militant Stern Gang (both men were to later become prime ministers of the State of Israel).

"It was an outburst from below with no one to control it," reported Meir Pa'il, a member of David Ben Gurion's mainstream Haganah militia and an eyewitness at Deir Yasseen. "Groups of men went from house to house looting and shooting, shooting and looting. You could hear the cries from within the houses of Arab women, Arab elders, Arab kids. I tried to find the commanders, but I did not succeed. I tried to shout and to hold them, but they took no notice. Their eyes were glazed. It was as if they were drugged, mentally poisoned, in ecstasy."[17]

Yehoshua Gorodentchik was an Irgun officer who participated in the fighting at Deir Yasseen: "We had prisoners, and before the retreat we decided to liquidate them. We also liquidated the wounded, as anyway we could not give them first aid. In one place, about eighty Arab prisoners were killed after some of them had opened fire and killed one of the people who came to give them first aid. Arabs who were dressed up as women were also found, and so they started to shoot women also who did not hurry to the area where the prisoners where concentrated."[18]

In his memoir, *The Revolt*, Begin denied that there was a premeditated slaughter of innocents at Deir Yasseen:

> One of our tenders carrying a loud speaker was stationed at the entrance to the village and it exhorted in Arabic all women, children and aged to leave their houses and to take shelter on the slope of the hill. By giving this humane warning our fighters threw away the element of complete surprise, and thus increased their own risk in the ensuing battle. A substantial number of inhabitants obeyed the warning and they were unhurt. A few did not leave their stone houses—perhaps because of their confusion. The fire of the enemy was murderous—to which the number of our casualties bears eloquent testimony. Our men were compelled to fight for every house; to overcome the enemy they used large numbers of hand-grenades. And the civilians who disregarded our warnings, suffered inevitable casualties.[19]

Despite Irgun denials, there have been numerous allegations that the killing of helpless fighters and civilians at Deir Yasseen was deliberate, that Jewish commandos raped the women, slaughtered infants, and even shot a woman who was nine months pregnant and "cut her stomach open with a butcher's knife," all in an attempt to sow panic among the Arab people and force them to flee the country.[20]

"Deir Yasseen was not an isolated, inexplicable atrocity in a war of defence against Arab invasion," Rosemary Sayigh wrote in her study of Palestinian refugees, "but part of a systematic campaign to terrorize the Palestinian peasants and force them to give up resistance."[21]

The realities of what took place at Deir Yasseen are still being debated within Israel and the Jewish Diaspora, with Begin and Shamir being held responsible for a massacre of innocents by their Zionist adversaries as well as by their opponents in the Arab world. At the time of the attack, the majority of Jews adopted the view that Deir Yasseen was a stain upon Jewish history. The incident was quickly denounced by mainstream Zionist leaders as an unofficial act of brutality that perverted the essence of Jewish teaching. Upon hearing of Deir Yasseen, David Ben-Gurion dispatched a telegram expressing his condolences to King Abdullah in Amman, Jordan.

Whether one subscribed to Begin's or Ben-Gurion's version of events or not, the furor over Deir Yasseen revealed that the deliberate slaughter of innocents would not be sanctioned by the Zionist leadership. Only the courage and dedication of the Old Testament Hebrew warriors, not the drive for total annihilation, was to be emulated by contemporary Jews.

The Zionist rejection of massacre as an instrument of state policy surfaced again during Operation Peace for the Galilee in 1982, when Lebanese Christian Phalangist militiamen slaughtered Palestinian civilians in the Sabra and Shatilla refugee camps in Beirut while Israeli troops were in control of the city. Nine days later, more than 300 thousand Israelis, over 8 percent of the entire population, took to the streets of Tel Aviv in the midst of a war to protest the Israeli army's failure to protect the Palestinian civilians from the Phalangist militiamen.

Three days later, a commission of inquiry was established in Israel to investigate the massacre, chaired by Yitzhak Kahan, president of the Israeli Supreme Court. Though it was clear from the outset that the killings were the work of Lebanese Christian forces, the Israeli public and the government wanted concrete assurances that Jewish forces were not involved.

On 8 February 1983, the commission issued its final report in which it concluded that "the atrocities in the refugee camps were perpetrated by members of the Phalangists, and that absolutely no direct responsibility devolves upon Israel or upon those who acted in its behalf."[22]

Because of the ongoing ferocity of the Arab rejection of the Jews, however, the commission felt compelled to remind the world of Israel's political and spiritual isolation in the region:

> Among the responses to the commission from the public, there were those who expressed dissatisfaction with the holding of an inquiry on a subject not directly related to Israel's responsibility. The argument was advanced that in previous instances of massacre in Lebanon, when the lives of many more people were taken than those of the victims who fell in Sabra and Shatilla, world opinion was not shocked and no inquiry commissions were

established. We cannot justify this approach to the issue of holding an inquiry, and not only for the formal reason that it was not we who decided to
hold the inquiry, but rather the Israeli Government resolved thereon. The
main purpose of the inquiry was to bring to light all the important facts
relating to the perpetration of the atrocities; it therefore has importance
from the perspective of Israel's moral fortitude and its functioning as a
democratic state that scrupulously maintains the fundamental principles of
the civilized world.

We do not deceive ourselves that the results of this inquiry will convince or satisfy those who have prejudices or selective consciences, but
this inquiry was not intended for such people.[23]

Shortly before his death in 1977, Kamal Joumblatt, a co-founder of the
Arab Front for Participation in the Palestinian Revolution and a man often at
odds with Israel, acknowledged the evolution of the Jews since their days as
Old Testament fighters and the uniqueness of the Zionist presence in the
Middle East:

There is, in the Jewish consciousness, a 'detachment from mundane history which has characterized the Jewish people's remarkable contribution
to the march of ideas and which has enabled them to retain a sense of the
human and the cosmic: And the spirit of God moved upon the waters.'
This Jewish awareness of permanence is noticeable in their music, in what
they have given the world in terms of philosophy and art, and even in their
behaviour in Israel. Until now, practically no fedayeen [Arab guerrilla]
prisoners have ever been executed; by contrast, most of the supposedly
progressive Arab regimes have liquidated dozens or even hundreds of
people, often without any real trial.[24]

The Middle East has been home to several ethnic minorities who have
fallen victim to regimes of all sorts: progressive, radical, traditional, fundamentalist. Repression, mass slayings, and official crackdowns have
haunted the Kurds in Iraq, the Copts in Egypt, the Shiites in Lebanon, the
Jews in Iran.

Notwithstanding the harshness of various ancient Hebraic writings, it
often appeared that it was modern Israel's neighbors who invoked Old Testament ideas of unyielding slaughter of one's enemies and "eye for an eye"
notions of justice.

It was at places like Damour in 1976, when Arab Moslems conducted
their massacre of Arab Christians, that Old Testament fury achieved an eery
revival: "In a frenzy to destroy their enemies utterly," Jillian Becker

reported, "as if even the absolute limits of nature could not stop them, the invaders broke open tombs and flung the bones of the dead into the streets."[25]

Deir Yasseen witnessed the tragedy of Arab victims and Jewish bullets. The 1982 Israeli siege of Beirut saw the relentless fury of Jewish bombs hurled at Arab targets. Both were born of the generations-old clash between Jewish nationalism and Arab claims to historic Palestine. But in places like Karantina, Damour, Sabra, Shatilla, Hama, Bourj al-Barajneh, Ain al-Hilweh, Rashidieyh, and Maghdushah, the region was presented with the spectre of Arab vs. Arab, of religious hatred and communal rivalries so stark that they made the eventual emergence of tolerant, pluralistic Arab regimes as remote and irrelevant as the onetime phrase that heralded Lebanon as the "Switzerland of the Middle East." For the region's most vulnerable ethnic minorities—Kurds, Jews, Bahais, Circassians—the dim prospects for peaceful coexistence were plainly seen and frighteningly real.

2

Caucasia's Legacy

IN 1980, a clandestine PLO broadcast by the Voice of Palestine was monitored by the United States government:

> Two Palestinian strugglers, William Nassar and Muhammad Mahdi Busayu, arrived in Beirut last night after their release from the Zionist prisons in exchange for Zionist spy Dina al-Asan [a pseudonym]. The exchange took place in Larnaca. The two strugglers were received at the airport by a representative of brother leader Abu Ammar [the code name for Yassir Arafat] and a number of the cadres of the Palestinian revolution.

Dina al-Asan had indeed been working for the Israelis. "Women make the best spies," an Israeli intelligence expert once said while discussing Dina, "No one checks their bedrooms."

Dina's task had been to infiltrate the Palestinian neighborhoods in Lebanon and locate the PLO's military installations. Her reports enabled Israel's air force and anti-terrorist squads to pinpoint PLO targets hidden among the civilians living in the crowded refugee camps. They also helped to launch the hidden diplomacy that culminated in Anwar Sadat's dramatic visit to Jerusalem.

Unlike many of the Mossad's agents stationed in Arab lands, Dina al-Asan was not a Jewish immigrant from Egypt, Morocco, Iraq, or one of the other Arabic-speaking countries. She was a native of Jordan and a Moslem, her Circassian ancestors members of the Islamic community that had fled religious persecution in the Caucasus mountains, a region currently under Soviet control.

The Jews of Israel are a population of barely 4 million in the midst of 200 million Arabs. The Circassians in Jordan number fewer than seventy thousand. Though followers of Islam like the region's other ethnic minorities, there have been Circassians who have voiced concern over the insecurity of their status. Like the Jews, they have been conscious of their particular vulnerability as a non-Arab people living in the Middle East. The bloodletting in Lebanon, the massacres of Kurds in Iraq, the repression of Copts in Egypt have made some Circassians fearful that an Arab-Islamic version of Old Testament wrath might one day threaten their own existence as well as Israel's.

These Circassians have heard the cries of men like General Azzam Pasha, the Arab League secretary general who vowed, "This will be a war of extermination and a momentous massacre which will be spoken of like the Mongolian massacres and the Crusades," a promise issued on 15 May 1948, the day six Arab armies invaded the newly formed Jewish state.[1]

They have listened to the speeches of PLO chief Yassir Arafat, who, on 29 March 1970, summed up a long-held Arab position for the *Washington Post:* "The goal of our struggle is the end of Israel, and there can be no compromise."[2]

Fifteen years later, on 16 May 1985, Arafat renewed this commitment during an Arab League summit in Tunis. When asked if he would ever accept Israel's right to exist, he replied, "no, never."[3]

Forty years of uncompromising declarations by Arab leaders, from General Pasha to Chairman Arafat, have carried an ominous message to some Circassians. Might not the day come when they are on the receiving end of such rhetoric?

The Middle East has been rife with talk of expulsion, liquidation, revenge. Khomeini's Shiite fundamentalists have appeared determined to liquidate the Bahai "infidels" in their midst; Lebanese Christians have sought to avenge their comrades through massive retaliations against their Moslem countrymen; PLO commandos have promised to expel the Jews and return Palestine to Arab rule. Could the Circassians be next? Would their countrymen in the Arab world one day see them as a fifth column to be subdued or expelled?

According to Dr. Jamal Shurdom, a Circassian professor of Palestinian history at the University of Jordan in Amman and a former Fulbright scholar, there is in fact little reason to believe that they would. The insecurity of the Jews in the Middle East cannot be compared with the situation faced by the Circassians in the region, insisted Shurdom, because the Circassians "did not occupy Arab lands, they are Moslems," and "they share the same beliefs with the Arabs."[4]

Nevertheless, while many Circassians, perhaps the majority, have shared the Arab hostility to the concept of a Jewish state in Palestine, others have seen the continued survival of the Jews as a guarantor of ethnic freedom and toleration in the area. If Israel could hold out against its neighbors, then moderate Arab forces recognizing the need to adapt to the reality of a Jewish state might come to power, bringing with them an acceptance of pluralism that could foster a benevolent approach toward the region's other minorities. Just as many Maronite Christians in Lebanon have looked upon the Jews of Israel as a group sharing a common struggle for minority rights in the Middle East, so some Circassians have identified with the Zionist cause. And, like the Jews, there were Circassians in Jordan who felt that they, too, could not afford to lose a battle with their neighbors. There might be no room for the vanquished, they reasoned, only utter destruction.

Circassian fighters have long been considered among the most effective in the Middle East. Circassian soldiers once formed the backbone of King Hussein's army in Jordan. It was the Circassians who founded the city of Amman, now the capital of Hussein's Hashemite kingdom.

The majority of the Circassians emigrated to Jordan in the late 1800s, making the long trek from their homeland in the Caucasus mountains, where three hundred years of Ottoman rule had established Sunni Islam as the religion of the area. (There are, however, Circassian Jews. According to a Circassian Moslem immigrant from Soviet Caucasia with friends among the Circassian Jewish community, nearly half of the Circassian town of Nalchik—located in the Caucasus region with a population of 100,000—is estimated to be Jewish, and the city of Dhegistan is said at one time to have been ruled by Jews. He recalled that there had never been any friction between the Circassian Moslems and the small Circassian Jewish communities.[5])

The Circassians did not leave the mountains of Caucasia by choice. In 1763, the forces of Czarist Russia converted the city of Mozdok into a military outpost, in effect triggering the long Russo-Circassian War that lasted nearly a century.[6] In 1774, Russian troops began moving into positions along the Black Sea. By 1829, they had taken control of the region from the Turks. It took nearly twenty years for the Russians to subdue the fierce Circassian fighters who steadfastly clung to their ancient lands and Islamic heritage. The triumph of St. Petersburg's Christian army threatened eventually to destroy the Moslem inhabitants of Caucasia.

The Russian occupation of the Caucasus was brutal. "Russia regarded the Circassian tribes as backward," historian K. H. Karpart explained, "and it took it upon itself to 'civilize' them by conversion—forcefully if necessary—to Orthodox Christianity. The tribes rejected the Russian demands, and consequently, were attacked and massacred."[7]

By 1863, nearly 1.6 million Circassians had been forced to flee south.

They moved into the Ottoman controlled areas of Bulgaria and Turkey, with many then making their way to Syria, Palestine, and Jordan.

The Circassian writer Kadir Natho boasts that in Jordan, the offspring of the original tribes of Caucasia continue to possess a ''warlike indomitable spirit'' and ''love for freedom,'' exhibiting the same ''unmatched pride and skill with which they defended their dignity and right wherever they went.''[8]

Circassians carry an exuberant nostalgia for their mountain homeland, expressed in a literature recounting grand conquests over oppressors and folktales extolling native glories like the ''Cherkesska,'' the traditional dress of the Circassian tribesmen:

Caucasus is the mighty, the wondrous! Cherkesska is a symbolic reflection of this Titan. His proud head the Mighty Caucasus held high. The clouds were his head-gear, white shrouds of eternal snow his cloak, and that is why the mountaineers of Caucasus donned with dignity a tall sheepskin hat with long white curling wool resembling the white snowy drifts on the mountain tops. Elbrus and Kazbek are the eyes of the Mighty Caucasus. The forbidding rocky Caucasian range is the bosom of the mighty one. That is why Caucasian men adorned their mighty bosoms with hazirs. The long skirts of the Cherkesska are the wide expansive valleys of the Caucasus.[9]

The Caucasus ''is the land of wonders, the land of knights,'' says the folktale, ''the land of the treasures of all the world;'' for many Circassians, the ancestral home beneath the snow-capped peaks of Caucasia still arouses a deep longing to return, stirring the nationalist spirit.[10]

As recently as May 1986, an open letter by Dr. Shurdom advocated an increased awareness of ''the bleak conditions represented in the human tragedy of the Circassian people and their wretchedness as a result of the occupation of Circassia.'' The document called for the start of political negotiations between Circassian leaders and Soviet government officials and asked the international community's support in the struggle to ''revive the Circassian national conscience.''[11]

Circassians everywhere continue to revere their traditions, endowing their homeland with an almost mystical significance. Their warrior heritage is still proudly displayed in the Cherkesska's *hazirs*, elaborately engraved silver cartridges sewn into the garment where shirt pockets might be, lined up in sets of six. Originally designed to hold premeasured charges for muskets, *hazirs* are prized as family heirlooms and handed down through generations.

The glory of the ancestral homeland is embodied in the Circassian names for settings like Mt. Elbruz, the highest mountain in Europe with a western peak reaching 18,480 feet. The Circassian word for Elbruz means "hill-blessed" or "god-place," and the mountain is still held to be an ancient holy site, its peaks associated with a "Prometheus-like giant or hero."[12]

Their allegiance to Caucasia's customs and values has at times brought Circassian refugee communities into conflict with their neighbors, a phenomenon which Shurdom observed is not unlike the interethnic rivalries that have plagued other parts of the world.[13] Indeed, such strife has existed in America's racially mixed urban areas and even in the towns and cities of Israel, where bitter rivalries among various Orthodox and secular Jewish groups once led to the burning of a particular sect's synogogue by fellow Jews. In commenting on the diversity of Israel's population and the denominational conflict within the Jewish community in Jerusalem, journalist Shai Franklin reported that the city's mayor, Teddy Kollek, told American students at Hebrew University that "It is only remotely possible that even Jews may unite by the end of the next century, leaving aside any chances for Arab-Jewish integration."[14] As for the Circassians of Jordan, despite their adherence to Islam, sharp cultural differences have periodically divided the tiny population from the surrounding Arab communities.

Circassians have their own language and traditional dress (the costumes are worn primarily on special social occasions) and their own customs regarding marriage and family relationships. Some of them still follow such unique tribal practices as "brother avoidance," in which younger brothers minimize contact with their older brothers in order to reduce sibling rivalries. Some also adhere to the traditional rules governing father-son relationships. In 1961, Professor George Weightman, who studied Circassian life in Jordan, revealed that there were adult males who had never had a direct conversation with their fathers. "Such a situation is considered a commendable example of proper filial respect," he explained.[15]

Politically and economically, the Circassian communities have tried to keep a relatively low profile in Arab lands, but their fidelity to their own cultural traditions has frequently created an unwelcome contrast to the traditional bedouin landscape. Their unusual customs and bold agricultural enterprises bring the Circassian presence into bold relief when viewed against the backdrop of the surrounding nomadic Arab culture.

In 1900, fighting broke out between Circassian settlers in Amman and local Arabs from the Balqawi and Bani Sakhr tribes. The Circassians managed to prevail in the Balqawiyeh War, but they remained keenly aware of the ongoing dangers.

Circassians have historically tried to protect their interests by supporting the regime in power. When the struggle between Arab and Jew in Palestine erupted into war, those living in the Galilee enlisted in the Israeli army, while those across the border made up 75–80 percent of King Hussein's elite military unit, Al Quat al-Khasa (the Jordanian Special Forces). Jan Bazell (a pseudonym), a prominent member of Jordan's Circassian community whose relatives have served in senior level positions within the Hashemite regime, explained: "Circassians are always loyal to their host governments."[16]

In Jordan, the Circassians have spent the past thirty years establishing key positions within the country. "Although the Circassian minority constitutes only about 1% of the population," U.S. Army officer and Middle East specialist Bruce Mackey observed in his study of Jordan's Circassian community, "it occupies a disproportionately influential political and economic position."[17]

Many of Jordan's Circassians have extensive land holdings in Amman, no doubt a result of their long history there, and the community is among the best educated. Many are trilingual, speaking Circassian, Arabic, and English, and are graduates of universities in Lebanon, Egypt, England, and the United States. Several Circassians have served in the Jordanian cabinet, including Said al-Mufti, who was prime minister in 1950, 1955, and 1956. By the 1980s, four Circassians had served in succession as directors of Jordanian security, and Walid Tash, a respected Circassian leader, has served as secretary general of Jordan's Foreign Ministry. In 1987, another prominent Circassian, Mohammed Ali Amin, was appointed governor of Amman.

However, according to Shurdom, the majority of Circassians in Jordan are far from wealthy and do not have any particular influence with the government, and thus, lacking an economic and political stake in the country, they "do not have to share the assumption that they are loyal" to the Hashemite regime. A number of them have "joined the PLO and other (even) radical organizations against Hussein" and are "still siding with the Palestinians," Shurdom reported.[18]

Yet, for the most part, the Circassian soldier has distinguished himself as an excellent fighter and loyal defender of the king. In 1970, Circassian officers and fighting men played a critical role in crushing an effort to overthrow Hussein's Hashemite monarchy. The challenge to the king came from militant Palestinian Arabs (refugees from the lands west of the Jordan River and their descendents), who make up over 50 percent of Jordan's population. Many of them felt that they were entitled to rule in Amman as well as in Jerusalem, Nablus, and Tel Aviv; their PLO leaders still speak of the liberation of Palestine as encompassing lands on both the east and west banks of the Jordan River.

The Circassian rally behind Hussein followed the PLO offensive unleashed against the king on 13 September 1970, an offensive resulting in the capture of the city of Irbid and in Palestinian control of nearly all of northern Jordan. Two days later, high-ranking officers made a midnight visit to the royal palace and urged the king to counterattack. According to Jacques Derogy and Hesi Carmel, the group included Circassian officers who pressed for an all-out assault against the PLO forces, though Shurdom doubts that such men would have been in much of a position to press the king on anything since Circassian officers had not reached a rank higher than that of first lieutenant, captain, or major.[19]

The role of the Circassians in the Jordanian army has been a subject of some contention, with Shurdom pointing out that at the time of the September 1970 uprising the Jordanian Special Forces was led by a bedouin Arab commander operating under orders of the Jordanian General Command, and that Hussein's army "is made up of mostly Bedouins and pro-Hussein Palestinians. Circassians are less than 0.0005%." There are virtually no Circassian enlisted men in the elite unit and no more than seven or eight officers, Shurdom insisted.[20] However, according to a U.S. Marine officer stationed in Jordan as an adviser to the Jordanian army, while it is true that Circassians constitute 10 percent of the officer corps (about six to seven officers), at least one third, perhaps as much as one half, of the enlisted men in the Jordanian Special Forces are indeed Circassian.[21] Whatever the exact numbers (a Pentagon intelligence report detailing the exact make-up of the Jordanian Special Forces remained classified as of this writing), Shurdom's emphasis aimed at dispelling any notion that during the September 1970 fighting there was "a special militia unit made up of Circassian[s] and under a Circassian Command, who implemented these operations and killed the Palestinians."[22]

Less than a week after the 15 September midnight visit by army officers to the king's royal palace during which they urged him to launch an assault against the Palestinian commandos, Hussein gave the order, pressing his troops into service against the PLO. Regardless of their degree of influence in the decision and the extent of their participation within the Jordanian Special Forces, some of the Circassian fighters in Hussein's army were eager to even the score with the Palestinians; their families had often been victimized by PLO power in Jordan.

Because of their reputed wealth and intense loyalty to the king, PLO members had singled out Circassian homes over the years, targeting them for "fundraising activities." Ahmad Suweilih, a Circassian captain in the Jordanian Special Forces, described one incident where three PLO members armed with machine guns entered his house:

They were Palestinians and told us they were collecting money for the PLO. This was something strange to me and I didn't know what to do, but we gave them some money and told them it was all we had. They knew I was an officer and said I should pay more since I would not fight to get back their homeland, but I told them I didn't have any more money. They left and I asked my family about this and they said that it had already happened twice in the past and the Palestinians took a lot of money from the Adigah [the native term used by Circassians to identify themselves] because they thought that they were all rich. This made me damn mad and when I talked to the other fellows in my unit I found out it was true. After that I was stopped at several road blocks and if they knew I was Circassian they would always demand money. My unit had several meetings with the King (over a period of several months) to tell him about these things and demand we be allowed to take some action but he always was able to persuade us to be patient. King Hussein is a great leader and he felt sympathy for all his people and wanted only peace.[23]

The PLO managed to build such a powerful military force in Jordan prior to 1970 that its members routinely patrolled the cities and controlled much of the traffic entering Amman. According to Mrs. Bazell, many Jordanian Arabs, not just Circassians, experienced the kind of victimization experienced by Captain Suweilih; Circassians were challenged because of their support for the king—which they shared with many other Jordanian Arabs—not because of any particular ethnic animosity between them and the Palestinians.[24] Bazell explained that "hard feelings" have "not grown as Circassian versus Palestinian" but "as Jordanian versus Palestinian . . . and these things happen between brothers." Commenting on the PLO targeting of Circassian homes in Amman prior to the 1970 uprising, Bazell asserted that the residences were singled out not because they belonged to Circassians, but because they were owned by "East-Bank Jordanians" as opposed to "West-Bank Jordanians [Palestinian refugees]." As for the new generation of Circassians, "some of them," Bazell said, "as is the case with the rest of the youth of Jordan, joined with the PLO" and "other extremist parties and their being Circassians does not put their minds into blinkers." The Circassians "are free each to his own belief, as individuals!"[25]

Moreover, Shurdom claimed that the Circassian loyalty to Hussein had not really inflamed relations with the Palestinians. "We have no problem with the PLO," Shurdom wrote. "For example myself, I have good relations with the PLO, and at the same time with King Hussein." Shurdom did admit that "there is some negative attitudes from Palestinians toward Circassians," but that there is not much negativity on the part of the Circassians toward the Palestinians. "I do not blame the Palestinians, because they feel that Circassians sided with Hussein (their enemy), so it is natural to develop such relations [feelings]." According to Shurdom, "educated Palestinians understand that there is no connection" between loyalty to Hussein and hostility toward the Palestinian cause.[26]

Though harassed by the PLO, the Circassians would not resist unless given the order by their king. "We were his soldiers and would obey him in everything," Captain Suweilih said, but in September 1970, however, the PLO "pushed even him too far and we got our chance."[27] An ancient Circassian *kindjal*, a two-foot dagger inlaid with gold and ivory, had once been inscribed, "I am slow to offend, quick to avenge."[28]

Although the Circassians supported the monarchy during the 1970 uprising, many of them believed that they, along with Hussein and the rest of the Jordanian Arab community, remained loyal to the Palestinian cause despite their confrontation with the PLO. Tahsheen Shurdom, a cousin of Jamal Shurdom who as a brigadier general served as General Commander of the Jordanian Special Forces, was a captain at the time of the civil war, in charge of the Special Forces 62nd brigade. He recalled the events that led up to the crackdown on the Palestinian commandos. "We were attempting to avoid friction with the guerrillas," he explained. "Can you imagine the Jordanian army members, especially the Special Forces, hiding from the guerrillas? Do you think we were afraid of them?" he said in a conversation with his cousin Jamal in Amman. "No, but the government was honest in attempting to avoid problems. We had received a military order not to intervene against the guerrillas as much as possible by following instructions not to carry weapons on leave to the city." But the fight with the PLO proved inevitable. Nevertheless, "we sacrificed very much for the Palestinian cause as a Jordanian army," the captain pointed out. "Why don't they go back into history and check the stand of the Jordanian army," he said of the PLO guerrillas. "I am a military man. I do what my commander tells me to do. But when it comes to the part of nationalism, we do not accept anyone's doubts as to our sincerity and sacrifices for the Palestinian cause. We here in Jordan are the defenders of the Palestinian people and their cause. It is actually our problem and we do actually carry the burden of the Palestinians. *Not the guerrillas*."[29]

The Syrians, who entered the 1970 fighting on behalf of the Palestinian commandos, abandoned the PLO shortly after the king launched his counteroffensive, leaving them to face the 150 millimeter cannon of Hussein's army and the guns of his crack Special Forces. The refugee camps were decimated. According to the American military analyst Richard Gabriel, an Israeli intelligence report estimated that Hussein's troops slaughtered as much as 30 percent of the PLO's key fighting force.[30]

On 22 September, President Jaafar Numairy of the Sudan led an Arab delegation to Jordan in search of a peace agreement. "We came out of Amman with the collective conviction that there was a full plan to exterminate all men of the valiant Palestinian Resistance and all the Palestinians in Amman," Numairy later reported.[31]

Thousands of Palestinians were killed or left homeless. Many of them poured across the border into Lebanon to escape the onslaught. Ironically, some even sought refuge in Israel rather than risk falling into the hands of Jordanian soldiers. "I saw the Jordanians killing people even though they were lying wounded," said Mohammad Masoud Abu Abed, a nineteen-year-old Palestinian guerrilla who swam across the Jordan River into Israel. "I am ready to join the Israeli Army against Jordan and Syria—because these are worse enemies of the Palestinians. We are better off in the West Bank under the Israelis than we were under the Jordanians, and better than we are in the East Bank today."[32] The PLO termed its defeat in Jordan "Black September," and it formed a special terrorist cell under that name to symbolize its defiance. Nearly twelve years were to pass before the wounds of Black September could begin to heal.

The mending started during the summer of 1982, when the Israeli siege of Beirut forced thousands of PLO fighters to evacuate the city. In the face of their desperate need for asylum, Hussein allowed some of them to return to Jordan. In the fall, Yassir Arafat flew to Amman for a meeting with the king. Afterwards, Arafat confessed that the meeting had been his first real talk with the Jordanian monarch since the 1970 civil war.

On 11 February 1985, Arafat and Hussein signed an eight-point PLO-Jordanian agreement that called for "the termination of Israeli occupation of the occupied Arab territories, including Jerusalem," and proposed in its place the formation of "confederated Arab states of Jordan and Palestine."[33]

A year later, however, Arafat and Hussein would again part company over the failure to fulfill the goals of the 11 February agreement, and Fateh's offices in Amman were ordered closed. The following year, Arafat, in a bid to woo PLO radical elements, bowed to extremist demands during the 18th session of the Palestine National Council held in Algiers in April 1987 and agreed formally to abrogate the two-year old accord with Hussein.

Although some observers predict yet another series of reconciliations and disputes between the two Arab leaders, the animosity between Hussein and Arafat brought on by the bloodshed of Black September had not even begun to subside over the decade following the uprising, and relations between Palestinian militants and supporters of the king were particularly raw. What emerged from the tension was Dina al-Asan, a Moslem woman from Jordan who was willing to work for the Israeli secret service.

3

The Human Factor

DINA al-Asan was born on 3 January 1935 in Amman, Jordan. Her ancestors in the Caucasus had originally been part of a prominent Circassian clan. After emigrating to Jordan, Dina's grandfather served as a foreman overseeing agricultural work.

One of three sisters, Dina grew up witnessing firsthand how the loyalty of the Circassian community to King Hussein frequently put her people at odds with the surrounding Palestinian refugee population.

In her study of Jordan's Circassians, Dr. Seteney Shami, professor of anthropology at Jordan's Yarmouk University, observed that by the early 1970s, "The insecure position of the Circassians became especially obvious as the Palestinian movement grew in strength in Jordan. Although some Circassian youth joined the Palestinian movement, Circassians in general were regarded suspiciously by the Palestinians as a pro-monarchical group."[1]

As a member of the Circassian minority, Dina al-Asan believed that she had reason to look upon the PLO as her enemy. The Circassian role in the 1970 Black September expulsion of Palestinian guerrillas held out the possibility that a brutal revenge might one day be visited upon her people, should radical Palestinians ever attain power in Amman.

But working for the Jews is not necessarily the same as opposing Palestinian militants. Not everyone holds to the dictum that "the enemy of my enemy is my friend." To King Hussein and the majority of Jordanians, Israel was still a bitter foe. A broadcast by Radio Amman on 17 November 1970, just two months after Black September, expressed the feeling Dina's countrymen had held since 1948, the year the Jewish state was established: "Israel's existence in the heart of the Arab people is an absurdity and ought to be got rid of by any means whatsoever."[2]

Despite the tense political and social climate confronting Dina during her early life, her initial interest was not politics, but medicine. She pursued a career as a physician, reportedly studying psychology in Iraq and setting up her own practice in Amman, a bold move for a woman living in an Arab country. She also married a Palestinian, which was an unpopular step for a member of the close-knit Circassian community. Even more unusual, when she separated from her husband, Dina befriended an Israeli. (Intermarriage between Arabs and Circassians is increasingly common, though it is most often between a Circassian bride and an Arab groom, and rare for a Circassian man to marry an Arab woman.)

Dina's marriage was a disaster. Members of the Circassian community claimed that her husband beat her. A Circassian woman from Jordan now living in the United States said that he actually threw Dina out of a window during one of their fights, nearly killing her.[3] While her marriage to a Palestinian may have alienated her from the clannish Circassian community, her husband's brutality most likely added to Dina's contempt for the Palestinians. In addition to her problems with the Palestinians and her fellow Circassians, some have claimed that Dina was at odds with the Hashemite authorities. Dina's uncle in Amman said that she never completed her medical studies and resented the Jordanian government for barring her from practicing medicine.[4] Jan Bazell, a friend of Dina's family, explained that Dina had opened up an office in Amman and practiced medicine without a license until the government discovered her activities and ordered the clinic shut down. "She was a disturbed girl," Bazell insisted, "not normal, unbalanced."[5]

The subject of Dina al-Asan arouses deep passions among the Circassians in Jordan. Jamal Shurdom asserted that Dina's actions in no way represent the thinking of her people and that she is viewed as an outcast for taking up with the Israelis.

Shurdom acknowledged that relations between the Circassians and the Palestinians are precarious, but emphasized that the Circassians in Jordan support the Arab position that the Zionists in Israel have inflicted an injustice on the Palestinians. Attainment of their full rights would give the Palestinians control over Jerusalem and all of Israel, he said; at the least they are owed an independent Palestinian state on the West Bank. Explaining that he was not necessarily speaking for the Circassian community in Jordan as a whole, his personal view of the conflict was that there must be compromise, that defending the national cause is not synonymous with "liberating all of Palestine." He would support a settlement based on an acceptance of Israel within its 1948 borders and the establishment of a Palestinian state on the West Bank and Gaza, with Jerusalem under international jurisdiction. One must recognize that in order "to save human lives" one cannot insist on getting everything one wants, Shurdom said. The moderate course is to accommodate Israel's security concerns, which could be worked out by military experts to establish secure borders for the Jewish state, and allow the Palestinians to create an independent state in the territories captured by Israel during the 1967 Six-Day War.

Shurdom added that if Dina's actions are taken as evidence that the Circassians in Jordan are less than loyal to the Arab cause, the Circassian community there would be in great danger. Radical Palestinians already view Circassians as non-Arab traitors, he explained; Circassians are particularly sensitive to any suggestion that they might have a dual loyalty (to Circassia, of course, not Israel) that precludes them from supporting the Arabs. Marxist PLO factions such as the Popular Front for the Liberation of Palestine (PFLP) headed by George Habash are particularly hostile to the Circassians. This arises out of the Circassian opposition to the Soviet Union's continued occupation of the Caucasus. With Moscow a key patron of these Marxist factions, and the Circassians steadfast in their rejection of communism, their backing of Hussein, and their support for the liberation of the Caucasus from Russian control, relations between them and the Circassians have been especially poor.[6]

Dr. Shami's research discussed an aspect of the "dualism" question raised by Shurdom's point about competing loyalties. In her anthropological study, Dr. Shami related a conversation among a group of college-educated government employees in their thirties: "Someone said to me, 'you are a Circassian, but you speak Arabic well!' It was as if he stabbed me with a knife. We have been 100 years in this country and he is surprised that I speak Arabic?" Another Circassian replied, "These are the pains of dualism. There is not a Circassian who is not sad."[7]

Shami observed that the confusion by certain Circassian youths over the status of their cultural identity in Jordan was a reaction to an evolution of the power structure within the country that saw the rise of a commercial industrial class in which the Circassians play no part. This was coupled with a "sharp sense of loss experienced by the Circassians upon the retirement of their national leaders," which demonstrated "that a large gap had been created between them and the community."[8]

According to Shami, the older generation of Circassians, though sensitive to the erosion of traditional customs and the weakening of their political standing, "do not experience doubts about their identity, or their perfect right to be Jordanian citizens. They point out that Circassians participated fully in the history of Jordan, and that 'there has never been a Circassian traitor.'" (Dina al-Asan is the obvious and perhaps sole exception.) But for some members of the younger generation, the "marginalization of the Circassians as a group from the national political structure" presented pressing problems revolving around questions of national and cultural identity within the Arab world. "For them being a Circassian and a Jordanian is almost bordering on a contradiction," Shami wrote. "Some also expressed the feeling of being 'outsiders.' "[9]

Shami attributes this reaction to the "class position of this age sector" as "this group of low-level bureaucrats and newly starting professionals are the ones most excluded from political power. They tend also to have lost most of their family land-holdings because of improvident sales by their parents." Hence, "these politically unconnected people feel insecure. This insecurity is then translated into a feeling of not belonging to the polity. They then begin to look beyond the nation-state, to a wider ethnic affiliation." According to Shami, for some, this look beyond was aimed at "the 'motherland' in the Causasus [*sic*]" and "to the Circassian communities in other countries, especially the extremely active Turkish Circassians."[10]

Dina al-Asan, responding to the gradual undermining of the Circassian cultural identity in Jordan, appears to have turned elsewhere. She may have concluded that: (1) despite their adherence to Islam, her people possessed a non-Arab cultural identity; (2) their national identity had traditionally been rooted in either a Jordanian identification or an Arab (or pan-Arab) one, and yet, in fact was neither, being simply Circassian rather than Jordanian or Arab; and (3) the erosion of their political power was presenting an increasing challenge to their political identity within the Hashemite / Palestinian state. Thus, Dina's own insecurity over the future of her fellow Circassians in Jordan may have drawn her closer to the region's other non-Arab minorities, perhaps even to the Circassians of Israel instead of "the extremely active Turkish Circassians" or those living under Soviet rule back home in the "motherland."

Yet, according to Shurdom, to conclude that Dina's work for the Mossad was endorsed by her people or represented their thinking in any way is not only erroneous but would only serve to isolate the Circassians of Jordan even further and give their enemies an excuse to move against them. In the Middle East, the stakes are high whenever the balance among minorities is compromised. And the Circassians are particularly keen on their longstanding role as loyal supporters of their respective host countries. Israeli historian Ori Stendel pointed out that as far back as the eighth century, when the Abbasid dynasty's rulers in Baghdad were recruiting foreign soldiers to protect them from internal enemies, warriors from the Caucasus were specifically sought out to serve as their personal bodyguards. The combination of military prowess and abiding loyalty made the Circassian fighters a valued asset throughout the region.[11]

In the Hashemite kingdom of Jordan, those qualities were amply demonstrated as early as 1923, when an uprising against King Abdullah was smashed by a Circassian battalion. "It's a matter of trust," historian Mohammed Haghandouqa said when discussing the ongoing special status of his Circassian countrymen in Jordan. "Whenever there is money or security involved, they put a Circassian in charge. There's never been a Circassian convicted of embezzlement or treason. For us, it's a religious conviction."[12] Again, the case of Dina al-Asan offers a rather blunt and indeed embarrassing challenge to Haghandouqa's assertion; her role as a highly visible exception to the Circassian tradition of loyalty to one's host government is why her name arouses such sensitive feelings in Jordan. But, ironically, for a while it was a Circassian from Israel, not from Jordan, who appeared to offer the most troubling exception.

In 1980, the same year that Dina was secretly freed from a PLO cell in a prisoner exchange with her Mossad sponsors, Israel's internal security service, Shin Bet, arrested Izat Nafsu, a lieutenant in the Israel Defense Forces and a Circassian. The charge was treason. Nafsu had left the army in October 1979 after having served in southern Lebanon as a liaison officer to Israel's Lebanese Christian allies. Soon after, Shin Bet accused him of selling secrets to Syria and pro-Syrian PLO factions in Lebanon and of smuggling weapons from Lebanon to West Bank Palestinians. Nafsu insisted on his innocence, eventually confessed, then retracted his confession at a secret trial held before a military court. His confession, he claimed, had been extracted from him under duress after nearly two weeks of brutal interrogation. In a later appeal before the Israeli Supreme Court, Nafsu reportedly testified that "his interrogators deprived him of sleep for days and nights, forced him to stand outside his interrogation room for hours during winter and then to take a bitterly cold shower, made him strip, spat in his face, threw him on the floor, pulled him around by the hair and threatened to arrest his wife and mother."[13] Nafsu was convicted of espionage and sentenced to eighteen years in prison. When the Israeli Knesset passed a law allowing military verdicts to be appealed before the Supreme Court, Nafsu's case again came to light.

On 24 May 1987, after Nafu had served seven and a half years in jail, the high court ruled that Shin Bet officers had framed the Circassian officer by using "unethical interrogation methods" which forced him to confess to crimes he did not commit and by perjuring themselves during Nafsu's trial. (The court declined to overturn Nafsu's conviction on a lesser charge of having exceeded his authority by failing to report two meetings with a senior Palestinian guerrilla leader during his tenure in south Lebanon, for which he received a two-year sentence and a demotion to sergeant major.

Because he had already served over seven years in prison, the court ordered that he be freed immediately.) The case became a cause célèbre among the Jewish state's Circassian community, and upon his release Nafsu was given a hero's welcome by the 1,800 residents of his home village of Kfar Kama. Nevertheless, he returned to a shattered life after seven years of wrongful imprisonment. After his conviction in 1981, Nafsu had divorced his wife to free her from having to be bound to an imprisoned man. "How do you begin putting the pieces of your life back together after something like this?" a friend asked following Nafsu's release. Israeli President Chaim Herzog hailed Nafsu's exoneration and said that the case made him feel "ashamed." Nafsu himself said that the outcome upheld his "faith in Israeli justice."[14]

But, on the other side of the Jordan River, many of the Hashemite kingdom's Circassians had disdain for, rather than faith in, Israeli justice. In Amman, the Circassian wife of a well-to-do pilot for the Jordanian airline Alia proudly discussed her family's plans to add a new room to their suburban house, then suddenly concluded with the bitter comment, "We build a new house, and the Israelis will come and take it." The future was not good, she said; she wanted to move to America and become a U.S. citizen. That way, she reasoned, if the Jews came she would be protected because "they will not take the property of an American." Reflecting the widely held Arab view, the Circassian housewife cautioned, "The Israelis want everything from the Nile to the Euphrates, even if it takes them two hundred, three hundred years."[15]

Shurdom offered a stern rebuke to those Circassians who might find virtue in their support for Israel:

We Circassians are part of the Arab cause, because we believe strongly in the Palestinian cause. We feel with them, because we share the same human tragedy of foreign forces: Palestine and Circassia, the same cause. We are Muslims and it is part of our duty to defend the rights of the Palestinian people. The higher national interests of the Arab people are part of our interests. We are proudly Jordanians and we are morally and religiously obligated to defend the principles of justice in this conflict.

I strongly denounce what some Circassians who are living in Palestine say in support of the other side. I think it is very shameful to have such few who gave themselves to their self-interests, instead of supporting the logical position of siding with our brothers in Islam who have hosted us during this period. Where is the logic behind a Circassian supporting Israel? I think this is (if true) the position of exceptions.[16]

Other Circassians, however, have understood the logic of supporting Israel. A Circassian businessman who emigrated to southern California explained that Circassians have it "in their blood" to serve their superiors faithfully, and echoing the qualities of loyalty espoused by people like Haghandouqa and Bazell, he affirmed that they will support whatever regime is in power, whether it be Palestinian, Turkish, Jordanian, Syrian, Israeli, British, American, or French. Indeed, in 1947, during Israel's War of Independence, the Circassian town of Rihaniya, though surrounded by Arab villages, threw in their lot with the Jews and were thus supplied with weapons by the Haganah. In 1956, the Circassians of Israel voluntarily asked David Ben-Gurion to draft them into the Israel Defense Forces, and nearly 40 percent of Rihaniya's residents now willingly serve in the various branches of the Israeli armed forces.[17] Still, according to Circassian spokesmen like the one who settled in the Circassian immigrant community in southern California, despite conflicting loyalties, "There is no hatred between the Circassians in Jordan and those in Israel." As for the overall dispute between Arabs and Jews, the community leader said that he had learned of "a Circassian village that raised a white flag to signal their neutrality during one of the [Arab-Israeli] wars."[18]

But in Dina al-Asan's case, it wasn't neutrality that she sought, but a part in the struggle against the PLO. Circassians on both sides of the Jordan River had been victimized by Palestinian violence.

On the evening of 30 November 1974, two PLO commandos crossed the Lebanese border and moved three miles south to Rihaniya, the small Circassian settlement of approximately seven hundred people located in the Israeli Galilee. At about 10:30 P.M., just after the lights were turned off for the night, the guerrillas approached a two-story house. When the thirty-five-year-old resident, Subhi Abzak, opened the door, the attackers fired two bursts of gunfire, killing Mr. Abzak and wounding his wife, Samira.[19]

The Circassian villagers came running into the streets after the shots were fired and surrounded the building. The PLO gunmen placed Subhi Abzak's nine-year-old daughter in front of a window and had her relay messages to the crowd outside. Her seven-year-old brother, who had managed to escape, told the neighbors that his father was dead.

Thirty minutes after the attack, Israeli forces arrived on the scene and the terrorists surrendered. Mrs. Abzak underwent surgery at a hospital in Safad, five miles south of the village.

An Israeli officer said that the PLO raid at Rihaniya had been launched to mark the anniversary of the 29 November 1947 decision by the United Nations to partition British-controlled Palestine into Jewish and Arab states. The PLO gunmen were apparently surprised to learn that the Israeli village was inhabited by Arabic-speaking Moslems, and they offered their apologies to the Circassian residents following the attack. The Circassians reportedly rejected the apology, reaffirming their allegiance to Israel and asking the authorities to arm them so that they could fend off future attacks.[20]

Eleven years later, the Circassians were again shaken by a Palestinian terrorist attack, though this time it was a man from the community across the river in Jordan that fell victim, not someone living in Israel.

On 4 December 1985, Azmi al-Mufti was assassinated in the parking lot of Romania's Bucuresti Hotel as he was taking his child to school. Azmi al-Mufti was a high-level Jordanian diplomat and a Circassian. The official Romanian press agency said that authorities immediately arrested the killer, Ahmed Mohd Ali Hersh, a twenty-seven-year-old native of the Israeli-occupied West Bank town of Nablus. The Palestinian had been attending the Bucharest Institute for Construction and was traveling on a Jordanian passport. In a telephone call to the London office of an international news agency, the terrorist unit of the Palestinian Black September Organization claimed responsibility for the murder.[21] According to terrorist experts, this Black September cell was unrelated to Arafat's strike force of the 1970s, being in fact a cover name used by the renegade ex-Fateh member, Abu Nidal. The murder of Azmi al-Mufti in Bucharest—who was probably singled out not because he was a Circassian but because he was simply an emissary of Hussein's—was most likely carried out by Abu Nidal's extremists, who were opposed to the PLO-Jordanian dialogue then under way between the king and Yassir Arafat.

Israeli sources said that it was Dina al-Asan's opposition to such PLO extremism and terror—not a rejection of Palestinian nationalism—that prompted her to join the Mossad. She saw PLO violence as a threat to both the Jewish and Circassian communities of the Middle East.

Yet, in a highly charged conversation, Dina's sister flatly rejected the proposition that she freely volunteered to work for the Israeli secret service. "Dina was trapped from both sides," she angrily declared. "It was a mistake, and she regrets it."[22]

Israeli intelligence officials, however, have pointed out that though coercion or blackmail may serve short-term ends, agents can function reliably and efficiently over the long run only if they act from deeply held convictions arrived at independently and without pressure. That is why the Mossad, unlike the Soviet KGB and other intelligence organizations, does not prevent an operative from resigning from the agency once the individual loses the desire to serve.

There is also Israel's adherence to the tenet that a country's citizens have the right to choose for themselves the kind of work they wish to pursue. And beyond the moral consideration is the practical issue: Israeli intelligence experts have adopted a policy that allows agents to resign their positions because they are convinced that the resentment felt by operatives involuntarily pressed into service will inevitably lead to carelessness, lack of initiative, and perhaps betrayal as double-agents for a foreign power.

In Dina's case, Israel's acceptance of the services of a Moslem woman from an Arab country for a long-term assignment with the Mossad held enough risks without the additional burden of attempting to hold her loyalty through entrapment or blackmail. As for her mental state, the insistence by various Jordanian Circassians that Dina was disturbed and unbalanced, a medical charlatan whose sufferings at the hands of an ex-husband drove her into the hands of the Zionist enemy, drew the Israeli response that the Mossad does not allow criminals, deranged adventurers, or unstable volunteers to perform delicate undercover work. Again, the risks are too high: a botched operation could expose an entire intelligence network, jeopardizing the lives of fellow agents and compromising the security of the state. Indeed, there were Circassians who remarked that Dina may not have been so "crazy" after all, with one Jordanian woman commenting that perhaps Dina was "smart" to work against the PLO.[23]

The Mossad is considered by many to be the best intelligence agency in the world. Its reputation was not built by enlisting the services of unwilling agents or unstable recruits. Espionage failures like that of the American naval analyst Jonathan Jay Pollard, who was arrested in Washington on 21 November 1986 on charges of spying for Israel and later sentenced to life imprisonment, are the exceptions that prove the rule: Pollard's reported indiscretions and emotionalism prior to his work for Israel should ordinarily have disqualified him as a candidate for the Israeli secret service. "I think a lot of people were surprised because it didn't fit the pattern of Israeli intelligence," said FBI director William Webster. "The utilization of Pollard was unusual."[24]

The Mossad's recruitment of Dina al-Asan did fit the pattern. The accusations of mental instability and professional fraud leveled against Dina al-Asan by Circassians in her native Jordan were dismissed as outlandish by the Israelis. According to the Mossad, Dina al-Asan was one of their most successful agents, a strong, courageous woman with a clear sense of purpose and a profound belief in the rightness of her mission.

Dina's mission actually came about as a result of a chance meeting during an extended stay in Vienna, when, after first visiting her sister in Rome, Dina landed in Austria to continue her medical studies.

Police records in Austria show her arriving in Vienna at the end of

1972, residing briefly at the Hotel Goldene, and leaving the country a year later. It was presumably during this period that Dina began her training as a Mossad agent. Though the police in Vienna also indicated that Dina enrolled in a local trade school, a check of the major educational institutions, including the University of Vienna, failed to uncover any evidence that Dina was ever a student.

She apparently returned to Austria, either for business or pleasure, the following year. The files of the central archives in Vienna indicate that Dina registered with their office on 15 May 1974. Yet police records failed to disclose this second trip. When first questioned about Dina, Viennese Police Inspector Kolvarnik—a man whose specialty was to keep tabs on potential PLO clashes with Jews—cavalierly dismissed allegations that she had been recruited by the Israelis while living in Austria.[25] But there were indications that Dina had indeed come to the attention of the Austrian authorities.

A Czechoslovakian refugee who had rented an apartment for Dina said that at one point police officials approached neighbors inquiring about her.[26] Yet Inspector Kolvarnik insisted that the Viennese police had no record of Dina. During an interview Kolvarnik at first calmly agreed to telephone headquarters to verify his statement that Dina had not run afoul of the police. But moments after speaking with his colleagues, Kolvarnik tensely hung up the phone and excused himself, disappearing into the next office. When he returned, red-faced, he demanded to know the purpose of the questioning about Dina. Apparently Kolvarnik had not been aware of Dina's history, and it appeared that a check of the records may have turned up something that the Austrian authorities were not eager to disclose.

Because of its location as a corridor between Western Europe and the East-bloc countries, Austria has long been a center of international diplomacy and intrigue. Vienna houses an important United Nations outpost and serves as the headquarters for the Organization of Petroleum Exporting Countries (OPEC). At the time of Dina's stay, the sympathies of Austria's pro-Arab Jewish Chancellor Bruno Kreisky, the visibility of numerous anti-Israeli representatives stationed at the United Nation's Vienna office, and the presence of visiting OPEC ministers and sheiks had turned Austria into a hot-spot for Arab-Israeli confrontation.

It is possible that the Austrians had learned of Dina's involvement with the Mossad prior to her return in 1974 and did not want to go on record as having been aware of her activities. They may have decided to launch a secret investigation of their own, compiling a dossier for future reference, keeping track of her movements to avoid a diplomatic incident on Austrian soil. They may have had plans to deport her; they may even have quietly expelled her; or they may have chosen to turn a blind eye in an attempt to remain neutral and avoid offending either the Israeli or Arab diplomats within their borders.

It is not known if the Austrian authorities were implicated in Dina's activities: whether they abetted the Mossad, acquiescing in her recruitment, or actually strove to sabotage her work. Whatever the truth, Dina's behavior in Vienna did arouse suspicion.

While renting the apartment from her Czechoslovakian landlord, Dina befriended a neighbor. Both the landlord and the neighbor say that at the time Dina was calling herself Dianne Schwartz. (Friends and family in and out of Jordan continue to refer to Dina as Dianne.) When Dina stopped paying the rent on her apartment, her landlord was forced to ask Dina to move out, and the neighbor agreed to take her in. The elderly neighbor, a Jew who later moved to Germany in January 1983, found Dina's behavior quite strange. She recalled that Dina frequently received telephone calls from Switzerland at midnight, the callers conducting their conversations in Arabic. Yet Dina often talked about her affection for Jews, the neighbor said, and often met a Jewish pilot at the Cafe Puckel or the Cafe Eos. Both the landlord and the neighbor say they had discussed with each other the possibility that Dina was involved in espionage, and that the news of her association with the Mossad was not a total surprise.[27]

According to Israeli sources, it was a romance with an Israeli pilot during Dina's initial stay in Vienna that led her to join the Mossad. She had fallen in love with the Israeli, and, as a non-Arab native of Jordan, she was able to relate to the precarious position of his fellow Jews in the Middle East. The pilot eventually introduced Dina to a Mossad operative, and Dina decided to join the organization. It was suggested that she open a clinic in Beirut to serve as a cover for a secret intelligence gathering operation. Her 1974 return trip to Vienna may have been to rendezvous with her Mossad contact, meet up with her Israeli pilot, or both.

A seasoned Israeli observer of intelligence affairs once said that, almost by definition, the mentality of a spy is mysterious. A spy's life is based on duplicity. You can never be sure if the face presented to you is the real one. The observer was referring to Anwar Sadat, who worked as a spy for the Germans during World War II, and he was commenting on the Israeli skepticism surrounding Sadat's motives for his sudden visit to Jerusalem. A similar skepticism might be applicable to Dina; it is difficult to determine which face she presented to the young Israeli captain she met while living in Vienna. Yet their relationship led to an introduction to a Mossad operative who became convinced that she would make a dependable agent.

It may have been the prospect of running a clinic again that prompted

Dina to accept the Mossad offer, or it may have been a desire for vengeance against her Palestinian ex-husband that led her to spy for his Zionist enemies. One former CIA agent observed that Dina's recruitment had all the markings of the classic "honey-pot" technique where a member of the opposite sex is used to lure a potential agent into the ranks.[28] Dina's decision may have rested less on romance than on a sincere conviction that the fate of the Circassians in Jordan hinged on the eradication of the PLO, who at the time were headquartered in Beirut. Or she may have just felt a simple bond with the Jews, another non-Arab minority threatened by a common enemy. Whatever her reasons, early in 1973, after receiving intensive training in the use of clandestine radio transmitters, message coding devices, and photographic surveillance techniques, Dina al-Asan arrived in Beirut to set up operations for the Mossad.

4

Retribution

WHEN Dina arrived in Beirut in 1973, the city had not yet plunged into chaos. The Place des Cannons, called the *Burj* by the Lebanese, bustled with Mercedes, Coca-Cola signs, and splashy discos blaring Mick Jagger's *Honky Tonk Women*. European bankers and oil-rich sheiks kept the city's neon blazing afterhours. The Byblos Cinema featured Faye Dunaway and Warren Beatty in *Bonnie & Clyde*, the luxurious Phoenicia-Intercontinental Hotel, overlooking the scenic Bay of St. George, served up stuffed grape leaves, spicy lamb shish-kebob, and authentic Arab flat bread.

The seventy-three financial institutions lining Bank Street competed for the petro-dollar deposits pouring in from Kuwait, Bahrain, Iraq, Qatar, Iran, Dhubai, and Saudi Arabia. Moscow's Narodny Bank operated alongside the First National Bank of Chicago, the Bank of Nova Scotia traded with the Arab Bank Limited, all profiting from Lebanon's liberal currency laws. Beirut was hailed as having the best of Times Square and Zurich.

Before the 1975-76 civil war drove the investors back to London and reduced much of the city to rubble, Beirut was the link between the cultures of East and West. There were outboards gliding across the Mediterranean, the skiers riding the waters shared by Europe; there were pilgrims hiking past the Cedars of Lebanon, touching the fir that was used to build Solomon's Temple in Jerusalem. Shoppers bartered with merchants carrying classical hand-crafted copper pots on donkeys ambling across Hamra Street; others browsed among the latest fashions from Calvin Klein in posh boutiques on Patriarch Hoyek Street. In the crowded Moslem quarters where Dina worked and slept, the narrow streets held the heavy smoke of hookah-pipes and the forlorn looks of refugees dreaming of a return to Palestine.

Dina catered to the sick and the wounded, treating PLO members, Palestinian civilians, Lebanese citizens. She would travel south to the refugee camps at Sidon and Tyre where dysentery, hepatitis, and malnutrition

32

flourished in squalid shacks lacking toilets, heat, and running water. She would visit Red Crescent facilities—the Palestinian equivalent of the Red Cross, run by Yassir Arafat's brother, Fatih—ostensibly to check on medical supplies, but, as in everything else she did throughout the camps, in fact to gather intelligence on PLO officials: the location of their arms caches, their plans for military action. At times she found crates of Soviet-made rocket launchers and explosives marked "Medicine" in the basements of Red Crescent hospitals.

During Israel's 1982 invasion of Lebanon, there were numerous accusations that Israeli troops deliberately launched artillery against civilian medical facilities. Journalist Michael Jansen charged that "Israeli 'pin-point' shelling and bombing" during the siege of Beirut "hit hospitals, killing people they had injured when they bombed them out of their houses."[1] Yet other observers, including Richard Gabriel, reported that, just as Dina discovered, Palestinian guerrillas were using civilian medical facilities to camouflage weapons depots and combat units. The PLO used "the sick and wounded as shields," Gabriel reported. "In the Ein Hilwe camp, the PLO staged military operations out of hospitals and put guns on their roofs."[2] Part of Dina's assignment was to distinguish the civilian institutions from the military ones, but often the two were so intertwined that civilian casualties in an attack on a military target were inevitable; this was often the case during the 1982 invasion of Lebanon.

In the early 1970s, a series of terrorist attacks against Israeli citizens was staged by Palestinian guerrillas headquartered in the refugee camps of Lebanon. There was the Munich massacre of eleven members of the Israeli Olympic Team in 1972; the April 1974 raid on a civilian apartment building in the border town of Qiryat Shemona, which claimed the lives of eighteen men, women, and children; and the following month's attack on a schoolhouse in Maalot in which twenty high school students were killed and seventy wounded. When such attacks took place, the Israelis retaliated by sending warplanes into Lebanon to knock out PLO positions. Dina's reports from Beirut were in part designed to keep bombs from falling on Arab civilians. It is likely that some of the PLO members killed or wounded by the Israeli fighter jets guided by her reports had previously been her patients in the camps.

Since the 1950s, the Israelis have executed a policy of quick retaliatory strikes against Palestinian guerrilla bases in neighboring Arab states in an attempt to discourage terrorist attacks against Jews. A significant step in the evolution of Israel's counterterrorist policy was taken in May 1953, when continued cross-border raids by Palestinian guerrillas resulted in the General Staff's consideration of a proposal issued by Brigadier Michael Shacham. It advocated the formation of a special commando squad devoted to the implementation of retaliatory strikes against Palestinian terrorists stationed in Arab countries.

A few months later, Chief of Staff Mordechai Makleff established Army Camp 101. Major Ariel Sharon was asked to command the all-volunteer squad of about fifty men. During a discussion with his troops, Sharon explained the rationale for Israel's policy of reprisal and formation of the elite squad, dubbed Commando Unit 101:

> In order to understand what's going on in the Israel of 1953, we must detach ourselves from the situation, and survey it from a distance.
>
> We have won the war. That is a fact. And as far as the Arabs are concerned, it's an irritating one. The Arab states that were defeated, possessed trained and well equipped armies. They were aided by foreign consultants. And nonetheless, they were beaten by a small, unequipped and isolated nation. It's a hard fact to swallow. And to top it all, Israel is ruling over a greater part of Palestine than was allotted to her by the U.N. in 1947.
>
> We—needless to say—are pleased. We're concentrating on development, immigration, and on protecting the land we have won. But they are ashamed and disappointed. They want to change the present reality. They can't bear to see us triumph, they seek only to destroy our achievements. And since we wish to retain all we have to avoid military confrontations, we try not to retaliate. This effort of ours is interpreted by them as weakness and cowardice. Thus, they increase their hostile activities and force us to respond. And again—as long as the reprisals are on a minor scale, it appears as though we are helpless. Thus we lose the power of intimidating them. They cease to fear us, and do not heed our warnings and threats. Simultaneously their belief in their own military prowess grows, and they renew the hope of reconquering Palestine. At the same time, on our part, since the terrorism does not lessen, despite our responses, we lose confidence in our ability to defend ourselves.[3]

Sharon's solution to the debilitating effects of terrorism was to "prove that we can strike hardest and best." The method would be to "strike secretly and efficiently, without employing large forces," the result that "we'll have taught the Arabs a thing or two about our power without having gotten involved in international conflicts."[4]

Three years later, Moshe Dayan—who as chief of staff had earlier merged Unit 101 with the paratroopers, placing Sharon in charge of the entire battalion—supported Ben-Gurion's call for a continuation of Israel's policy of reprisal:

We had to convince Jordan that her attacks—or attacks by terrorists using her territory as a base—on Israeli civilians could end only in a loss of prestige of her government. The Arab public might regard terrorism against Israel as part of a noble national war, satisfying their yearning for vengeance, restoring something of their honor after the defeat of their armies in Israel's War of Independence. To overseas critics, the Arab governments, including Jordan's King Hussein, claimed that they were powerless to prevent acts of terror, which they said were the acts of Palestinian refugees. Among their own people, however, they made no secret of their encouragement of terrorism. I had no doubt that the only way to put an end to their attacks on Israeli civilians was to take sharp action against specifically military objectives in the countries from which the attacks were launched. This alone would have the desired impact on their governments, showing them that it was in their own interest to prevent fedayeen activity. If they did not, the Israeli army would strike back, demonstrate the weakness of the Arab armies, and expose them as incapable of meeting the Israeli army in the field. The consequence to the Arab leaders could only be a loss of standing in the eyes of their people.[5]

Sharon's tactics indeed led to a loss of standing for Arab leaders, though many would claim that they likewise led to the tarnishing of the Israeli soldier's image as a humane fighter. He sent his men on daring missions, in which they penetrated deep into Arab territory on foot and wearing civilian clothes to conduct lightening strikes behind enemy lines, openly flaunting his ability to pursue the enemy at any time and in any place.

In October 1953, when a mother and two small children were murdered in their sleep by Arab infiltrators, Sharon asked to lead a reprisal against Kibya, a Jordanian town of about 2,000 people that served as a sanctuary for Arab terrorists operating against Israel. The reprisal resulted in the deaths of sixty-nine Arabs, nearly half of them women and children. Sharon's troops had carried thirteen hundred pounds of explosives into Kibya, blowing up forty-five buildings. The men of Unit 101 later insisted that most of the deaths occurred accidently during the explosions: despite a quick search of the buildings, many were not empty when the demolition teams set their charges. To this day, Kibya is held by both Arabs and Israelis as one example among many of Sharon's willingness to sacrifice Arab civilians, including women and children. At the time, Prime Minister Ben-Gurion distanced himself from the raid, but nevertheless overlooked its apparent carelessness (or callousness) out of a regard for Sharon's ability to avenge the deaths of innocent Jews. ''One consequence of this action was to restore a measure of confidence to the General Staff in the ability of the IDF [the Israel Defense Forces] to act effectively against the Arab guerrillas,'' wrote Sharon biographer Uzi Benziman. According to Benziman, Sharon believed that the raid had served to "prove that any mission was possible if one believed in its urgency.[6]"

This urgency to combat Arab terrorism led to more and more daring blows by Israeli commandos operating behind enemy lines. The reprisal raids appeared to yield results: in January 1965, Ahmad Musa was killed after returning from a raid on Israel's Eilaboun tunnel, part of a water diversion project leading from the Sea of Galilee. The commando was shot after re-crossing the border into Jordan by King Hussein's troops. "The first 'Martyr' of Fatah," Jillian Becker points out, "was the victim not of Israeli but of Jordanian response."[7]

Hussein's biographer Peter Snow wrote that by 1965 the king was determined to "stop the guerrillas from inflaming his border with Israel," even if it meant killing PLO fighters like Ahmad Musa, and that Nasser had likewise also acted to prevent guerrilla raids on Israel from the Egyptian-occupied Gaza Strip because he too believed that he was not yet prepared for a war with Israel.[8] Israel's reprisal policy meant that a price would be paid by countries supporting terrorist attacks against Jews, and for some Arab governments, that price was unacceptable.

Yet, despite the tight reins being imposed on Palestinians guerrillas by their host Arab states, terrorism continued. By PLO leader Abu Iyad's own account, nearly two hundred guerrilla attacks against Israel were launched by Palestinian commandos between 1965 and 1967.[9] It wasn't until the 1970 Black September crackdown on Palestinian forces in Amman that terrorism along the Jordanian frontier dropped significantly.

Critics of military retaliation point to the fact that despite Israel's stand, the nation has never been free of terrorism. Others defend the Israeli position by claiming that though reprisal raids have failed to completely eliminate terrorism, their absence would have allowed even more instances of terror. For Moshe Dayan, one of the chief architects of Israel's counter-terrorist strategy, the decrease in guerrilla activity during the 1960s and 1970s could be directly traced to Israel's policy of reprisal: "If Israel had not reacted so sharply to sabotage operations undertaken from Jordanian territory, the government of Jordan would have reached a modus vivendi with the terrorists," Dayan insisted. "Hussein finally resolved to stamp out terrorism because the alternative would have been the destruction of ordered life in Jordan."[10]

But, as Dayan also observed, the destruction of the PLO in Jordan only served to send them north "where they operated from bases in the refugee camps of what became known as Fatah-land in Lebanon."[11]

Fatah-land was Dina's field of operation. The Mossad stationed her there as part of an overall Israeli effort aimed at repeating the relative success with Jordan that brought about a reduction in Jordanian-based terrorism, the hope being that both the Lebanese and the Palestinians might move to stamp out PLO terrorism operating from Lebanese soil in order to shield themselves from Israel's policy of military retaliation.

For the Israelis, the merit of their reprisal policy was demonstrated a decade later, when the Shiite Amal militia, determined to protect themselves from inevitable Israeli retaliation, moved against armed Palestinians in southern Lebanon and Beirut to block PLO raids into Israel. The Shiites, who had earlier fought off the Israelis in Southern Lebanon by launching a series of guerrilla commando strikes and suicide car bombings, no doubt also sought to capitalize on the Israeli withdrawal from Lebanon by consolidating their power base in Beirut. Prior to Israel's rout of the PLO during its 1982 invasion, the Shiites, especially in the south of Lebanon, had suffered under the weight of PLO dominance, which they had come to resent with such force that at first they welcomed the Israeli soldiers as liberators. Later, with the Israelis out and Shiite power and prestige in the ascendancy, the Amal leaders felt it was time to eliminate the PLO's challenge to their authority. But fear that the re-establishment of a Palestinian military presence in Lebanon would bring Israeli bombers, possibly troops, back to Beirut was a contributing factor in the Shiite drive to oust the PLO fighters.

Many observers, including those in Israel, found the Amal "Battle of the Camps" attacks against Palestinians to be unnecessarily brutal. Yet it seemed obvious that the same counterterrorist strategy that Dina had helped execute in the mid-1970s again had relevance in the mid-1980s.

"Amal wants to stop the PLO because they know they'll pay the price," a Western diplomat reported after the Shiite takeover of Palestinian positions that followed in the wake of Israel's withdrawal from the area. Like many residents in neighboring Arab states, many Lebanese knew that the price of terrorism against Jews would be swift Israeli reprisals. "The Israelis will retaliate against this area and these people," the diplomat said. And so, like the Egyptians, the Syrians, and the Jordanians before them, the Lebanese Shiite Muslims came down hard on the Palestinian guerrillas, hoping to destroy the PLO's ability to launch attacks against Israel from Shiite neighborhoods and thus remove the threat of Israeli retaliation against Shiite communities. [12]

On 24 June 1984, U.S. Secretary of State George Shultz made a public appeal that seemed to mirror the counterterrorist stance that Dina had felt compelled to embrace ten years earlier. The secretary called on Western nations to fashion specialized intelligence networks that could help implement a unified policy of military retaliation against terrorists:

From a practical standpoint, a purely passive defense does not provide enough of a deterrent to terrorism and the states that sponsor it. It is time to think long, hard, and seriously about more active means of defense—about defense through appropriate preventive or pre-emptive actions against terrorist groups before they strike.

We will need to strengthen our capabilities in the area of intelligence and quick reaction. Human intelligence will be particularly important, since our societies demand that we know with reasonable clarity just what we are doing. Experience has taught us over the years that one of the best deterrents to terrorism is the certainty that swift and sure measures will be taken against those who engage in it.[13]

Most likely, it was the Israeli experience which Secretary Shultz referred to when discussing the lessons that had been learned about "deterrents to terrorism." The Americans had long been privy to Zionist decision-making regarding the interplay between intelligence and reprisal in the formation of counterterrorist policy. The intelligence agencies of the United States and Israel enjoyed a close working relationship, dating back to James Angleton's contacts with Jewish underground leaders in London on behalf of the U.S. Office of Strategic Services during World War II. When the OSS was dissolved in 1945, Angleton moved on to the newly-formed Central Intelligence Agency and used his wartime contacts to establish an intelligence exchange agreement with the Mossad.[14] The exchanges continued for the next forty years.

Dina's own intelligence work in Lebanon enabled the Israelis to mount a series of devastating blows against the region's guerrilla organizations, but though she vehemently opposed terrorism, she nevertheless sympathized with the plight of the Palestinian people. She could not endorse the methods of "freedom fighters" who hurled grenades into a packed Tel Aviv movie theatre or gunned down unarmed Jewish athletes. But she could not overlook the tragedy that had engulfed the Palestinian people since their defeat in 1948.

5

The Camps

IN 1974, Beirut may have been a modern financial capital brimming with prosperous Lebanese bankers, chauffeur-driven Saudi princes, and elegant nightclub patrons, but the Palestinian camps Dina visited resembled urban ghetto slums. Many of the refugees still lived in canvas tents that barely kept out the cold and the rain.

In 1976, there were fifteen Palestinian refugee camps scattered throughout Lebanon: Nahr al-Bared and Beddawi in the north near Tripoli, Wavell to the east in the Bekaa Valley near Baalbeck; in the south Ain al-Hilweh and Mieh-Mieh outside of Sidon; Nabatieh above the Litani River; al-Bass, Bourj al-Shemal, and Rashidiyeh on the outskirts of Tyre; and around Beirut, Bourj al-Barajneh, Shatilla, Dbayeh, Tal Zaatar, Mar Elias, and Jisr al-Basha.

Dina found nearly 200 thousand Palestinians living in the overcrowded camps. She would walk past the rows of concrete shelters where the sewage ran through open, fly-infested ditches, the human waste steamed by the summer sun, giving off a perpetual foul odor. Tal Zaatar had been designed to accommodate five thousand people. In 1974, it was packed with fifteen thousand. A 1971 survey of the camps by the Statistics Department of the Lebanese Ministry of Planning revealed that an average of six to seven people lived in houses with two rooms or fewer.[1] Douglas Watson, a journalist for the *Washington Post*, reported that in the Rashidiyeh camp there were no street lights and no street names, and the lanes between the shelters were "barely wide enough for a truck to squeeze past the usual congregations of wandering children and goats."[2]

The unsanitary conditions in the camps made it impossible for Dina to prevent outbreaks of childhood diseases like chickenpox, poliomyelitis, and measles. According to the United Nations Relief and Works Agency for Palestine Refugees (UNWRA), the biggest killer of refugee babies was gastroenteritis, which rapidly dehydrated small infants, often killing them within the first year of life.[3]

Dina had established her practice for children, and she toured the camps to ferret out these cases of gastroenteritis. Those suffering from the disease were rushed to special UNRWA rehydration centers. The dying babies would be given anti-diarrhoeal drugs and fed salt solutions through emergency internasal drip procedures to restore bodily fluids. Then they would be placed on high-protein diets to add weight to their emaciated bodies. Eight-month-old children were brought in weighing less than they had at two months. "Sudden deterioration, and even death, can occur within hours," one UNRWA report explained. "Anyone who has seen the distended abdomen and shrunken face of a dehydrated baby has some idea of the brutality of this disease. Even in milder cases, malnutrition as a result of gastro-enteritis can take weeks or sometimes months to treat."[4]

Dina also worked closely with the *dayahs*, the traditional midwives who delivered the majority of the babies in the camps, trying to ensure that complications arising from premature births and Caesarian section deliveries were properly treated. Dealing with trachoma was another priority. The highly contagious eye disease has been one of the biggest causes of progressive blindness in the Middle East. Irritation from dust and wind enable the trachoma virus to grow unchecked, producing a granular thickening of the eyelids that leads to the formation of ulcers in the eyes. These ulcers could scar the cornea, resulting eventually in blindness. The disease can be transmitted by hand or even through contaminated objects, as was often the case in refugee families owning only one towel.

"The usual carrier of trachoma is the common fly," UNRWA reported, "which becomes particularly obnoxious in overcrowded conditions and in hot weather. The sight of a swarm of flies clustering around a refugee baby's eyes is all too common."[5] By dispensing tubes of chlortetracyline that cost less than thirty cents each, Dina was able to prevent blindness in scores of refugees.

Palestinians refer to the establishment of Israel as the "Great Disaster." Dina understood why after seeing their misery in Lebanon. Her dedication and empathy did not go unnoticed by her patients, and she was welcomed into the homes of refugees living in the camps as well as of those fortunate enough to have apartments in Beirut proper. UNRWA doctors might examine more than two hundred patients in one day, with women seated on hard benches and floors for hours, nursing their sick babies. A camp of sixteen thousand would be served by a single nurse and a doctor who could manage only two visits a week. Dina's clinic helped ease UNRWA's workload while providing personal attention to distraught refugee families.

At first, Dina began operating within regular office hours, working from a small building that also housed her own apartment. But once it became obvious to the refugees that she was willing to travel great distances at any hour to treat a patient, the clinic became an important center for the Palestinian community.

The clinic had been established with secret Israeli funds. Dina's cover story was that she had used money from her savings account in Geneva to start her practice in Beirut. She explained that she came from an Arab family that had moved to Europe when she was still a young girl, and that she had spent most of her adult life in Switzerland. She said she still had a brother in Geneva, but that she had decided to return to the Middle East to help her fellow Arabs and that she sympathized with the Palestinian cause. The addresses she gave concerning friends, relatives, and finances were provided by the Israelis so that if anyone should check her story, the Mossad would have agents available to back it up. They could pose as family members, answer correspondence, and process the necessary paper work with the bank that held Dina's account in Geneva.

Dina's work in Lebanon deepened her conviction that the Palestinians needed a nation of their own, not in place of Israel but rather alongside it, to be established on the West Bank and in Gaza, lands captured by Israel during the 1967 war. She continued to oppose the PLO's strategy for attaining a Palestinian state, rejecting armed struggle and the use of terror. She was completely candid on this point with whomever she met, and had numerous heated debates with PLO members and supporters. Her honesty reinforced the trust that she had already built up among the refugees while treating patients throughout the camps. Dina used that trust to search the camps and sabotage PLO operations. She was not always successful: on 11 April 1974, three members of the PLO faction known as the Popular Front for the Liberation of Palestine—General Command (PFLP-GC) shot their way into an apartment house at Qiryat Shemona, a small settlement town located in northern Israel. They rigged the buildings with explosives and four hours later blew themselves up along with the residents, killing eight children, eight adults, and two Israeli soldiers.

The PFLP-GC was hoping to prevent policy-makers within the Arab world from seeking an agreement that might allow for the establishment of an independent Palestinian state in the territories conquered by Israel in the 1967 Six Day War. In 1947, Arab militants were opposed to any compromise that would partition Palestine into two states, one Jewish, one Arab. "We carried out the operation at Qiryat Shemona," the terrorists' communique stated, "to underline that our liberation struggle is not limited to the West Bank or Gaza but covers all Palestinian territory." The next day, an official spokesman for the PFLP-GC, Mohammad Abbas (who later masterminded the Achille Lauro hijacking), held a news conference, telling reporters that the guerrilla "campaign is aimed at blocking an Arab-Israeli peace settlement."[6]

The following month, on 15 May, another PLO faction, the Popular Democratic Front for the Liberation of Palestine (PDFLP), sent three commandos into Maalot, an Israeli settlement in the Galilee. They crept in at 3:30 A.M., when thirty-five hundred impoverished Jewish immigrants lay sleeping in their new refuge. The commandos broke into Block No. 34, a weatherworn three-story apartment building, and raced through the halls shouting in Hebrew, "Open up! This is the police!" Yosef Cohen jumped up from his bed and opened the door. He was cut down in a hail of bullets along with his four-year-old son. His wife, seven months pregnant, fled toward the staircase with her wounded daughter at her side. She was struck by a barrage of machine-gun fire.

The Netif Meir school was next. Bursting through the door, the commandos asked the fifty-year-old janitor one question: "Are there children inside?" The janitor answered yes. Seconds later he was dead. The commandos moved on. Slipping into the classrooms, they found nearly one hundred sleeping teenagers in the midst of a three-day outing, huddled inside their sleeping bags on the floor. The PLO guerrillas began firing into the walls and ceilings, herding the students together, kicking and clubbing them.

The next evening, fourteen hours later, the Israelis attempted a rescue. The battle lasted nine minutes. One of the commandos was shot as he dashed down the stairs to the first floor in order to detonate pre-set explosives. The other two had immediately raised their guns as the rescue began, opening up on the captive children. When they were finally silenced by Israeli soldiers, twenty-one children lay dead or dying on the bloodsplattered floors of the schoolhouse, along with the seventy-four other survivors, their flesh shredded from shrapnel and their lungs wincing from gunpowder and lead.[7]

Like their counterparts in the PFLP-GC, the PDFLP faction decided to hold a news conference to justify their assault at Maalot. The leader and founder of the PDFLP, Nayef Hawatmeh, chose to conduct the meeting personally. "To put it bluntly," he told reporters, "we will spare no effort to foil the Kissinger mission."[8]

The shuttle diplomacy by the American secretary of state had already succeeded in bringing about a disengagement of Egyptian and Israeli forces along the Suez Canal, stationed there as a result of the 1973 Yom Kippur War. The likelihood of Kissinger attaining a similar accord on the Golan

Heights between Israel and Syria spurred hardliners like Hawatmeh and Jibril into launching attacks like the ones at Maalot and Qiryat Shemona.

The Kissinger mission succeeded nevertheless: on 18 January 1974, a disengagement agreement was signed by Egypt and Israel; on 31 May, Syria and Israel concluded a similar agreement. But the documents clearly stated that they did not constitute peace agreements and served only as first steps toward a "just and durable peace" between Israel and its Arab neighbors.[9]

The events of 1974 put Beirut squarely on the map as the capital of international terrorism and the headquarters of the political infighting among the PLO's rival factions. The spate of terrorist atrocities had sickened Dina, but as she continued to comb the streets of Beirut on behalf of the Mossad she began to notice that the climate emerging out of the Kissinger agreements seemed to hold out hope that her own vision of a peaceful solution to the conflict might one day be realized.

In July, the twelfth session of the Palestine National Council (PNC) was held in Cairo. The PLO's policy-making body adopted a resolution calling for the establishment of a Palestinian "national authority" on any portion of Palestine that might be relinquished by Israel, which in essence meant a Palestinian state on the West Bank and Gaza as envisioned by Dina. It was a move designed to give the PLO leadership a place at a planned follow-up to the previous December's Middle East peace conference in Geneva, where negotiations were to be held among Israel, Egypt, Syria, Jordan, the United States, the Soviet Union, and the United Nations. The PLO resolution, however, accommodated Hawatmeh, Jibril, and ideological comrades like George Habash and Waddieh Haddad by assuring them that the establishment of a Palestinian "national authority" on the West Bank and Gaza would not mark the end of the Palestinian struggle with Israel. "The 'national authority'," PLO expert Helena Cobban wrote, "would only be a transitional step towards the creation of a secular democratic state in the whole of Palestine," which meant in effect the dismantling of the Israeli state.[10] This of course, was at odds with Dina's vision of peaceful coexistence between Arabs and Jews in Palestine.

Aaron David Miller, a former State Department analyst, explained that the PNC's call for the creation of a Palestinian state in the territories occupied by the Arab countries in 1948 and seized by Israel in 1967 was not the expression of a newfound willingness to embrace a territorial compromise in Palestine. "It attempted," he said, "to create a new consensus around the concept of *marhaliyya*—the liberation of Palestine in stages—and to convince the Palestinian community that this was a tactical imperative essential to exploiting the post 1973 environment. The resolution enhanced the PLO's negotiating position and helped to create a more moderate image abroad without giving up the right to continue the struggle for all of Palestine or the right to return.[11]

The success of Kissinger's shuttle diplomacy and the gradual acceptance of the *marhaliyya* concept of a phased liberation of Palestine did not mean that the PLO had abandoned its commitment to armed struggle. In July 1981, the Popular Front for the Liberation of Palestine (PFLP), a Marxist faction of the PLO, affirmed its commitment to a step-by-step dismantling of the Jewish state:

> The battle to liberate Palestine will be a long, complex and difficult process, politically and militarily. It is not to the benefit of the Revolution to forget this fact. The liberation of any part of Palestine demands the creation of the objective Arab conditions. In order to begin liberating Palestinian land, the Palestinian Revolution needs a progressive Arab depth that guarantees the strategic national dimension of the battle.
>
> Moreover, there is an objective difference between the areas occupied by Zionism in 1948 and those occupied in 1967. This means that there is a difference between the balance of forces required to impose the liberation of those parts occupied in 1967, and that which can liberate all of Palestine. We believe that the process of changing the balance of forces will take place gradually through confrontation with the enemy. In this process, one part after another of Palestine will be liberated. Our war is a protracted people's war, not a sudden one. It is possible that some parts will be liberated, followed by a number of years before the liberation of other parts. The strategy of liberation entails depending on these areas for the continuation of the battle against the enemy until its entity is completely destroyed.[12]

Dina favored the PLO's call for the establishment of an independent Palestinian state on "those parts occupied [by Israel] in 1967," but parted company with the group when its leaders spoke of battling "the enemy until its entity is completely destroyed." Her frankness in dealing with both Arabs and Jews served her well: instead of adopting an extremist position that would have meant the complete abandonment of her fellow Moslems and a total rejection of the Arab culture in which she was raised, Dina's qualified support for the Palestinian cause gave the Mossad reason to believe that her dedication to Israel was the result of a carefully thought-out position that would stand the test of time. To the PLO, Dina's boldness in disclosing her acceptance of the Zionist presence in Palestine dispelled whatever suspicion they might have had regarding her activities in Lebanon: surely an Israeli intelligence agent would not want to do less than win the hearts of her PLO adversaries by proving that she was more anti-Zionist than they.

The Palestinians Dina met lived in the shadows of Lebanese society, a people without a country. To Dina, righteous ideologies, passionate debates, and clever politicians could not obscure the suffering of the refugees, nor could the assertion by her colleagues in Israel that it was the Arabs who had helped initiate the Palestinian dispersion by rejecting the 1947 Partition Resolution dividing historic Palestine between Arabs and Jews and by going to war against the newly-formed Israeli nation.

Dina's feelings about the legitimacy of Palestinian nationalism did not align with the sentiments of many Zionists. In fact, at times they tended to parallel the beliefs of people like PLO member Fawaz Turki, someone who represented the group Dina had pledged to oppose:

I have discovered that with enough diligence, the historian can present a devastatingly convincing version of the Zionist / Israeli / Jewish (call it what you wish) claim in modern Palestine. Another historian, with equal reserves of diligence and partisan to our own claims and grievances, can come up with a perfectly valid and at the same time diametrically opposite view.

"The vexatious issue," as the problem of my people was called during the Truman and Mandate years, has now expanded and become the "Arab-Israeli" conflict; and it is felt that the solution of it by the big powers is as mandatory now as it was mandatory then.

Mine is not a vexatious issue, nor has it much to do with the conflict now raging between the Arabs and the Zionists. Nor is its solution dependent upon, nor will I allow it to be, the whims of the big powers. Mine is an existential problem having to do with the yearning for my homeland, with being part of a culture, with winning the battle to remain myself, as a Palestinian belonging to a people with a distinctly Palestinian consciousness.

If I was not a Palestinian when I left Haifa as a child, I am one now. Living in Beirut as a stateless person for most of my growing-up years, many of them in a refugee camp, I did not feel I was living among my "Arab brothers." I did not feel I was an Arab, a Lebanese, or as some wretchedly pious writers claimed, a "southern Syrian." I was a Palestinian.[13]

Dina embraced the national aspirations of the Palestinian; what she fought was his use of terror.

As a physician working in the refugee camps throughout Lebanon, Dina may not have been able to convince many Palestinians to adopt her more moderate stance toward the conflict with Israel or prevent the PLO from conducting its protracted guerrilla war against the Jews, but, as a highly trained Mossad agent, she was in a position to help Israel carry out its policy of retribution. Her chance came shortly after the next guerrilla attack on 24 June 1974. Three terrorists from Arafat's Fateh faction landed on the Israeli coast by boat during the night and entered Nahariya, a town built by German Jews in the 1930s and located four miles south of the Lebanese border. Bursts of automatic gunfire suddenly broke through the night air as the PLO guerrillas dashed across the once quiet roads. They stormed into the apartment building at 19 Balfour and killed three Israeli civilians. Two hours later, a fifteen-minute gun battle erupted when Israeli troops under the command of Major General Raphael Eitan—the man who would later serve as chief of staff during Israel's 1982 war against the PLO in Lebanon—stormed the building, rescuing seventeen people. All three of Arafat's terrorists, and one Israeli soldier, died in the rescue operation.[14]

The bloodshed at Nahariya was to be repeated five years later, in April 1979, when a four-man PLO team was sent into Nahariya by Mohammad Abbas, the commando leader who had offered the press a justification for the slaughter at Qiryat Shemona. Abbas's terrorists entered the home of an Israeli family, Dani and Smadar and their two children, Anat and Yael. The commandos took Dani and his daughter Anat to the shore. Dani was shot on the beach. They picked up Anat by her feet and smashed her skull against the rocks. Dani's wife Smadar hid inside a closet with her two-year-old girl, Yael. Yossi Klein, the Israeli journalist who interviewed her in 1982, tried to capture the thoughts that might have ran through Smadar's mind as the PLO gunmen held the building hostage:

> —Yael and I pressed in the closet . . . Yael don't they'll hear us please no you mustn't there is nothing to fear we can stay in here forever learn to sleep standing we are not hiding we are not quarantined we are not locked in here like lunatics no one waits outside the door for us to weaken and surrender Yael no they will hear us please no you must not cry . . . And I press Yael deep within me—hard until I can't breathe—I burst, split wide, heave her in, her cries muffled like gentle kicks. And when the neighbors come upon my corpse they will hear a baby knocking from within: A miracle! The baby lives . . .[15]

But the baby did not live. Yael was inadvertently smothered by her mother while hiding in the closet.

Smadar remained in Narahriya. Her mother was a Holocaust survivor whose entire family perished in the Nazi death camps. "It's important for me to show we can live normally," Smadar said, "even in the midst of all of this. I suppose I am a symbol for people here."[16]

By 1984, Mohammad Abbas—apologist for the attack at Qiryat Shemona, organizer of the killings at Nahariya—was sitting on the PLO's executive committee, personally appointed by Yassir Arafat. The following year, in October 1985, Abbas sent four men to Genoa, Italy, ordering them to smuggle weapons aboard the Achille Lauro cruise ship and open fire upon docking at the Israeli port of Ashdod, south of Tel Aviv. When an Achille Lauro waiter discovered the PLO gunmen cleaning their weapons in their cabin, they seized the ship, holding 97 tourists and 331 crew-members hostage for three days, killing the disabled Jewish-American tourist Leon Klinghoffer and dumping both his body and his wheelchair into the sea. "We came on behalf of Mr. Arafat," the hijackers said. They demanded the release of fifty Palestinians being held in Israeli jails and permission to land in Syria. The only prisoner they demanded by name was Samir al-Qantari, arrested by Israel for his role in the 1979 slaughter of Smadar's family at Nahariya.[17] (During an April 1987 meeting in Algeria of the 462-member Palestine National Council, the PLO's "parliament in exile," Abbas was given a front row seat during Arafat's opening speech to the gathering. Following a flurry of media attention surrounding the presence of Abbas—who had been in hiding and against whom arrest warrants had been issued by both the United States and Italy for his role in the Achille Lauro operation—it was announced that Abbas had been dismissed from the PLO executive committee because, in the words of an Arafat aide, he had "become too much of an embarrassment and a political liability to the organization." Abbas, however, was in fact reelected to the executive committee chaired by Arafat and retained his leadership post as general secretary of the Palestine Liberation Front faction of the PLO.)[18]

Two weeks after the first PLO strike at Nahariya in 1974, Israel retaliated by launching a naval raid on the Lebanese port cities of Tyre, Sidon, and Ras a-Shak. It was Dina who had furnished the reports detailing the locations of the PLO targets. She had secretly photographed the harbors during her trips to the coast to treat Palestinian children.

Dina had been trained to distinguish between the scores of ordinary Lebanese fishing boats and the specially equipped military vessels camouflaged by the PLO. The PLO ships were fitted with customized cranes used to lower the rubber dinghies that brought guerrillas to the Israeli coast for nighttime assaults. The standard cranes affixed to the other ships were designed to handle fishing nets. Dina's photographs of the PLO ships were sent to Israel via courier, enabling planners to pinpoint their targets.

Dina never knew the identity of the Mossad courier in Beirut. She communicated with the Israeli secret service officers in Tel Aviv via an intricately constructed transmitter—no larger than a pack of cigarettes, yet with a range of up to 250 miles—which she kept hidden in her bathroom scale. When she had pictures to send, she would receive instructions to bring them to a certain hotel at a specified time, check into a room, hide the package, and then leave. The Mossad courier would then enter the room with a pass key, pick up the photographs, and head for Tel Aviv on the next plane. The location, day, and hour for each transaction was always different.

When Israel's frogmen slipped into the Lebanese ports during the night of 9 July 1974, Dina's intelligence reports led them straight to the PLO ships. They destroyed thirty. The demolition teams left leaflets printed in Arabic aboard some of the remaining Lebanese fishing boats: "It was from your harbors that the terrorists set out who murdered a peaceful woman and her children and we know that they are planning additional operations from your harbors, using your boats," the leaflets said. "It's up to you," they cautioned. "Don't let them operate out of your homes. Take this warning to heart before it is too late."[19]

The next day, *New York Times* correspondent Juan de Onis filed a story from Beirut: "Israel's latest raid on fishing ports in southern Lebanon was regarded here as restrained in comparison with the threats of violent reprisals issued by Israeli officials after a Palestinian guerrilla raid from the sea on the beach resort of Nahariya two weeks ago."[20] Israeli intelligence sources have claimed that the restraint was made possible by Dina's espionage in Beirut. By touring the Lebanese countryside as a physician and smuggling reports about Palestinian guerrilla emplacements to the Mossad, the Israeli commandos were able to retaliate against PLO targets nestled in the ports without inflicting casualties on the civilian residents. But not all of Dina's work met with such success.

6

Fellow Travelers

ON 10 August 1973, Defense Minister Moshe Dayan and Chief of Staff David Elazar received approval from Prime Minister Golda Meir to proceed with a plan to intercept a civilian Middle East Airlines flight from Lebanon to Iraq. The seventy-four passengers were mostly Iraqis returning from a summer vacation in Beirut. They were originally scheduled to return to Baghdad via flight 006, a Lebanese Caravelle jet that had been leased by the Iraqi airline. The plane was scheduled to arrive in Beirut from Vienna and then continue on to Iraq, but the flight's arrival from Austria was running four hours late so the passengers in Lebanon were shifted to a Middle East Airlines Caravelle and the flight number was changed to E006.

At 9:45 P.M., the seventy-four passengers and seven crew members of flight E006 took off for Baghdad. As the plane gained altitude and marked a course north of Beirut, jet fighters approached from both sides and tried to make radio contact with the Lebanese captain, George Mata. The captain quickly radioed the Lebanese control tower, telling them that enemy fighter jets were ordering him to shift direction and head south. He was then interrupted by a broadcast instructing him to change radio frequency and follow the lead of the jet fighters.

"I will not follow you," the captain declared. "Who are you?" The fighter pilot answered, "There is an exercise in the skies of Lebanon and I want to get you out." The captain continued to object, explaining that the skies were clear. Captain Mata then saw several Mirage fighter planes converging on his aircraft. The jet fighters had no markings. The pilot threatened to open fire unless the captain broke off radio contact with the Lebanese control tower. Captain Mata was then told to follow the Mirage jets southward.[1]

A state of emergency was declared at the Beirut airport when the control tower learned that the Middle East Airlines flight was on its way to Israel. The runway lights were extinguished, warning sirens went off, and Lebanese fighter jets were scrambled from the Kliat air base northeast of Beirut. But by the time they were in position, the Israeli Mirages and their hijacked Lebanese Caravelle airliner had crossed the border, and the Lebanese air force chose not to pursue them into Israeli territory.

The Lebanese airliner touched down at an Israeli military airfield. Most of the passengers were not aware of the hijacking and thought they had landed in Baghdad. Searchlights flooded the aircraft as ambulances, fire trucks, and four Israeli army buses pulled up alongside. When the plane's doors opened, the astonished passengers were met by Israeli commandos who leapt inside and ordered them in Arabic to raise their hands. The male passengers were put aboard an Israeli army bus. Each one was placed in front of the interrogator and told to display his passport. Dina had sent word to Israeli intelligence that PLO leader George Habash was on the flight from Beirut to Iraq.

George Habash was born in Lydda in 1926. His family was Greek Orthodox, his father a successful corn merchant. In 1944, Habash enrolled as a medical student at the American University of Beirut. During the fighting in 1948, while Habash was home on summer vacation from his studies at the university, Moshe Dayan's forces overran Lydda and Habash fled to Ramallah on the Arab-held West Bank of the Jordan River, along with thousands of other refugees. His sister died from an illness shortly thereafter and Habash is said to have blamed the Jews for her death. The 1948 war transformed him into a lifelong revolutionary dedicated to the expulsion of the Zionists and the eventual return to an Arab Palestine.

Habash received a medical degree in 1951 and opened a practice in Amman. It was while studying at the AUB that he immersed himself in the fight against Israel and against the Arab regimes whose rulers he deemed backward and corrupt, holding them responsible for the Palestinian defeat.

Habash aligned himself with militant Arab groups like Young Egypt, which conspired to overthrow the governments of Iraqi Prime Minister Nuri Said, Jordan's King Abdullah, and Syrian strongman Adib Shishakly. It was during his stay in Damascus from 1949 to 1950 that Habash worked with the Young Egypt organization. After a plot to assassinate President Shishakly was uncovered, Habash moved back to Beirut to continue the struggle to topple certain Arab regimes and replace them with "progressive" leaders likely to join forces for the successful liberation of Palestine.

At this point, Habash was still opposed to communism, which he believed would only distract the Arab world from its true cause, that of expelling the Zionists from Palestine and uniting the region into a single pan-

Arab nation stretching from Morocco's Atlantic coast to Saudi Arabia's Persian Gulf. As a student, Habash had won election to the executive committee of a campus nationalist literary association called Jam 'iyat al-Urwa al-Wathqa, the Society of the Close Bond, and he eventually recruited members from the committee to form a secret organization called the Young Arab Men Association. In 1952, after instigating clashes with university officials and Lebanese police in order to promote their call for a new Arab order, the Young Arab Men began to actively lure followers from among the Palestinian refugee camps in Syria and Jordan. Habash, along with fellow physician Waddieh Haddad, toured the camps dispensing medicine and political propaganda, mixing health care and clandestine activity in a manner that was to find its match in Dina's work twenty years later.

Habash's close association with Egypt's President Gamal Nasser came after a March 1954 campus demonstration against the British-sponsored Baghdad Pact, an anti-Soviet alliance of Middle Eastern nations designed to secure British military bases and prevent Moscow's access to Middle Eastern oil. During the protest at AUB, one student was killed by Lebanese riot police and twenty-nine others were injured. Administrators singled out twenty-two students and expelled them for organizing the rally. Nasser—who denounced the pact as a perpetuation of European domination and a threat to Arab unity—demonstrated his support for the student activists by granting them admission to Cairo University. Several of the twenty-two were members of Habash's Young Arab Men Association.

In 1955, the first congress of the Young Arab Men was held. Its name was changed to the Arab National Movement and plans were approved to open branches in Jordan and Syria. Returning to Jordan, Habash began publishing a weekly echoing President Nasser's pan-Arab philosophy, while still insisting that conservative Arab regimes should be replaced by progressive governments who could serve the Arab cause and free Palestine from Zionist control. One of the slogans he adopted was "Unity, Liberation, Revenge."[2]

In April 1957, during a power struggle between King Hussein and his prime minister, Suleiman Naboulsi, riots erupted in Amman and several villages on the West Bank. Naboulsi's government had been the first democratically elected government in Jordan, but the prime minister's shift to the left and his blatant challenges to the king's authority prompted the twenty-one-year-old Hussein to remove him from office. Jordanian officials in Amman and mobs in Ramallah demonstrated in support of Naboulsi. On 23 April, representatives from a coalition of left-wing parties met with the new prime minister, Hussein Khalidi. They demanded that Jordan enter into a union with Egypt and Syria and reject plans to accept U.S. financial assistance. George Habash was a member of the left-wing delegation, and was among those involved in the rioting against Hussein.[3] The king's army managed to restore order, instituting curfews and conducting military tribunals to prevent further outbreaks of violence. Hussein's biographer, Peter Snow, wrote that Hussein's actions delivered the deathblow to Jordanian democracy: "The effect of this on Jordan was to emphasize further the political rift between its two parts. Generally, the East Bank Transjordanians greeted the King's takeover with relief and satisfaction. It appeared to them likely to restore stability in the country and security for their interests. The Palestinians, on the other hand, saw the demise of the Naboulsi government as a blow to any chance they might have had of genuine participation in the running of the country. They felt it inevitable that their interests would now be less well represented to the King, and thus further neglected."[4]

Prime Minister Naboulsi was seen as an advocate of pan-Arabism who might eventually replace the monarchy with a republic, guaranteeing the Palestinians a voice in Jordanian affairs and perhaps uniting the other Arab states in a second strike against Israel. In the wake of Naboulsi's removal, Habash moved back to Damascus. By 1967, following the defeat of the Arab armies in the Six Day War, Habash had already replaced pan-Arab Nasserism with Marxist-Leninism as the ideological path to liberation. The international working class, he believed, had to unite in armed struggle against the American / European / Imperialist / Zionist / Arab Reactionary schemes that kept Palestinians and other Third World peoples oppressed and enslaved. Calling for Arab solidarity with the socialist nations led by the Soviet Union, Habash adopted the line of Ho Chi Minh, Mao Zedong, Fidel Castro, and Che Guevara, advocating a protracted people's war to topple reactionary rulers and replace them with Marxist regimes. He linked the fate of the Palestinian Arabs to the triumph of revolutionary socialism over world capitalism. Habash claimed that the destruction of Zionism required guerrilla warfare against Israel's capitalist supporters in Europe and America and the "liquidation" of the Arab "puppet" reactionary regimes that served them. Following the devastating defeat of the Arabs in 1967, Che Guevara's words had an even greater urgency and validity for Habash and his followers:

> Revolutionary violence as the highest expression of the people's struggle is not only the path, but it is the most concrete and the most direct potential for the defeat of imperialism.[5]
> The guerrilla is a social reformer. The guerrilla takes up weapons as the wrathful protest of the people against their oppressors; the guerrilla

fights to change the social system that subjects his unarmed brothers to approbrium [*sic*] and poverty. He acts against the special conditions of the Establishment at a given moment. And he is determined to smash the Establishment's patterns, with all the force that circumstances permit.[6]

For Habash, the Establishment was responsible for the loss of Arab Palestine. Hijackings, assassination, and terror against targets ranging from American airliners to Jordanian officials to Israeli civilians would bring about the necessary disruption of establishment patterns prescribed by the Cuban revolutionary.

In September 1967, Habash formed the Popular Front for the Liberation of Palestine (PFLP), made up of a Palestinian wing of the Arab National Movement that had been established in 1964, and two other guerrilla groups, Heroes of the Return and the Palestinian Liberation Front, both reportedly linked to the former Syrian officer, Ahmed Jibril. The PFLP's first public statement paralleled the words of Che: "The only weapon left in the hands of the people," it said, "is revolutionary violence."[7]

On 23 July 1968, Habash ushered in the age of hijackings; the PFLP commandeered El Al flight 426 on its regular run from Rome to Tel Aviv. Three of his terrorists forced Captain Oded Abarbanel to fly the plane to Algeria after striking the first officer, Maoz Proaz, in the face with a pistol. The non-Israeli passengers were flown to Paris and a short time later the Israeli women and children were released. But the remaining passengers and crew sat on the ground in the Boeing 707 for forty days until Israel agreed to release fifteen PLO guerrillas (one account sets the number at sixteen) in exchange for the safe release of the hostages.[8] It appeared that Habash's daring revolutionary violence had paid off. The group captured the world's headlines and attracted new recruits among the refugees. "The incident was an eye opener for me," wrote Leila Khaled. "It was the beginning of the end of my exile. I was about to be liberated," she said, "and I sought to make contacts with the PFLP."[9]

A series of other terrorist attacks followed. On 26 December 1968, PFLP commandos stormed an El Al aircraft on the ground at Athens airport. Armed with hand grenades and machine guns, the terrorists attacked the plane carrying forty-one passengers and ten crew-members, screaming, "We want to kill Jews!" One passenger died in the attack and two stewardesses were wounded.[10] On 29 August 1969, Leila Khaled and another PFLP commando hijacked TWA flight 840 shortly after it left Rome and diverted it to Damascus. After touching down at the Syrian airport, the passengers and crew were evacuated and the Boeing 707 blown up. "It was an act of protest against the West for its pro-Zionist (therefore anti-Palestinian) posture," Khaled wrote. "The list of the sins of the West is overwhelming."[11]

On 10 February 1970, a Swiss airline flight with thirty-eight passengers and nine crew-members aboard exploded in mid-air fifteen minutes after taking off from Zurich's airport. A bomb set to detonate at ten thousand feet had been placed inside a package and mailed to an Israeli address, the terrorists hoping that all mail to Israel would be carried aboard an El Al flight.[12]

On 22 July 1970, six PFLP commandos hijacked a Greek Olympic Airlines jet and demanded the release of terrorists imprisoned by the Greek government.

On 6 September 1970, Khaled and several other PFLP members hijacked four planes: a DC-8 Swiss airlines plane en-route from Zurich to New York, an El Al Boeing 707 flying to New York from Tel Aviv via Amsterdam, a Pan American Boeing 747 on its way to New York from Amsterdam, and a TWA Boeing 707 flying to New York from Frankfurt. The El Al hijacking failed when an Israeli security guard shot PFLP operative Patrick Arguello while passengers and crew wrestled his accomplice, Leila Khaled, to the ground. The other hijackings succeeded: the Pan American jumbo jet was taken to Cairo and blown up after the hostages were set free, and the other two planes were ordered to land at Dawson Field, an airstrip in the Zarka Desert north of Amman. Two days later, on 9 September, the PFLP took over a British airlines VC-10 flying to London from Bombay via Dubai and Bahrain; that plane joined the others at Jordan's Dawson Field. The PFLP hijackers agreed to free the non-Israeli passengers in exchange for the release of three colleagues who had been imprisoned by Swiss authorities for an attack on an El Al airliner in Zurich, of Leila Khaled by British police, and of three other Arabs serving sentences in West Germany for a terrorist raid against Israeli civilians at the El Al lounge in Munich's airport. The Israeli hostages were to be freed too, providing Israel released a number of guerrillas from its jails. A total of more than 450 hostages sat inside the planes for six days, sweltering in the desert heat. The planes were then evacuated and blown up. All the hostages were released, except for 56 Jewish passengers. Britain, West Germany, and Switzerland all caved in to the PFLP's demands, releasing the imprisoned terrorists. Israel took a hardline, rounding up nearly 450 Palestinians on the West Bank, many of them PFLP sympathizers. The Israelis were showing that they, too, could play the hostage game. Eventually, all of the remaining 56 Jews were freed unconditionally.

King Hussein was outraged over the blatant use of Jordanian territory as a staging area for acts of international terrorism. The multiple hijackings triggered a crackdown on PLO forces by the king culminating in their "Black September" expulsion from Jordan.[13]

The PFLP did more than employ terrorism in its struggle against Israel and its supporters; it also involved itself in the various revolutionary struggles being waged by guerrilla groups around the world. In a single issue of the *PFLP Bulletin*, Habash's organization aligned itself with the National Liberation Front of South Yemen, the Irish Republican Army, Guatemala's Guerrilla Army of the Poor, the Sudanese Communist Party, and the Faragundo Marti National Liberation Front of El Salvador. Another issue offered a "salute" to the Marxist regimes of Bulgaria, East Germany, and Czechoslovakia, and reaffirmed PFLP support for the government of Babrak Karmal in Afghanistan, whose rule required the presence of thousands of Soviet troops.[14]

When Israeli intelligence received word from Dina that PFLP leader Habash would be aboard the Lebanese airliner destined for Iraq, Defense Minister Dayan, Chief of Staff Elazar, and Prime Minister Meir decided that they could not pass up the chance. Risking the international condemnation that would surely follow, they ordered their air force to bring the civilian airliner into Israel.

After conducting their search, the Israelis quickly discovered that Habash was not aboard. The PLO leader had indeed booked passage on the aircraft. But the flight, which had originated in Vienna, was running late. After Habash had waited for hours at the airport, he began to feel pains in his chest. He had an ongoing heart ailment and had already suffered at least one heart attack. Fearing the risk of a two and one half hour flight to Baghdad, he canceled his plans.

The incident boosted the morale of the Palestinians. Political commentators denounced the Israelis, charging them with air piracy. The day after the hijacking, Habash conducted an interview in his Beirut office: "Israeli fighter planes come to Beirut, take control of a civilian aircraft and force it to land in Israel. That is the height of terrorism. It is time world public opinion knew who the terrorists actually are."[15]

Back in Tel Aviv, senior Mossad officers speculated that Habash's people were on to Dina and that they had set her up, purposely disclosing false leads indicating that the PLO chief would be flying to Baghdad in order to lure her into a trap. If true, there was more at stake in the Middle East Airlines hijacking than Israel's faltering public image. The PLO would deal ruthlessly with Dina if she were discovered to be working for the Mossad.

Writing shortly after the Habash incident and unaware of Dina's role in it, British journalist Christopher Dobson echoed the sentiments of the Mossad officers overseeing Dina's operations:

> From the intelligence point of view, the hijacking showed intimate knowledge of the movements of one of the most closely guarded and secretive of the Palestinian leaders. Such knowledge could only have come from someone very close to Habash. Only his bad heart made that knowledge useless at the last moment.
>
> The Palestinian organizations have in fact been penetrated through and through by the Israelis and the Jordanians—King Hussein's intelligence service is estimated to have three-hundred men working in Beirut—at various levels. But the super-spy, the man [or woman?] at the top, must be an extremely brave and resourceful character. The fedayeen security checks are stringent and each time the Israelis carry out a coup there is a flurry of anti-spy activity throughout the various groups. So if the super-spy is an Israeli he must have a perfect cover and eat, drink, sleep and think not only like an Arab but like an Arab terrorist, and if he is an Arab turned traitor he must consider every movement he makes, every word he says. In either case a dreadful death awaits him if he is caught.[16]

Carlos Marighella, the Brazilian rebel admired by the Palestinian militants, once declared that "terrorism is an arm the revolutionary can never relinquish," and his Middle Eastern disciples had faithfully followed the creed. In his *Minimanual of the Urban Guerrilla*, virtually required reading for the aspiring PLO commando, Marighella had also warned that "the worst enemy of the urban guerrilla and the major danger we run is infiltration into our organization by a spy or an informer." His remedy was simple: "For their part the urban guerrilla must not evade the duty—once he knows who the spy or informer is—of wiping him out physically. This is the correct method, approved by the people, and it minimizes considerably the incidence of infiltration or enemy spying."[17]

7

The Circle Closes

INCIDENTS like the debacle involving the Middle East Airlines flight were rare. Dina won high praise from the Mossad for her espionage operation in Lebanon. She had managed to penetrate the highest echelons of the PLO, befriending the family of a top assistant to Abu Iyad, chief of military planning for Arafat's Fateh and reputed architect of the Black September terrorist strike force that carried out the Munich Olympic massacre.

Born Salah Khalaf in Jaffa in 1933, Abu Iyad fled with his family by boat to Arab-controlled Gaza on 13 May 1948, the day after Israel proclaimed itself a state. According to Iyad, it was the news of Deir Yasseen and the military superiority of the Jews that prompted the exodus of the 100 thousand Arab residents of his native town.

Iyad's father had been raised in Gaza, and it seemed natural to seek refuge there until the Arab armies had a chance to secure victory over the Zionist forces, enabling the family to return home. "Confident of a speedy return," Iyad wrote, "they [his parents] left all their furniture and possessions behind, taking with them only the bare necessities. I can still see my father, clutching our apartment keys in his hand, telling us reassuringly that it wouldn't be long before we could move back."[1]

During his youth, Iyad managed to pick up a little Hebrew while working in his father's grocery store in Carmel, just outside Tel Aviv. His father, however, spoke Hebrew frequently and one of Iyad's uncles had married a Jewish woman. Despite his family's apparently long-standing cordial relations with Jews, as World War II came to a close Iyad joined the "lion cubs" youth section of the Najjadehs, an anti-Zionist Palestinian group cofounded by the principal of his school, Muhammad al-Hawari. Not yet twelve, the young Iyad was exposed through the Najjadehs to the causes being championed by the Arab leaders of the time: opposition to continued Jewish immigration and to the purchase of Arab lands by Jews. The flight from Jaffa in 1948, during which Iyad witnessed the drowning of a distraught woman who tried to swim ashore to search for her missing child, injected a bitter personal element into the boy's rejection of the Zionist presence in Palestine.

In 1951, Iyad enrolled in Dar al-Ulum, a teachers' college in Cairo, and it was during his association with the Palestine Student Union that he met Yassir Arafat. In 1952, Iyad and Arafat formed a unified ticket dubbed the "Student Union" and ran for seats on the executive committee of the Palestinian organization. The nine-member Student Union slate won the election and Arafat—who had received training in explosives at the Egyptian Military Academy and was in charge of training fellow engineering students volunteering for guerrilla action against the British in the Suez Canal Zone—took office as president, with Iyad serving as vice-president. In 1956, after Arafat completed his studies and left the university, Iyad took over as president of the Palestinian student group.

In 1957, Iyad returned to Gaza with a degree in psychology and philosophy from Dar al-Ulum and a teaching certificate from Ain Shams University. The Egyptian authorities assigned Iyad to Al Zahra, a girls' school where he taught Arabic and psychology. In his memoirs, Iyad claimed that the Egyptian regime deliberately appointed him to the post in order to keep him from organizing an effective political movement among disenchanted Palestinian residents in Gaza. Ordinarily, only married men were allowed to teach in an all-girls school, and many Moslems believed it was an embarrassment for a man to work among females. But according to Iyad the Egyptian authorities made an exception in order to put him in a situation where he would be "treated like a pariah."[2]

During his tenure at Al Zahra, Iyad organized student groups to debate political questions during school hours. After he had been there for six months, the Egyptian authorities transferred him to a crowded, make-shift boys' school in the Gaza desert, filled with poor refugee children. As at Al Zahra, Iyad worked to arouse the political consciousness of these students, at one point establishing a committee in support of the Algerian revolution, which collected small sums to send to the Arab rebels. He also continued underground work, recruiting Palestinian militants in coordination with colleagues like Arafat who were working in the gulf states of Kuwait and Qatar. Iyad published pamphlets openly criticizing the Egyptian regime in Gaza while secretly recruiting and training fighters for his clandestine army. In 1959, Arafat asked Iyad to join him in Kuwait. Arafat had worked for the Kuwaiti Ministry of Public Works, and afterwards set-up his own construction company, raising funds and gathering followers to expand the underground resistance movement. Iyad accepted Arafat's call, leaving Gaza after

Kuwait's director of instruction, Abdel Aziz Hussein, offered him a teaching post at one of the country's secondary schools. In Kuwait, Iyad—along with Arafat, Farouk al-Qaddumi, Khaled al-Hassan, Abd al-Muhsin al-Qattan, and Khalil Ibrahim al-Wazir—formed Harakat al-Tahrir al-Watani al-Filastini, the Movement for the National Liberation of Palestine. The initials for the group were reversed to read FATEH, which means "conquest" in Arabic.[3]

Kuwait had become a haven for Palestinian workers, and the high wages of the oil-rich nation provided a generous pool for Fateh's fundraising efforts. Not being one of the confrontation states bordering Israel, Kuwait's more liberalized climate afforded Arafat's group greater freedom to operate. Iyad did not suffer the type of harassment meted out by the Egyptian authorities in Gaza.

In 1967, following the Israeli victory in the Six Day War, Iyad left Kuwait for Damascus, where he took up the post as Fateh's liaison with the Arab regimes. He obtained financial support for Fateh from Iraq's President Abdul Rahman Aref, and military aid from President Nasser. In the summer of 1968, Iyad received a pledge from Saudi Arabia's King Faisal to deduct 7 percent of the salary of every Palestinian working in the country and to turn the funds over to Fateh. In addition, the monarch offered to provide the group with an equivalent amount donated by the kingdom. Iyad was also one of the first Palestinian leaders to be granted an audience with Muammar Qaddafi following the 1969 coup that overthrew Libya's King Idris.

Along with his role as Fateh's ambassador to the Arab world, Iyad served as chief of Jihaz el Razd, the security wing of Fateh. It was in this capacity that he recruited Ali Hassan Salameh, the man identified by Israeli intelligence as the mastermind behind the Munich Olympic massacre. Iyad reportedly chose a core group of men from the Jihaz to form the nucleus of Black September, Fateh's covert terrorist squad. It was these guerrillas, along with Iyad, who had been singled out by the Israelis for their role at Munich. Iyad denied having any overt connection with Black September, though he acknowledged his close association with the commando unit: "It acted as an auxiliary of the Resistance, when the Resistance was no longer in a position to fully assume its military and political tasks. Its members always insisted that they had no organic tie with Fateh or the PLO. But I knew a number of them and I can assure you than most of them belonged to various fedayeen organizations. Coming out of the ranks, they accurately reflected the profound feelings of frustration and indignation shared by the entire Palestinian people regarding the Jordanian massacres and the complicities that made them possible."[4]

As chief of Fateh's security division, Iyad's proximity to the Palestinian family Dina had befriended was particularly dangerous. One of Ali Hassan Salameh's first missions for Iyad had been to ferret out Fateh members who had been recruited by Israeli intelligence. During his first year under Iyad, Salameh reportedly executed twenty Arab guerrillas who had been secretly working for Israel, acts in line with Carlos Marighella's call for the prompt physical liquidation of spies.

Iyad was acutely aware of the dangers posed by Israeli agents. Many PLO operations had been blocked while still in the planning stages, as a result of information passed on to the Mossad by Arab informers. At first, Dina did not know that the PLO official for whom she had been baby-sitting was a close associate of Iyad. While Salameh did talk openly of his PLO affiliation, it wasn't until Dina transmitted his name and address to Tel Aviv that she learned of his relationship to Iyad. She had managed to penetrate into the core of the PLO leadership, closing the circle around Abu Iyad, the man whose job it was to expose informers like Dina and exact the appropriate punishment.

During her visits to Iyad's lieutenant in Beirut, Dina would secretly listen in on his telephone conversations. Generally, everything was discussed in code, but occasionally there were slip-ups and Dina would be able to relay pieces of information to Tel Aviv for analysis at Mossad headquarters. Her transmissions were based on a precise routine. In Egypt and Syria, there were strict monitorings of all radio broadcasts. But in Lebanon there were a number of private transmitters, and government regulations were much more lax. Dina and her Mossad supervisors had worked out a timetable allowing for transmissions every second Monday at 6 A.M., or alternate Wednesdays at 8 P.M.

Iyad's lieutenant had never told her that he was directly involved in the PLO, though it was near common knowledge among the refugees in the camps. Instead, he dropped hints, telling her that he was "emotionally and politically" committed to the Palestinian organization. Dina would try to detect trends within the PLO by initiating discussions about recent terrorist attacks. She commented on the deaths of innocent schoolchildren at Ma'alot, asking him why it was necessary to continue to harm civilians. She hoped his answer might offer a clue about future PLO plans regarding assaults on civilian targets. Iyad's assistant denied that civilians were deliberately attacked by Palestinian commandos, claiming that innocent people suffered only when something went wrong with the PLO's original plans. This claim was a recurring theme in the arguments used by the defenders of PLO tactics: it was the Israeli policy of refusing to negotiate with terrorists that was responsible for the PLO killings of civilians.

Despite the protestations of Abu Iyad's lieutenant and his PLO associates, Dina was convinced that the Palestinians' weakness in the face of Israeli military might had led their leaders to endorse a deliberate, premeditated war against civilians, and that only a policy of swift reprisal and repeated assaults on the PLO infrastructure would stop the killing, not appeasement by Israeli policy-makers.

In his preface to Abu Iyad's biography (which he co-authored with the PLO leader), Eric Rouleau, a Cairo-born Jewish journalist living in Paris, put forth the Palestinian rationale for terrorist violence: "Isn't terrorism, as atrocious as it is, the last weapon of the weak?"[5] Such sentiments made it easy for PLO leaders to justify attacks against civilians, as did the contention, expressed by Arab intellectuals like Fawaz Turki, that "only when we took to armed violence did the world stop calling us 'the Arab refugees' and start calling us Palestinians."[6] To make the world aware of the plight of the Palestinians, George Habash's PFLP faction embraced hijackings, bombings of Israeli shopping centers and cinemas, and international acts of sabotage: "We believe to kill a Jew from the battleground has more of an effect than killing 100 of them in battle; it attracts more attention. And when we set fire to a store in London, those few flames are worth the burning down of two kibbutzim."

Habash elaborated: "Has it been said that these operations expose the lives of innocent people to danger? In today's world, no one is innocent, no one is neutral. A man is either with the oppressor or the oppressed."[7]

Yassir Arafat's Fateh agreed that the PLO fighter need not confine himself to military targets on the field of battle: "The Palestine revolution, owing to the nature of Zionist society, does not recognize this distinction between the enemy's armed forces and people. The colonialist Zionist society is a military society root and branch and there can be no distinction between military and civilian "[8]

It was this failure to distinguish between military and civilian targets, coupled with the steadfast Arab refusal to compromise over the issue of a Jewish homeland in Palestine, that fueled Dina's drive to sabotage PLO schemes in Lebanon. When fighting broke out between Moslem and Christian factions during the 1975-76 civil war, Dina was forced to evacuate her Beirut apartment to avoid being caught in the battle. She was ordered to fly to Switzerland to personally review her situation with a Mossad officer. With Lebanon in the throes of civil war, the Israelis wanted to make sure it was safe for her to continue her operation. Dina insisted that it was, and returned to Beirut to continue her surveillance of her PLO associates.

While baby-sitting alone in the home of Abu Iyad's lieutenant, Dina went through stacks of hidden military directives, carefully photographing each one for transfer to the Mossad office in Tel Aviv. There were names of

PLO members, forged identification papers, times and places of impending attacks. Some of the documents she discovered were similar to the one captured by the Israeli army during its 1982 invasion of Lebanon:

TARGET SELECTION AND TIMING OF THE OPERATION

1. The blow must be directed at the enemy's weak point. His greatest weakness is his small population. Therefore, operations must be launched which will liquidate immigration into Israel. This can be achieved by various means: attacking absorption centres for new immigrants; creating problems for them in their new homes by sabotaging their water and electricity supply; using weapons in terrifying ways against them where they live, and using arson whenever possible.

2. Any installation which is designated as a target must meet the criterion of importance to the civilian population. Blows directed at secondary or isolated targets, whose impact passes unnoticed, are of no use.

3. Attacks can be made to multiply their impact. For instance, attacking a tourist installation during the height of the season is much more useful than dealing the same blow at another time. If fuel tanks are set on fire during an energy crisis, this can be much more useful than at another time. Likewise, dealing a blow to the enemy immediately following his own attack constitutes an excellent reprisal which is beneficial to morale.

4. Density of the population in the streets and market places of cities tends to increase on special occasions like holidays and vacations. One ought to bear this in mind in order to better select the place of action and improve the impact of the blow.

5. Attention should be given to the safety of our people. The type of action should take their safety into consideration.[9]

In addition to documents similar to the one cited above, among the materials Dina uncovered were two false Kuwaiti passports that had been issued to Palestinian commandos. The men were on their way to London. When the Mossad agents in Tel Aviv decoded Dina's message about the two PLO operatives, their warning lights went on.

8

The Flesh of the Usurper

DINA'S broadcast about the departure of two Palestinians from Lebanon was apparently a routine warning. Beirut had been dubbed the capital of international terrorism: Palestinians, along with mercenaries from West Germany, Ireland, Japan, France, Cuba, and neighboring Arab states, moved freely in and out of Lebanon, organizing hit squads, hijackings, and terrorist bombings. But Israeli intelligence had linked the two men to Waddieh Haddad, chief of operations for George Habash's PFLP faction of the PLO.

Haddad was born in Safad, Palestine, to a Greek Orthodox family. His father was a successful school teacher who fled with his family to Arab territory following the creation of Israel in 1948. Haddad met George Habash while studying medicine at the American University of Beirut. The two men, along with Ahmad Yamani and Abdul Karim Hamad, formed the nucleus of the PFLP, gathering followers, disseminating their political line through a magazine called *Revenge*, establishing the beginnings of a covert militiary capability for guerrilla action against Israel. Haddad's close ties with Habash, dating back to their shared journeys through the refugee camps, treating patients while recruiting new members to their underground organization, put him in the number two spot in Habash's PFLP. As chief of operations, Haddad was responsible for carrying out some of Habash's most spectacular terrorist raids. It was Haddad who planned the five airline hijackings of September 1970, and the simultaneous assassination plot against King Hussein. The murder attempt, which Leila Khaled claimed was falsely attributed to the PFLP by Hussein in order to split the Palestinian movement, was uncovered by Jordan's security forces, but the success of the hijacking scheme demonstrated Haddad's ability to mount a complex worldwide operation.[1]

The Israelis had already identified Haddad as an all too competent adversary. In the spring of 1969, Haddad had organized a murder plot against

David Ben-Gurion. A private citizen at the time, the former Israeli prime minister was planning to tour Jewish communities in Latin America. Haddad decided to send a Palestinian named Ishmael Souhail, along with a Swedish mercenary, to Argentina to attack Ben-Gurion. They were to first meet up with Mona Soudi, a Palestinian painter enrolled in the school of fine arts at Copenhagen, and then proceed to South America. Soudi had established a support group for the PFLP, and her apartment served as a European base for the operation against the Israeli leader. But the day before the hit-team was to leave for Buenos Aires, the Danish police arrested the would-be assassins.[2]

Two months before Haddad's Black September hijackings were to prompt Hussein's war against the PLO, the Israelis already initiated their own strike against the Palestinian leader. On 11 July, six Soviet-made Katyusha anti-tank rockets were detonated shortly after 2 A.M. from a rented room across the street from Haddad's Beirut apartment on rue Mukhi Eldin Alkhayat. His wife, Samia, and eight-year-old son, Hani, were asleep in the bedroom while Haddad and Leila Khaled were up formulating PFLP strategy in the living room. The rockets had been triggered by an electronic timing device, two of them crashing into the apartment, scorching the carpets as they landed but failing to explode, the other four bursting upon impact. Aside from a small cut on Haddad's hand, neither he nor Khaled were hurt, but the apartment went up in flames. Samia and Hani came out of the bedroom screaming. The woman had been cut by shrapnel from the blast and the boy was badly burned, bleeding from the chest. Haddad's fifteen-year-old maid, Adla Khaled el-Zayn, was wounded in the attack. The electricity went dead as Haddad and Khaled tried to battle the flames to no avail. Hani was then rushed to the American University Hospital by Khaled and Abu Dardock, a fellow PFLP member who arrived on the scene shortly after the bombing; Hani was disfigured from the burns.

The assault against Haddad was reported to have been the first time the Israelis attempted to strike at a particular Palestinian resistance leader. Haddad went underground, hiding out first in the Beddawi refugee camp outside Tripoli, and then, fearing the presence of Israeli agents, moving to Baghdad, where he refused to sleep more than two nights in the same bed. He set up a printing press there to produce forged documents, thereby assuring the security of his operatives. Toward the end of 1971, in a bid to free himself from attempts by his Iraqi hosts to control his organization, Haddad shifted his headquarters to the port city of Aden, capital of the Marxist-led People's Democratic Republic of Yemen. The ruling National Liberation Front shared the same roots as the PFLP, having emerged from the Arab Nationalist Movement in the 1950s in order to wrest control of the then British-controlled colony.[3]

The assassination attempt drove Haddad deeper into the shadows, but not away from his commitment to dismantle the Jewish state. Leila Khaled underwent plastic surgery in order to avoid detection. In March 1970, after undergoing three painful operations to alter her appearance, Khaled gave a man who was visiting his wife in the hospital room next door a present for his new daughter: "a necklace made of bullets" with a wish for her to one day assume "a long, long revolutionary career."[4] Haddad was no less ardent in his determination to continue his struggle, and he too was reported to have had plastic surgery to disguise his identity.

In February 1972, Haddad's forces hijacked a Lufthansa 747 jet carrying 170 passengers, including the late Robert Kennedy's son, Joseph, and flew it to Aden. The hijackers demanded and received a $5 million ransom, reportedly paying the South Yemeni government between $1 million and $2 million for "landing rights." On 7 March 1972, after facing increasing criticism from George Habash over his insistence that airline hijackings were still an effective instrument for Palestinian nationalists, Haddad broke with his long-time ally and created a splinter faction, the Popular Front for the Liberation of Palestine—Foreign Operations Branch.

Two months later, Haddad attended a conference of international terrorist groups in the Beddawi refugee camp. Representatives included members of the Irish Republican Army, West Germany's Baader-Meinhof gang, the Liberation Front of Iran, the Japanese Red Army, Turkey's People's Liberation Army, Habash's PFLP, Arafat's Fateh and his deputy Iyad's Black September. They coordinated plans to assist each other by providing safe houses and escape routes, and procuring weapons and intelligence data. They also agreed to exchange personnel for participation in future operations. George Habash had noted that a foreigner would have a better chance than a native of eluding detection by a police force geared toward apprehending native terrorists. British authorities would be less likely to suspect a Turkish national in Ulster than an Irishman, though both might be acting on orders from the IRA. Likewise, the West German police, alert to possible bombing attacks by Baader-Meinhof members, would be more apt to investigate the erratic movements of a German citizen that those of an Iranian, who would be judged to be crisscrossing the country as a tourist. Though the suggestion to exchange personnel was reportedly put forward by Habash during the Tripoli conference, the technique of recruiting foreign nationals for terrorist strikes had been pioneered by Waddieh Haddad.[5]

Haddad's operation employed a string of foreigners: Christopher Moreau, a Swiss national, arrested on 25 July 1970, following his arrival in Tel Aviv aboard a Greek ocean liner while carrying five pounds of Soviet-made explosives; Patrick Arguello, son of an Irish-English mother and Nicaraguan father and member of the Sandinistas in pre-revolutionary

Nicaragua, killed during Leila Khaled's ill-fated attempt to hijack an El Al jet on 6 September 1970; and Evelyn and Nadia Bardeli, Moroccan sisters who were arrested on 11 April 1971 while trying to smuggle weapons into Israel. When they were taken into custody upon landing at Lod Airport, a search disclosed false linings in their bras stuffed with powdered explosives and Tampax soaked in inflammable liquid.

It was also Haddad who recruited the notorious Venezuelan terrorist Carlos, who was to later carry out a series of dramatic attacks including the 21 December 1975 raid on a gathering of OPEC oil ministers in Vienna, in which an Austrian police guard, an Iraqi security officer, and a Libyan economist were killed.[6]

The acceptance of Habash's proposals to adopt Haddad's international approach to terrorist activity spawned the 30 May 1972 Lod Airport massacre, carried out by three Japanese Red Army commandos in collusion with the PFLP followers of Habash and Haddad and with members of the Arafat-Iyad Black September unit. Takeshi Okidoro, Yasuiki Yashuda, and Kozo Okamoto boarded Air France flight 132 during a stopover in Rome, landing at the airport outside Tel Aviv. Their hand-luggage had been checked by Italian police, but their suitcases were sent through without a search. When they landed in Israel, the three Japanese commandos waited by the Number 3 luggage conveyer belt until their bags arrived. Then they quickly opened them, each man pulling out a Czech-made VZT-58 submachine-gun. Armed with the assault rifles and several shrapnel grenades, they fired into the crowd and hurled grenades at the shocked passengers. Twenty-seven people were killed in the airport lounge, sixteen of them Roman Catholic pilgrims from Puerto Rico about to embark on a tour of the Holy Land. Professor Aharon Katzir, a distinguished chemist and personal friend of David Ben-Gurion, was also killed in the attack. Seventy-eight others were wounded. One of the Japanese terrorists was accidentally killed by his comrade's burst of gunfire; a second was decapitated by the explosion from one of his own grenades. The third, Kozo Okamoto, was apprehended by an unarmed El Al employee. Okamoto was later released in the 22 May 1985, prisoner exchange in which 1,150 Palestinian commandos were exchanged for 3 Israeli soldiers captured during the 1982 invasion of Lebanon.[7]

The killing of unarmed passengers at the Lod Airport terminal exemplified Waddieh Haddad's approach to the Arab-Israeli conflict: utilize the combined might of international terrorist groups, hit civilian targets to inflict maximum suffering on the enemy. In explaining the rationale for the attack, a PFLP spokesman declared: "Our purpose was to kill as many people as possible at the airport. Israelis, of course, but anyone else who

was there. There is a war going on in Palestine. People should know that.''
The spokesman admitted that the ordinary Englishman would label the
Palestinians cold-blooded murders. "But he will think three times before
coming to Israel.''[8]

The Lod massacre embodied the sentiments of many PLO patriots,
sending a signal to the Jews of Palestine that had a poetic counterpart in the
words of the Palestinian writer, Mahmoud Darwish:

Put it on record.
    I am an Arab.
You stole my forefathers' vineyards.
    And land I used to till,
    I and all my children,
    And you left us and all my grandchildren,
    Nothing but these rocks.
    Will your government be taking them too
    As is being said

So!
    Put it on record at the top of page one:
    I don't hate people,
    I trespass on no one's property.
And yet, if I were to become hungry
    I shall eat the flesh of my usurper.
    Beware of my hunger.
    And of my anger![9]

After suffering a string of hijackings and mass slayings, the Israelis
were careful to take note of those willing to turn their rage into military action against civilian targets. They would not dismiss a ''routine'' warning
about two Palestinians on a mission to London when they were in the
employ of an adversary like Waddieh Haddad.

When Dina's warning came in over the transmitter from Beirut, Mossad
officials dispatched two agents to London to await the arrival of the two
Palestinians. Identifying the Palestinians as they entered the country, these
agents began tracking their every move, watching them as they traveled
from one hotel to the next, apparently roaming at random through the streets
of the city, perhaps hoping to avoid being followed. Eventually, the PLO
operatives met up with an Englishman named Brad Kirkland [a
pseudonym]. The meeting took place in the lobby of one of London's most
elegant hotels while the Israeli intelligence agents secretly photographed the
encounter. Words were exchanged, then Kirkland handed the Palestinians a

medium-sized briefcase and left the hotel. A Mossad officer immediately followed the Englishman into the street. Photographs of the hotel meeting were sent via courier to Tel Aviv for identification and analysis. Surveillance of the two Palestinians in London continued.

The PLO men headed back to Heathrow Airport and the Israelis agents watched as they purchased two tickets for an El Al flight to Tel Aviv. They would be taking the briefcase received from Kirkland in the hotel lobby on board with them. The Mossad allowed the men to board, but upon arrival in Israel they were quickly taken into custody and the briefcase was searched. Carefully hidden inside were two machine guns and five hand-grenades.

A military trial was quietly held. Neither Kirkland nor the PLO men in Beirut knew what was responsible for their sudden disappearance. The military censor had blocked publication of the story in the Israeli press. The two Palestinians confessed to charges that they were plotting a commando strike against Israel. Their statements revealed that Brad Kirkland was supplying military equipment to Waddieh Haddad's faction, and that the money was being funnelled in from Libya.

Over the next several months, Israeli intelligence agents kept up a close surveillance of Kirkland, waiting for a clue that might uncover the full scope of his activities. Kirkland traveled constantly, flying to Zurich, Geneva, and Paris several times a month. Mossad analysts discovered that he had once served as an officer in Britain's Special Air Service Regiment, an elite commando unit and anti-guerrilla squad. He had been stationed in Northern Ireland and was no stranger to terrorism, having spent most of his young adult life fighting the underground Irish Republican Army. Later he left the British military, charging that his commanders were growing too mild with the Irish Catholic militants. Kirkland had been convinced that the situation in British-ruled Northern Ireland demanded harsher measures, but his superiors were not prepared to go along with his recommendations. Bitter and frustrated, Kirkland quit the army in protest. In a cynical drive for adventure and cash, he began working for Arab terrorists in the Middle East, people whose inclination toward restraint was measurably less than that found among the British leadership in Northern Ireland. Such lack of inhibition on the part of international terrorists nevertheless does not necessarily explain why a former British military officer would choose to throw in his lot with radical Arab forces when similar mercenaries were choosing to carry on the fight on behalf of the West by enlisting in the counterinsurgency forces of pro-Western Arab regimes like Qatar, Bahrain, the United Arab Emirates, North Yemen, and Oman. Perhaps the coffers of radical Soviet-backed oil states like Libya and Iraq enabled Kirkland to extract a higher price for his services. Maybe it was simply that the first group to knock at Kirkland's door happened to be PLO operatives rather than recruiters for the Sultan of Oman.

Whatever his motivation, Kirkland's expertise and access to Western resources heightened the chances that one or more terrorist attacks against Israel might succeed in the coming months, and the Mossad case officer felt he had little choice but to maintain a close watch over the British mercenary.

Kirkland lived in the exclusive London neighborhood of Eton Place with his wife and three children. Always properly groomed and elegantly dressed, his life seemed typical of the well-mannered English gentleman. To the outsider, Brad Kirkland was a quiet, responsible family man. His flights to France and Switzerland continued with bland regularity. Eventually, the Mossad considered turning the case over to Scotland Yard. Months had gone by with nothing new turning up. The operation was going nowhere. The swollen Israeli defense budget had always created great pressures on the intelligence community. Mossad superiors could not afford to see their money squandered on low-level surveillance operations that could easily grind on week after week with no end in sight. There had to be results soon or the investigation of Kirkland would have to be canceled.

Weeks passed without incident. Pressures within the Mossad to drop the case increased, but the agents in the field were convinced that their watch over Kirkland would bear fruit, and they resisted suggestions to terminate their mission. Finally, following one of his trips to Paris, Kirkland flew to Tripoli. It was now clear that he was directly involved with the Libyans and was playing a role in the terrorist network being underwritten by Muammar Qaddafi.

Other cities were soon added to Kirkland's itinerary. He traveled to Rome and Hamburg as well as Paris, London, Zurich, Geneva, and Tripoli. In Hamburg, he visited a so-called electronics company managed by an elderly German war veteran. Mossad agents observed Kirkland enter the factory, and later emerge with suitcases resembling the one carried aboard the El Al jetliner by the two Palestinians. The Israelis soon learned that the German company specialized in surveillance equipment and high explosives, providing the weapons illegally to various international terrorist groups. In Kirkland's case, an order would be placed with the West German factory by Qaddafi's second-in-command, Major Abdel Salem Jalloud, upon recommendation by Kirkland. The Englishman would then pick up funds that had been transferred to a Swiss bank account and travel on to Hamburg to secure the supplies. Kirkland's contract with the Libyans amounted to weapons' sales worth more than $250,000 a year.

It was in Paris that Kirkland met up with Pierre Bujold, a former member of the clandestine French OAS (Organisation Armée Secrète), the right-wing paramilitary organization responsible for the "Day of the Jackal" assassination of Charles de Gaulle.

Like Vietnam, the Algerian War had produced thousands of disgruntled veterans who felt betrayed by a nation that had sent them into battle only to deny them the moral and spiritual support necessary to win. A fraction joined the underground OAS. The majority quietly slipped back into civilian life. Some resumed their military careers, albeit chastened by the experience of fighting an unconventional colonial war that had lacked popular support. Others signed on as mercenaries, fighting against African liberation movements in places like Rhodesia and Angola, still committed to the notion that decolonization masked communist expansion and spurred the triumph of forces opposed to Western values like parliamentary democracy, economic self-determination, and religious freedom.

Yet for a few, the loss of French colonies in Indochina and Algeria revealed the futility of fighting for Western governments, institutions forced into retreat not by a superior enemy but by shortsighted leaders and enervated populaces; one of these veterans, Pierre Bujold (his real name remains classified by the Israeli government), rejected the official policies of the West and decided to continue his own ideological struggle by contracting with the PLO.

Bujold had served as an officer in both Indochina and Algeria, achieving the rank of lieutenant colonel in the paratroopers, and an excellent service record. His disgust over his country's "abandonment" of Algeria, however, purportedly pushed him into the ranks of the OAS underground. The irony was that many of his PLO clients had as their patrons Bujold's former adversaries: Marxist Vietnam, FLN-led Algeria, the Eastern-bloc nations of Russia, Bulgaria, Hungary, and Cuba.

Bujold's one-time arch-enemy, Gammal Nasser, was the man who actually gave birth to the Palestine Liberation Organization in 1964, a ploy designed to control the burgeoning nationalism of displaced Palestinians as well as to put pressure on Israel through the use of PLO terrorists operating from the Egyptian-controlled Gaza Strip. In 1956, when Israel, Britain, and France united against Egypt, the leadership in Tel Aviv had already claimed that Palestinian guerrilla actions could be traced to Nasser's hand.

By the time Bujold joined forces with the PLO, the guerrilla organization's connection with his former foes was unmistakable. In December 1962, Ahmad Ben Bella, now president of a newly independent Algeria, met with representatives of Arafat's Fateh faction and granted them permission to set up an office on Victor Hugo Street in Algiers under the name, Palestine National Libération Committee. The victorious rebel leader offered the Palestinians the expertise of his FLN (Front de Liberation Nationale) resistance group—which had come from the long years of fighting with the French—and agreed to set up training camps in Algeria for courses in guerrilla warfare.

"The guerrilla war in Algeria," wrote Abu Iyad, Arafat's second-in-command, "had a profound influence on us. We were impressed by the Algerian nationalists' ability to form a solid front, wage war against an army a thousand times superior to their own, obtain many forms of aid from various Arab governments (often at odds with one another), and at the same time avoid becoming dependent on any of them. They symbolized the success we dreamed of."[10]

During her first public speech on 15 May 1961 in Saida, Lebanon, Leila Khaled—whose two airplane hijackings in 1969 and 1970 brought George Habash's PFLP faction to the world stage—echoed the widespread sentiment of the Palestinian leadership: "We must learn to emulate our Algerian brethren in order to liberate Palestine."[11]

Ben Bella lent further assistance to the Palestinian guerrillas by establishing a policy whereby Palestinians living in Algeria would be allowed employment provided they registered for work permits, to be issued on the condition that they turn over a percentage of their salaries to the Palestinian resistance movement.[12] This "resistance tax" is still being levied: Palestinians living in Arab countries pay between 5 percent and 7 percent of their gross income to the PLO-controlled Palestine National Fund.[13]

When George Habash's PFLP inaugurated the era of international terrorism in 1968 by hijacking an Israeli El Al flight, the guerrillas chose Algeria as their destination. Once the plane was on the ground, the Algerian authorities immediately agreed to assist the hijackers. Israeli passengers and crew were held inside the plane for forty days while Algeria's official press praised the guerrilla action.

It was the Algerian connection that enabled Fateh to forge a long-term relationship with the People's Republic of China. In 1964, Fateh co-founder Khalil Wazir was invited to join an official Algerian delegation to Beijing. Wazir quickly followed up this first visit with another on 17 March 1964, this time traveling to Beijing with Arafat and holding talks with Liao Ch'eng-chih, the chairman of the Chinese Committee for Afro-Asian Solidarity.[14]

The following year, in March 1965, the PLO chairman at the time, Ahmed Shuqairy, was received by Mao Zedong in Beijing and a Chinese statement was issued expressing support for the "Arab people of Palestine in their struggle to return to their homeland by all means, political and otherwise."[15]

The Communist Chinese republic became the first nation to grant the PLO diplomatic recognition with ambassadorial status. According to Israeli intelligence, an estimated $5 million in arms was sent by the Chinese to the PLO between 1965 and 1969.[16] The chief of the PLO mission in Beijing claimed that throughout the early 1970s, the Palestinian guerrillas received 75 percent of their weapons from China.[17]

Following a trip to the People's Republic in March 1970, Arafat, by then the PLO chairman, was able to structure another important alliance when he flew to North Vietnam aboard a Chinese military plane.

"Everything I had read and heard about the Vietnamese resistance, first to the French occupation and then to the American aggression, filled me with a sense of hope," recalled Abu Iyad, who accompanied Arafat on his mission to Hanoi. "Everything I was to see in North Vietnam was a source of enrichment and inspiration for me." During the visit, General Vo Nguyen Giap outlined the Vietcong strategy for conquering South Vietnam, and Hanoi's Politburo offered to train PLO guerrillas at Vietnamese camps.[18]

It was Nasser who introduced Arafat to the Soviet leadership in 1968. Traveling under an Egyptian passport in the name of Muhsin Amin, Arafat was taken to Moscow by the Egyptian president for meetings with Chairman Leonid Brezhnev, President Nikolai Podgorny, Premier Aleksei Kosygin, and the Central Committee official in charge of national liberation movements, Kyril Mazurov.[19] A few weeks later, the Soviet Central Committee accepted Nasser's recommendation to provide the Palestinian guerrillas with $500,000 in arms.[20] In 1970, the Soviets began a systematic program of providing military and ideological instruction to Palestinian fighters. In 1981, they granted embassy status to the PLO diplomatic office in Moscow.

The training and support of Palestinian guerrillas by the Algerians, the Egyptians, the Soviets, and the Vietcong had become a significant factor in the development of the PLO's capacity to conduct guerrilla warfare. In 1968, Faisal Muhammad al-Sheikh Yussuf went to Moscow to receive training as a PLO battalion commander. In 1969, PLO member Jawad Ahmad 'Abd al-Ghani attended a course at a military college in Algeria. In 1977, Fadl Muhammad 'Uthman was instructed as a PLO company commander in Vietnam. In 1978, PLO member Ahmad Muhammed Ahamd Mar'i al-Sharqawi graduated from a course held at a military academy in Egypt.[21]

These PLO fighters represented just a fraction of those trained and equipped by the people Bujold had pledged to resist during his years in Indochina, Algeria, and his time with the OAS. Bujold's PLO allies were receiving training and supplies from elements he had once opposed so fiercely that in order to crush them he had been willing to risk his life with the clandestine OAS and bring about the violent overthrow of French President de Gaulle's democratically elected government.

A decade after his right-wing OAS involvement, Bujold had opted out of the East-West/Third World struggle being waged by Western governments and gone into business for himself, acting as a paid military adviser to PLO terrorists and other Arab radicals. The PLO faction employing Bujold had aligned itself with Colonel Muammar Qaddafi's Libya, an implacable foe of Egypt's President Sadat. The Frenchman justified his work by noting that Egypt had assisted the FLN rebels in Algeria, and that Qaddafi would use the PLO faction Bujold was training to damage Egypt's influence in the Arab world. Support for Libya would therefore provide a circuitous route for revenge against Egypt. Bujold received somewhere between $250,000 and $500,000 for his work as organizer and commander of Qaddafi's special PLO commando unit.

To men like Bujold, Charles de Gaulle had once represented the triumph of French Algeria and the preservation of French values, which they had believed were under siege by Third World revolutions spearheaded by Vietnam's Ho Chi Minh, Egypt's Gammel Nasser, and Algeria's Ahmad Ben Bella. Such right-wing supporters of de Gaulle were to see their hopes dashed, however, when the French president eventually pushed for Algerian self-determination and later adopted an openly pro-Arab policy despite his country's longtime alliance with Israel.

Like other members of the French right, Bujold had once envisioned himself as a footsoldier in defense of French honor, protecting European civilization from the onslaught mounted by anti-Western elements. In a curious way, like his onetime hero and subsequent rival, Bujold seemed to embrace the Gaullist philosophy that causes do not have friends, only interests; he was willing to collaborate with Arab revolutionaries and Third World leaders dedicated to the eradication of European dominance in North Africa and the dismantling of the Jewish state in the Middle East if it helped bring about the downfall of Nasser's heir, Anwar Sadat.

Bujold's alliance with Qaddafi and his PLO commandos may have been tactical, part of a sincere strategy to undermine Egypt's role as leader of the Arab world. Or it may have been based partly on a warrior's thirst for adventure, partly on monetary gain. Perhaps Bujold's ideological conviction that he had to forge short-term alliances with lesser enemies in order to take on greater ones was simply an attempt to put a respectable gloss on the impulses of a confused, ambitious mercenary.

Regardless of the murky reasoning behind the ex-OAS commando's alliance with Arab terror, Israeli intelligence, by the spring of 1977, was unraveling Bujold's convoluted path to Qaddafi and the PLO.

During their liaisons in Paris, Bujold exposed fellow mercenary Brad Kirkland to a life quite different from that of Eton Place. The conservative family man tasted the lush Paris nightlife in supreme fashion, guided through the discos and bordellos by the experienced Bujold. While they were gone on one such outing, Mossad men moved in and searched Kirkland's apartment. Once inside, they discovered numerous documents detailing several Swiss bank holdings and illegal financial transfers among various accounts in Paris, Zurich, Bonn, and Geneva, the amounts totalling hundreds of thousands of dollars. The intelligence agents methodically photographed each one of the documents, including the names of various fictitious companies that had been used as covers for the illegal bank transfers. The folder of incriminating evidence against Kirkland was beginning to thicken. The intelligence officers decided it was time to make their move.

One morning, two men knocked on Kirkland's door in Paris. They deliberately chose to hold the meeting outside Kirkland's native Britain, knowing that foreign soil would heighten the intimidation. When Kirkland answered, the two men quickly entered the apartment and confronted Kirkland with their evidence. Shoving open the file, they displayed microfilmed copies of the Swiss bank transactions, photographs of Kirkland handing the suitcase of arms to the two Palestinians in the London hotel lobby, documents detailing his trips to Libya, reports on his visits to the Hamburg weapons factory. Stunned and frightened, Kirkland demanded that the two men identify themselves.

"You don't need to do much thinking to figure out who we are," one of them told Kirkland. "You are collaborating with international terrorists. You are being paid by Libyan agents. You should know who we are."

"You are connected with French intelligence?" Kirkland asked, assuming that since he was on French soil he was most likely under their jurisdiction.

"We are Israelis," the Mossad officer told him. Kirkland began to panic.

"You do have some choices," the other Israeli told him. "You can surrender to the British authorities back home, who will certainly send you to prison. Or you can move your wife and children from their beautiful home in Eton Place and flee to Libya to join your comrades. Or you can continue with your work."

"What do you mean, continue with my work?" Kirkland asked.

"You'll just have a new boss," the Mossad man explained. "We can't pay you as much as the Libyans. But Israel will pay your expenses." Kirkland was silent. "Of course you can continue collecting money from Qaddafi," the Israeli added. "We don't mind that. But you will be taking orders from us."

The British mercenary at first flatly denied that he was working under contract for Libyan intelligence, but he soon confessed. "It's your chance to get out of this terrible operation," the Israeli told him.

Kirkland accepted the offer to go over to the Israeli side. He was interrogated for days until every detail of his operation was on tape. He described how the Libyans were training twenty commandos from Haddad's group for a special assignment, but insisted that he was unaware of their actual mission. His role was merely to acquire supplies while Bujold organized the operation and drew up the plans.

The Mossad struggled to unravel the details of the PLO-Libyan plot, but the security-minded Waddieh Haddad kept a tight cloak around his organization and Mossad agents were unable to learn anything further. To make matters worse, the organization had lost a valuable resource: Dina al-Asan had been arrested in Beirut. After spending almost eighteen lonely months undercover, she had taken a Lebanese lover and, through carelessness, had allowed him to suspect her true purpose in Lebanon. An anti-Zionist and PLO sympathizer, the man informed the Lebanese police and Dina was promptly taken into custody by the Christian-dominated regime in Beirut. Shortly after the outbreak of the Lebanese civil war, she was turned over to the PLO, possibly as part of a deal to gain the release of captured Lebanese Christian militiamen being held by Palestinian rebel forces or their Lebanese Moslem allies.

9

Palestinian Prison

THE woman who had led the Israelis to Brad Kirkland and his Libyan clients was now behind bars in a PLO cell. Her Palestinian jailers ordinarily displayed a grudging respect for their Israeli prisoners, but faced with a Moslem woman like Dina they felt little need for restraint. She was one of their own, and a woman; their comrades had been humiliated by her. A price had to be paid. At first, she was kept in a cell six feet by six feet, with no running water and no toilet. She was often chained to the bars on the window and starved for days at a time. The torturers blamed her for the success the Israelis were having in reducing PLO raids on Jewish targets. Hoping to learn more about Israel's counterterrorist tactics, they coaxed information out of her by repeatedly pressing burning cigarette butts into her skin and sticking a hot electric curling-iron into her mouth. Mock executions were staged where Dina would sit down to write a farewell letter to her family convinced that she would soon be killed.

The PLO also devised a new method of torture: Dina would be placed inside an empty truck tire with her arms and legs tied around the outside. Then someone would pound the soles of her feet with a broomstick until they were soft and bloody. When she would finally faint from the pain, the jailers would revive her by rolling the tire back and forth, drenching her body with ice water.

At one point, when Israeli warplanes intensified their retaliatory strikes against PLO positions near Beirut, Dina's captors thought that the Mossad was attempting a rescue and they hastily moved her to an underground cave near Sidon. It was one of the first of dozens of caves that would eventually be built by the PLO to store weapons ranging from Soviet-made Katyusha rocket launchers to attack helicopters disassembled for storage. Dina had no idea if an attempt was being made to rescue her or not. She did not even know if the Mossad knew that she had been captured. She languished in the tiny wooden box that had been constructed inside the cave while her twenty-two-year-old guard tormented her, often taking his Gustav rifle, heating up the barrel in a kerosene lamp, and touching it against her lips. His questions ranged from demands for details of Mossad procedures to queries about the sexual appetites of Israeli woman. Dina's interrogators also pressed her for the home addresses of Moshe Dayan, Ezer Weizman, Ariel Sharon, and Menachem Begin. Dina eventually broke, revealing several state secrets. But she held back on three aspects of her mission in Beirut that she believed were vital to Israeli security: her activities concerning the detection of PLO munitions depots hidden within the refugee camps; her surveillance of foreign mercenaries and their connection to international terrorist groups like the Japanese Red Army, the Baader-Meinhoff gang, and the IRA; and her efforts to locate Ali Hassan Salameh, Arafat's trusted aide who had planned the Munich Olympic attack for Abu Iyad's Black September organization. Dina was determined not to jeopardize the Mossad's future efforts in these three areas by revealing the specifics of her work concerning them to PLO interrogators. The Israelis, however, did not expect captured agents to endure prolonged torture. They made new plans on the assumption that Dina had confessed everything, disclosing the details of her entire operation in Beirut.

Dina's loneliness during her captivity was so intense at times that she waited days for a fly to appear. A compassionate PLO woman encouraged her by bringing Red Cross boxes filled with food and cosmetics which had been packed by the Israelis and forwarded to Lebanon as if sent by Dina's family. There would be months of quiet and then suddenly the interrogations would begin again, usually prompted by a successful Israeli raid and the subsequent urge of a PLO commando to take vengeance against the imprisoned Mossad agent. Dina was also visited by an East German intelligence officer and later on by a Russian KGB operative. They were both more thorough and systematic than the Palestinians in their questioning of her, meticulously going over the details of her recruitment by the Israelis, the training she received, and the contacts she had made in Beirut.

Throughout her imprisonment, the Israeli government worked behind-the-scenes to get Dina out. Their policy had always been to spare no effort in seeking the release of Israeli POWs, and in Dina's case, perhaps sensitive to charges that they might be less vigilant because the imprisoned agent was a non-Jew, the Israelis pushed even harder than usual for her release. They contacted intermediaries in Europe, notifying the PLO that they were willing to pay a high ransom for her release, but the offers were rejected; Dina was to spend five years in an isolated cave in war-torn Lebanon until suitable terms for her freedom could be worked out. Her imprisonment nearly destroyed her. "I saw her before and I saw her after," Dina's sister said. "You can't imagine what it did to her."[1]

On 24 February, 1980, Dina was taken to Larnaca airport in Cyprus. Under the supervision of the International Red Cross, she was placed in Israeli custody in exchange for two Palestinian prisoners: William Naguib Nassar, a member of Arafat's Fateh faction, and his fellow PLO member Muhammad Mahdi Busayu, known as Abu Ali. Busayu had been arrested in the Gaza Strip in 1971. Nassar had been arrested in 1968 in Jerusalem, charged with murder and sabotage. Both men had been serving life sentences in Israeli jails.[2]

Nassar had joined Arafat's group in 1965. He traveled to the People's Republic of China to receive training in guerrilla warfare and was one of the first members of Fateh to be arrested by the Israelis. Repeated demands for his freedom had been made by Palestinian hijackers, including those who carried out the hijacking to Entebbe. Nassar's mother was Jewish and his father an Arab Christian. Though Nassar claimed to be a nonobservant Christian, according to Jewish tradition and Israeli law, anyone born of a Jewish mother is considered a Jew.

While still in prison, Nassar was asked if there would ever be a peaceful solution to the Arab-Israeli conflict. He replied: "There is no solution, only war. The only solution is that the full privileges and rights to this land will be in the hands of the Palestinians and not the Israelis. This will come only in war because we are stubborn and you are no less stubborn."[3]

Dina al-Asan, a Moslem woman from Jordan who had worked as a spy for the Israeli Mossad, had been exchanged for two PLO commandos, one of them a Palestinian Jew. After her release, Dina began work as a physician under an assumed name in northern Israel. Her clinic there faced the main invasion route taken by the Israeli army during its 1982 invasion of Lebanon, when troops uncovered numerous PLO hideouts like the one which had held Dina for nearly five years.

10

"Magnoun"

THE loss of Dina's operation in Lebanon had weakened the Mossad's ability to penetrate Waddieh Haddad's group in Beirut. Her special access to Abu Iyad's lieutenant had enabled intelligence agents to identify Brad Kirkland as Haddad's weapons supplier, Pierre Bujold as his operational planner, and Muammar Qaddafi as his financier. Yet the specific purpose of the link between Haddad and Libya remained unclear. At the time, with Dina still in prison and Haddad's team nearing the end of their training, it fell to Kirkland, now working as a Mossad agent (which is why his real name remains classified by Israeli intelligence), to uncover the nature and purpose of Libya's PLO strike force.

There were twenty members in Haddad's group. Kirkland was told to try to identify each one, though they were all operating under pseudonyms. The Mossad ordered him to initiate meetings in Paris and Tripoli in an effort to gather more details about the Libyan underground network. But the Israelis were careful to do a follow-up check on Kirkland's information. If the Englishman indicated that on a certain day two Palestinians would be traveling from Tripoli to Athens under false passports, Israeli agents would be waiting in Greece to verify the report. Though afraid that his Arab companions might uncover his Israeli connection, Kirkland grudgingly agreed to carry out Mossad directives. He was not trusted, however. An agent operating out of fear rather than loyalty may quickly switch sides the moment he or she feels that the threat has been lifted. Working with reluctant informers is dangerous for an intelligence operation, which is why the Mossad hesitated to coerce adversaries into working as double-agents. Operatives like Kirkland who had been pressured into service by Israel might offer temporary rewards, but their resentment could easily drive them, if not back into the hands of their original employers, then perhaps into the arms of some other enemy. Qaddafi wasn't the only Arab leader willing to employ foreign mercenaries against Israel.

After several more weeks of continued meetings between Kirkland and Bujold, and numerous trips to Tripoli for meetings with Major Jalloud and members of Haddad's commando unit, the objective of the strike force was eventually revealed: to assassinate Anwar Sadat.

Qaddafi was bent on eliminating Sadat. He had long admired the Egyptian's predecessor, Gamal Nasser, and viewed himself as the rightful heir to Nasser's pan-Arab throne. His resentment of Sadat as usurper of this position was deep and vengeful.

Qaddafi's infatuation with Nasser began in 1959 when he was fifteen and attending high school in the Fezzan desert city of Sebha in eastern Libya. It was then that he started listening to the Egyptian leader's speeches over Cairo's "Voice of the Arabs." The young boy became enthralled by Nasser's calls for Arab unity, the elimination of Western hegemony in the region, and the expulsion of Jews from Palestine. With fellow classmates that included Abdel Salem Jalloud, the young Qaddafi began to form a series of revolutionary cells dedicated to the creation of Nasser's new order.

While still a student, Qaddafi led public demonstrations against Libya's King Idris al-Sunussi, condemning the monarch for his failure to embrace Nasserism and champion the destruction of Israel. The young Qaddafi was eventually expelled from Sebha for his political activities. He then moved north to the city of Misurata to complete his studies, and continued to expand his network of revolutionary cells among fellow students. Modeling himself after Nasser and the Free Officers that toppled Egypt's King Farouk, Qaddafi convinced his followers to pursue military careers in order to place themselves in a position to launch a similar overthrow of King Idris. Qaddafi attended a special signal corps training course in Beaconsfield, England, following his graduation from the University of Benghazi military college. Other members of his underground network traveled to Cairo to study at Egypt's Military Academy where they were to deepen their attachment to Nasser's brand of pan-Arabism.

Soon after taking power from King Idris in a coup on 1 September, 1969, the twenty-seven-year-old Qaddafi welcomed Nasser's emissary, *Al Ahram* editor Mohamed Heikal, and offered to forge a union between Egypt and Libya and hand over complete power to the Egyptian leader. "All we have done is our duty as Arab nationalists. Now it is for President Nasser to take over himself and guide Libya from the reactionary camp, where it was, to the progressive camp, where it should be." He explained that such a union was needed in order to give Egypt a second front in its struggle against Israel. "We have hundreds of miles of Mediterranean coastline; we have the airfields; we have the money; we have everything! Tell President Nasser we made this revolution for him. He can take everything of ours and add it to the rest of the Arab world's resources to be used for battle."[1]

Not yet ready to accept the total union Qaddafi was suggesting, Nasser did agree to enter into a pact with the new leader, along with the Sudan's Jaafar al-Numeiry, another advocate of pan-Arabism who had recently seized power in a military coup. On 27 December, 1969, an alliance among Egypt, Libya, and the Sudan was formed to resist Israel and block U.S.-European influence in the region.

Qaddafi remained enamored of Nasser. During his official visit to Tripoli, Nasser was hoisted in the air and heroically paraded through the streets by Qaddafi's followers. On 4 August, 1970, when the Egyptian president endorsed the proposal by American Secretary of State William Rogers for a cease-fire with Israel along the Suez Canal, Qaddafi was willing to depart from his usual hard-line position in order to spiritedly defend Nasser from Palestinian critics who condemned the move as an appeasement that weakened the Arab cause.

The following month, at the height of the Black September fighting between the Jordanian army and Palestinian commandos, Qaddafi agreed to join Nasser in Cairo to attend an Arab summit conference that the Egyptian president had called to help seek an end to the fighting. Qaddafi "was an eye-catching character, with a revolver that never left his belt," recalled Anwar Sadat, who was Nasser's vice-president at the time. "He attacked King Hussein constantly, describing him as a madman who should be confined to a lunatic asylum; until then I had put his attacks down to over-enthusiasm and youthful impetuosity."[2]

For several years, Sadat was to view Qaddafi as little more than an undisciplined nuisance, a boy whose tendency to misbehave had to be checked now and again by a stern hand. According to a story told by Egyptian journalist Hamdi Fuad, Qaddafi's mother, during a meeting in Algeria with Qaddafi and Sadat, asked Sadat to look after her son and not take his misdeeds too seriously. Sadat then turned to Qaddafi, chastising him like a grand uncle, and told him to listen to his mother and start acting responsibly. Sadat later confessed that he knew that such a possibility was hopeless.[3]

Qaddafi may have showed a childlike affection for Nasser, but he reacted to Sadat's paternalistic attitude with scorn. When Nasser died of a heart-attack on 28 September, 1970, at only fifty-two years of age, the Libyan leader was taken by surprise by his mentor's death and took it especially hard. He continued to remain loyal to Nasser's pan-Arab legacy, however, and on 8 November, 1970, Qaddafi went to Cairo to meet with Sadat, Numeiry, and Hafez Assad, who had just taken power in Syria. They agreed to join their nations into a Confederation of Arab Republics, which would provide the framework for a proposed unification of the four Arab nations. The following year, on 17 April, 1971, Egypt, Syria, and Libya formed the Union of Arab Republics, with Sadat as president and Cairo the capital of the new nation. No significant transfer of power ever took place, however.

Sudan refrained from entering the union because Numeiry was engaged in a power struggle at the time. Qaddafi, however, had already voiced his opposition to a Sudanese role because of communist participation in Numeiry's government. Qaddafi was a strident anti-communist, which accounted for the CIA's initial backing of his regime. He once declared that he would have liked to travel overland from Libya to Egypt but that he could not stand the thought of passing the Soviet-manned bases in the Egyptian desert.

During a 23 January, 1974, meeting with Egypt's Foreign Minister Ismail Fahmy, Soviet President Leonid Brezhnev raised the issue of Qaddafi's virulent anti-communism. "That young man is crazy," Brezhnev said. "He is always attacking the Soviet Union vehemently, without any justification whatsoever. Until now I have refused to meet him, although Nasser told me that he was a nice boy." According to Fahmy, the Soviet leader concluded that Qaddafi was "an unbalanced fanatic."[4] Two years earlier, when Sadat had ordered all fifteen thousand Soviet military experts to leave the country, Qaddafi was so elated that he decided to renew his call for the total unification of Egypt and Libya along the lines first proposed to Mohamed Heikal following the September 1969 coup.

Sadat had responded favorably to Qaddafi's new call for unification, flying to Benghazi to discuss the proposed merger. On 2 August, 1972, Egypt and Libya agreed to "create a unified state and to establish a unified political command," with Sadat serving as president and Qaddafi as vice-president. But Qaddafi's rash behavior and his particular mix of socialism and Islamic fundamentalism soon began to alienate the Egyptian hierarchy.

Qaddafi had embraced the struggle against Israel with a vengeance, even denouncing the Palestinian guerrilla leadership for being too cautious, extolling instead the heroism of those responsible for the Lod Airport massacre that had been carried out by Japanese Red Army commandos. In a speech on 7 October, Qaddafi spoke of those who had fired into the unarmed crowd of civilian passengers at the Israeli airport lounge:

> Indeed, feda'i [guerrilla] action must be of the type of the operation carried out by Japanese feda'iyin. The Japanese feda'i who was tried said they had carried out the operation to stir the Arab world, which lacked spiritual zeal. This statement should have an impact upon the Arabs who are still slumbering.

Feda'i action has not yet reached the level of the true spirit of the feda'iyin. We demand that feda'i action be able to carry out operations similar to the operation carried out by the Japanese. Why should a Palestinian not carry out such an operation? Go to the Popular Front, the Democratic Front, the Revolutionary Popular Front, the General Command, or the Special Command. You will see them all writing books and magazines full of theories, but otherwise unable to carry out one daring operation like that carried out by the Japanese.[5]

Qaddafi's pronouncements on fedayeen terror did not go unnoticed in Jerusalem. On 21 February, 1973, a Libyan Boeing 727 airliner with 108 passengers aboard was shot down by Israel's American-built Phantom fighter aircraft. The Libyan plane was on its way to Cairo when it lost direction in a sandstorm and flew passed the Nile Delta into Israeli-occupied Sinai airspace. The Israelis feared that the plane was on a secret reconnaissance mission or a Kamikaze-type suicide raid—similar to the ones carried out by Shiite Moslem car-bombers in South Lebanon a decade later—its aim being to plunge into an Israeli city or crash into Israel's top-secret nuclear reactor at Dimona in the Negev Desert. Israeli fighter jets approached the Libyan aircraft and ordered it to land at the Refidim airstrip, but the French pilot either did not hear or misunderstood the command. Mistaking the Phantoms for an escort of friendly Egyptian MIGs, the French crew continued the journey through Israeli-occupied territory. Warning shots were fired, then Israel's Chief of Staff David Elazar radioed the order to bring the plane down. Israeli gunfire turned toward the wings of the aircraft and the burning Libyan airliner crash-landed twelve miles from the Suez canal, killing all 108 people aboard. Among the dead was Libya's former foreign minister, Salah Buassir.[6]

Qaddafi, enraged by the incident, told Sadat that he planned to attack Haifa. Sadat restrained him, hinting of war plans that were to culminate in the surprise Yom Kippur attack the following October. The upcoming war would satisfy the demands for retribution, Sadat assured Qaddafi; a premature attack by Libya would only bring an Israeli reprisal against Libyan airfields that would damage Arab ability to launch a combined strike. Qaddafi went along with Sadat, but riots erupted in Benghazi and Tripoli when the bodies of the victims arrived home. Charges were also leveled against Egypt for failing to use its fighter jets to protect the Libyan airliner. Salah Buassir's son printed leaflets blaming his father's death on Egyptian cowardice, and two days after the downing of the Libyan airliner, mobs attacked the Egyptian consulate in Benghazi.

The following month, Qaddafi told Black September representatives in Tripoli that he was willing to pay them $10 million to blow up an El Al plane with passengers still on board. On 4 April, two Black September members were arrested in Rome carrying guns and hand-grenades meant to be used in an attack against an El Al plane at the airport there.

A week later, on 17 April, Qaddafi issued an order to the commander of a Soviet-built Egyptian submarine that had been stationed in Libyan waters under the joint-defense agreement worked out during Nasser's rule. A group of Jews and and other supporters of Israel, which included the wife of Shimon Peres, had embarked on the *Queen Elizabeth II* for a special cruise to commemorate the upcoming twenty-fifth anniversary of Israel's independence on 15 May. Qaddafi told the submarine captain that according to the Egyptian-Libyan defense agreement, the vessel and crew were part of Libya's armed forces and therefore under his jurisdiction. Showing him a map of the Mediterranean, Qaddafi ordered the captain to intercept the *Queen Elizabeth II* on its journey from Southampton to the Israeli port of Ashdod and sink the ship with two torpedoes. According to reports by Mohamed Heikal and American journalist John Cooley, the submarine captain sailed out of Tripoli harbor and transmitted a coded report to the naval base at Alexandria describing his mission for Qaddafi. Sadat, awakened at 1 A.M., immediately canceled the order, later telling Qaddafi that the submarine had been unable to locate the luxury liner. Sadat himself described the incident in one of his memoirs, explaining that he was informed of Qaddafi's plan by the Egyptian naval command in Alexandria at 1:30 P.M., and that due to a radio blackout he was forced to wait two hours until the submarine made its next scheduled contact with the Alexandria base before his order to abort the mission could be transmitted.[7]

In their book, *The Untold History of Israel*, Jacques Derogy and Hesi Carmel disputed the Heikal version regarding the Egyptian captain's coded message to Alexandria, claiming that the submarine had been proceeding to Malta on its mission for Qaddafi when British planes detected its movements. Prime Minister Edward Heath ordered his ambassador in Cairo to awaken the Egyptian president, and Sadat's personal secretary was informed of the plan at 1:30 A.M. As with Qaddafi's plan to attack Haifa in the wake of the Libyan airline shooting, Derogy and Hesi charged that Sadat cancelled the submarine mission out of a reluctance to jeopardize his upcoming plans for a surprise attack against Israel by engaging in a premature military strike.[8] Whatever the true version, the *QE II* incident, along with the aborted plan to attack Haifa, demonstrated that Qaddafi's thinking was not in line with Sadat's and could dangerously threaten the latter's strategy toward Israel.

"Try to imagine what would have happened if Qaddafi had succeeded in sinking the *QE2*," Sadat wrote. "First of all, Egypt would have lost its submarine and her crew. The [U.S.] Sixth Fleet would not have allowed it to escape. Secondly, the world would never have forgiven the Arabs for committing this criminal and barbaric act, involving innocent women and children who had nothing in the world to do with the Arab-Israeli conflict. This would have been the shameful consequence of giving arms to a teen-ager—or a mad man. Qaddafi has the mentality of a small child. The tragedy is that the toys he plays with are real weapons."[9]

According to a statement made to journalist John Cooley by a former Libyan official, Qaddafi "became like a different person" following the failure of the *QE II* affair. "He withdrew into the desert, raging at anyone who tried to speak to him. If ever he showed signs of being a manic depressive, it was after the submarine incident."[10]

The Libyan leader felt betrayed by Sadat, and he decided to quit Libya's ruling Revolution Command Council, publishing the text of his resignation and personally handing out copies to passersby on the streets of Tripoli. Several days later, after consulting with Jalloud and other RCC members, Qaddafi agreed to withdraw his resignation and travel to Egypt to mend fences with Sadat.

On 22 June, Qaddafi arrived in Cairo with his wife and small child. Sadat offered Tahra Palace as a residence for Qaddafi during his visit and advised him to travel throughout Egypt and meet with groups of professionals, students, and community leaders. During one of Qaddafi's talks, discussion turned to feminist issues. In the audience was Aminah es-Said (known as the "Arab Katherine Graham"), the female publisher of the huge publishing company, Dar al-Hilal. Founded in the late 1800's, Dar al-Hilal had become one of the largest publishing firms in the Middle East, and Mrs. Said ran the entire operation, producing millions of books and mass-circulation weeklies. In the 1930s, she had been one of the first five women to gain entry into Cairo University. When she started out as a journalist she had been forced to write under a male pseudonym. At least she found work; many of her fellow women had had to leave Egypt in order to pursue professional careers.[11] Given such early trials, Mrs. Said was not receptive when Qaddafi stated his opposition to women entering the traditionally male-dominated work force and expounded on the importance of their fulfilling their proper roles as wives and mothers. In his *Green Book*, the three-volume work in which he put forward his philosophy regarding political, economic, and social problems, Qaddafi acknowledged the equal status of men and women, but insisted that female rights should be expressed within the constraints of marriage and child-bearing:

> Men and women must perform, not abandon the role for which they were
> created. Abandoning the role or even a part of it only occurs as a result of

coercive conditions. The woman who rejects pregnancy, marriage, make up and femininity for reasons of health, abandons her natural role in life under these coercive conditions of health. The woman who rejects marriage, pregnancy or motherhood etc., because of work, abandons her natural role as a result of a coercive condition, which is a moral deviation from the norm. Thus, abandoning the natural role of female and male in life can occur under unnatural conditions which are contrary to nature and a threat to survival. Consequently, there must be a world revolution which puts an end to all materialistic conditions hindering woman from performing her natural role in life and driving her to carry out man's duties in order to be equal in rights.[12]

Several members of the Egyptian intellectual community, many of whom were struggling to reform traditions that had oppressed Moslem women for centuries, were offended by Qaddafi's remarks about the role of women in society. His views on Islam also clashed with the modernized leadership in Cairo. Qaddafi returned to Tripoli on 9 July, depressed at his lukewarm reception in Egypt. He persisted, however, in his calls for a unified Egyptian-Libyan state, albeit one created on his own terms.

On 18 July, 1973, thousands of Libyans massed along the border at Ras Jedir for a "people's march" into Egypt in support of Qaddafi's call for unity. Egyptian leaders were worried that the Libyans might be armed, and that aroused by the cries of Moslem extremists, they might begin destroying the bars and nightclubs of Cairo upon entering the city. Egypt installed land-mines and sent a railway car to block the road into the capital. When the column of forty thousand marchers reached Fuka, the group was persuaded to halt its advance by Egyptian authorities.[13]

On 23 July, Qaddafi announced that a "people's revolution" was needed in order to end the "corruption, bureaucracy and favoritism which reign in Egypt today." On 29 August, Sadat attempted to placate Qaddafi by agreeing to a series of measures to be adopted by the Egyptian-Libyan Unified Political Command. The moves, however, lacked substance and Qaddafi continued to play a disruptive role in Egyptian politics.

Journalist Hamdi Fuad claimed that Qaddafi circulated rumors that Sadat's wife Jihan had tried to seduce the Libyan leader, and that she wanted her daughter to marry him. At one point, Qaddafi reportedly declared that he was going to travel to the south of France to convince the French to convert to Islam.[14]

During another episode, when Sadat attempted to enlist his aid in preparing for his upcoming strike against Israel, Qaddafi responded by telling him that Libya was not prepared for war, that indeed the entire Arab world was not prepared, and that what they needed was the ultimate weapon to destroy Israel. Qaddafi was determined to obtain an atomic bomb. He sent his deputy Jalloud to Peking and offered Zhou Enlai cash to buy a nuclear device. The Chinese refused; Qaddafi simply decided to shop elsewhere.[15]

As tensions with Sadat continued to increase, Qaddafi began accusing Egypt of adopting Western values and turning away from Islam. In 1973, when Sadat agreed to a cease-fire with the Israelis in the aftermath of the Yom Kippur War, and later when he cooperated with Henry Kissinger's shuttle diplomacy to reduce Arab-Israeli tensions, Qaddafi labeled Sadat a traitor and a coward and eventually called for his overthrow.[16]

In 1974, following the signing of the U.S.-engineered Sinai I disengagement agreement between Egypt and Israel, Qaddafi backed a plot by the terrorist Carlos to assassinate the American ambassador to Cairo, Hermann Eilts. The plot was foiled when a member of the hit team, which was stationed at the former U.S. air force base in northern Libya, sold the plans to the CIA.[17] In an interview with John Cooley before leaving for the Arab summit conference in Rabat in October 1974, Sadat said that he believed Qaddafi to be mentally unbalanced.[18] Qaddafi provided steady support for the Egyptian Moslem Brotherhood in its opposition to the ruling regime and stepped up his campaign for Sadat's ouster. Sadat increasingly began referring to Qaddafi as *magnoun*, the Arabic word for insane. "How deceived I was in the person of Muammar al-Qaddafi!," the Egyptian leader wrote shortly before his death. "I discovered he had a double personality: the first impressing you with its idealism, enthusiasm and devotion; the second appalling you with its evil, bitterness, violence, and bloodthirstiness."[19]

In the spring of 1977, Qaddafi and Jalloud bought arms from the ex-British commando, Brad Kirkland, hired the former OAS officer Pierre Bujold as a military planner, and recruited Waddieh Haddad's PLO guerrillas in preparation for the murder of the Egyptian president. "What we could not do with de Gaulle, we will do with Sadat," the French mercenary assured Qaddafi.

11

Begin's Ploy

THE details of the assassination plot against Sadat, relayed to the Mossad by Brad Kirkland, were sketchy. All that was known was that there were two plans: one involving a sea-launched attack on Sadat's resort home at Alexandria, the other consisting of an assault during a presidential parade in Cairo. Kirkland was ordered to initiate contacts within Libya in an effort to gather more information. As the days and weeks passed, the target date grew imminent and details of the Libyan-PLO plot began to unfold. Realizing that the Egyptian president's life was in increasing danger, the Mossad decided to take its findings to the newly-elected prime minister, Menachem Begin.

Begin astonished the Israeli intelligence community. He wanted the information turned over directly to Anwar Sadat. At first, the seasoned Mossad officers reacted with doubt, but Begin held firm. He wanted the file turned over to the Egyptians, and he called his cabinet into session to debate his proposal.

Many observers considered Begin an unrepentant hawk; he was branded a terrorist by Arab detractors for his activities as head of the Irgun Zvai Leumi underground in pre-state Israel and labeled an uncompromising militant fanatic by adversaries in Israel. Until the polling on 17 May, 1977, his Herut faction had never achieved an electoral victory in the twenty-nine-year history of the Jewish state. It had appeared as if David Ben-Gurion's Mapai party and his heirs in the Labor Zionist Movement had established an unshakeable hold on the reins of government, leaving for Begin's followers in the Revisionist Labor Movement little more than the thankless role of loyal opposition.

To many, Menachem Begin represented a strident, offensive Zionism, one that gave no quarter to Jewish moderates advocating reconciliation with their enemies through appeasement, but also one seeming to similarly reject a reasoned accommodation for the sake of peace. It was Begin who led the opposition to the United Nations, 1947 decision to partition Palestine into separate Jewish and Arab states. Like his fellow Zionists, Begin claimed the right of Jews to establish a homeland in British Mandate Palestine, which included territory on both sides of the Jordan River. But unlike the majority of Zionist leaders, such as David Ben-Gurion and Chaim Weizmann, who reluctantly accepted partition in hopes of satisfying Arab demands in the region and thereby averting further bloodshed, Begin fought on for the realization of Jewish sovereignty over all of Eretz Israel, the ancient biblical kingdom that spanned all of Palestine.

Despite his opposition to the U.N. plan, Begin did agree to accept the authority of the newly-formed state, and although the original borders of the area given to the Jews under partition were expanded as a result of their subsequent victory against invading Arab armies in 1948, Israeli authority did not extend to the West Bank territories of Judea and Samaria until the 1967 Six Day War. Practical realities led to abandonment of the drive to achieve Jewish sovereignty over the East Bank of the Jordan, on which the Hashemite Kingdom of Transjordan had been established under British auspices in 1922, covering 80 percent of the historic land of Palestine. Begin was to eventually agree to the dismantling of Jewish settlements in the Sinai, the return of the peninsula to Egyptian control, and the granting of autonomy to the Palestinians in Israeli-occupied Gaza and the West Bank. But he would not relinquish his belief in the right of Jews to settle anywhere in the ancient Land of Israel west of the Jordan River, whether it be under Israeli, Egyptian, Hashemite, or Palestinian authority.

Begin's fervent nationalism had been nourished by his father, Ze'ev Dov, while still a boy in his native Brest-Litovsk, a village in Eastern Europe that alternately fell under Lithuanian, Russian, Polish, and German rule, now the capital of the Brest region of the Belorussian Soviet Socialist Republic. Ze'ev, along with Mordechai Sheinerman, the grandfather of Ariel Sharon, were staunch followers of Theodor Herzl's burgeoning Zionist movement. The young Begin was raised amid his father's displays of a proudly defiant Judaism. Ze'ev spoke of the *pogroms*, the periodic outbreaks of anti-Semitic violence that would erupt across Eastern Europe. He taught his son the lessons of the Dreyfus affair, when the Jewish captain was wrongly convicted of treason in France and the crowd cried "Death to the Jews" while a startled Theodor Herzl looked on. He lectured about the Beilis case, when a thirty-seven-year old Jew in Kiev was falsely charged with the ritual slaughter of a twelve-year-old Christian boy, adding strength to the popular anti-Semitic refrain that Jews killed gentile children and used their blood for secret religious ceremonies.[1] (The "blood libel" persists to this day: in 1985, Syrian Defense Minister Mustafa Tlas published a book entitled *The Matzoh of Zion*, purporting to prove that in 1840 the Jews of Damascus killed two Christians and used their blood to bake matzoh. "This violence was not the first of its kind," Tlas wrote.[2])

Ze'ev Begin's reaction to the virulent anti-Semitism of his native Europe was one of defiance. He walked through the streets carrying a cane with a silver knob on the top bearing the likeness of Emile Zola, the French novelist who had written a spirited defense of the maligned Captain Dreyfus. On one occasion, Ze'ev was carrying the cane while walking with a rabbi when a Polish sergeant tried to engage in the popular anti-Jewish sport of cutting off the religious man's beard. "My father did not hesitate," Menachem later recalled. He "hit him with his cane on his hand. In those days, hitting a Polish sergeant had to be a signal for a pogrom. Both the rabbi and my father were arrested. They were taken to the river Bug, and their captors threatened to throw them in. They were beaten until they bled. My father came home in bad shape, but he was happy. He said he had defended the honour of the Jewish people and the honour of the rabbi. So I remember these two things from my childhood: Jews being persecuted and the courage of the Jews."[3]

Despite Ze'ev Begin's courage, he, like millions of other Jews, was to meet his end at the hands of Adolph Hitler's Nazis. According to Menachem, his father was taken by the Nazis to the Bug River with five hundred other Jews, where they were all machine-gunned to death. "We were told that at his intitiative the Jews started to sing *Hatikva* [the Zionist anthem]," Begin recalled. His sister Rachel offered a different version of her father's final moments: "What I know, what my friends in Brisk told me, is that the Germans passed a law forbidding Jews from burying their dead. My father went to bury a Jew in the cemetery. A German approached him and asked what he was doing. He told him in German and the soldier killed him on the spot."[4]

Both accounts reveal the defiant quality in Ze'ev that the younger Begin grew to emulate. "I have never known a man braver than him," Menachem said. "I shall never forget how my father fought to defend Jewish honour."[5]

The image of the fighting Jew was to dominate Menachem Begin from childhood on, first envisioned as a burgeoning ideal while he was under the sway of his Zionist father's vision, later judged an absolute necessity in the wake of Hitler's Third Reich. (Most of Menachem Begin's family perished in the Holocaust, the few survivors being himself and his wife Aliza and his sister Rachel and her husband Yehoshua. His older brother Herzl, Rachel's baby son, and both of his parents were murdered by the Nazis.)

As a young boy of ten, Begin had originally aligned himself with Hashomer Hatzair, the left-wing Zionist faction supported by his father. But its increasing emphasis on a Marxist call for international class struggle prompted the family to join the more nationalistic movement of Vladimir Jabotinsky's Union of Zionist Revisionists. "You must first of all fight for your own freedom," Begin's father explained, "and when you are free, you will fight for the freedom of the world."[6]

As an adult, Begin became commander of the Irgun Zvai Leumi, the National Military Organization that had broken away from the Haganah (the main Jewish militia unit operating in Palestine). Its reputation for unreserved militancy stemmed from the principles of its founder, Jabotinsky:

> It was a wise philosopher who said "man is a wolf to man"; worse than the wolf is man to man, and this will not change for many days to come. We will not change this through political reforms, nor through culture and even bitter experience will not change it. Stupid is the person who believes in his neighbour, good and loving as the neighbour may be; stupid is the person who relies on justice. Justice exists only for those whose fists and stubbornness make it possible for them to realize it. When I am criticized for my insistence on apartness, on not believing in anyone and on other matters which are difficult for delicate persons to accept, I sometimes want to answer: I am guilty. Do not believe anyone, be always on guard, carry your stick always with you—this is the only way of surviving in this wolfish battle of all against all.[7]

Originally under the direct leadership of Jabotinsky, who died in 1940 while on a speaking tour of the United States, the Irgun drew the bulk of its recruits from the Betar youth movement in Poland, guided by Begin. At the third World Congress of Betar, held in Warsaw in September 1938, the twenty-five-year-old Begin boldly clashed with his mentor Jabotinsky, who had advocated restraint in the struggle against Britain while she was fighting against Hitler. On 1 February, 1944, with England continuing to enforce its 1939 White Paper restrictions on Jewish immigration into Palestine (which was applied despite the imminent extinction of European Jewry in Nazi concentration camps), the Irgun's new commander was able to finally act on his 1938 call for a war against British rule. Begin issued a public appeal to the Jews of Palestine, urging that they cease honoring the truce that had placed them fighting alongside English soldiers in the war against the Nazis:

> Four years have passed since the war began, and all the hopes that beat in your hearts then have evaporated without a trace. We have not been ac-

corded international status, no Jewish Army has been set up, the gates of the country have not been opened. The British regime has sealed its shameful betrayal of the Jewish people and there is no moral basis whatsoever for its presence in Eretz Israel [the Land of Israel].

We shall fearlessly draw conclusions. There is no longer any armistice between the Jewish people and the British Administration in Eretz Israel which hands our brothers over to Hitler. Our people is at war with this regime—war to the end . . .

We shall fight, every Jew in the Homeland will fight. The God of Israel, the Lord of Hosts, will aid us. There will be no retreat. Freedom—or death.[8]

A year later, when it became evident that England would indeed continue to uphold its White Paper restrictions on Jewish immigration into Palestine, keeping thousands of Holocaust survivors stranded in refugee camps, David Ben-Gurion invited Begin to join forces with his Haganah in a unified front against the British. On 31 October, 1945, the united T'nuat Hameri Haivri (Hebrew Resistance Movement) launched a coordinated attack against British targets: three British police vessels were sunk in Haifa and Jaffa by the Haganah's elite strike force, the Palmach; railway installations were blown up by Haganah soldiers; commandos from the extremist Lohamei Herut Israel faction attempted to sabotage storage tanks at the oil refinery in Haifa (LEHI had been formed in 1940 by several hundred Irgun commandos who rejected the four thousand-member group's earlier participation in the wartime truce with Great Britain); and Begin's Irgun troops destroyed a locomotive at the Lydda Railway Station.[9]

On 29 June 1946, the British authorities in Palestine retaliated against the Ben-Gurion–Begin forces and launched "Operation Agatha." They raided Zionist offices and twenty-five Jewish settlements throughout the country, placing hundreds of Jews in barbed-wire detention centers, sending planes and setting up roadblocks to impose a curfew on Jewish neighborhoods. Remembered as "Black Saturday" by the Palestinian Jewish community, the British operation led to the arrests of 2,718 Jews.[10]

It was in response to Black Saturday that Begin's Irgun carried out the infamous attack at the King David Hotel on 22 July, 1946. Six years earlier, the British army had taken over the hotel's fourth floor as headquarters for its operations in Palestine. The following year, they moved into a portion of the third floor and set up a communications center in the basement and bottom two floors of the garden annex. "The King David was the British Mandate's equivalent of the American Pentagon and Congress," wrote historian Thurston Clarke. "To penetrate and destroy it would be an act of guerrilla warfare unequalled in history. No partisan band in the Second

World War had succeeded in destroying German headquarters in any occupied European country."[11]

At first, Ben-Gurion's Haganah approved the strike against the King David Hotel (Clarke says the militia leaders actually requested it). Later, the Haganah high command reportedly canceled the operation, though Begin subsequently denied that they had rescinded the order. The Irgun went ahead with "Operation *Molonchick* [small hotel]", planting 350 kilograms of TNT in the hotel basement under the empty Régence restaurant. An Irgun warning to evacuate the premises went unheeded: the blast left ninety-one people dead and forty-six others wounded. The victims included twenty-eight Englishmen, forty-one Arabs, two Armenians, one Russian, one Greek, one Egyptian, and seventeen Jews. Most were civilian workers: typists, clerks, messengers, hotel employees.[12]

Begin was denounced as a terrorist. The Irgun/Haganah alliance came to an abrupt end, with Ben-Gurion ordering a cessation of anti-British violence. Begin defied the ban: in March 1947, the Irgun launched a frontal assault against a Jerusalem officers' club, hurling satchel bombs into the building under cover of machine-gun fire, killing seventeen British soldiers and three civilian telephone operators; in July 1947, two British soldiers were hanged by the Irgun's chief of operations, Amihai Paglin, in reprisal for the hanging of three Irgun commandos by the British authorities; in that same summer two Irgun commandos were dispatched to London to assassinate the former British commander in Palestine, General Evelyn Barker, but Scotland Yard detectives ordered them to leave the country before the plan could be carried out (one of the members of the hit team was Chaim Weizmann's nephew, Ezer, who later became Begin's minister of defense, referred to as "my friend Ezer" by Sadat after the ex-Irgun fighter managed to establish a warm relationship with the Arab president during the Israeli-Egyptian peace negotiations).[13]

The King David hotel bombing, the hanging of British soldiers, the massacre at Deir Yasseen, the opposition to the 1947 U.N. partition plan, the steadfast loyalty to Jabotinsky's militant legacy, the rejection of the Israeli Labor Party's willingness to accept a territorial compromise in the West Bank lands of Judea and Samaria in exchange for peace with the Arabs—these events over the past forty years gave both Arabs and Jews reason to believe that Menachem Begin represented Israel's hardest line, the exponent of "gun Zionism," the term coined by a former Irgun member turned dissident Israeli peace activist, Uri Avnery.

An Arab analyst at *Al Ahram's* Center for Political Strategic Studies in Cairo, Abd el Moniem Said, once noted that even strong Zionists like Moshe Dayan had proclaimed that the Arab-Israeli problem is a question of two equal rights to the land, which was why, in Dayan's view, force would ultimately have to decide the issue. But Begin denied that the Palestinians had a historical right to the land that had been divinely delivered to the Jews centuries ago. Therefore, Said contended, in Begin's view and among those sharing his brand of Zionism, the Palestinians were not even relevant to a just solution to the Arab-Israeli conflict.[14]

For anti-Zionist Arab observers like Said, even the hawkish General Dayan—who had once said he preferred Israel's continued occupation of the Sinai's Sharm el-Sheikh without peace to a peace without Sharm el-Sheikh—appeared in a positive light when compared with the former Irgun commander, Menachem Begin.[15]

Ben-Gurion himself had reportedly referred to Begin's mentor as "Vladimir Hitler" and warned that if Begin were to ever take charge of Israel his rule would make its name "an abomination throughout the civilized world." Golda Meir labeled Begin a "rabble-rousing crypto-fascist," while other Jews denounced him as a murderer, a fanatic, and a devout militarist."[16] Indeed, Begin unabashedly wrote of his commitment to armed struggle: "When Descartes said: 'I think, therefore I am', he uttered a very profound thought. But there are times in the history of peoples when thought alone does not prove their existence. A people may 'think' and yet its sons, with their thoughts and in spite of them, may be turned into a herd of slaves—or into soap. There are times when everything in you cries out: your very self-respect as a human being lies in your resistance to evil.

"We fight, therefore we are."[17]

It is no wonder that the Mossad men who delivered the report of Waddieh Haddad's plot against Sadat were startled to discover that, after decades of relative powerlessness in the no man's land of Israel's political establishment, this Biblically driven advocate of "gun Zionism" was calling for direct contact with the leader of the Arab world's largest state in order to prevent his assassination by Muammar Qadaffi's PLO hit squad. It appeared to some observers that Begin was determined to signal that he, too, was willing to seek an accommodation with his Moslem neighbors, hoping to use his newfound power to exchange his militant role for that of peacemaker.

12

Second Thoughts

THE Israeli leadership was not unanimous in its support for Menachem Begin's decision to turn over the Mossad file to the Egyptians. In the spring of 1977, Israel was still technically in a state of war with Egypt, it had no obligation to save the life of its president. Why intervene in what was essentially an inter-Arab struggle? If the Arabs wanted to assassinate each other's leaders, why not let them? Wouldn't it only weaken their ability to mount another combined assault against Israel?

On the other hand, the possibility that Qaddafi might emerge the victor in a power struggle with Sadat worried Israeli analysts. "The sound rule is that every nation should have a religion. The contrary to that is the abnormal," the Libyan strongman had written. "There is no other solution but to be in harmony with the natural rule that each nation has one religion."[1] Israel is a Jewish nation with Christian and Moslem minorities. Few Israelis believed that Qaddafi's brand of Islamic fundamentalism would tolerate the continuation of their pluralistic state ruled by a Jewish majority. Such an "abnormality" might require a solution based on the "natural rule" that each nation embody a single religion: the Jewish State of Israel would have to be replaced by the Islamic Republic of Palestine. Jews and Christians in the new Moslem state would either become followers of Islam voluntarily (perhaps through the kind of proselytizing Qaddafi planned to employ in the south of France), or suffer the oppression reserved for "unbelievers." (Christian churches in Libya were closed down in 1971, some converted to cafes; the Cathedral of the Sacred Heart in Tripoli became the Gamal Abdel Mosque in 1979.[2])

There was no doubt that the triumph of Qaddafi's ideology in the region would not bode well for Israel (or, for that matter, for Palestinian Christians like PFLP leaders George Habash and Waddieh Haddad, who struck a perhaps temporary alliance with Islamic Arab nationalists like Qaddafi in order to do battle with the Jews). Though a Qaddafi-led Libyan hegemony in the area would be a disaster, some Israelis also reasoned that to assist Sadat at Qaddafi's expense might provoke an-all-too devastating Egyptian blow against Libya that could neutralize what had for some become a welcomed source of Arab disunity. There were those who saw the value in Qaddafi's continued rule. One Israeli ex-military intelligence chief explained: "in the long run, of course we have to take Qaddafi seriously. He is a man with a single purpose: the destruction of Israel. In the long run, he has the money, the arms, and the means to cause us all serious harm . . .

"In the medium and short runs, it's a different story. You might even say that for Israel, Qaddafi can be a kind of asset. Who else, in all his frantic attempts to unite the Arabs, is keeping them divided to the extent Qaddafi is? He is a strategic threat, but perhaps a tactical asset; an agent of division in the Arab World."[3]

That the destruction of Israel was Qaddafi's single purpose may be overstating the case: the Libyan strongman had taken Gamal Nasser's pan-Arabism as his central goal and aspired to lead a united Arab world ruled according to his own revolutionary model, as outlined in his three-volume *Green Book*; this is why many of his resources were marshaled in the attempt to subvert rival "anti-progressive" Arab regimes in Chad, the Sudan, and Egypt. But there was no doubt that the destruction of Israel was an inherent element in Qaddafi's drive for revolutionary change in the Middle East, and his dogged, almost obsessive pursuit of that aim at times did appear to transcend his larger dream of uniting the Arab world. Almost more than any other criteria, devotion to the extinction of the Jewish state often became a benchmark for Qaddafi's measure of his fellow Arab leaders: Christian Marxists like Habash and Haddad were preferable to anti-communist Moslems like King Hussein and President Sadat because their anti-Zionist credentials proved more unassailable (and their ability to challenge Qaddafi's aspiration for the pan-Arab throne less threatening).

Yet despite Qaddafi's unwavering hatred of Israel, most analysts agreed with the former Israeli military chief that, barring some unforeseen catastrophe like the successful development of a Libyan atomic bomb, Qaddafi's regime did not pose much of an immediate threat to Israel's survival. Instead, some observers, like Hamdi Fuad, the Washington-based columnist for Cairo's *Al Ahram*, have insisted that from the beginning, Begin's real strategy had been to try to isolate Egypt from the Arab world. Sending the report about Qaddafi was just one more opportunity for the prime minister to accomplish his aim. According to Fuad, the Israeli leader was fond of telling Sadat that there was no such thing as an eastern front, only a western front. The danger to Egypt had traditionally been viewed as emanating from the east, from Israel, said Fuad, but Begin began emphasizing the Libyan threat in order to convince Sadat that the geopolitical map had changed, making an alliance with Israel a necessity (the long-simmering dispute between Qaddafi and Sadat made it likely that the Egyptian president did not need much convincing of the dangers from his western neighbor). The United States was a party to the plan, Fuad claimed; American leaders continually referred to Libya as an outlaw nation and issued repeated denunciations of Qaddafi as the world's foremost terrorist, branding him a dangerous fanatic bent on fomenting revolution in neighboring countries. But the Libyans are like younger brothers to the Egyptians, Fuad said; therefore the Israeli-U.S. strategy could never prompt a real shift by Egypt away from Libya toward a permanent alliance with the Jewish State.[4]

Fuad asserted that the Israeli strategy toward Cairo persisted even after the two countries reached agreement on the 1979 peace treaty. Begin's continued push for Jewish settlement in the Israeli-occupied West Bank, his destruction of the Iraqi nuclear reactor at Osirak in 1981, the 1982 invasion of Lebanon—each action, Fuad has claimed, was calculated to force Egypt into honoring its peace commitment in the face of Israeli agression toward its Arab brothers. A pariah among Moslem states, its military and financial ties with the Arab world broken, Egypt, so Begin reckoned, would have no choice but to turn to Israel and its American patrons for defense assistance and economic support. (Sadat's break with the Soviets back in 1972 had already signaled his own desire to throw in with the Americans sans the Israeli-orchestrated pressure alleged by Fuad.) Fuad may be guilty of offering a solipsistic analysis of Israeli policies in the Middle East, ignoring Begin's historical dedication to the establishment of a Jewish presence on the West Bank, his fears of a virulently anti-Israeli Iraq armed with nuclear weapons, and his assessment of the direct threat posed by a Soviet-backed Syrian and PLO-dominated Lebanon on Israel's northern border. Yet, as the comments of the Israeli ex-military intelligence chief demonstrate, the Egyptian journalist was not alone in thinking that Muammar Qaddafi, already a source of inter-Arab rivalry, could be put to further use as a tool for Arab dissension, and that at least "in the short run" this could serve Jerusalem's interests.

The cabinet meeting called by Begin to discuss whether the Mossad report on the Libyan plot against Sadat should be turned over to Egypt as he had suggested led to a stormy debate focusing on Qaddafi's role in the region. It also highlighted the greater dangers that Israel faced from the existing regime in Cairo. Sadat commanded the most powerful Arab army in the world, and he had proved to be no friend to Israel. His surprise attack on 6 October, 1973, nearly forced Israel into suffering its first defeat in its thirty-five-year-old history. Some were quick to point out that such a debacle would also have been Israel's last defeat, for Sadat's army would have expelled or imprisoned the vanquished Jewish leadership, installing an Arab regime in its stead. "It is relevant to recall that Anwar Sadat was perhaps the most vehement of the Arab leaders in pronouncements on Israel," Shmuel Katz later wrote, "and at the same time the most competent in conducting war on her."[5] Katz, a former Irgun member, eventually resigned as Begin's foreign press secretary over his opposition to the prime minister's decision to grant Arab autonomy in the West Bank and return the Sinai to Egypt in exchange for a peace agreement with Sadat.

Despite the praise of Katz and others for Sadat's military competence, most historians agree that the surprise attack in 1973 was never intended to achieve—and had no possibility of bringing—an Arab victory over Israel. Sadat's real purpose, they argue, was twofold: to restore Arab confidence after their devastating defeat in 1967, and to shift the region's balance of power, the successful demonstration of combined Arab strength bringing the kind of pressure that might prompt Israel's leaders into granting concessions during post-war negotiations.

Sadat's acumen as a military strategist, however, had nevertheless painfully impressed itself on the Israelis. The Yom Kippur War had inflicted the highest casualties ever on the Jewish state: 2,297 killed, 6,067 wounded.[6] In his review of the 1973 attack, Israeli President Chaim Herzog wrote: "The massive Egyptian crossing of the Suez Canal, including the transfer of five divisions simultaneously in the course of 24 hours while engaged in battle with a surprised enemy, must be considered a major military achievement. In general, both the planning and execution of the Egyptian Army, above all the technical and organizational ability which enabled them in the course of a night to throw across the Canal ten bridges over which they transferred tanks and vehicles, and a further ten bridges for infantry, all point to a very successful organizational military operation."[7]

In the spring of 1977, on the eve of Sadat's dramatic November visit to Jerusalem, there were many members of Begin's government who looked warily upon the Egyptian leader's intentions toward Israel, either concerned about his ability to wage future wars against the Jewish state or alarmed by the political concessions he demanded, which called for Israel's total withdrawal from all of the territories occupied in 1967. Since coming to power in 1970 after Nasser's death, Sadat had indeed sent mixed signals. Ten days after the Yom Kippur attack, Sadat gave a speech to the People's Assembly in Cairo, declaring that he was willing to attend a United Nations peace conference in order to resolve the conflict with Israel. Nevertheless, he did not fail to air his all too familiar assessment of the Jewish state: "By its racist claims and its reasoning of expansion through brute force, Zionism is nothing but a feeble replica of Fascism and Nazism which is contemptible rather than frightening and calls for disdain more than for hatred."[8]

As a political leader, Sadat's ability to secretly plan a coordinated strike with Syria's rulers demonstrated his facility for marshaling a significant measure of the Arab world's resources, later put to use during the OPEC oil embargo against Western nations supporting Israel. His success in outwitting the much renowned Israeli intelligence apparatus proved equally daunting:

> The first outstanding Arab military success—and indeed the most important—was the strategic and tactical surprise they achieved. While this success was aided to no small degree by mistakes made by Israeli Intellence and the political and military leadership in Israel, the bulk of the credit must go to the sophisticated deception plan mounted by the Egyptians and the Syrians. They succeeded in convincing the Israeli Command that the intensive military activity in Egypt to the west of the Canal during the summer and autumn of 1973 was nothing more than a series of training operations and manoeuvres. This deception must be marked out as one of the outstanding plans of deception mounted in the course of military history.[9]

Sadat's talent for deception—which he had tapped during the days when he fought against British rule in Egypt by working as a spy for the Nazis during World War II—would later prompt right-wing Israelis like Shmuel Katz to charge that the real purpose of the Egyptian president's 1977 diplomatic offensive was to lull Israel into a false state of complacency, undermining its security through Egypt's reacquisition of the Sinai and creating an atmosphere in which the Jews would willingly decrease their taxing defenses in their desperate embrace of the promise of peace, only to be faced with another onslaught of Arab aggression that would result in the "extinction of the Zionist dream."[10] Left-wing Israelis like Golda Meir also felt compelled to respond skeptically to Sadat's peaceful overtures, the former prime minister remarking that history would judge whether the Egyptian leader deserved the Nobel Peace Prize or the Oscar for his journey to Jerusalem. Prior to the visit, Chief of Staff Mordechai Gur put his forces in the Sinai on alert in case Cairo's talk of diplomacy turned out to be a propaganda blitz aimed at encouraging a temporary relaxation of Israeli preparedness, during which time Egypt would launch another bold strike across its borders.[11] Israeli troops were also deployed at the airport in case the Sadat visit was merely a ruse whereby Egyptian commandos could burst from the presidential plane and slaughter the Israeli leaders awaiting Sadat's arrival. The lessons of Yom Kippur were not easily forgotten: Sadat had succeeded in orchestrating a devastating deception in 1973; the Israelis did not want to see him repeat one four years later.

There had also been the experience with President de Gaulle, when Jerusalem repeatedly intervened in OAS plots against the president's life, allowing the Mossad to use its resources to foil assassination schemes on several occasions. Israel had turned its back on the French rightist officers opposed to de Gaulle despite their longstanding solidarity with the Jewish state, only to be abandoned by the French president when he found himself no longer encumbered by the war in Algeria and free to pursue a reconciliation with oil-rich Arab states (in 1967, de Gaulle cut off military arms shipments to Israel). But prior to the falling out with Paris, during the years when Israeli decisionmakers were choosing de Gaulle over the OAS, the French president, at least, was demonstrating his support for Israel in both word and deed, providing the Jewish state with military, economic, and diplomatic backing. Anwar Sadat had no such history.

A cursory glance back at the Sadat rhetoric only seemed to bolster the thesis that Sadat's deception did not end with the Yom Kippur War:

> The Zionist conquest to which we are being subjected will not be terminated by the return of the occupied territories. This is a new Crusaders' war which will persist during our generation and through the coming one.
>
> The liberation of the territories [lost in June 1967] is what we have chosen for this stage. Revolutionary Arab thought must define the stages of a consistent and diligent policy out of the necessity that all the various strategies used in the confrontation with the enemy should flow out of one grand strategy.
>
> The effort of our generation is to return to the 1967 borders. Afterward the next generation will carry the responsibility.[12]

With Israel's return to the 1967 borders, the only responsibility left to the next generation of Arabs would be the liquidation of Jewish control within the 1948 armistice lines—in effect, the end of Israel as a nation. For Sadat, the establishment of a true moral order in the Middle East demanded an ongoing struggle against the Zionist state: "We may say that our war [against Israel] is a continuation of humanity's war against Fascism and Nazism."[13]

Along with the dire predictions regarding the political fate of Zionism in the Middle East and the denunciations of the Zionist ideal came Sadat's views on the social status of the Jewish people:

They talk today about direct negotiations. They [the Jews] were the neighbors of Mohammad in Medina. They were his neighbors and he negotiated with them, but they eventually proved to be a mean, traitorous and treacherous people when they allied themselves with his enemies to strike at him in Medina from within. [The Jews had refused to renounce their Judaism and embrace Mohammad's new religion.] The most splendid thing our Prophet Mohammad did was that he evicted them from the entire Arabian Peninsula. This is what our Prophet did. We shall never negotiate with them directly. We know our history and we know their history with our Prophet. They are a mean, treacherous people. They are a conspiratorial people who have been raised to be treacherous. I declare here, on this anniversary [of Mohammad's birth], that their dreams which they talk about today and the elation from the conceit of victory which they now talk about and which they thought they had achieved in 1967, I tell them: We shall not give up one inch of our territory and we shall not negotiate with Israel under any circumstances; we shall not bargain over any right of the Palestinian people.

This year, I promise you, we shall celebrate on the next anniversary, God willing, and in this place with God's help, not only the liberation of our land but also the defeat and vanquishment of the Israeli conceit and arrogance so that they may once again return to the condition as decreed in our Holy Book: "Abasement and submissiveness have been pitched upon them."

We shall not renounce this. The matter is no longer one of liberating our territory alone, but it is a matter which is linked to our honour, dignity and the message in which we believe. We shall turn them back to what they were.[14]

Could such vituperative language be dismissed, as one Middle East analyst has suggested, as mere reflexive declarations peddled as pablum to Arab masses by practically every Arab leader? It is true that many Arab diplomats and intellectuals have become prisoners of Arab contemporary politics, which demands unfaltering opposition to Zionism in all its forms as a measure of national pride, independence, and integrity, much the way twentieth century American patriotism has become synonymous with a fundamental opposition to communism. Indeed, some Arab officials feel compelled to denounce in public what they dare to utter in private: compromise and co-existence with the State of Israel is the only solution to the Arab-Israeli conflict. Yet the violence and despair that have marred Arab-Jewish relations over the decades have convinced many that the true sentiments of the Arab world are voiced when Arab leaders speak plainly in Arabic to fellow Arabs, not when Arab diplomats whisper cryptic messages of peace in French and English into the ears of Western journalists and government officials.

As much as anyone, Prime Minister Begin harbored deep suspicions about his Middle Eastern neighbors, always insisting that Israel rely on Jewish might to preserve its existence, not on behind-the-scenes assurances by Arab leaders and bold promises by American diplomats. Yet the Mossad report on Qaddafi's murder scheme was an opportunity for him to demonstrate that the new leadership in Israel was capable of striking a deal with the Arabs. If the Sinai disengagement agreements forged by Henry Kissinger in 1974-75 following the Yom Kippur War had indeed provided the impetus for a peace process between Egypt and Israel, then Begin would not be the one to block its progress. Despite the assessments of Qaddafi's value as a force for Arab division and the misgivings about Sadat's role as a future negotiating partner, Begin's cabinet ruled in favor of the decision to warn the Egyptians about the plot against their president.

13

Sadat's Initiative

AN Israeli intelligence file concerning a threat against an Arab regime was ordinarily turned over to the CIA, who then passed it along to the appropriate government as a U.S. document. The lack of any permanent direct channel between Jerusalem and the Arab states often meant that intermediaries would have to be used if Israeli information was to quickly get into the right hands. There was also the question of credibility: if it were deemed to be in Israel's interest to ensure that the Saudi Arabian monarchy be protected from an impending coup attempt by a Soviet-supported Arab colonel, then it could be vital that the rulers in Riyadh respond swiftly to a given Israeli intelligence report detailing rebel plans. Coming from the Mossad, the Saudi sheikhs might very well hesitate, preferring to launch a thorough investigation of their own before acting on a report by agents of the "Zionist entity" which in their judgement could easily be a false alarm designed to sow dissension within the kingdom. By the time the independent Saudi investigation got underway, it could be too late. But the same report coming from the Americans would get priority treatment. There was little doubt that Washington wanted to preserve the rule of the anti-communist Saudi princes and maintain the Arab nation's lucrative ties to U.S. oil companies. There would be no need to second-guess the CIA: the Saudis would round up the conspirators and ask questions later. The same would hold true for the Egyptians. Sadat had expelled the Russians, turned away from Nasser's socialism by instituting the *infitah* "open door" policy (which favored Western-oriented capital investment and a laissez-faire economic environment), and, following the success of Henry Kissinger's shuttle diplomacy, he came to rely on the United States as the key mediator in the Arab-Israeli conflict. Washington clearly had an interest in helping Sadat maintain power in Cairo.

Menachem Begin had sat on the opposition benches for twenty-nine years and was relatively unschooled in the wily ways of international diplomacy. He had not been aware of the CIA role as front-man for Israel, and when he was informed of the fact he refused to go along. Why should the Jews use an American courier to save an Arab president's life? The file on Qaddafi's plot would prove itself to the Egyptians, and when it did their leaders should know who had delivered it to them. Begin wanted the Mossad report turned over directly to Egypt. Now that he was in power, the predecessors who had scorned him as a hardline fanatic and the Arabs who had vilified him as a brutal terrorist would soon learn that he would succeed where others had failed. "I must bring peace to my people," he had confided to his associates upon assuming office.[1] Begin wanted to mark his era with efforts to end a half-century of bloodshed between Arab and Jew.

It was decided that the Mossad's report to the Egyptians would have to take place on neutral ground, with the help of an intermediary who was trusted by both sides. King Hassan II of Morocco, a personal friend of Sadat, had already talked privately with Israel's representatives, indicating his desire to see a peaceful settlement of the Arab-Israeli conflict. Though he had sent a Moroccan brigade to fight alongside his Arab brothers during the Yom Kippur War, Hassan nevertheless ruled over a large Jewish minority of nearly twenty thousand and wanted to help bridge the gap between Israel and its neighbors. The year before, Prime Minister Yitzak Rabin had traveled incognito to Morocco for an unpublicized meeting with the king, and he asked the monarch to help arrange a secret talk with President Sadat. Hassan relayed the message, but Sadat reportedly felt that the Israeli leadership had been so weakened in the aftermath of the Yom Kippur War that the time was not right for negotiations, opting instead for a continuation of American mediation.[2] "I got the impression that he was a do-gooder by nature," Moshe Dayan later wrote after holding his own secret meeting with the king.[3] (In July 1986, Hassan became the second Arab leader after Sadat to hold public talks with Israeli officials, inviting Prime Minister Shimon Peres to his summer palace at Ifrane.)

The Moroccan channel seemed like a solid choice for Begin, and King Hassan agreed to host the unprecedented encounter between Israel's Mossad chief Yitzak Hofi and his Egyptian counterpart Kemal Hasan Ali.

During the secret meeting at Hassan's palace in Rabat, General Hofi handed the Mossad file on the Libyan-PLO operation over to Lieutenant General Ali, head of the Egyptian intelligence network (he went on to serve as prime minister under Sadat's successor, President Mubarak).[4] Other accounts suggest that the exchange was made between Mossad officials and Sadat's close adviser, Egyptian Deputy Premier Hassan Tuhami, who did secretly meet later with Israeli Foreign Minister Moshe Dayan in Morocco for a private talk that acted as a catalyst for Sadat's visit to Jerusalem.[5]

Whether it was Ali or Tuhami who first saw the Mossad file, the presence of an outside party like King Hassan was essential. The Israelis reckoned that given the shifting matrix of Mideast politics, it was conceivable that an Egyptian intelligence official or presidential adviser could be a party to Qaddafi's plot against Sadat. At the very least, he might not wish to see it thwarted, and would therefore refrain from passing along the Mossad report to the Egyptian president. Or the Israeli warning might be hastily dismissed because of the Egyptian representative's fear that his career would be jeopardized if it were known that the Mossad had upstaged him by uncovering a plot against the regime he had pledged to protect. Hence the reason for Hassan: the king had a close relationship with Sadat; he would surely follow-up a report of a plot against his life with a direct telephone call to the Egyptian leader. No doubt the Egyptian representative attending the meeting with the Mossad chief would figure likewise. With the king as a witness, he would have little choice but to deliver the contents of the Israeli file to his president.

The assassination plot against Sadat involved two alternative plans: a sea-launched commando raid on Sadat's resort home at Alexandria and an armed attack during a presidential parade in Cairo, similar to the one that eventually succeeded in taking the Egyptian leader's life four years later. The Mossad report contained details on both plans, plus the names of Haddad's seven-man hit squad and the addresses of the hidden arsenals that had been stockpiled throughout the Egyptian capital.

The murder team's weapons had been smuggled in through an undisclosed foreign embassy's diplomatic mail service, which is traditionally immune from search by host governments. This was the same technique used on 17 April, 1984, when a gunman opened fire from the window of the Libyan embassy in London, shooting into a crowd of anti-Qaddafi protesters, wounding eleven demonstrators and killing a twenty-five-year-old British policewoman.

The Libyan diplomats were eventually declared *person non grata* and ordered out of the country, but their luggage was protected from search by British officials. The 1961 Vienna Convention on Diplomatic Relations grants immunity to foreign diplomats and bars the search of embassy pouches. After the Libyans evacuated the London building, Scotland Yard investigators entered the premises and discovered three .38-caliber Colt revolvers, a .32-caliber Smith and Wesson handgun, a Barreta pistol, a Browning pistol, two pistol grips, forty-nine rounds of ammunition, eight suits of body armor, a spent cartridge, and two magazines used for machine-guns. Although embassies often maintain their own armed security staff, British policemen were surprised at the unusually large number of weapons, especially since they suspected the Libyans of having packed most of their arsenal into diplomatic bags for removal during their evacuation from London.

The Reagan administration, possibly as a result of shared intelligence among the Israelis and Egyptians, had already been on the alert against Qaddafi's use of Libyan embassies for terrorist purposes. Three years before the London shooting, in May 1981, the Reagan administration closed the Libyan embassy in Washington and expelled all Libyan diplomats from the country, charging that the embassy was being used as a base for terrorist attacks against anti-Qaddafi dissidents.[6] Unlike other clandestine groups, Libya's guerrilla squads were able to exploit the privileges afforded to sovereign governments under international law, using its embassies and diplomats to transfer weapons and supply hit teams, as it did in 1977 when dispatching Haddad's men to Cairo.

Hofi's Mossad file also revealed that Soviet KGB trainers had been present at Haddad's base in the Libyan desert, and there was evidence that Moscow was actively supporting the mission to kill Sadat.[7] Two years earlier, Libya had signed an agreement with the Soviet Union, contracting for $2 billion worth of arms that included twenty-four MIG aircraft, eleven hundred tanks, and fifty batteries of anti-aircraft missiles. According to a *Washington Star* report, "while the Soviet Union officially opposed terrorism, much of the terrorists' weaponry passed from Russia through Arab countries, particularly Libya and Syria." By June 1977, the West German newspaper *Die Welt* was reporting that Qaddafi was spending an average of $75 million on terrorist operations.[8] Libya's oil wealth, Russian weaponry, PLO personnel, and KGB expertise had enabled Qaddafi to plant an assassination squad in Cairo. Yet Egyptian intelligence remained skeptical about the Mossad report.

Indeed, the Israelis could have been just using Qaddafi to drive a wedge between Egypt and Libya. Sadat's people were certainly familiar with the views of men like the Israeli ex-military intelligence chief who recognized Qaddafi's ability to breed discord in the Arab ranks. Perhaps the entire file was a hoax, the devious Mossad strategists hoping to provoke an even wider breech between Qaddafi and Sadat that would further dampen the prospects of a united Arab front against Israel. In his 1983 account of the plot that succeeded in killing the Egyptian president, the Arab world's leading journalist, Mohamed Heikal, still clung to the position of the skeptics, writing that in 1977, the Mossad "produced an implausible story about a conspiracy to assassinate Sadat being hatched by Qaddafi."[9]

A further cause for Cairo's coolness toward General Hofi's report stemmed from a nagging question: Was it likely that Egypt's own intelligence network would fail to detect a plot in their own country against their own president, and that the Israelis would be the ones to discover it? Both Sadat and his predecessor Nasser had ruled with a firm hand, building up a powerful secret police to monitor any hints of domestic unrest. The Moukhabarat el-Amma (the general intelligence agency, GSI) and the Moukhabarat el-Kharbeya (the military intelligence division) had agents dispatched throughout Egypt and the Middle East, bolstered by sophisticated electronic surveillance and an array of paid informants. Wolfgang Lotz, the agent who spent four years in Egypt spying for the Israelis, had earlier detailed the scope of Cairo's intelligence operation:

> Practically every servant, doorman, taxi-driver, shopkeeper, hotel employee, waiter, vendor, and beggar was a potential or actual police informer who would report to anyone he came into contact with. To refuse to do so would have resulted in the cancellation of one's business permit or worse. In this way the GIA and Secret Police found it easy to keep track of almost everyone's activities at almost all times. Naturally the information obtained in this way was not always reliable. In many cases informers who had nothing of importance to report simply fabricated items of information to gain favour with the police. In other instances, people were denounced for reasons of personal revenge. In cases of denunciation the procedure was to arrest and torture first and to check facts afterwards, if at all.
>
> Hidden microphones and phone tapping devices were a matter of routine installation in most of the Europeans' houses and apartments. I vividly recall how, when I rented my first flat in Rue Ismail Mohammad, in the Zamalek quarter, an American who turned out to be the vice-consul of the US Consulate in Cairo called on me. He explained that he had been the previous tenant, and then proceeded to show me a microphone concealed in the mouthpiece of my telephone. I disconnected it and the following day a telephone engineer appeared to check on the connection and put things right again.[10]

Some observers have claimed that Sadat deliberately kept hundreds of low-level informers on the dole as a means of fostering the population's dependency on the regime. To proud professionals like Kemal Ali, the notion that Israel succeeded where Egypt's own vast intelligence apparatus had failed simply did not ring true. Furthermore, assuming the Mossad report was accurate, here was Israel brazenly acknowledging that it had established an effective clandestine network in Cairo. Ali was obliged to tell Hofi that Israeli covert activities in his country should cease. Hofi assured him that the information had not been gathered in Egypt. He also expressed the notion that perhaps some of his country's interests coincided with those of Egypt, and that the two nations might work together to avoid situations undesirable to both.

After the Rabat meeting between Hofi and Ali, a week went by with no word from the Egyptians. The Mossad report had indicated that the assassination plot was in its final stages; Sadat's delay could be fatal. Bujold, the French mercenary who had traveled to Cairo to oversee the attack, suddenly dropped out of sight. Telling his comrades that he had to return to Tripoli for consultations, he left for Paris and went underground.

Israeli intelligence soon learned that the Egyptian secret police had in fact acted on its warning. Sadat's security forces rounded up the conspirators in the hideouts that had been pinpointed in the Mossad report. Word of their impending arrest may have been what prompted Bujold to go underground. After ten days of interrogation, which corroborated the Israeli claim of Libyan-Soviet involvement in the PLO plan, a secret military trial was held. Not a word of the plot was mentioned in the Egyptian press. Then a tiny item finally appeared in a Cairo newspaper: several men had been executed for conspiring against the state. The names were given, nothing more. Five days later, Sadat launched an attack against Libya.

The official Egyptian military communiqué stated that the 21 July, 1977, raid across Libya's border was "in retaliation for Libyan aggression," and it accused Qaddafi of trying to overthrow Sadat by engaging in a "large-scale terrorist plot" with members of an Egyptian Moslem extremist group, dubbed by Sadat's security forces as *takfirv wa hijra*, the Society for Repentance and Holy Flight. Earlier in July, *takfir wa hijra* had kidnapped Sheikh Mohamed al-Dhahabi, a former minister of Waqf (religious endowments), demanding that the Sadat regime admit over state radio that it had not governed according to Islamic principles and that it pledged to do so in the future. When the request was turned down, *takfir wa hijra* militants murdered Sheikh al-Dhahabi. Sadat blamed Qaddafi for the crime.

The day after Egyptian forces invaded Libya, Sadat again denounced the Libyan leader, charging him with hatching a series of plots against Egypt. In his 22 July speech at Cairo University, commemorating the twenty-fifth anniversary of the coup led by Gamal Nasser, Sadat announced that Libyan saboteurs arrested in Egypt for placing a bomb in a government building had been hanged, and that Egyptian troops operating in Libya had taught Qaddafi a lesson. "We are ready to repeat this lesson unless this maniac stops playing with fire," Sadat vowed.[11]

Meanwhile, prior to the Egyptian invasion of Libya, the Israelis received word from King Hassan that Sadat would like them to avoid instigating any aggressive moves along the Suez Canal. The king stated the request delicately, implying that it came from Cairo but that it would also be in Morocco's interest if things were quiet along the Israeli-Egyptian frontier. The king had his own feud with Qaddafi, he reminded the Israelis. The Libyan leader was providing support to rebels in the former Spanish Sahara, the region annexed by Morocco where Polisario Front fighters hoped to set up their own independent state. Now that Egypt was about to launch an operation against Qaddafi, it was important for both Hassan and Sadat that the Israelis refrain from exploiting the situation. Indeed, after two days of fighting, Egypt was forced to transfer reinforcements from the Sinai front with Israel to the border region with Libya. In the Knesset, Begin took the podium and declared that Israel would do nothing to disturb the Egyptians in the Sinai while they were engaged in battle against the Libyans. Many Israelis wondered why their hawkish prime minister would provide Cairo with such reassurance.[12]

With Egyptian troops pressing their attack into the Libyan desert, Sadat denounced Qaddafi as an "agent of a foreign power," an obvious reference to his ties with the Soviet Union. He had long been concerned that the Russians were attempting to encircle Egypt with a string of radical states, using Qaddafi to destabilize the regimes in Zaire, Sudan, and Chad. With Marxist Ethiopia already well within the Soviet orbit, the Red Sea would no longer be the "lake of peace" linking Egypt with the rest of Africa, but rather a "revolutionary sea" threatening the independence of the pro-Western government in Cairo. "If your aim is to say that you are stronger than Egypt we will strike you," Sadat warned during his speech at Cairo University, publicly addressing Qaddafi and including a reference to the Soviets: "If someone else has pushed you to act against us we will strike you again."[13] It was ironic that Qaddafi—the man who once despaired over not being able to drive overland from Libya to Cairo because it would warrant his passing Soviet bases en route, the fervent anti-communist who delighted in Sadat's expulsion of Soviet military advisers—was now being denounced by an Egyptian president for taking arms from Moscow and sowing revolution in collusion with the Russians and their Marxist allies.

Though many observers, including pro-Israeli writers like Jacques Derogy and Hesi Carmel and Arab critics of Israel like Mohamed Heikal, were to claim that Sadat's border strike against Libya in the summer of 1977 was a direct response to the Mossad report on Qaddafi's hit team, other analysts saw things differently. Hermann Eilts, who was serving as U.S. ambassador to Egypt during the fighting, said that Sadat had been itching for an excuse to launch a military operation against Qaddafi, and the Israeli report was just one more element pushing him to act, certainly not the deciding factor.[14] The Libyan ruler's opposition to Egypt's signing of the Sinai disengagement agreements with Israel, his use of Soviet equipment and advisers to support a massive military buildup, his attempts to bring radicals to power through covert operations like the 1976 coup attempt against President Numeiry of Sudan, which the Egyptian president believed had been instigated by Qaddafi, all contributed to Sadat's growing conviction that Qaddafi had to be eliminated.

According to Eilts, in late summer 1976, Sadat decided to take action against Qaddafi. He had been receiving reports from disaffected members of Qaddafi's ruling Revolution Command Council (RCC) requesting that Egypt assist them in ousting the Libyan strongman. Cairo had already offered asylum to Omar al-Meheishi, one of the original RCC members who took power following the coup against King Idris and an associate of Qaddafi's since their school days in Misurata. In May 1975, Meheishi broke with Qaddafi over a dispute involving the enactment of economic austerity measures. He criticized the country's costly expenditures on arms and its financing of international terrorist operations, which he said amounted to "the dissipation of public funds in order to foment unrest" in neighboring Arab countries. In the summer of 1975, Meheisha, along with fellow RCC members Basshir Hawadi, Awad Hamza, and about twenty other Libyan officers, attempted to overthrow Qaddafi in a military coup, but the plot was discovered and Hawadi and Hamza were arrested. Meheisha fled to Tunisia and then sought refuge in Cairo, where he continued to offer a steady stream of anti-Qaddafi pronouncements. Though he denied orchestrating the coup attempt, Meheisha described Qaddafi as a "dangerous psychopath" and urged that he be removed from power.[15]

Although Sadat was bent on toppling Qaddafi, Eilts said that he needed a "political hook" on which he could hang his justification for launching an attack against his Libyan brothers. Sadat's military advisers were concerned that young Egyptian soldiers might resent having to fight their fellow Arabs instead of the Israelis. They also doubted that their army had the capability to engage in a full-scale ground assault across the Libyan desert. Meheisha's rebellious RCC members seemed to offer Sadat the hook he needed: they would rise against Qaddafi and Egypt would merely come to their aid, assisting the Libyan people in their struggle to topple an unbalanced dictator. Sadat would not be condemned as the aggressor, but rather hailed as the patron of Libyan democracy. Sadat contacted Washington to enlist its support for his planned intervention. The Libyans, he explained, had installed Soviet-supplied missiles with a range of 200-250 miles, capable of threatening Alexandria, and he wanted U.S. backing for his move against Qaddafi.

Egypt's military leaders were still reluctant to wage war with Libya, and they kept stalling Sadat when pressed for a decision to act. The Americans gave Sadat the-go ahead, then withdrew it when President Carter came into office. Sadat was not deterred, but when Meheisha's planned RCC uprising failed to materialize, he was again left searching for a political hook.

On 16 July, 1977, Qaddafi apparently handed Sadat the hook he needed: a Libyan patrol attacked an Egyptian border post sixty miles south of Salum, located inside a disputed border strip that includes the Bardia port and the oases of Jarabub, Arkinu, Uwaynut, Sara. The Egyptian government claimed that while under British rule in 1925, part of the area had been illegally ceded to Italy in order to help it solidify control of Libya, and the territory actually belonged to Egypt. Libya rejected the charge.[16] According to Michael Austrian, head of the U.S. State Department desk on Near East and South Asian affairs, the series of events that sparked the 1977 Libyan-Egyptian border war was that a fence had been erected by Egyptian bedouins that cut into Libyan territory, while Libya maintained control over the remaining lands claimed by Egypt. This left a high potential for a Libyan-Egyptian clash along the border. According to Austrian, Qaddafi decided to unilaterally move his forces into the disputed area where the Egyptian bedouins had erected their fence, openly challenging Cairo's sovereignty.[17] Libya asserted that it was the Egyptians who had initiated hostilities, bombing civilian installations in Musaid and then seizing the Libyan city.

On 20 July, 1977, a four-hour battle took place between defending Egyptian troops and Libyan forces who attacked several checkpoints inside Egypt's border, supported by tanks and helicopter gunships. Nine Egyptian soldiers were killed in the fighting. On 21 July, a Libyan armored car unit, backed by artillery fire, stormed the Egyptian outpost at Salum and attacked a border police station. "I could not hold back our armed forces any longer," Sadat declared, and he threw mechanized infantry units from two divisions of the First Egyptian Army, along with tanks, a dozen commando and paratroop battalions, and three squadrons of MIG fighter jets into the war against Qaddafi.[18] As Eilts pointed out, however, Sadat refrained from placing his army in direct confrontation with Libyan troops, perhaps bowing to pressures from his military officers to avoid ordering Egyptian soldiers to shed the blood of fellow Arabs. Instead, Sadat called on his air force to carry out the bulk of the fighting.

Sadat sent his planes deep into Libya, flying over villages at rooftop level without bombing or firing on civilians, a tactic reportedly employed in the hope that the air raids would create panic among the population, turn public opinion against the leadership in Tripoli, and provoke a split within the Libyan military that would prompt moderate officers to remove Qaddafi from office. At the time, Egyptian officials disclosed that they were "intent on overthrowing" the Libyan leader.[19]

Sadat's air force struck hard at Libya's military installations, however, sending Sukhoi-20 fighter bombers on a raid against the El Aden air base south of Tobruk, destroying its modern Soviet-built radar station and killing three Soviet military technicians. Airborne commandos attacked another Soviet-built installation in the Jarabub oasis, twenty miles inside the Libyan border and one hundred miles south of the Mediterranean Sea.[20]

The Libyan border clash lasted six days. Egyptian troops overran the desert training base that had been used by Waddieh Haddad's would-be assassins. Sadat denounced Libya's PLO desert compounds as being the "nests of terrorists."[21] Two months later, on 9 September, the Israelis received word from King Hassan that President Sadat was willing to meet secretly with Prime Minister Begin. The Israelis quickly agreed, but Sadat then retreated, calling for a preliminary lower-level meeting between Foreign Minister Moshe Dayan and Deputy Premier Hassan Tuhami. Former Egyptian Foreign Minister Ismail Fahmy said that the initial suggestion for a secret Begin-Sadat meeting was King Hassan's proposal, and had not originated with Cairo. Nevertheless, Dayan and Tuhami met privately in Morocco on 16 September. The following month, on 9 November, Sadat declared his readiness to address the Israeli Knesset. Ten days later, he flew to Jerusalem.[22]

Ambassador Eilts insisted that the Mossad report on the Qaddafi plot did not play a significant role in Anwar Sadat's decision to initiate the peace process with Israel. The Israelis did tell Sadat of the Libyan assassination attempt, Eilts admitted, but Egyptian intelligence officials were doubtful about its validity because the information lacked essential details, such as the names of the conspirators. Moreover, the United States, Eilts said, had also informed the Egyptians of similar attempts by Qaddafi on other occasions, the ambassador having personally passed along such reports to Sadat. According to Eilts, the Egyptian president did not give the Qaddafi plot great weight; he felt no sense of obligation to the Israelis, the murder plan was not a key element in the decision to strike at Libya, the Mossad report was not the catalyst for Sadat's decision to negotiate a peace treaty with Menachem Begin.

Philip Stoddard, a longtime observer of Arab-Israeli affairs and executive director of Washington's pro-Arab Middle East Institute, expressed the widely held view that Sadat's main mission in going to Jerusalem was to remove Israel as an obstacle to United States-Egyptian relations. He wanted his nation to get on the American "gravy train." He had garnered his political victory in the Yom Kippur War, restoring Arab honor, and thus felt able to put the forty-year-old conflict with Israel behind him and grapple instead with the desperate economic conditions facing Egypt.

However, Stoddard said, although it had adopted the "territory for peace" formula following the 1967 Six Day War, the Labor Party of former Prime Minister Yitzak Rabin had still called for a limited Israeli presence in the Sinai, insisting that it provided the strategic depth necessary to enable the tiny Jewish state to absorb a first strike by Egypt, giving it time to call up its reserves without putting its major population centers at risk. Sadat knew, said Stoddard, that Begin held the West Bank and Gaza dear but did not buy the Labor Party line regarding the Sinai, and that he would easily consent to a complete Israeli withdrawal in exchange for a peace agreement with Cairo, hence Sadat's eagerness to respond to Begin's overtures.[23]

The tough bargaining at Camp David over the question of whether Israel would dismantle its fourteen Sinai settlements and three airfields might belie the notion that the return of the peninsula to Egypt was a sure thing under Begin, and that it was such an implicit guarantee that had prompted Sadat into taking advantage of the Labor Party's ouster by offering to cut a deal with the new leaders in Jerusalem. Paradoxically, even if Begin had sent a signal to Sadat that the Sinai could be had, Fahmy insisted that this was the very reason why the Egyptian president should *not* embark on a journey to Jerusalem.

Fahmy recalled that Sadat first raised the subject of a visit to Israel during their October 1977 trip to Romania, when President Ceausescu followed up an earlier talk with Begin by informing the Egyptian leader that the newly-elected Israeli prime minister was serious about concluding a peace treaty with Egypt. Fahmy immediately opposed the idea of a Jerusalem trip, explaining that such a visit would automatically imply recognition of Israel and the end of the state of belligerency, leaving Egypt in the position of having played its two most important cards, without gaining anything substantive in return:

I then argued that if the aim of the trip to Jerusalem was to secure the return of Sinai, it was unnecessary. Sinai was never and would never be a problem. The Israelis knew that there would be no peace in the area if they did not withdraw completely from that region. Three successive American administrations had also been aware of this fact. The proof was that the American draft for a peace treaty between Israel and Egypt stipulated clearly that the Israeli forces would withdraw from the entire peninsula to the international borders which separated Egypt and Palestine under the British mandate.[24]

Sitting in the guest house in Romania, hoping to dash Sadat's burgeoning notion of a bold peace inititiative, Fahmy argued that Egypt's economic needs required more than a ride on the American gravy train: "So, Mr. President, Sinai was not and will never be a problem. Now, if your move to go to Jerusalem was motivated by other reasons, such as the domestic economic situation, this again must be handled in a different way, not through a simple visit to Jerusalem. It takes time and specific concrete measures to improve the economic conditions of a country, Mr. President. In this regard, we need measures at home and we need the close cooperation of the Gulf states, the United States and all Western powers."[25]

In his autobiography, Sadat wrote that during his talks with President Ceausescu, he asked the Romanian leader point blank: "Can an extremist like Begin really want peace?" Ceausescu's answer was an unequivocal yes.[26] The assertion came against the backdrop of Begin's warning about Qaddafi's assassination attempt, his Knesset declaration that Israel would not exploit Egypt's position in the Sinai while its army was engaged in battle along the Libyan frontier, and his willingness to meet with the Egyptian president in face to face talks, later authorizing Dayan to go to Rabat for the session with Tuhami. Dayan attributed Sadat's receptivity toward an Egyptian-Israeli peace inititiative to "the mediation of the King of Morocco" and Sadat's "trust in Begin's Government."[27] For his part, despite Fahmy's objections, Sadat became convinced that the time was ripe to break the psychological barrier that had separated Arabs and Jews for decades, and that was threatening to sabotage the resumption of the Geneva peace talks: "I realized that we were about to be caught up in a terrible vicious cycle precisely like the one we'd lived through over the last thirty years. *And the root cause was none other than that very psychological barrier I have referred to.*"[28]

Sadat deduced that a dramatic change was needed if the cycle of Mideast violence was to be broken:

What was it, then, that I needed to change? We had been accustomed (and a whole generation had been brought up) to regard Israel as taboo—as an entity whose emotional associations simply prevented anyone from approaching it. The situation went from bad to worse as the cumulative effect of things said and done over the years rendered any change difficult, if it didn't actually preclude that possibility for both the Arabs and the Israelis. So I concluded that any possible change should occur to the *substance* of that attitude itself. If indeed we wanted to get to grips with the substance of the dispute—with the basis of the problem—in order to establish a durable peace, I reasoned, we ought to find a completely new approach that would bypass all formalities and procedural technicalities by pulling down the barrier of mutual distrust. Only thus, I decided, could we hope to break out of the vicious circle and avert the blind alley of the past.[29]

The Egyptian leader, however, was well aware of the risks involved in pulling down the barriers of past generations, for it would surely unleash the hatred of those who had relied on him to carry on the struggle against the Jews. It would also stir the wrath of many Israelis whose loved ones had fallen at the hands of his army and the guerrilla terrorists he supported. Writing just months before his assassination in 1981, Sadat recalled how in 1977 he had questioned whether his decision to go to Israel to talk face to face with his enemies might not simply give the Israelis the chance to murder him in the streets of Jerusalem. His answer spoke to both Arab and Jew alike: "No man can escape his fate. The day of my death is set beforehand by God. It might take place in Jerusalem or in Cairo, on a bridge or under a bridge. The hour is coming, have no doubt. How can we forget the words of God almighty: 'Wherever you may be, death shall overtake you, even though you be in fortified castles.'"[30]

14

The Price of Peace

TWO years after the signing of the peace treaty with Egypt, when Sadat put forward a proposal to President Reagan that the PLO be included in the Israel-Egyptian autonomy talks covering the future of the West Bank and Gaza territories, Begin made his first public reference to the 1977 incident with Qaddafi and Waddieh Haddad's Palestinian commandos. The prime minister told reporters that he would tell the Egyptian president he was flatly opposed to "bringing in that murderous organization which, by-the-by, from time to time tries to assassinate Sadat. Once we learned from a very serious source (of a PLO plot to kill the Egyptian leader) and we didn't leave it a secret as far as the proper authorities were concerned."[1]

The following year, in the summer of 1982, Begin wrote a letter to President Mubarak defending Israel's invasion of Lebanon, reminding him that his predecessor had exercised a similar right of self-defense by invading neighboring Libya after the Israelis had informed him of Qaddafi's assassination plot.[2] The letter did not keep Mubarak from recalling his ambassador from Tel Aviv to protest the Israeli action in Lebanon, but the new relationship with Israel, by then already downgraded to a "cold peace" but a peace nevertheless, remained intact.

Muammar Qaddafi, meanwhile, was still playing a role in Egyptian politics, occupying the extremist end of the Rejection Front of Arab nations that had lined up against the Camp David accords and Sadat's separate peace with Israel. Tripoli issued a flow of invective against the Egyptian leader, branding him a traitor to the Arab cause and a pawn of the Americans and the Zionists: "Egypt with its resources and its 40 million people, its large army, the Suez Canal, its eternal Nile, its Pyramids, regretably fell, capitulated, fell to its knees and signed with all humiliation the document of capitulation, the document of slavery, the document of shame at Stable David, at the dirtiest place, under the bayonets of the enemy and the flag of imperialism, the flag of the United States—the enemy of the Arab nation.''[3]

Libya provided a haven for hardline PLO terrorists who would accept nothing short of Sadat's overthrow and Israel's eventual destruction. Qaddafi even issued a call to the PLO to destroy the Suez canal because Sadat had opened it to Israeli shipping.[4] (In 1984, the U.S. State Department concluded that Libya was involved in the planting of mines in the Red Sea that damaged at least nineteen ships.[5])

During a meeting at Alexandria in the summer of 1979, General Mahmoud Labib, the top-ranking Egyptian intelligence officer, was asked by an Israeli journalist how Cairo planned to deal with the increasingly volatile Qaddafi :

> *Israeli*: When are you going to conquer Libya?
> *Labib*: When are you going to *liberate* Libya?
> *Israeli*: When are you going to liberate Libya?
> *Labib*: We are not going to liberate Libya.
> *Israeli*: You must be planning something.
> *Labib*: (smiling) What do you think of the definition—we are going to help the people liberate Libya themselves?[6]

Instead of Sadat fomenting unrest in Tripoli that would lead to Qaddafi's ouster and the ''liberation'' of Libya, however, the opposite was to unfold. The Libyan ruler had aligned himself with Islamic militants like the ones from the Society for Repentance and Holy Flight—known by the Egyptian media as *takfir wa hijra*—who had kidnapped and executed Sheik al-Dhahabi, the former Egyptian Minister of Waqfs (religious property) in July 1977. Though the Society for Repentance and Holy Flight needed no prompting from its Arab neighbors in carrying out its ''holy'' mission, many believed that the Libyans were partly to blame for the Egyptian official's murder. The same would hold true five years later: Egypt's Islamic militants were organizing against Sadat on their own, but Qaddafi was behind the scenes ready to assist.

The bulk of Egypt's Moslem fundamentalists resented the country's turn toward the West, blaming Sadat for the influx of foreign goods and culture, the continuing economic crisis, and the country's isolation from the Islamic world that followed the signing of the peace agreement with Israel. Cairo's acute housing shortage still forced families to sleep between cemetery tombstones. Fresh Egyptian lamb, once a staple among local women buyers was now reserved for the wealthy elite who could afford the high prices, the poorer classes having to make do with frozen American hamburger patties. The television airways beamed the intrigues of Texas tycoons on "Dallas" while slick commercials promoted underarm deodorants to peasants who had been working the fields all day, sweating under the hot Egyptian sun. According to the Egyptian anthropologist Fadwa el-Guindi, Sadat's embrace of the West, consisting of the *infitah* open-door economic policy and the U.S. gravy train that headed for Cairo following the Israeli peace treaty, had alienated the local peasantry:

> What the people are faced with is the fact that the promised cargo comes down to false eyelashes, wigs, and hamburger patties. Their local grown produce is rarely in the market. The peasant buys imported food to eat. And while the Egyptian people are struggling to survive and make ends meet, Israel continues her belligerent acts in attempts to eliminate the Arabs, using different dehumanizing tactics to justify her acts to the world.
>
> In other words, the open-door economic policy (capitalism) actually translates into elitism, consumerism, and foreign imposition of goods and values instead of production and development; and peace translates into isolation, indignity, deception and imposed silence in the face of massacres and genocides of fellow Arabs and Palestinian women and children. Israel proved to be a disappointing partner. The Egyptians felt betrayed.[7]

There were indeed signs that Sadat's policies were coming under increasing attack: there was the 1976 murder of former Minister of Religious Endowments Sheik al-Dhahabi, which prompted a crackdown on Islamic militants that left 6 dead, 57 wounded, and 620 members of the Society for Repentance and Holy Flight arrested. There were the riots of January 1977, when, as a condition for new loans from the International Monetary Fund, the government decided to reduce or eliminate various food subsidies, triggering a dramatic surge in prices. The ongoing inability of the Egyptian worker to pay for basic necessities of life forced Sadat to reinstate the pricing system, covering commodities like wheat, flour, sugar, rice, cooking oil, tea, and butane gas, costing the state more than $2.9 billion in 1981.[8] And there was the 1979 Israeli peace treaty, after which many Egyptians were left watching in dismay as Israel carried out its pre-emptive strike against the Iraqi nuclear reactor, its cross border reprisals against PLO camps in Lebanon, and continued its settlement of the West Bank territories of Judea and Samaria.

With all other outlets for political dissent blocked by Sadat's security forces, the Islamic movement emerged as the vehicle for public protest. Fearing the wrath of Moslem militants, cognizant of the Khomeinist forces that had brought down his friend, the shah of Iran, Sadat was at first reluctant to use the might of his army to try to crush the Islamic associations. Yet as the power of the Moslem zealots grew, their comparisons between Egypt and pre-revolutionary Iran became more frequent.

Sadat was infuriated by the persistent comparisons of himself to the shah. Prior to his August 1981 visit to Washington, the videotape of an ABC television special prepared for the occasion, which suggested parallels between the Iranian monarch and the Egyptian president, was confiscated by police at the Cairo airport. Sadat then issued an emotional condemnation of the program, rebuking those in the American media who implied that Khomeinism had taken root in Egypt. He lashed out at press accounts equating the overthrow of the shah by Moslem extremists with the growing anti-Sadat activism of Egypt's own Islamic militants.

A few weeks later, on 3 September, Sadat decided to act against his country's Moslem dissidents. Egyptian security forces launched a massive crackdown against Sadat's opponents, rounding up more than three thousand people, including political leaders, journalists, lawyers, students, Coptic priests, and Moslem sheikhs. Among those arrested was an Islamic activist named Mohamad, the older brother of Khaled Ahmad Shawki el-Islambouli, a first lieutenant in an Egyptian army artillery unit.[9]

Islambouli belonged to one of the many militant groups associated with the Islamic movement, known as '*anquds*, Arabic for "grapes," named to reflect their self-sufficient nature: if any one of them was plucked, the others would continue to thrive. The twenty-four-year-old lieutenant had embraced these groups' demand that a new Islamic state be built on the ruins of the Sadat regime, one that would free devoted followers of the Prophet, like his imprisoned brother Mohamad, and roll back the sacrilegious peace that had been made with the Jews.

Sadat, known as "the pious president" for his public displays of worship at mosques across the nation, had tried to demonstrate a religious basis for his peace efforts, quoting from the Koran (2:135) to bolster his call for the acceptance of Israel: "We believe in God and in what has been revealed to us and what was revealed to Abraham, Ishamael, Isaac, Jacob and the 13 Jewish tribes. And in the books given to Moses and Jesus and the prophets from their Lord, who made no distinction between them."[10]

Other passages from the Koran seemed to fly in the face of the Egyptian president's pact with Palestine's Jews and their Christian allies in America:

> Believers, take neither the Jews nor Christians for your friends. They are friends with one another. Whoever of you seeks their friendship shall become one of their number. (5:49)

Had the People of the Book [the Jews] accepted Islam, it would surely have been better for them. Few of them are true believers, and most of them are evil doers. (3:110)

Because of their iniquity, We forbade the Jews good things which were formerly allowed them; because time after time they have debarred others from the path of Allah; because they practice usury—although they were forbidden it—and cheat others of their possessions. We have prepared a stern chastisement for those of them that disbelieve. (4:159)[11]

To Egypt's Moslem militants, it was obvious that true followers of the Prophet would never condone a peace with Zionist Israel or accept the permanence of a Jewish state in the heart of Islam:

Do not be deceived by the activities of the unbelievers in this land. Their prosperity is brief. Hell shall be their home, a dismal resting place. (3:194)

Mohammad is Allah's apostle. Those who follow him are ruthless to the unbelievers but merciful to one another. (48:26)

When We resolve to annihilate a people, We first warn those of them that live in comfort. If they persist in sin, We rightly pass our judgement and utterly destroy them. (17:16)

Tell the unbelievers that if they mend their ways their past shall be forgiven; but if they persist in sin, let them reflect upon the fate of their forefathers.
    Make war on them until idolatry is no more and Allah's religion reigns supreme. (8:36)[12]

As the French scholar Dr. Gilles Kepel has pointed out, many in Egypt's Islamic movement hailed peace as a worthy goal, but nevertheless said that the problem lay with the fact that the Jews were to be a partner to this peace. "The inclination to betrayal and belligerence is deeply implanted in the soul of every Jew," wrote the editors of *al-Da'wa* (The Mission), the popular magazine of the Moslem fundamentalists. In October 1980, they published a children's supplement, called *The Lion Cubs of al-Da'wa*, in which they labeled the Jews "the enemies of God" and called upon their young readers to "annihilate their existence." The Zionist state, with whom Sadat had made peace, was roundly condemned: "It may happen that a man lies or falls into error, but for a people to build their society on lies, that is the speciality of the children of Israel alone."[13]

When Lieutenant Khaled Ahmad Shawki el-Islambouli learned that the members of his Islamic militant group had met with fellow Islamic militants Mohamed Abdel-Salam Farag Attiya and Lieutenant-Colonel Abboud Abdel-Latif Hassan el-Zumr to plot the Egyptian president's murder, it occurred to him that here was an opportunity to offer himself as a sacrifice to Islam and fulfill his role in the *jihad* (holy war) against the apostate Sadat and his allies among the unbelievers. It was Abdel-Salam Farag's own book, *The Hidden Imperative*, that had already convinced Islambouli of the righteousness of assassinating "hypocritical" Moslem rulers:

> In the Islamic countries, the enemy is at home; indeed, it is he who is in command. He is represented by those governments that have seized power over the Muslims, and that is why *jihad* is an imperative for every individual.
>
> Now, there is no doubt whatever that the false gods of this earth will disappear only at sword-point. That is why the prophet said: *I was sent sword in hand, that they might worship only God . . . Those who do not govern according to what god has revealed are wrongdoers . . .*
>
> There are people who say that the goal of *jihad* today is the liberation [from the Jews] of Jerusalem, the holy land. Of course, this is a legal obligation and a duty for all Muslims . . . but:
>
> First: the fight against the enemy at home takes priority over the fight against the enemy abroad.[14]

On 23 September, 1981, the young lieutenant received word from his commanding officer that he had been selected to lead an artillery detachment of twelve 131mm guns in the 6 October parade commemorating Sadat's 1973 Yom Kippur attack against Israel. It quickly dawned on him that he would be in a unique position to carry out his "sacred mission." All he needed was three assistants and the right ammunition.

According to Israeli intelligence, it wasn't pure chance that an Islamic extremist was given orders to participate in the 6 October parade. Abdel-Salam Farag had indeed met Lieutenant Islambouli the previous summer, when the young militant was hoping to find an apartment of his own in the cramped quarters of Cairo. Aware of the asset of his position as a military officer, Farag personally assisted Islambouli in his apartment search, using the opportunity to indoctrinate him with ideas about martyrdom and the need to reverse Egypt's drift toward the West. Later, during the meeting with Farag, Colonel Zumr, and the members of Islambouli's Islamic militant group held at the beginning of 1981, the presidential parade was specifically discussed as the occasion for a possible assassination attempt. The advantage of staging an attack during a military procession had been recognized once before, when Muammar Qaddafi's and Waddieh Haddad's PLO commandos slated it as one of two alternatives for their strike against Sadat in 1977.

Following Sadat's assassination in 1981, Egyptian security officials in the southern city of Assiut found nearly $20,000 in the home of Mufti Omar Abdel-Rahman Ali Abdel-Rhaman, an associate of Colonel Zumr since 1974 and the murder team's spiritual leader who had earlier ruled that it was lawful to shed the blood of a leader if he failed to uphold the laws of Islam. It was Mufti Omar's ruling that gave rise to the reports circulating within the Islamic associations at the start of 1981 that Sadat had been condemned to death. The money discovered at Assiut after Sadat's murder had been delivered to Sheik Omar by a Libyan emissary.

Israeli intelligence experts concluded that Qaddafi's agents had worked closely with Egyptian conspirators in the military to arrange for Islambouli's assignment in the 6 October parade, in addition to providing training for his hit team. And the ammunition, originating in East Germany, came to Abdel-Salam Farag and eventually to Islambouli by way of Libyan intelligence. Security measures instituted by Egyptian authorities had prohibited parade participants from carrying ammunition for their weapons; it was the Libyans who had managed to provide the assassins with the 120 rounds of ammunition used to kill Sadat.[15]

Less than a month before the attack against Egypt's president, Israel's intelligence chief reportedly flew to Cairo to express his concern that Qaddafi had infiltrated the Egyptian army and the Islamic underground, and that Sadat's opponents were on the verge of launching a coordinated strike.[16] This time, unlike their initial reaction to Begin's report on Qaddafi's 1977 plot against Sadat, the Egyptians did not hesitate to take Israel's warnings seriously. Richard Allen, a former head of the National Security Council under President Reagan, revealed the depth of Cairo's concern at the time:

I can recall a situation that occurred, a very eerie situation that occurred just days before the assassination of President Sadat. Mr. Mubarak came to Washington to meet with President Reagan and raised again the concerns that President Sadat himself had raised with President Reagan—on the basis of great urgency, the need to do something about Libya, which was a festering sore. And while no specific solutions were brought to the fore, it was clear that the Egyptians were very agitated. And I for one could never quite get it out of my mind that there had to be or there ought likely to be some connection between that Egyptian concern and what eventually happened to President Sadat.[17]

According to *New York Times* reporter Seymour Hersh, the Reagan administration had early on come to the conclusion that something had to be done about Libya. One former cabinet-level official told Hersh that it was obvious that the "only thing to do with Qaddafi was to kill him." But blocked by President Carter's 1978 executive order prohibiting the United States government from carrying out assassinations, the Reagan White House was forced to search for a third party to get rid of Qaddafi. President Sadat seemed the likely candidate. In August 1981, the Egyptian president expressed support for the shooting down of two Libyan bombers by U.S. Navy fighter planes after the Sixth Fleet, operating through the Gulf of Sidre off the coast of Libya in the eastern Mediterranean, was challenged in international waters by Libya's air force. Sadat also denounced his Arab colleagues for siding with Qaddafi after learning that his planes had been shot down. "Do you not think of the seriousness of what this maniac is doing?" Sadat asked. "Do you not think of the innocent lives that could be lost because of Qaddafi's dangerous games? Or have the lives of innocent people also become a game in the hands of our countries' rulers?"[18] Hersh reported that there were those in the White House who believed that by the following month, toward the end of September 1981, Sadat himself "was within a few days of moving against Qaddafi."[19] If true, the timetable was to nevertheless prove too late.

On the morning of 6 October, 1981, Khaled Islambouli slipped four hand grenades under the seat of the truck that was to lead his artillery detachment in the military parade. He had already sent one regular member of his unit on leave and placed another on special assignment. A third had conveniently fallen ill. The lieutenant had replaced the men with three of his accomplices, though plans to drug the truck's regular driver went astray. At about 12:40 P.M., an hour into the parade, Islambouli's vehicle pulled to within forty yards of the presidential reviewing stand. He pulled his pistol on the driver, ordered him to stop, and jumped from the truck, hurling a grenade to create a diversion. A second gunman immediately stood up and sprayed the official platform with machine-gun fire. Islambouli charged toward Sadat, who had already taken a bullet in the neck, unloading his rounds into the president nonstop, the second gunman firing from behind, the two others shooting from both sides, pinning down the security detail. As the crowd looked on, stunned, and the military and security officials dove for cover, Islambouli and the second gunman stood unharassed against the reviewing stand wall for nearly thirty seconds, stretching themselves up on tiptoe, their rifles raised above their heads, steadily shooting at Sadat and the mob of bodies around him at point-blank range. Only when they finally turned to flee did Sadat's security men move toward the attackers. Islambouli and two others were wounded and taken into custody. The fourth managed to escape, but was arrested two days later.

In addition to Sadat, seven others died in the attack, and twenty were wounded, including the Israeli security officer guarding Jerusalem's ambassador to Cairo.

On the second day following Sadat's death, rioting erupted in Assiut, the hometown of Mufti Omar, the forty-five-year-old blind theologian who reputedly issued the death sentence against the Egyptian president. Eighty-seven people were killed, including sixty-six policeman, and hundreds were arrested. Egyptian officials charged that the uprising had been instigated by Islamic extremists who wanted to trigger a general revolution in the aftermath of Sadat's assassination.[20] To some observers, the violence appeared linked to a wider conspiracy. Certainly the precision timing involved in the 6 October murder hinted at a well-orchestrated operation going well beyond a handful of killers.[21]

Only two weeks had gone by since Lieutenant Islambouli first asked Abdel-Salam Farag to provide him with three volunteers who could help him carry out the plot against Sadat. The day after the request, Farag showed up with a twenty-seven-year-old reserve officer, Ata Tayel Hemeida Reheil, and an expert marksman who served as an instructor in the Civil Defense School, Hussein Abbas Mohamed. "For Farag to be able to produce within twenty-four hours two such well-qualified assistants for such a desperate enterprise," Mohamed Heikal wrote, "shows what a wide pool of like-minded men he must have been able to call upon."[22] The Israelis saw things differently. To them, Farag's speed reaffirmed their belief that the operation did not stem from a spur-of-the-moment plan hatched by a lone lieutenant, but was instead the result of a carefully prepared scheme involving Libyan, and probably Soviet, funds and advisers. This was not a case where an unbalanced attention seeker walked into a pawn shop, bought a Saturday night special, and jumped through a crowd to fire a shot at a poorly guarded public figure. Egypt was a closed society. As an American-educated journalist at Cairo's *Al Ahram* once remarked, the country was no democracy. The nation's dissidents were carefully monitored, and the regime dealt forcefully with its political opponents. Security around Sadat was tight, especially in the aftermath of the 3 September crackdown on religious extremists. Under the prevailing conditions, Israeli intelligence analysts concluded that the logistics of obtaining ammunition, talented accomplices, and the right opportunity to strike had to require more than a two-week period of last-minute planning. Preliminary plans had to have been already crafted, the agents already in place, the weapons and funds readily available, the conspirators poised to move at a moment's notice.

Such an operation would ordinarily require months, not days, to set up. And in the repressive atmosphere of Egypt, it would require outside funds and training by people experienced in underground acts of terror, bombings, and murder. The Israelis were not surprised to discover that Qaddafi had furnished the ammunition to Sadat's killers, or that Libyan funds were found in Mufti Omar's possession in the city where an anti-government uprising was to break out forty-eight hours after the Egyptian president's murder.

Despite Qaddafi's urgings, the tragic loss of Sadat did not bring revolution to Egypt, nor did it break the peace with Israel. Michael Austrian, the U.S. diplomat with special expertise in Egyptian affairs, said that though it became fashionable for Egyptians to complain about Sadat's policies and profess their disdain for his agreement with Israel, the truth is that the average Egyptian sincerely liked Sadat and was tired of war. The journalists who remained critical of the Egyptian leader for supposedly selling out Arab interests did not represent the masses, being in large measure holdovers from the Nasser regime, leftists and intellectuals still enamored of the pan-Arab ideal. Such people found it difficult to adjust to Sadat's dramatic shift, to suddenly discard their anti-Israeli ideology. They resented having to endure the isolation and vitriol that the Arab world brought down upon them in the aftermath of their president's visit to Jerusalem. But Austrian insisted that the ordinary Egyptian did not even fully grasp Zionism and did not wish to continue shedding blood in a seemingly endless battle against it. Sadat was indeed in tune with his countrymen, claimed Austrian, and the main elements of his legacy reflected that: the Egyptian people did not want to fight yet another war with Israel.[23]

In the week following Sadat's assassination, Henry Kissinger wrote:

> When he died, the peace process was a commonplace; Egypt's friendship with America was a cornerstone of Mideast stability. By his journey to Jerusalem he had demonstrated to our country, obsessed with the tangible, the transcendence of nobility. In the process he had accomplished more for the Arab cause than those of his brethren whose speciality was belligerent rhetoric. He had recovered more territory, obtained more help from the West, and done more to make the Arab case reputable internationally than any of the leaders who regularly abused him at meetings of the so-called rejectionist front.[24]

In the same week, Qaddafi's flag-waving followers in Tripoli celebrated Sadat's murder, PLO commandos in Beirut danced in the streets, Radio Damascus declared that "the traitor is dead," and Yassir Arafat offered to shake the hand of the assassin.[25]

At his trial, Lieutenant Islambouli clutched a copy of the Koran and proudly announced: "It was I who killed the Pharoah." Twenty-three others were charged with direct involvement in the plot against Sadat, and as they crowded into the courtroom on 22 November, 1981 (one of them was hospitalized and could not attend), the defendants chanted in unison: "We acted for the sake of God, not for the sake of earth or homeland. We sacrifice ourselves for religion. Today is a glorious day for religion on which blood is spilt."[26]

The following year, on 15 April 1982, the core group of four gunmen were executed by the Egyptian government. The military men, Lt. Islambouli, 24, and Sgt. Hussein Abbas Mohammed, 28, were shot by a ten-man firing squad at an army base near Cairo. Ata Tayel Hemeida Reheil, 29, a civilian, was hanged in the capital's central prison. The other civilian, Mohamed Abdel-Salam Farag Attiya, 25, author of *The Hidden Imperative*, was also hanged. Seventeen of the remaining conspirators received prison terms ranging from five years to life. Among them was Colonel Zumr, the Islamic militant who had attended the 1981 meeting with Farag and members of Islambouli's Islamic militant group to plan Sadat's murder.[27]

On 30 September 1984, Chief Judge Abdel-Ghaffar Ahmed sentenced 107 Moslem extremists to prison for their role in the Assiut uprising that followed Sadat's murder. The defendants hung banners from the bars of the make-shift jail that held them in the courtroom: "God is our only judge," the banners read. "Holy war against lackeys, Jews, Christians, and atheists." The defendants also shouted slogans, including "Moslem blood should not be sacrificed for the Jews and the Americans!" Mufti Omar Abdel-Rahman Ali Abdel-Rhaman, the guiding light of the Moslem militants, who had given an implied blessing to Sadat's murder by pronouncing that the proper remedy for a leader who strayed from Islam was death, delivered a courtroom sermon on the subject of martyrdom. He had already been found innocent of charges arising out of the Assiut riots as well as of those alleging his involvement in the Sadat killing.[28]

On 16 July 1985, nearly four years after Sadat's murder, President Hosni Mubarak's government arrested forty-four Islamic activists in what was described as a new campaign to curb Moslem extremism. Mubarak had pledged to uphold the terms of the peace treaty with the Jewish state, assuring one Israeli reporter within days of Sadat's death, "Go tell your people, don't worry."[29] Following his 16 July crackdown, a spokesman for Mubarak charged that one of those arrested, Sheik Hafez Salama, a prominent fundamentalist leader, had distributed pamphlets which "instigated the people against the regime," urging them to "destabilize" the government. Twenty-two of those apprehended by Mubarak's forces were members of a militant Islamic group from the village of Fayoum, southwest of Cairo. The previous Friday, they had tried to prevent a government-appointed sheik from conducting the noon prayers, attempting instead to have them led by Mufti Omar.[30]

The following year, in April 1986, thirty-three members of a militant Moslem organization, including four military officers, were arrested by Egyptian security forces for plotting to assassinate President Mubarak.[31]

Across the River Jordan

I sincerely tell you also that before us today lies the appropriate chance for peace. If we are really serious in our endeavor for peace, it is a chance that may never come again. It is a chance that if lost or wasted, the resulting slaughter would bear the curse of humanity and of history.

Anwar Sadat
Israeli Knesset
19 November 1977

15

The Diplomatic-Military Mix

ISRAEL'S approach to Middle East peace has been twofold: (1) to use its military strength to deliver crushing defeats sufficient to convince its Arab neighbors that future wars will not bring about the destruction of the Jewish State and therefore should not be employed in the search for a solution to the conflict; and (2) to use its diplomatic leverage with the West and exploit whatever parallel interests it shares with the region's moderate Arab regimes to lure its adversaries into public negotiations that could bring about a political settlement. In Lebanon, the military option has been at the forefront for more than a decade. Israel has employed covert paramilitary means such as hit teams, intelligence agents, and commando strikes in addition to more conventional military tactics such as aerial bombardment and invasion by ground forces to carry out reprisals for PLO terrorist raids and to destroy the Palestinian guerrilla movement's political and military infrastructure. Dina al-Asan was one of many agents working on behalf of the Mossad in Beirut, providing Israeli counterterrorist strategists with information on PLO movements, arms depots, international contacts, and planned terrorist assaults. Because of the nature of terrorist warfare, with faceless attackers perched alongside airline ticket counters, school rooms, buses, mailboxes, and synagogues, operating across national boundaries and funded by an array of governments from Moscow to Riyadh, Israel's battle against terrorism to a large degree has relied on intelligence agents working undercover, stalking terrorists in the shadows of civilian life.

In Egypt, the 1970s saw a series of Israeli behind-the-scenes diplomatic encounters aimed at bringing the two sides closer together, tapping their common desire for peace as well as their mutual rejection of Soviet influence in the area and opposition to the spread of radical Khomeini-style Islamic forces.

On Israel's northern border, the secret warfare in Lebanon foreshadowed the full-scale Israeli invasion in 1982 that drove the PLO from Beirut. On the southern front, the clandestine meetings between Israeli and Egyptian officials helped lay the groundwork for the public negotiations at Camp David and the 1979 peace treaty between Egypt and Israel.

Meanwhile, to the east, across the Jordan River, a combination of covert military arrangements and secret diplomatic talks, already in place for more than twenty years, were working to shape a possible settlement with King Hussein's Jordan, a key factor in any solution to the Palestinian-Israeli dispute.

16

King of the Arabs, Guardian of Islam

KING Hussein of Jordan is a first-generation Jordanian. His father, King Talal, was born in 1909 in the eastern region of Saudi Arabia, then known as the Hejaz. His grandfather, King Abdullah, was placed at the helm of the newly-formed Kingdom of Transjordan by the British in 1921 in partial fulfillment of a pledge to turn over Ottoman-controlled territories to the Hashemite clan as compensation for its role in spearheading the Arab Revolt against Turkish rule during World War I.

King Hussein ibn Talal's great-grandfather was Hussein ibn 'Ali, King of the Hejaz, Grand Sharif of Mecca, Supreme Guardian of the Holy Places of Mecca and Medina, and leader of the House of Bani Hashem, the distinguished Arab family that traced its male lineage back to the Prophet Muhammad's daughter, Fatima. It was Sharif Hussein who launched the Arab Revolt on 5 June 1916, waging a relentless guerrilla war against the Turks. It was Sharif Hussein's son Feisal who rode with T. E. Lawrence, sabotaging Turkey's supply lines along the Hejaz Railway, evicting the Turkish army from the strategic port of Aqaba, driving Turkey's forces into retreat in tandem with the British. And it was the sharif's other son, Abdullah, who took control of eastern Palestine, only to be shot down by a Palestinian assassin while his young grandson, Hussein ibn Talal, stood helpless at his side.

When Hussein ibn Talal took the throne of Jordan on 11 August 1952, the seventeen-year-old king fell heir to a weighty legacy embracing both Islam and modern Arab nationalism. He was a direct descendant of the Prophet; head of the powerful family from the Arabian Peninsula that had once ruled the Holy Places of Mecca and Medina; great-grandson of Sharif Hussein, the desert chief who masterminded the Arab Revolt; nephew of Ali and Feisal, the warriors who helped liberate the Arabs from Turkish rule; and grandson of Abdullah, founder of the Transjordan nation, who led the nation to independence in 1946 and christened it The Hashemite Kingdom of Jordan, establishing the groundwork for one-man rule by the family from Arabia in the lands east of the Jordan some six hundred miles away from the Hashemite's traditional tribal homeland.

Like his namesake, Sharif Hussein of Mecca, King Hussein of Jordan has been both burdened and emboldened by his dual lordship over Islamic purity and Arab nationalism. In his day, the sharif had boldly embraced his role as protector of Islam and champion of the Arab cause, proudly proclaiming himself King of the Arabs and taking upon himself the responsibility for negotiating a post-war settlement with Great Britain and France that would guarantee the security of the Holy Places and grant Arab rule in the lands once held by the defeated Ottoman Empire.

Though the other Arab tribes of the Peninsula, namely the Idrisi of Asr and the Saudis of Najd, welcomed the sharif's leadership of the Arab Revolt against Turkey, they resented his pretensions to all-consuming sovereignty, reflected in his self-proclaimed title of King of All the Arab Countries.[1] The conservative Saudis, members of the fundamentalist Islamic Wahabi sect, not only opposed his political aims but also rejected the sharif's status as guardian of Islam, believing that most of their fellow Moslems, including the sharif, had corrupted the Prophet's teaching.

More than a half-century after Sharif Hussein's Arab Revolt, the sharif's great-great grandson Hussein ibn Talal was to face similar difficulties in trying to reconcile his status as chief of the Hashemites with his role as ruler over the Arabs in other lands, in this case, the Arabs of Palestine. "He believes naïvely, passionately in his family's divine right—and duty—to rule, even if it is assailed from all sides," wrote Hussein's biographer, Peter Snow, in 1972.[2]

Just as the sharif's aspirations as King of the Arabs eventually prompted a revolt by the Saudi tribe and the eventual expulsion of the Hashemites from the Arabian Peninsula in 1926, King Hussein's rule over the Arabs of Palestine eventually embroiled him in a bloody civil war, leading him in 1970 to fight against Palestinian Arab forces spearheaded by the PLO. Though he avoided the defeat suffered by his ancestors on the peninsula and managed to crush Palestinian power in Jordan, the PLO's longstanding hostility to Hussein's attempts to serve as spokesman for the Palestinian cause continued to threaten his throne.

The king's former standing as the Arab ruler of Jerusalem, the third holiest city in Islam, gave him the added responsibility of safeguarding the rights of Moslems. There is the echo of the sharif in Hussein: the Hashemite monarch of Jordan, the guarantor of Arab national rights, the savior of Islam.

Yet Hussein has been a cautious ruler, eschewing the unexpected move, the bold confrontation, the provocative adventure, opting instead for the carefully structured alliance, the co-optation of rivals, the safety of playing the second fiddle in Middle Eastern politics. Among the powerful chieftains of the Arab world—Nasser, Sadat, Assad, Arafat—Hussein remained in the background, letting the initiative fall to others, whether in battle or diplomacy. It was Nasser who won the title of Pan-Arabism's great visionary champion. The modern day incarnation of the Arab Revolt had "death to Israel" as its battle cry, and it was Nasser, not Hussein, who rallied the masses to the cause, leaving the king little choice but to follow the Egyptian president's lead in a course that ended disastrously in the 1967 Six Day War when Jordan lost Jerusalem and the West Bank territories to the Jews. Later, it was an Egyptian, not a Hashemite, who salvaged Arab honor in 1973, when Anwar Sadat's surprise attack shook the Jewish State and demonstrated the might of a united Arab world. And it was Sadat, not Hussein, who became the first Arab leader to sign a peace treaty with the Zionists, enabling the king to begin his own tentative moves toward a settlement with Israel.

Hussein's caution may have stemmed in part from the shock of his grandfather's murder and in part from the lessons gleaned from the plight of the sharif, whose desire to parlay the victory of the Arab Revolt into Hashemite sovereignty beyond his native Hejaz nearly ended in the eradication of his family's leadership everywhere. During the early 1920s, the sharif attempted to extend Hashemite control over the rest of the Arabian Peninsula. But beginning in the early 1920s the rival House of Saud in central Arabia began sending its bedouin fighters out from their bases in Najd to challenge the sharif's reign. Under Abdul-Aziz Ibn Saud's leadership, the Saudis vanquished the armies of Sharif Hussein and his son King Ali in the Hejaz. The Saudis also managed to subdue the competing forces of Ibn Rashid in the northern principality of Shammar in addition to seizing control of the Idrisi clan's region to the south in 'Asir, thus consolidating Ibn Saud's control over almost the entire Arabian Peninsula. Only in the southernmost territory of Yemen did the Saudi conquest come to a halt.

Sharif Hussein, who had abdicated in favor of his eldest son Ali in 1925 hoping to placate Ibn Saud, had to eventually flee Mecca and take refuge north in Aqaba. He was then forced to abandon the Peninsula and settle on the island of Cyprus where he lived in exile until 1930. Then, after suffering a stroke, the sharif journeyed to Amman to spend his remaining days in his son Abdullah's Kingdom of Transjordan in eastern Palestine. He died the following year, an embittered man cut off from his native Hejaz.

After Ibn Saud's expulsion of the Hashemites, King Ali was forced to flee to Baghdad where his brother Feisal had been installed by the British. Feisal had earlier been dethroned by the French as the monarch of Syria. Refusing to indulge Feisal's dreams of Arab independence in Damascus, the French ended his rule. The British then stepped in to assist their wartime ally, placing him at the head of a restless Iraq in a ploy to establish a cooperative pro-British, Arab-ruled regime in the region. While the French were not averse to a direct confrontation with the Arab nationalists if it would secure their interests in the area, the British were more politic. London's diplomats preferred to bargain for their spoils in the Middle East, trading territory and money in exchange for British influence. Yet Britain's sponsorship of the Hashemite dynasty in the Hejaz did not prevent the family's demise on the Arabian Peninsula, and the clan's transfer to Iraq was to only end in failure.

On 14 July 1958, Sharif Hussein's great-grandson (and King Hussein's cousin), King Feisal II, was machine-gunned to death in his palace court-yard during a military coup led by Brigadier Abd al-Karim Kassem; the Hashemite dynasty in Iraq was destroyed. On 20 July, 1951, Abdullah, the architect of the modern state of Jordan, was assassinated by a Palestinian gunman who feared the king's secret overtures to the Jews. King Hussein of Jordan was thus to become the only member of the Hashemite family to remain in power, the sole surviving heir of Sharif Hussein's Arab Revolt. The Hashemites had been pushed from their own base on the Arabian Penin-sula and forced from their thrones in Damascus and Baghdad. Hussein, the lone ruling survivor from the House of Bani Hashem, was left to lord over a domestic population that increasingly saw Hashemite rule as a foreign presence in Palestine, albeit an Arab one and therefore preferable to a regime governed by Jews. The young monarch knew all too well that the history of the dynasty from the Hejaz in the lands beyond the Arabian Peninsula had been littered with betrayal, disillusionment, and death.

Despite the murder of Abdullah and growing opposition to the regime in Amman, there were still Palestinians on both banks of the Jordan River who looked to the Hashemites for leadership in their war against the Jews. Keeping Palestine Arab, free from European (and later Zionist) dominance, had been a near-sacred goal of the Hashemites since the days of Sharif Hus-sein.

Prior to his joining forces with Great Britain against the Turks under the banner of the Arab Revolt, the sharif had sought assurances from London that Arab demands for independent rule in the Middle East would be ful-filled in any post-war settlement. In 1914, Oriental Secretary Ronald Storrs had been authorized by the British agent in Cairo, Lord Kitchener, to ask the sharif's son Abdullah whether or not the Hashemites would fight with the British if Turkey entered World War I on the side of Germany. Following further contacts among Storrs, Kitchener, and the Hashemites, and after Turkey's entry into the war against Great Britain, the sharif dispatched a letter on 14 July, 1915, from his base in Mecca, to Sir Henry McMahon, British high commissioner for Egypt and the Sudan. In it he indicated his willingness to commit Arab forces in the fight against the Turks provided that certain conditions were met:

> Great Britain recognizes the independence of the Arab countries which are bounded: on the north, by the line Mersin-Adana to parallel 37° N and thence along the line Birejik-Urfa-Mardin-Midiat-Jazirat (ibn 'Umar) - Amadia to the Persian frontier; on the east, by the Persian frontier down to the Persian Gulf; on the south, by the Indian Ocean (with the exclusion of Aden whose status will remain as at present); on the west, by the Red Sea and the Mediterranean Sea back to Mersin.[3] [See map, page 138]

Sir Henry McMahon's response came in a letter from Cairo, dated 24 October 1915:

> The two districts of Mersina and Alexandretta and portions of Syria lying to the west of the districts of Damascus, Hama and Aleppo cannot be said to be purely Arab, and should be excluded from the limits demanded.
>
> With the above modification, and without prejudice to our existing treaties with Arab chiefs, we accept those limits.
>
> As for the regions lying within those frontiers wherein Great Britain is free to act without detriment to the interests of her ally, France, I am empowered in the name of the Government of Great Britain to give the following assurances and make the following reply to your letter:
>
> (1) Subject to the above modifications, Great Britain is prepared to recognize and support the independence of the Arabs in all regions within the limits demanded by the Sherif [sic] of Mecca.
>
> (2) Great Britain will guarantee the Holy Places against all external aggression and will recognize their inviolability.
>
> (3) When the situation admits, Great Britain will give to the Arabs her advice and will assist them to establish what may appear to be the most suitable forms of government in those various territories.[4]

Ten letters in all were exchanged between the sharif and Sir Henry, but McMahon's response of 24 October is the one cited by Arab nationalists and supporters as offering an explicit promise by Great Britain to deliver

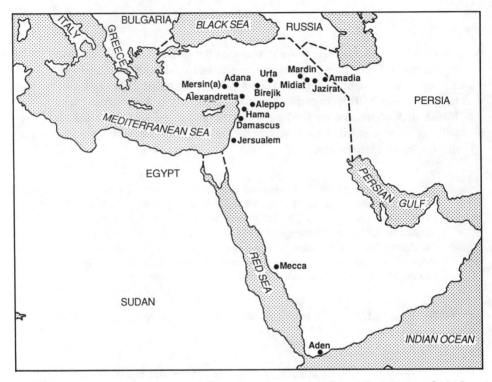

Middle East Territories Delineated in the McMahon-Sharif Correspondence of 1915

Palestine into Arab hands once the hostilities with the Turks came to a close. As the Arab historian George Antonius wrote, the McMahon letter "may perhaps be regarded as the most important international document in the history of the Arab national movement."[5]

The Arab interpretation of McMahon's reservations regarding the "portions of Syria lying to the west of the districts of Damascus, Hama and Aleppo" did not go unchallenged. Later, when the furor over the establishment of a Jewish homeland in the Middle East erupted, the position put forward by the British government was that what McMahon had meant by those "portions of Syria lying to the west" in fact constituted the land west of the Jordan River, from Jerusalem to the Mediterranean Sea, known as western Palestine.

But the controversy over western Palestine was yet to come, for on the heels of the McMahon correspondence came the Sykes-Picot Agreement among France, Great Britain, and Russia, which called into question the larger issue of Arab sovereignty in the Middle East. Concluded in May 1916, the agreement called for the establishment of independent Arab states or confederations of Arab states on the lands seized from the Turkish rulers under a post-war settlement. In Iraq, the British would retain the power to "establish such direct or indirect administration or control as they desire and as they may think fit to arrange with the Arab State or Confederation of States."[6] The French would reserve the same prerogatives in Syria, which at the time included territory as far north as Turkey and as far south as the city of Tyre in Lebanon and Gaza in Palestine. In addition, Great Britain pledged to put Palestine east of the Jordan "under the suzerainty of an Arab chief," with London enjoying the "priority of right of enterprise and local loans" and alone supplying "advisers or foreign functionaries at the request of the Arab State or Confederation of Arab States."[7] But the region to the west of the Jordan River, owing to its special nature as home to the Christian holy places of Nazareth, Bethlehem, and Jerusalem, would be severed from French-controlled Syria and placed under an international administration to be coordinated among France, Great Britain, and Russia, in consultation with the sharif of Mecca.

Upon learning of the Sykes-Picot Agreement, the Arabs cried betrayal, but the British assured the sharif personally that the agreement did not compromise their commitment to the cause of Arab independence. The Sykes-Picot Agreement, which had been negotiated in secret and withheld from the sharif, came to light in December 1917, a month after the Bolsheviks seized power in Moscow and made public various classified documents from the

Russian Imperial Ministry of Foreign Affairs. Maneuvering to win favor with the leadership of the Arab Revolt, the Turkish leader Jemal Pasha made a direct appeal to the sharif, inviting him to "turn against the British and return to the fold of the Caliph and of Islam," and with it he provided the Arab leader with a copy of the Sykes-Picot Agreement.[8] Reginald Wingate, the British high commissioner in Egypt, telegrammed the sharif on behalf of British Foreign Secretary Alfred James Balfour:

> Documents found by Bolsheviki in Petrograd Foreign Ministry do not constitute an actually concluded agreement but consist of records of provisional exchanges and conversations between Great Britain, France and Russia, which were held in the early days of the War, and before the Arab Revolt, with a view to avoiding difficulties between the Powers in the prosecution of the war with Turkey.[9]

Lt.-Col. Bassett, the acting British agent in Jedda, followed-up the telegram with a formal note to Sharif Hussein dated 8 February, 1918:

> His Majesty's Government and their allies stand steadfastly by every cause aiming at the liberation of the oppressed nations, and they are determined to stand by the Arab peoples in their struggle for the establishment of an Arab world in which law shall replace Ottoman injustice, and in which unity shall prevail over the rivalries artificially provoked by the policy of Turkish officials. His Majesty's Government re-affirm their former pledge in regard to the liberation of the Arab peoples.[10]

Though the terms of the Sykes-Picot Agreement were altered in the post-war settlement, its spirit lived on in the division of Turkey's Middle Eastern territories into spheres of influence apportioned to France and Great Britain. The Treaty of Versailles and the Covenant of the newly-established League of Nations granted mandates sanctioning French and British rule in the region. At the San Remo Conference of 25 April 1920, the Supreme Allied Council of France, Great Britain, and Italy drew the boundaries, splitting the Syrian province into three separate states—Lebanon, Palestine, and what was left of Syria—with Lebanon and the newly altered Syria coming under French rule and Palestine and Iraq subject to the British.

For most Arabs, Palestinian nationalism had not yet been born, the notion of an independent Palestinian state on either side of the Jordan River being nearly as far-fetched as a move to make the American state of New Hampshire a sovereign nation of its own would be. The Palestinian identity was subsumed by the Syrian one, if not by the larger sense of pan-Arabism that had been stirred by the sharif's Arab Revolt in the Hejaz. For the Arabs, the betrayal they saw in the San Remo Conference was not merely in the transfer of eastern and western Palestine from Ottoman to European rule, but in the breakup of Turkey's Syrian district into three separate states. George Antonius put forward the Arab position:

> The country [Syria] had a unity of its own in more ways than one. In spite of the great diversity of its physical features, it was geographically one and formed a self-contained unit enclosed by well-defined natural frontiers. In the economic field, it had developed its agricultural and commercial life on a foundation of natural resources, and the whole country was criss-crossed with a close network of inter-dependent lines of activity, linking region to region, the countryside to the cities and the coast to the interior. It had also cultural and historical traditions of unity: ever since the Arab conquest, except for the interlude of the Crusades, it had formed one political unity and kept the language and the customs which it had begun to acquire in the seventh century. On every essential count, it was clear that the well-being and the future development of the country were bound to be retarded if its unity were to be destroyed. Nor had indications been lacking to show the strength of feeling in the country itself on the subject of unity. But all those considerations were ignored; and the Supreme Allied Council, mindful only of the appetites of its members, found that the only way to satisfy Great Britain and France was to divide Syria between them.[11]

To this day, the Arab world has been beset by leaders, scholars, and activists who denigrate Palestinian nationalism along with Lebanese independence not in deference to the Maronite Christian minority in Beirut or the Jews of Tel Aviv but rather in service to their historical opposition to San Remo. In 1977, Druze chieftain Kemal Joumblatt emphasized that the dream of an independent "Greater Syria" as envisioned during the Arab Revolt is still very much alive in the corridors of the ruling Ba'ath Party of present-day Syria:

> They refuse to forget the days before the carve-up of 1919, when the Lebanese, the Palestinians, the Jordanians and the Syrians formed a single people, the people of historic Syria, covering the area from the Taurus Mountains to Sinai and from the Iraqi steppes to the sea. Indeed, President Assad confirmed this quite unambiguously to Yasser Arafat not so long ago (around April 1976): "You do not represent Palestine as much as we do. Never forget this one point; there is no such thing as the Palestinian people, there is no Palestinian entity, there is only Syria! You are an in-

tegral part of the Syrian people, Palestine is an integral part of Syria. Therefore, it is we, the Syrian authorities, who are the true representatives of the Palestinian people.'' On this occasion, at least, the ''Lion of Greater Syria'' put his viewpoint frankly enough.[12]

Despite the Arab hostility to the dismemberment of Turkey's former Syrian province and the establishment of European-controlled states in the region under the terms set forth at San Remo, the British aspired to deliver on their original pledges made to the sharif on the eve of the Arab Revolt. Moreover, the 1920 rebellion against British rule in Iraq had demonstrated to London the wisdom of jettisoning direct administration over the bulk of its Middle East mandate in favor of a policy promoting the installation of friendly indigenous Arab regimes. By taking such an approach, London could at once avoid the costly and frequently bloody burdens of empire while fulfilling its promise to the sharif to reward him for his role in leading the Arab uprising against the Turks.

On 23 August, 1921, British-controlled Iraq was turned over to the sharif's son, Feisal. The year before, it had been Feisal's brother Abdullah who was appointed king of Iraq by a group of Iraqi leaders, and Feisal who had been proclaimed king of United Syria (meant to include Lebanon and Palestine) by the General Syrian Congress of 8 March, 1920. But Feisal's expulsion from Damascus by the French had made him England's number one candidate for the throne in Iraq. Abdullah, though, was determined to have his share of power. With his father's blessing, he gathered a force at Ma'an in eastern Palestine and prepared to invade Syria to avenge his brother's eviction from the throne. Although they disapproved of France's move against Feisal in Syria, the British could not countenance the raising of an Arab army aimed at their French allies. England had agreed to grant France jurisdiction over northern Syria (which included Lebanon) at San Remo, in turn receiving France's pledge to respect the British position in Iraq and southern Syria (Palestine, east and west). The French would surely hold England responsible for an Arab insurrection against France emanating from British-controlled lands.

Arriving in Jerusalem on 24 March, 1921, therefore, British Colonial Secretary Winston Churchill attempted to assuage Abdullah by asking him to set up a provisional government in Amman and await further developments that might expand the scope of his rule. Churchill realized that Abdullah would not be content to govern eastern Palestine only, telling his prime minister, Lloyd George, that the Arab leader would ''almost certainly think it too small.''[13] But the British were not prepared to offer up the entire Palestine province, so Churchill sweetened the deal by offering to use his government's influence with its wartime ally France to restore Hashemite power in Syria with Abdullah as its king. In the meantime, Abdullah was to temporarily administrate Palestine east of the Jordan River, an area formerly part of Feisal's Syrian domain but one which Britain had earlier managed to wrest from the French, with their consent. The region, known as Transjordan, consisted of thirty-five thousand square miles, 80 percent of the entire Palestine Mandate recognized by the League of Nations.

Abdullah accepted Churchill's offer, which included a monthly grant of five thousand British pounds, and on 27 March, 1921, an agreement was signed whereby the British established the Kingdom of Transjordan in eastern Palestine. Abdullah was to serve as its king, with a pledge to refrain from hostile acts against French rule in Damascus and against British jurisdiction in western Palestine.[14]

"He had come to Trans-Jordania hoping for great things and now he realized that he had no hope either north or east," wrote the British representative in Amman at the time. "If he went back from here to the Hejaz, he would look ridiculous." And so, "Abdullah agreed to act in accordance with Mr. Churchill's wishes and with British policy, as he did not wish to be the cause of any friction between the British and their allies."[15]

Feisal's British confidant, T.E. Lawrence, had accompanied Churchill to Amman. "You are well known for sacrificing your personal ambitions for your country, so stay here," he told the Hashemite leader. "If you succeed, you will achieve the unity of Syria in six months. God willing, we will visit you in Damascus to offer our congratulations."[16]

Of the lands that fell to Britain under the Sykes-Picot and San Remo agreements and the League of Nations Covenant, the only portion not under direct Arab administration by 1921 was the remaining 20 percent of the original Palestine Mandate, the territory west of the Jordan River. Though Abdullah tried to persuade Churchill to grant him jurisdiction over western Palestine, the British government held firm. Three years earlier, on 2 November, 1917, Foreign Secretary Balfour had made other commitments regarding Palestine, contained in a letter written to the British banker and Jewish leader Lord Rothschild:

Dear Lord Rothschild,
I have much pleasure in conveying to you, on behalf of His Majesty's Government, the following declaration of sympathy with Jewish Zionist aspirations which has been submitted to, and approved by, the Cabinet.
"His Majesty's Government view with favour the establishment in Palestine of a national home for the Jewish people, and will use their best

endeavours to facilitate the achievement of this object, it being clearly understood that nothing shall be done which may prejudice the civil and religious rights of existing non-Jewish communities in Palestine, or the rights and political status enjoyed by Jews in any other country."

I should be grateful if you would bring this declaration to the knowledge of the Zionist Federation.[17]

Having ceded nearly 80 percent of Palestine to Arab rule under Abdullah in 1921, the British felt compelled to retain at least the remaining 20 percent as a site for the Jewish homeland mentioned in Secretary Balfour's statement to Lord Rothschild and to the Zionist Federation. The Arab leadership saw the declaration as a violation of Britain's wartime pledge to the sharif, citing the McMahon letter of 24 October, 1916 as evidence that London had agreed to grant the Arabs sovereignty over the whole of Palestine. The British, however, disputed the Arab claim, pointing to McMahon's reservations concerning the "portions of Syria lying to the west of the districts of Damascus, Hama and Aleppo," which they said covered the Palestine Mandate. Various British statesmen challenged their government's position, stating that Palestine did not lie west of those districts but south, and thus fell within the area assigned to the Arabs. The minutes of a meeting of the War Cabinet's Eastern Committee held in London on 27 November 1918 appear to uphold their interpretation: "The Palestine position is this. If we deal with our commitments, there is the general pledge to Hussein in October 1915, under which Palestine was included in the areas to which Great Britain pledged itself that they should be Arab and independent in the future."[18]

A 1919 document compiled by the Political Intelligence Department of the British Foreign Service in preparation for the Paris Peace Conference also stated:

With regard to Palestine, His Majesty's Government arc committed by the Sir Henry McMahon's letter to the Sherif on October 24, 1915, to its inclusion in the boundaries of Arab independence.

The whole of Palestine, within the limits set out in the body of the Memorandum, lies within the limits which H.M.G. have pledged themselves to Sherif Hussein that they will recognize and uphold the independence of the Arabs.[19]

But in the White Paper of 1922, issued by Colonial Secretary Winston Churchill to sum up British policy in the region, a wholly different interpretation of the McMahon letter is presented:

It is not the case, as has been represented by the Arab Delegation, that during the war His Majesty's Government gave an undertaking that an independent national government should be at once established in Palestine. This representation mainly rests upon a letter dated the 24th October, 1915, from Sir Henry McMahon, then His Majesty's High Commissioner in Egypt, to the Sherif of Mecca, now King Hussein of the Kingdom of the Hejaz. That letter is quoted as conveying the promise to the Sherif of Mecca to recognise and support the independence of the Arabs within the territories proposed by him. But this promise was given subject to a reservation made in the same letter, which excluded from its scope, among other territories, the portions of Syria lying to the east of the district of Damascus. This reservation has always been regarded by His Majesty's Government as conveying the vilayet of Beirut and the independent Sanjak of Jerusalem [*vilayet* and *sanjak* were the terms for administrative districts during the Ottoman Empire]. The whole of Palestine west of the Jordan was thus excluded from Sir H. McMahon's pledge.[20]

In a published piece dated 23 July, 1937, McMahon himself embraced the view that the territory had been *excluded* from the commitments made to Sharif Hussein: "I feel it my duty to state, and I do so definitely and emphatically, that it was not intended by me in giving this pledge to King Hussein to include Palestine in the area in which Arab independence was promised. I also had every reason to believe at the time that the fact that Palestine was not included in my pledge was well understood by King Hussein [the sharif]."[21]

There was evidence that the Hashemites not only understood England's reservations regarding Palestine but in fact accepted, albeit grudgingly, its commitment to the Jews undertaken in the Balfour Declaration. While on his way to Paris to attend the 1919 Peace Conference following World War I, Feisal stopped in London and held a meeting with T. E. Lawrence and Dr. Chaim Weizmann, leader of the Zionist movement. Weizmann had already met with Feisal the year before at the Hashemite prince's camp in the Hills of Moab near Mann in eastern Palestine. The London meeting was a follow-up discussion about possible Arab-Jewish cooperation in the region. The Lawrence-Feisal-Weizmann encounters went well, and on 3 January, Feisal signed an agreement that gave an implicit endorsement to the national aspirations of the Jewish people and their determination to establish a homeland in Palestine:

The Arab State and Palestine in all their relations and undertakings shall be controlled by the most cordial goodwill and understanding, and to this end Arab and Jewish duly accredited agents shall be established and maintained in the respective territories.

In the establishment of the Constitution and Administration of Palestine all such measures shall be adopted as will afford the fullest guarantees for carrying into effect the British Government's Declaration of the 2d of November, 1917 [the Balfour Declaration].

All necessary measures shall be taken to encourage and stimulate immigration of Jews into Palestine on a large scale, and as quickly as possible to settle Jewish immigrants upon the land through closer settlement and intensive cultivation of the soil. In taking such measures the Arab peasant and tenant farmers shall be protected in their rights, and shall be assisted in forwarding their economic development.[22]

There has been speculation that Lawrence, anxious for an agreement between the Arabs and the Jews, misled Feisal about the agreement's implications for Zionist rule in Palestine, and that had he realized that Weizmann was setting the stage for the eventual establishment of a Jewish national authority he would never had signed the document.[23] Yet three months later, on 3 March, in a follow-up letter to the American jurist and Zionist leader Felix Frankfurter, Feisal wrote: "We are working together for a reformed and revived Near East, and our two movements complete one another. The Jewish movement is national and not imperialist. Our movement is national and not imperialist, and there is room in Syria for us both [Syria then included Lebanon and Palestine on both sides of the Jordan]."[24]

Feisal did attach a reservation to the agreement with Weizmann, stipulating that if his prior demands for Arab independence were not met by the British he would not be "answerable for failing to carry out" its terms. To many Arabs, London's decision to delegate a portion of Mandate Palestine to the Jews invalidated Feisal's accord with the Zionists. Yet why would British support of Jewish statehood jeopardize the agreement when Feisal himself observed that Arab and Jewish nationalism served to complete and not conflict with one another?

The controversy surrounding Feisal's initial responses to Zionism remains far from resolution. Writing some fifty years later, the Palestinian scholar Sami Hadawi claimed that "nowhere in the Feisal-Weizmann Agreement of January 1919 is there any mention of a Jewish state in Palestine," insisting that Feisal "certainly did not agree to turn Palestine over to the Jews or to establish a 'Jewish state' in Palestine."[25] If so, the purpose of the agreement's distinction between the "Arab State" and "Palestine" and its reference to "Arab and Jewish duly accredited agents" which "shall be established and maintained in the respective territories" remains elusive. Arab and Jewish agents to be established in their *respective* territories would presumably have meant the existence of separate Arab and Jewish territories. And if Palestine were to come under exclusive Arab rule, then agreements outlining relations between the "Arab State" and "Palestine" would appear peculiarly redundant to say the least. Feisal's letter to Frankfurter, equating the merits of Jewish national aspirations with those of the Arab movement would also seem disingenuous at best, for he would be denying the Jews any territorial base for their nationalism while demanding that the Arabs gain full reign from Baghdad to Damascus, Beirut, Jerusalem, Amman, and Mecca.

The rationale used to read Feisal's embrace of the Jewish national movement as something other than an implied endorsement of Jewish sovereignty resurfaced in the summer of 1919, when Woodrow Wilson's consent to Feisal's request for a political survey of the inhabitants of Syria and Palestine led to the issuance of a report by U.S. representatives Henry C. King and Charles R. Crane. In its official recommendation to President Wilson, the King-Crane Commission claimed that the Balfour Declaration's support for the establishment of a Jewish national home in Palestine "was not equivalent to making Palestine into a Jewish State," and it called for a sharp limitation of Jewish immigration into the area.[26]

British ministers like Lord Grey, however, later asserted that the Balfour Declaration did in fact promise a Zionist home in Palestine and as such implied "a Zionist government over the district in which the home is placed," and that others like Balfour himself had earlier only qualified the pledge to connote the "gradual" rather than "early" development of an independent Jewish state, to come about "in accordance with the ordinary laws of political evolution."[27]

Nevertheless, the King-Crane Commission took the position that a Jewish home did not imply Jewish self-determination and that the Balfour Declaration promoted neither the early nor the eventual establishment of a Jewish government in Palestine. The commission's actions seemed to have been foreshadowed by the statements of Feisal's Arab supporters in the wake of his agreement with Dr. Weizmann: not wanting to completely repudiate their ally and erstwhile leader, they read the agreement with the Zionist leader to mean an Arab acceptance of Jewish nationalism, providing it remained devoid of the apparatus of nationhood. The Arabs would tolerate a Jewish national presence in Palestine as long as it lacked the prerogatives of self-rule and independent statehood. This appeared to contradict Feisal's embrace of the equality of Jewish and Arab nationalism, for the Arab demand for self-rule was unequivocable.

The American members of the King-Crane Commission were apparently reticent about alienating their wartime ally, Great Britain, and reluctant to overtly denounce the Balfour Declaration as either unfair or unworkable, or both. Seeming to take a leaf from Feisal's Arab apologists by similarly overlaying a particular interpretation of a formal agreement by third parties, the commission read the Balfour Declaration to mean that the establishment of a Jewish national home in Palestine was not equivalent with statehood or the free immigration of Jews into the region, and that what London had called for was in actuality the kind of national home where the nation's brethren were denied access and its inhabitants denied the right of self-rule.

Ironically, in his agreement with Weizmann, Feisal himself recognized the need to "encourage and stimulate immigration of Jews into Palestine on a large scale." Yet regardless of Feisal's initial posture toward the Zionists, the continued vehemence of the Arab rejection of the Balfour Declaration and all subsequent steps toward the establishment of a Jewish homeland in any portion of Palestine rendered the agreement irrelevant.

At the General Syrian Congress held in Damascus six months after Feisal's London meeting with Weizmann, the Arab leaders who purported to "represent the Moslem, Christian and Jewish inhabitants of our respective districts" went on record as being officially opposed to Jewish immigration and Jewish self-rule: "We reject the claims of the Zionists for the establishment of a Jewish commonwealth in that part of Southern Syria which is known as Palestine, and we are opposed to Jewish immigration in to any part of the country. We do not acknowledge that they have a title, and we regard their claims as a grave menace to our national, political and economic life."[28]

The view that took hold among the Arabs was clearly not Feisal's vision of Arab and Jewish national movements that "complete one another," with room for both. Though the congress accepted Feisal as their king, they rejected his accord with Zionism. The following October, Feisal himself told an interviewer from the *Jewish Chronicle* that the Arabs would "fight to the last ditch against Palestine being other than part of the Kingdom and for the supremacy of the Arabs in the land."[29] The dominant Arab view was summed up by Antonius: "No room can be made in Palestine for a second nation except by dislodging or exterminating the nation in possession."[30]

What Antonius could have added was that no room could be made in Palestine for a second nation ruled by Jews. For although there had been an outcry against the separation of Lebanon and Transjordan from Syria, the Arab world had quickly accustomed itself to the post-war reality. Even the latter-day pan-Arab Nasserites in Cairo and Beirut and the Ba'ath proponents of a reunited "Greater Syria" in Damascus were unwilling to launch an all-out war against their Arab neighbors in order to realize their goal of establishing a single Arab nation. But when the 20 percent of Mandate Palestine that had been held by Britain following the creation of Transjordan under Abdullah was set aside for the Jews, there were anti-British and anti-Jewish uprisings, the anniversary of the Balfour Declaration was quickly branded as an Arab national day of mourning, and six Arab armies along with a host of Arab irregulars poised in unison, ready to march on the Jewish state the moment it came into being.

On 29 November, 1947, the United Nations voted to partition the final 20 percent of Mandate Palestine that had been administered by Great Britain, creating a second independent Arab state beside Jordan on 42 percent of the land in western Palestine, with 56 percent allotted to the Jews and 2 percent, including Jerusalem, to be governed under international jurisdiction.[31] Accounting for the previous establishment of the Arab state of Transjordan under the 1947 partition plan, the Jewish national homeland was to be established on 11 percent of Mandate Palestine. The Arabs rioted in Damascus, Beirut, and Amman.

By the time of the November Partition Resolution of 1947, the Kingdom of Transjordan had already been released from the British Mandate, achieving full independence. Abdullah had successfully transformed his "temporary" status as ruler, granted to him by Churchill in 1921, into a full-fledged monarchy governing the independent Kingdom of Transjordan in eastern Palestine. Though the goal of establishing a single unified nation embracing all the Arab lands formerly held by the Turks had long since vanished into the realm of the impractical, the victorious European powers of World Wars I and II had left in their wake an independent Arabian Peninsula and Arab-ruled regimes in Damascus, Cairo, Baghdad, Beirut, and Amman. Out of more than 660,000 square miles of Middle Eastern territory, less than 8,000 had been set aside for the Jews. But the Arabs objected, charging that Jewish settlement and sovereignty would displace the local non-Jewish population living in the 11 percent of Palestine that had been allotted to the Zionists, and that Jewish rule threatened the Arab character of Palestine. There were Arabs who campaigned for a united Arab land encompassing the borders of Syria, Iraq, and the Peninsula; there were Arabs like Ibn Saud who displayed a tribal or regional chauvinism that resisted the rule of rival dynasties like the Hashemites of the Hejaz. But to nearly all Arabs, acceptance of a neighboring state run by Jews was unthinkable. A monarchical clan from the Arabian Peninsula could be transplanted hundreds of miles to the north to rule in the cities of Damascus, Baghdad, and Amman without arousing universal Arab wrath; not so the attempt by the Jews to set up a state of their own on territory comprising less than 1.5 percent of all the lands claimed and eventually governed by the Arab world. Hashemite rule may have been vanquished by the Saudis of

Arabia and resented by the Palestinians of Amman, but its presence as a foreign, authoritarian regime in the capitals of Syria, Iraq, and Jordan did not yield generations of bloodshed and hatred. A Syrian-born leader jostling for power in Beirut or a Hashemite ruler from Arabia lording over Amman did not trigger a holy war against the foreign invaders by the native inhabitants. But an Iraqi-born Jew in Tel Aviv or a Polish-born Jew in Jerusalem aspiring to govern fellow Jews in Palestine sparked a century-old conflict with an Arab world that could yield no place for a Jewish state with Jewish rulers in their midst.

The Hashemites did share a common language, religion, and culture with the Arabs beyond the clan's native Hejaz not shared with the Jews. But though a tiny fraction of Palestine's inhabitants, Jews had maintained a continuous presence in the Holy Land for hundreds of years. There were Jews living in Jerusalem whose ancestors had immigrated to the city when King Hussein's great-grandfather the sharif was still a boy riding the deserts of Arabia. Still, the attempts by Jews to lay claim to a fraction of the Middle Eastern lands that had been held by the Turkish Empire for nearly four hundred years were met with cries of imperialism, colonialism, and *jihad*.

Admittedly, the perception of Zionism as simply a tool of the Western powers designed to consolidate Europe's imperialist gains in the region was a major element in the hostile Arab reaction to the Jewish return to Palestine. But anti-Semitism, prevalent in both the Arab and European cultures, was no doubt another factor in the vigorous resistance to Zionist goals in the Middle East. The Arabs were at least united in their common religion, even if their respective tribal homelands created cultural differences and national rivalries. There was no such bond to bridge the gap with the Jews, even with those Jews who were born in Arab lands and spoke Arabic as their mother tongue.

Although a factor in the Arab opposition to Zionist settlement in Palestine, anti-Semitism did not play a significant role in the conflict until the post-World War I period. Prior to that time, the Jewish communities of the Islamic east had traditionally been treated with a tolerance far greater than that experienced by the Jews of Christian Europe. As Princeton professor Bernard Lewis concluded, what can be said of the Jews who had lived under Islamic rule for the previous fourteen centuries is that they ''were never free from discrimination but only rarely subject to persecution; that their situation was never as bad as in Christendom at its worst, nor ever as good as in Christendom at its best. There is nothing in Islamic history to parallel the Spanish expulsion and Inquisition, the Russian pogroms, or the Nazi Holocaust; there is also nothing to compare with the progressive emancipation and acceptance accorded to Jews in the democratic West during the last three centuries.''[32]

According to Lewis, earliest Arab opposition to Jewish immigration centered on localized practical matters concerning the establishment of certain Zionist agricultural settlements where "disputes arose over such matters as grazing rights, land titles, and the differences of custom and usage that inevitably developed between neighbors of such vastly different backgrounds."[33] As for questions of ultimate sovereignty over Palestine, the Zionist threat seemed minimal to most Arabs, for the traditional status of Jews as second-class, albeit at times protected, citizens of Islamic culture appeared to have permanently nurtured Jewish weakness, engendering scorn for the Jews rather than fear among their Moslem neighbors.

In Christian Europe, the Jews had come to represent a central theological challenge, for the belief that Christianity had replaced Judaism as the legitimate heir to ancient Israel's promise was apparently being challenged by the stubborn persistence of a vibrant Jewish culture. But in the east, the Prophet's followers had subdued the Jews and taken up Islam as a new religion that served as an extension rather than a replacement of Judaism. And while many Christians continued to hold the Jews responsible for Christ's crucifixion, breeding charges of deicide and long-festering resentment, Muhammad had debased and humiliated the Jews during his own lifetime. The Jewish challenge to Muhammad had been settled long ago in the seventh century, when the Prophet's followers conquered the Jews of Medina and his successors expelled the Jews from nearly all of Arabia. For many Arabs, such political victories were testimonies to the triumph of their theological message as well. With the Jews devoid of any significant temporal power in the Middle East, Judaism could only remain discredited and weak, incapable of mounting any serious threat to Islam. Even up until the late 1800s and early 1900s, observes Lewis, to the Arabs, "Jews as Jews might be a nuisance, but could hardly be a danger, and their political ambitions were laughable."[34]

What wasn't laughable were the political ambitions of the European powers, and the notion that they might one day conspire with the Jews to catapult themselves into a position of dominion over the Middle East did worry some Arab leaders at the turn of the century. As Western influence in the region expanded and Ottoman power declined during World War I and its aftermath, the struggle for political spoils among the European powers, the local Arab tribes, and the Zionist settlers brought competing nationalisms into conflict and with it the specter of a revived Jewish culture in the Middle East freed from its second-class status. There were Moslem leaders who believed that such a development would in part undo the legacy of the Prophet's conquest of Arabia's Jews and hence undermine Islam's pre-eminence in the region. As long as the Jews had remained without political power, they reasoned, their religion and their culture remained without legitimacy, deserving on occasion a degree of paternal indulgence and protection or at other times ridicule or worse. But the vacuum left by the collapse of the Ottoman Empire was enabling Jewish immigrants, backed by their supporters in the West, to make inroads into the political fabric of the region, and Jews were thus no longer to be viewed as merely a "nuisance," but rather as potential rivals capable of challenging both Arab nationalism and Moslem theological hegemony.

By the 1920s, Arab thinkers were opposing Jewish immigration as a European-backed imperialist conspiracy to manipulate by proxy Arab national interests, while the prospect of an independently ruled Jewish state in the region, whether free or in alliance with the Western powers, was being resisted as an assault upon Islamic supremacy in the area. The latter element brought with it the earmarks of traditional anti-Semitism, where Jews were not to be accepted as equal partners in the governance of nation states. For many Arab nationalists, the realization of legitimate Arab rights not only meant the withdrawal of European powers from the region and the establishment of an independent Arab nation or constellation of states, but such a state or combination of states would have to be led by rulers who followed Islam. An independent Syrian nation with a Syrian Jew as head of government fell outside the very constructs of Arabist thought at the time. The Arab east's marking of the Jew as being unfit to rule either in the land of his birth or elsewhere, a view largely rooted in historical theological antagonisms, was shared by much of the Christian west, and its elements showed up in the King-Crane Commission report of 1919:

> There is a further consideration that cannot justly be ignored, if the world is to look forward to Palestine becoming a definitely Jewish State, however gradually that may take place. That consideration grows out of the fact that Palestine is the Holy Land for Jews, Christians, and Moslems alike. Millions of Christians and Moslems all over the world are quite as much concerned as the Jews with conditions in Palestine, especially with those conditions which touch upon religious feeling and rights. The relations in these matters in Palestine are most delicate and difficult. With the best possible intentions, it may be doubted whether the Jews could possibly seem to either Christians or Moslems proper guardians of the holy places, or custodians of the Holy Land as a whole.
>
> The reason is this: The places which are most sacred to Christians—those having to do with Jesus—and which are also sacred to Moslems, are not only not sacred to Jews, but abhorrent to them. It is simply impossible, under those circumstances, for Moslems and Christians to feel satisfied to have these places in Jewish hands, or under the custody of Jews.[35]

The King-Crane report did not speculate about Jewish concerns for the security of their holy places; it did not characterize the Moslem denunciation of the Jews for their failure to accept Muhammad as the Prophet of God as an abhorrence of Jewish tradition and belief; it did not suggest that there were Christians who abhorred the Jews for their refusal to embrace Jesus as the Son of God; and it did not attempt to reconcile the widespread Moslem view of both Christians and Jews as infidels with the prevalent Christian view of Moslems and Jews as unrepentant sinners. Only in the case of the Jews did the clash of doctrine imply an inability to respect the rights of others, and, despite the obvious inherent theological differences among all three religions, only the Jews were disqualified from having an authoritative presence in the Holy Land out of a fear that they alone would be unable to rise above the denominational strife and rule with a just hand. Such thinking fueled the crusade of the Mufti of Jerusalem in his campaign to rid the country of the Jews in the 1930s, and it persisted into the 1980s when Iran's Ayatollah Khomeini took up the Palestinian cause, not in deference to Arab rights but rather to help bring Palestine into the Moslem fold. The constant reminders by other Arab supporters that Jerusalem is the third holiest city in Islam was put forward as further justification for removing Israeli jurisdiction over the Jews' first and only holy city.

From the outset of his rule in 1952, Jordan's King Hussein found himself circumscribed by his role as guardian of Islam when struggling to come to terms with the reality of the Israeli nation. For Hussein, protector of Islam had to be synonymous with keeping Jerusalem in Arab hands. When the eastern half of the city was lost to the Jews in 1967, later to be officially reunited with the western region, Hussein protested: "Israel's annexation of the Arab eastern sector of the City has embittered the Arabs who revere the Islamic holy places there." The eastern sector also contains the Wailing Wall, the remnant of Solomon's ancient temple honored as Judaism's holiest site. Still, the king insisted that Arab rule must prevail; only then could Jerusalem become "the symbol of peace."[36]

In addition to the duties that fell to him as protector of Islam, Hussein was the leader of a Third World nation, a category that supposedly meant nonalignment but more often translated into anti-Americanism and hostility toward Washington's friends abroad. Hussein had no doubt been suckled on palace stories of alternating betrayal and patronage by the West, nurturing a home-grown suspicion of America and its allies. Yet he also cast a wary eye toward his fellow Arab rulers—after all, his great-grandfather had been deposed by the Saudis, his grandfather murdered by a Palestinian, his cousin killed by the Iraqis. Hussein's fear of neighboring regimes probably contributed to his decision to throw in his lot with the British and the

Americans despite Arab misgivings over United States-European involvement in the Middle East. But Jordan's ongoing historical ties with Great Britain and its rapidly increasing dependence on the United States left the king vulnerable to Arab critics who accused him of serving the interests of imperialism. The king was indeed exposed to Western statesmen who applied diplomatic pressure while dangling arms sales and cash subsidies before him in order to manipulate him. What emerged as a result was a condition whereby a harsh, intransigent stance toward Israel appeared to be the only acceptable demonstration of Jordanian independence.

Hussein was also saddled with the competing claims of Jordanian "East Bankers" who wished to concentrate on the development of their country, and those of the Palestinian "West Bankers" (the refugees), who held out for a return to an Arab-ruled state on the other side of the Jordan River. Moreover, the king was haunted by his role as the sole surviving Hashemite ruler, further reducing his inclination to lead his countrymen rather than merely seek their approval, especially when it came to peace with the Zionists.

Finessing his way through a policy of empathy toward anti-American, anti-Zionist Arab radicals and moderation toward America and Israel's supporters in the West may have secured his throne, but it kept the Jordanian king from attaining either a Nasser-like stature as beloved revolutionary of the Arab world or a Sadat-like status as courageous peacemaker hailed by the United States and Europe. Yet Hussein remained the only contemporary Arab ruler whose destiny had been so inextricably linked to the evolution of Arab nationalism in the twentieth century. Through it all, he managed to not only shoulder the mixed legacy of the Arab Revolt—the liberation from the Turks; Sykes-Picot; Balfour; San Remo; the Hashemite expulsion from Arabia; the division of Ottoman Syria; the emergence of independent Arab rule in Beirut, Amman, Damascus, Baghdad, and Cairo—but also to culture the penchant for diplomacy exhibited in his uncle Feisal's agreement with Zionist leader Chaim Weizmann and his grandfather Abdullah's secret negotiations with Israeli representatives Golda Meir, Eilias Sasson, Moshe Dayan, Yehoshafat Harkavi, Walter Eytan, Yigal Yadin, Reuven Shiloah, and Moshe Sharret.[37]

Feisal's public dealings with the Zionists had earned him the enmity of much of the Arab world, and Abdullah's private contacts (he met with Golda Meir twice, in 1947 and 1948, in an effort to avoid the subsequent outbreak of war) neither prevented war with Israel in 1948 nor led to a settlement when the fighting ceased. Moreover, Abdullah's talks with the Jews cost him his life. Hussein was a boy of fifteen when he saw his grandfather gunned down a few steps ahead of him as they headed into the al-Aksa

Mosque in Jerusalem for noonday prayers. He may have inherited a keen political sense from his Hashemite ancestors, but he had also experienced the danger of failure firsthand.

For Hussein, the risks of hidden diplomacy with the Jews had to be drastically cut: absolute secrecy would be the priority in any discussions, concrete results amenable to the majority of Arabs would have to be assured before any public negotiation could begin. As Golda Meir once wrote, "One of the first lessons that most Arab rulers learn is the connection between secrecy and longevity."[38] She also recalled what Egyptian President Nasser had told an intermediary working on behalf of the Israelis: "If Ben-Gurion came to Egypt to talk to me, he would return home as a conquering hero. But if I went to him, I would be shot when I came back."[39] With this in mind, the king launched his first round of private talks with Israeli leaders.

17

Cloak and Dagger Diplomacy

ON 25 April, 1957, following the Palestinian uprisings protesting Hussein's removal of Suleiman Naboulsi as prime minister, King Hussein was moved to defend himself by blackening his opponent with the name of Israel. Naboulsi had legalized the banned Communist Party newspaper, *Al Jamaheer*, and in his radio speech denouncing the former prime minister, the king reminded his listeners about Naboulsi's attitude toward the Jordanian communists. He then added, "The Communist party here are brothers of the Communist party in Israel and receive instructions from them."[1] Though the insinuation that Naboulsi was acting in collusion with the Jews was widely rebuffed, and the former prime minister's Palestinian supporters continued to rail against the king, the attempt to smear Naboulsi with the name of Israel was not an uncommon act in a region where almost any ailment could be attributed to the "disease" of Zionism.

Five years after excoriating his ex-prime minister for being clandestinely in league with the Jews, King Hussein initiated a secret meeting with the Israelis. Iraq and Syria had been taken over by regimes professing loyalty to Gamal Nasser's vision of pan-Arab unity. Hussein feared the Egyptian president's plans for a grand alliance of Arab states: he believed Nasser's ultimate goal spelled dissolution of his monarchy, removal of the Hashemites, and a disenfranchised Jordan subsumed under a union of Arab nations ruled from Cairo.

On 17 April, 1963, the newly-installed regimes in Baghdad and Damascus agreed to join in a union with Nasser. The Palestinians in Jordan rejoiced upon hearing the announcement. Acting collectively and fueled by a renewed wave of Arab nationalism, a federation of Iraq, Syria, and Egypt might be able to muster the might and the will to finally dislodge the Jews from Palestine. The Palestinians called upon Hussein to make his own contribution to the cause by bringing Jordan into the alliance. On 20 April, a riot broke out in the Jordanian sector of Jerusalem. Mobs ran through the streets shouting Nasser's name and holding his picture aloft. The Jordanian flag was ripped from a government building and replaced with a banner bearing four stars, three representing the union of Iraq, Syria, and Egypt, the fourth heralding the cry for Jordan to join in. Hussein had to call in the army to restore order. Four people were killed, thirty wounded. Samir Rifai, the prime minister appointed by the king just a month earlier, lost a vote of no confidence in the Jordanian Parliament. Hussein's new prime minister, Sherif Hussein bin Nasser, ordered the army into the countryside and imposed a curfew, finally bringing the demonstrations to a halt.[2]

The king would not be pushed into an Arab union led by Nasser that might deliver on its promise to defeat Israel but in the process remove the Hashemites from power in Amman. For their part, the Israelis, too, feared for their survival. The treaty of federation called for a military alliance "capable of liberating the Arab homelands from the dangers of Zionism." Prime Minister Ben-Gurion told his colleagues that there were "grounds to believe that the Arab countries *were* contemplating an attack on Israel" and that the declarations of the newly-formed federation could not be easily dismissed. After a two-day debate, the Israeli parliament passed a motion drawing "the attention of the Great Powers and world public opinion to the threat to Israel's existence contained in the plan of action of the Federation of Egypt, Syria, and Iraq, headed by Nasser."[3]

Neither Ben-Gurion nor Hussein wished to see Jordan join the alliance with Nasser. For Ben-Gurion, it would portend an invigorated Arab force on Israel's eastern border bolstered by the resources of three other countries committed to the destruction of the Jewish nation. For Hussein, the union would relegate his nation to second-rate status beside the alliance's more powerful member states and leave him with a diminished role in the shadow of the charismatic Nasser. Eventually, it was likely to bring the overthrow of his regime by revolutionaries encouraged by the fact that the federation's other leaders were all deeply opposed to monarchies: Egypt's Nasser had toppled the rule of King Farouk in a 1952 military coup; Syria's rulers belonged to the Ba'ath (Renaissance) Party, a leftist group preaching socialism and pan-Arabism, that had supported Naboulsi's 1957 challenge to Hussein; and Iraq was led by Colonel Abd al-Salam Aref, the second member of the two-man team that had forced the Hashemites from power in Baghdad, killing Hussein's cousin King Feisal II in the 1958 takeover.

Faced with a Palestinian-supported union of Arab radical governments that threatened to undermine his rule, Hussein turned to the one regime that he knew would also suffer the consequences of Nasser's success. In September 1963, the king sent word to Ben-Gurion's successor, Prime Minister

Levi Eshkol, that he wanted to meet privately with an Israel representative. Eshkol sent Yaacov Herzog, general-director of the prime minister's office and a confidant of Ben-Gurion. The secret meeting took place in London at the clinic of a Jewish physician who had treated the king. The memory of his grandfather's murder by a Palestinian gunmen in Jerusalem had a sobering effect on Hussein's encounter with the Israeli official. Even Nasser, the implacable foe of the Jewish state, had confided to President Eisenhower's Middle East envoy, Robert Anderson, that the threat of assassination was no small factor in his refusal to negotiate an accommodation with Israel. "I don't want to happen to me what happened to King Abdullah," Nasser told Anderson during a meeting in January 1956. "That is why I cannot risk an agreement with Israel."[4] In 1963, Hussein knew that the dangers were no less great than they had been seven years earlier, when Nasser had voiced his concerns to Anderson, and that in fact they were likely to continue for some time. The legitimacy of the king's fears was repeatedly substantiated by the threats of fellow Arabs over the next two decades; on 14 April, 1970, for example, a PLO leader in Arafat's Fateh faction openly promised that "any Arab leader signing a peaceful settlement with Israel will be signing his own death sentence."[5] The veracity of that prediction was sharply illustrated by the 1981 murder of Anwar Sadat. For Hussein, the secrecy of his meeting with Herzog and of subsequent encounters with Israeli leaders was more than a precaution: it was an obsession.

Leaving even his closest advisers in the dark, the king traveled to London to meet with Herzog and urgently pursued two things: a political dialogue outlining terms for a peaceful solution to the conflict with Israel, and a practical dialogue exploring mutual security concerns arising out of the radicalization of neighboring Arab regimes and the increasing militancy of Palestinian nationalists in Jordan.

The proposed terms for a political accommodation consisted of free access by Jordan to the Mediterranean port of Haifa (with the security of Jordanian ships guaranteed by Israeli troops) and permanent resettlement of the Palestinian refugees, with the United States providing financial assistance.

The Jordanian demand for a Mediterranean outlet had been agreed to more than a decade earlier in the draft peace agreement, "Principles of a Territorial Arrangement (Final)," secretly worked out by King Abdullah, Reuven Shiloah, and Moshe Dayan and initialed by Abdullah and Shiloah on 17 December, 1949. Abdullah later felt compelled to cancel the agreement and scuttle further moves toward a peace treaty in order to avoid the appearance of breaking ranks with the other Arab states, which were not yet ready to end the war with Israel.[6] Likewise, though Abdullah's grandson King Hussein had invited the Israelis to London fourteen years later to discuss peace, the climate in the Arab world at large was still not right for a comprehensive agreement ending the state of war with Israel. The Arab rebels in Algeria had succeeded in securing independence from France the year before, inflating the hopes of Palestinian guerrillas that they could finally oust the Zionists. The newly-formed federation of Iraq, Syria, and Egypt, with its lofty appeals for Arab solidarity and the eradication of Israel, stirred the Palestinian Arabs into pressing for a military solution to the conflict. Syria's Ba'ath regime encouraged this intransigence by overtly sponsoring acts of Arab sabotage and terror against Israel, using its strategic advantage atop the Golan Heights to shell Jewish schools, homes, and farms along the Huleh and Jordan Valleys below.[7] Palestinian students and intellectuals in Beirut were swept along by the renewed nationalist rhetoric and began agitating for a separate Palestinian presence in Arab affairs, proclaiming their rejection of Hashemite rule and demanding a state of their own on the then Jordanian-controlled territory on the West Bank of the Jordan River, a prelude to an expanded nation of Palestine that would include all of Israel.[8] Hussein became convinced that he was in no position to buck the tide: he told Herzog that he could not become the first Arab leader to make peace with Israel.

Attaining a political breakthrough between Hussein and the Israelis proved elusive during the London meeting with Herzog; achieving a security arrangement was rather straightforward. Jordan and Israel had a mutual interest in clamping down on Palestinian guerrilla activities.

The Palestinians, especially those living on the West Bank, had long resented Hashemite rule. The area had originally been allocated to the Palestinians in the 1947 U.N. Partition Resolution, which divided western Palestine into separate Arab and Jewish states. But in the ensuing fight against Israel, King Abdullah's Arab Legion crossed the Jordan River, capturing the old city in east Jerusalem, and seizing the West Bank region that had been intended for the creation of a second Arab state in Palestine. The Egyptians checked Abdullah's ambitions and took control of the Gaza region in the southern strip bordering the Sinai and the Mediterranean.

In September 1948, Palestinians under the leadership of the Jerusalem Mufti Haj Amin Husseini met in Gaza and announced the formation of a "Government of All Palestine" that would have sovereignty over the entire British Mandate for Palestine, including Abdullah's Transjordan, the conquered West Bank territory held by the king's Arab Legion, and the lands allotted to the Jews in their new State of Israel. All of the Arab League members except Transjordan recognized the Husseini government the following month. King Abdullah was not about to accept a "Government of All Palestine" led by the Palestinian Mufti, a longtime rival. Abdullah's dream of ruling over an expanded Transjordan united with Syria—as envisioned when he originally agreed to Winston Churchill's 1921 offer to head a provisional government in Amman and await a return to Damascus under British auspices—had long been shattered. The war with the Jews held out the possibility that even though he had been denied lordship over a powerful Greater Syria his reign might at least move beyond the deserts of eastern Palestine to include the prestigious city of Jerusalem and the rolling hills and fertile lands of the West Bank.

On 1 December, 1948, just two months after the Mufti's declaration of his All Palestine Government, an opposition Palestinian group sponsored by Amman held a conference in Jericho. Its members requested that the West Bank territories be united with Transjordan, and proclaimed Abdullah "King of Arab Palestine." Thirteen days later, Abdullah's parliament endorsed the Jericho declaration, and in April 1950, the West Bank was formally annexed. Transjordan of eastern Palestine became the Hashemite Kingdom of Jordan, incorporating the western region slated by the United Nations as the Arab state to be set up alongside Israel in fulfillment of the Partition Resolution. The Hashemites from the Hejaz now ruled over Palestinian Arabs on both sides of the Jordan River. For the "East Bankers," who had become accustomed to Hashemite rule since the formation of Transjordan twenty-nine years earlier, the annexation was understandably less disturbing than for the newly-incorporated "West Bankers." To many of the latter, who had aspired to self-rule in a land free of Jews, Abdullah's takeover was a violation of Palestinian rights: their nation had been stolen once by the Jews and a second time by the Arabs. Against this backdrop, the rise of Palestinian extremism, fueled by Nasser's 1963 union of Egypt, Iraq, and Syria and by the increasing talk of an independent Palestinian entity on a West Bank liberated from Hashemite rule, laid the groundwork for the practical dialogue sought by Hussein in his London meeting with Israel's Yaacov Herzog.

Hussein may not have been prepared to carry through on a real peace agreement with Israel, but he was ready to coordinate clandestine military operations with Tel Aviv in order to keep Palestinian extremists from undermining his authority. Intelligence data on guerrilla activities on both sides of the Jordan would be shared by the two nations in order to keep the Palestinians from inflaming the Israeli-Jordanian frontier through terrorist incursions. Hussein's cooperation in the prevention of terrorism would shield Jordan from costly military reprisals by Jewish forces and enable the king to improve relations with the United States, opening the way for increased American aid for his faltering economy. Shared security arrangements would keep the Palestinian guerrillas from building a separate military force that could threaten not only Israel but, one day, Hussein's monarchy in Amman.

The security arrangements initiated in London in 1963 created an ironic bond between Israel and an Arab neighbor who refused to acknowledge its existence and publicly vowed to dismantle the Jewish state by force of arms. As Mideast observers Ze'ev Schiff and Raphael Rothstein have noted, this unorthodox arrangement was not a paper alliance, but one involving concrete coordinated efforts to combat the PLO: "In the first years of Fateh operations Jordan willingly accepted from Israel lists of Jordanians collaborating with the fedayeen group. Israeli intelligence kept a close watch on Jordanian border villages and on several occasions extensive arrests of Jordanians were made on the basis of lists received from the Jewish enemy."[9]

For the moment, the need for the two nations to temporarily unite against a common military threat appeared to be more compelling than the ideologies that divided them.

18

Talking Peace, Making War

PALESTINIAN pressures on King Hussein reached new levels with the formation of the Palestine Liberation Organization, which had been launched at the Cairo gathering of thirteen Arab heads of state in January 1964, billed as "The First Arab Summit." Hosted by Nasser, it was held for the ostensible purpose of coordinating steps to block Israeli plans to divert a portion of the Jordan River.

Nearly a decade earlier, in 1955, President Eisenhower's envoy, Eric Johnston, had proposed an agreement whereby a series of pipelines would be built to enable Lebanon, Syria, Jordan, and Israel to use the waters of the Jordan and Yarmuk rivers to cultivate their lands, with 60 percent of the water going to the Arab states and 40 percent allocated to Israel. According to Miles Copeland, the former CIA man in Cairo, President Nasser reacted positively to the Jordan River project, but was nevertheless compelled to reject it, explaining to Johnston in 1956 that "you find me at a time when I am unable to take an unpopular action."[1] The Johnston Plan was vetoed by Egypt and the other Arab states, which reasoned that any cooperative venture with the Israelis would imply recognition and acceptance of the legitimacy of the Jewish state.

In 1963, the Israelis announced their plans to unilaterally implement the terms of the Johnston Plan by building a pipeline in northern Israel that would draw their 40 percent share of the Jordan River into the Negev Desert in the south for the irrigation of agricultural lands. Nasser then called his January 1964 summit conference to organize Arab resistance to the Israeli project.

The Arab summit passed several anti-Zionist resolutions: steps would be taken to draw off water at the Jordan River headwaters in Lebanon and Syria to reduce its southward flow into Israel; an Arab Defense Pact with a "Unified Arab Command" would be established to coordinate troop movements and military intelligence among the Arab nations in preparation for a confrontation with Israel; and a Palestinian resistance movement would be organized to enable the Palestinian people "to play their role in the liberation of their country and their self-determination."[2] The last item, though overtly aimed at Israel, held ominous implications for the future of Hashemite rule in Arab Palestine.

The formation of the Palestine Liberation Organization represented a direct challenge to Hussein's claim to speak for the Palestinian Arabs. The appointment of the pro-Egyptian Palestinian lawyer Ahmad Shuqairy, hand-picked by Nasser, to head the newly-created PLO planted the seeds for the growth of an indigenous power base in Jordan that could one day provide a Palestinian alternative to the Hashemite throne. The immediate threat was the future of the Jordanian-controlled West Bank. The Egyptian hold on the Gaza Strip was purported to be temporary. The Palestinian Arabs living there had been denied Egyptian citizenship, their status remaining as stateless natives and refugees awaiting the establishment of Arab rule over all of Palestine. A campaign by the pro-Egyptian Shuqairy to transfer control of the Gaza to a PLO dominated by Cairo would be welcomed by Nasser, who saw this as a way of undermining Hussein's rule on the West Bank, a step toward the eventual incorporation of all of Jordan's land into an Arab union led by Egypt.

The Hashemites, however, had formally annexed the West Bank, granting Jordanian citizenship to its inhabitants in keeping with Abdullah's proclamation on the eve of the 1948 assault against the Jews. "Palestine and Transjordan are one," the King had declared, "for Palestine is the coastline and Transjordan the hinterland of the same country."[3] The West Bank takeover by Abdullah's Arab Legion was not viewed by the rulers in Amman as an annexation of conquered territory, but rather as the reunification of a country. A call for a PLO state on the West Bank, linked with the Gaza Strip and under the leadership of the pro-Nasserite Shuqairy, meant the breakup of the Hashemite Kingdom forged by Abdullah and was thus unacceptable to Hussein.

In deference to the Hashemites, the Palestine National Covenant —adopted by the 422 members of the Palestine National Council who attended the PLO's founding conference in Jordanian-controlled East Jerusalem in May and June of 1964—specifically exempted the West Bank and Gaza from the demand for the liberation of Palestine. But just a few months later, on 2 July, 1964, PLO Chairman Shuqairy issued a statement in Amman asserting that the entire Kingdom of Jordan, including the Jordanian-controlled West Bank, was part of the original land of Palestine.[4] The defiant signal to Hussein was clear: the PLO would seek not only to dislodge the Jews from Palestine, but to end Hashemite rule in favor of Palestinian sovereignty. It was a position that had been foreshadowed by the Mufti's 1948 formation of a Government of All Palestine, which rejected Jordanian control of the West Bank, and it was one which Hussein hoped he had overcome when he clashed with Arab leaders at the 1960 Shtura Conference in Lebanon.

In September 1959, at the thirty-second session of the Arab League in Casablanca, Egypt had tabled a proposal for the creation of a "Palestine entity." At the follow-up conference in Cairo five months later, debate over Nasser's plan to establish a separate Palestinian entity and army erupted into a tense confrontation between Jordanian and Egyptian representatives. "We do not recognize the existence of a Palestine status," the Jordanian foreign minister, Moussa Nasser, declared, "because there exists but one people, which owes its allegiance to King Hussein."[5] The Iraqi leader, Brigadier Abd al-Karim Kassem—the man who had led the coup against the Hashemites that took the life of Hussein's cousin Feisal II the previous year—supported Nasser's advocacy of a distinct Palestinian state and military force, though he was determined to block any attempts toward Egyptian hegemony. The Jordanian delegation was reported to have vehemently denounced Egypt's "Palestinian entity" plan as "subversive to the union enforced in 1949 between the original nation of Transjordan and the Arab sector of Palestine."[6]

When the issue of a Palestinian homeland separate from Jordan arose again at the Arab League's Shtura Conference in September 1960, the debate ended in a deadlock, with the Egyptian proposal assigned to a committee charged with "the drafting of a plan to 'recover' Palestine and report such a plan to the League as soon as possible."[7] One Israeli observer at the time noted that at Shtura, the Hashemite ruler found himself locked in a struggle for his very survival, cornered by a two-pronged attack from an Iraq and Egypt in competition with each other yet nevertheless united in their determination to challenge the king's continued reign in western Palestine: "King Hussein's representatives were forced into a serious discussion of the possibility of putting into effect ideas whose realization would amount to the dismemberment of the Hashemite Kingdom. President Nasser's delegation kindly invited the Jordanian Foreign Minister to cooperate in political action that would assure the gradual suicide of the state whose existence and international status he was supposed to defend."[8]

Many Israelis were not eager to see Hussein submit to the "gradual suicide" that would find Jordanian rule on the West Bank replaced by an independent Palestinian entity backed by a powerful Egypt and a radical Iraq. Israel may have grudgingly reconciled itself to Hashemite sovereignty in eastern Palestine and Jordanian jurisdiction over portions of western Palestine (that is, the West Bank territories of Judea and Samaria), but the establishment of a Palestinian regime in the region whose legitimacy and purpose stemmed from an abiding dedication to the complete eradication of the Jewish state could have disastrous consequences.

The dark prediction regarding the dangers of a PLO state in the region was far from infallible. Some could assert, as Ariel Sharon did during the Black September uprising in 1970, that the overthrow of the Hashemite dynasty and its replacement with a Palestinian state ruled by an indigenous leadership would provide a legitimate outlet for Palestinian national aspirations and perhaps thereby dampen the need to continue the assault against Israel. Sharon remained convinced, however, that the West Bank territories of Judea and Samaria were crucial to Israeli security, and that therefore, a PLO state must not encompass those areas: the Palestinians could take power in Amman, not Jerusalem and Hebron, confining their jurisdiction to the lands east of the Jordan River. For Sharon, Israel could passively acquiesce or even actively encourage a PLO takeover in Jordan, but its political leadership, backed by the full weight of its army, would have to resist any Arab attempt to retake control of the strategic West Bank highlands.

Regardless of its possible implications for Israel, the creation of the PLO by the Arab Summit Conference of January 1964 and the creation of the Palestine Liberation Army during the PLO's first council meeting the following June, gave implicit recognition to a Palestinian leadership independent of Jordan. Several observers in Amman concluded that the immediate threat to the Hashemite Kingdom came not from the Jewish state but from their Arab brothers in Cairo, Baghdad, and the West Bank. In the fall of 1965, Hussein reportedly held meetings with the Israeli foreign minister. He wanted the cooperation between Israel and Jordan in blocking PLO power to continue.

Two years later, Hussein was unable to avoid being seduced into joining Nasser's war against Israel. The Egyptian president had convinced the king that a lightening victory over the Jews was imminent. On 17 May, 1967, Nasser had ordered United Nations peace-keeping forces stationed along the Egyptian-Israeli border to leave the area, and then turn over their positions in the Gaza Strip to the PLO's Palestine Liberation Army. On 22 May, he imposed a blockade of Israeli shipping through the Straits of Tiran. Hussein then summoned the Egyptian ambassador to Jordan and told him that he wanted to meet with Nasser in Cairo. On 30 May, the king flew to Egypt's Almaza Air Force Base, stepped into Nasser's limousine, and offered to sign a full-scale military pact with Egypt. His cooperation agreement with Israel concerning Palestinian terrorism was a short-term tactical maneuver; Hussein would not let it deter him from entering into an all out war to destroy the Jewish nation.

According to Peter Snow, Hussein's decision to join Nasser in 1967 was a ploy to win the hearts of the Palestinians, who were growing increasingly restless at the inability of the Hashemites to dislodge the Jews from Palestine: "Popular resentment against him [Hussein], particularly on the West Bank, would be uncontrollable if he refused to take up Nasser's challenge to Israel. His cousin, Zeid bin Shaker, who commanded one of Hussein's tank brigades at the time, says Hussein went to war in '67 because there would have been civil war if he had not. Hussein himself says that his reasons were essentially moral ones: he felt bound by the Arab Defense Pact of 1964 that they had all signed in Cairo, and says that he simply could not stand aside while all the other Arabs fought."[9]

The monarch's entry into the war was also essential if he was to avoid being left in isolation from the rest of the Arab world. No doubt the distinct possibility that the Arabs would emerge victorious in 1967 and leave Israel in ruins also proved an irresistible temptation for Hussein.

In 1956, when U.S. envoy Eric Johnston tried in vain to persuade Nasser to buck Arab public opinion and agree to the Jordan River Project worked out with Israel, he left a meeting in frustration, then turned to the Egyptian and said, "Mr. President, I am reminded of the words of the French revolutionary leader: 'The mob is in the streets. I must find out where it is going, for I am its leader.' "[10] Though directed at Nasser, the point was sadly appropos of Hussein in 1967, if reports regarding the king's reservations about joining the war are correct. Despite instincts that told him the Arabs were not yet ready for a fight with Israel, Hussein signed a military pact with Egypt, mobilized his forces, and accepted Nasser's conditions for joining the war effort, partly out of a need to align himself with fellow Arab leaders, partly from a hunger for victory, and partly from a desire to hang on to his throne by following the mob in its march against the Jews. "He had no alternative," Anwar Khatib, governor of the West Bank at the time, explained. "If he didn't take part all the people would blame him that because he didn't take an active part they lost the war. He couldn't behave otherwise."[11]

Whatever his motivation, be it the survival of his monarchy or the smell of victory against the Jews, Hussein's desire to enter the fighting in 1967 was fully exploited by Nasser, who insisted that PLO chief Shuqairy—based in the Gaza after having been expelled by Hussein for anti-Jordanian activity—be allowed to return with the king to Amman as a symbol of Jordanian-Palestinian solidarity. Nasser was determined to let the PLO share in the glory of the impending victory over the Jews, and the king felt he had little choice but to agree to the Egyptian president's preconditions for an alliance. Hussein was willing to subject his Kingdom to renewed challenges from Shuqairy's Palestinian nationalists if it would keep him from being left out of the *jihad* against Israel.

According to one observer on the scene, the king's decision to join Nasser's alliance and his acquiescence to the demand for Shuqairy's return to Jordan appeared to bear fruit: "That afternoon Hussein returned from his six-hour Cairo visit. There were massive ovations in Amman. Young men who had cursed his name the day before now lifted his car up from the street and carried the monarch and his Mercedes for a few steps of symbolic triumph."[12]

The Palestinian leader and the Hashemite king were now linked under the alliance orchestrated by Nasser. "Let's throw the Jews into the sea, to the last man," Shuqairy said, uttering for the first time the now-historic phrase. "Anywhere you find the Jews, kill them, with your weapons, with your fingernails, with your teeth," said Hussein.[13]

Despite the secret talks with the Israeli prime minister's emissary in London in 1963, the Paris meeting with the Israeli foreign minister in 1965, and the combined Israeli-Jordanian efforts against Palestinian terrorism that followed, the king was fully committed to the 1967 war against Israel. Two battalions of Egyptian commandos, consisting of 1,200 men, were flown into Amman and stationed along the West Bank. Plans called for the arrival of Iraqi, Syrian, and Saudi Arabian troops. The newly-appointed Israeli defense minister, Moshe Dayan, sent a personal appeal to Hussein: "If you do not stop mobilization of troops, the next time I speak to you will be through the antennas of my tanks."

On the morning of 5 June, after Israeli fighter pilots launched their pre-emptive strike against Egyptian targets, Prime Minister Eshkol sent a final urgent message to Jordan via the chief of the United Nations peace-keeping force, General Odd Bull, who was stationed in Jerusalem: "We shall not initiate any action whatsoever against Jordan. However, should Jordan open hostilities, we shall resist with all our might, and King Hussein will have to bear the consequences."[14]

Hussein ordered his air force into action. They bombed Tel Aviv, Netanya, and the airport at Lod. Jordanian ground forces launched an artillery barrage into the Israeli sector in west Jerusalem. Once Jordan joined the fray, Israeli intelligence switched from its role as courier, carrying appeals for Arab diplomacy and restraint, to one which called for the implementation of a sophisticated plan of deception designed to confuse the enemy and lure it into defeat. At a relay station in the Sinai, radio messages between the Arab commands in Cairo and Amman were intercepted by the Israelis, who had managed to crack the coded transmissions. New messages were quickly re-broadcast to both of the Arab capitals, a process referred to in intelligence circles as "cooking." Those sent to Amman gave false assurances to Hussein that the Egyptian front was going well, that Israeli warplanes on their way to destroy the Jordanian air force were in fact Egyptian aircraft, and that Jordan's forces should be re-routed to the Hebron area to support a fictional Egyptian counterattack in the Sinai, all of which helped the Israeli army press its advantage. Israel wound up capturing the entire West Bank, east Jerusalem, the Gaza Strip, the Sinai Peninsula, and the Golan Heights.[15]

Having previously joined Israel in a series of covert diplomatic encounters designed to block the common threat posed by Palestinian extremists who were eyeing Hussein's West Bank territories and possibly his throne in Amman as well, Hussein in 1967 felt compelled to reject a tacit understanding that would have prevented a direct confrontation with the Jewish state. The result was the loss of Jerusalem and the West Bank and a Palestinian disillusionment with the Hashemite regime that triggered an escalation of terrorism and the eventual Black September showdown between Hussein and the PLO in 1970.

With the loss of Jerusalem and the West Bank, it became even more evident to the king that covert security cooperation rather than open military confrontation with the Jews was the more prudent path to a safe monarchy in Jordan. After the devastating defeat of 1967, the prospects were dim for winning the return of Jordan's former territories in Jerusalem and the West Bank through force of arms. Similarly, the realization of Palestinian national aspirations in the region was unlikely to occur as a result of conditions imposed by Arab armies.

Three months after the Six Day War of June 1967, Hussein agreed to another secret meeting with an Israeli official in London.

19

All or Nothing

LONDON served as a convenient venue for the Hussein-Israeli talks. The king frequently traveled to the Jewish physician's clinic on Harley Street for medical check-ups. His ongoing visits there served as a useful cover for the secret contacts with Israeli officials. During his stays in London, the king was routinely guarded by Scotland Yard and British intelligence, yet both the Israelis and the Jordanians reasoned that it was best to keep the British authorities uninformed about the rendezvous at the clinic if absolute security was to be ensured. Neither side could be certain what the British position would be on the talks. Would they approve? Would they leak it to the press? Would they ask to play a direct role in the negotiations?

The king even took measures to keep all knowledge of the meetings from several of his own bodyguards. His grandfather Abdullah had been assassinated by Palestinian Arabs in the employ of a relative of Abdullah's rival, Mufti Haj Husseini. King Hussein was convinced that a similar conspiracy hatched by Palestinian gunmen in Jordan could easily penetrate the ranks of his inner circle. Nearly all of Hussein's most trusted advisers were excluded from the covert diplomacy with the Israelis. Only a small group of Jordanian security officials were privy to the meetings, and once in London, they worked closely with Israeli intelligence to protect the king.

Hussein's London encounters in the late 1960s involved a series of negotiating sessions with Israeli Foreign Minister Abba Eban and Deputy Prime Minister Yigal Allon. The Israeli official slated for the particular session would arrive at the clinic, reportedly on a private visit to receive medical treatment, and dismiss his British escorts as he remained alone in the waiting room. Hours later, King Hussein would show up, also telling his hosts that he was in need of medical treatment, excusing his British companions as he entered the doctor's office. The Jordanians and the Israelis would then slip out the back exits, regrouping in a nearby building to conduct their business.

169

On 24 December, 1968, Hussein flew to London for a reported "private visit" following an Arab summit conference held in Raabat, Morocco.[1] He had been suffering from a stress-induced jaw ailment and was grinding his teeth down on both sides. On 6 January, 1969, the king returned to London, telling reporters at the airport that he had arrived "for what he hoped would be the last stage of a protracted period of medical treatment."[2] His jaw was in fact operated on by London surgeons.[3] In 1968, Yigal Allon also traveled with his Israeli physician, Dr. Sadeh, to consult with British specialists regarding a weak muscle that was causing facial disfigurement. While in London, Allon held a meeting with Hussein.

Allon had come up with a proposal for a joint Israeli-Jordanian presence in the West Bank territories of Judea and Samaria barely six weeks after their capture from Hussein during the Six Day War of June 1967. The pre-1967 border had left Israel with 60 percent of its population confined to a coastal plain bordering the Mediterranean on the west and only fifteen miles deep at its widest point. The irregular armistice line separating Israel from the Jordanian-controlled West Bank territories curved its way through the countryside, narrowing the Jewish state down to a strip of land a mere nine miles wide before hitting the Jordanian frontier in the east. An armored vehicle traveling at 55 mph could set out from the Jordanian border and reach Israel's main population centers in ten minutes. The highlands of the West Bank and the densely populated Arab villages spread throughout offered an effective staging area for artillery strikes and terrorist raids against Israeli cities. With its tiny population, Israel lacked the manpower to organize a large standing army, and its defense had to rely on reserve forces that could be quickly mobilized in the early hours of an attack.

The long frontier with Jordan and the narrowness of the Jewish state denied Israel the strategic depth necessary for it to absorb the opening rounds of an assault against its borders. The closeness of the Jordanian front lines meant that Arab troops could reach Israeli homes before there was time for a full mobilization of the Israel Defense Forces. It also meant that the country could be cut in two by a concentrated attack aimed at its narrow nine-mile wide center. In addition, its capital, Jerusalem, was divided, with Arab forces deployed in the eastern sector. Its port at Haifa was only twenty-one miles from the Jordanian border, and Tel Aviv, its largest city, was a mere fifteen miles from the frontier.

Ezer Weizman, the former Israeli Air Force chief and minister of defense, wrote that Arab control over the highlands of western Palestine, which offered a strategic advantage over the Jewish urban areas centered in the lowlands along the coast, pushed Israeli military planners into adopting a posture based on a hair-trigger readiness to mobilize forces quickly and thrust the bulk of the fighting onto the other side of the border.

Prior to the 1967 war, Israel's strategy was defensive. Israel had no ambitions to expand its territory. However, in the event of an outbreak of war, our army would obviously be ordered to lose no time in carrying the battle into enemy territory—principally because of our lack of any strategic depth.

The West Bank was like a bone in Israel's throat. It was the ideal springboard for an attack on Israel. One of the first war games staged by our army was based on the assumption that the Jordanians and the Iraqis had moved into the West Bank, from which they would launch their thrust into Israel. The war game was conducted in the area lying between Ra'anana, Herzlia, and Beersheba. We calculated that Jordan would occupy Ramleh and Lod.[4]

The occupation of the West Bank in 1967 allowed Israeli planners to dispense with a military strategy that conceded the capture of Israeli cities such as Ramleh and Lod in a future war against Jordan. Initially, there was talk of reaching a political arrangement with the Arab inhabitants on the West Bank that might reduce the need for a defensive line against hostile forces along the western frontier. At last liberated from Hashemite rule, the West Bank Arabs might grasp at the opportunity to finally establish an independent state as outlined in the original 1947 U.N. Partition Resolution in exchange for a peace agreement with Israel.

Eight days after the cease-fire ending the Six Day War, a group of Arab notables agreed to meet with Chaim Herzog, the West Bank's military governor at the time, former director of military intelligence, future president of Israel, and brother of Yaacov Herzog, the emissary who had secretly met with Hussein in London. Gathering at the home of Jordan's ambassador to London, Anwar Nusseibeh, Herzog presented them with a plan to set up an Arab state on the West Bank with economic and political ties to Jordan, yet ruled independently by the local inhabitants. The solution (in essence, an autonomous Palestinian state federated with Jordan) that was to become the Arab magic formula for peace in the 1980s was being offered by Herzog within days of Israel's occupation of the West Bank. It was rejected out-of-hand by Arab Jerusalem's mayor, Rouhi al-Khatib, and the other city council members, government officials, and political leaders who had come to Nusseibeh's home to hear Herzog's proposal. Though there were some Palestinians who seriously considered the Israeli offer, such as the mayor of Hebron, Sheik Mohammed Ali Jaabari, many more either lacked the foresight to compromise, feared reprisals from the Hashemite regime, felt convinced of an inevitable Zionist exploitation of a foundering West Bank state under the thumb of Israeli political and military might, or merely remained unwilling to reach any kind of settlement with a Jewish nation.[5]

As the option of establishing a Palestinian state on the West Bank at peace with Israel was closed, the path was opened for Yigal Allon's plan for a string of military outposts to be built in the unpopulated regions of Judea in the southern portion of the West Bank and in the Jordan Valley area running northward, in effect creating a defensive line that moved the frontier straight up to the Jordan River. By expanding its strategic depth through the construction of army settlements on the West Bank, Israel's population centers along the Mediterranean would no longer be subject to a lightening strike from the eastern front, and Palestinian terrorists would no longer enjoy the freedom of operating from bases in the West Bank highlands. The importance for Israel of a continued military presence in the territories captured from Jordan in the Six Day War was outlined in the appendix to a memorandum prepared on 29 June, 1967 by the chairman of the U.S. Joint Chiefs of Staff, Earle G. Wheeler:

Discussion of Key Israeli Border Areas [see map, p. 173]
1. *The Jordanian West Bank*
    a. Threat. The Jordanian-Israeli border is 330 miles in length extending from the Gulf of Aqaba northward to the Dead Sea, thence following the armistice demarcation lines and the Jordan River northward to the Yarmuk River, thence along the Yarmuk River to the Syrian frontier. This border area has traditionally been lightly held by military forces and defenses consisted mainly of small, widely separated outposts and patrols and, therefore, afforded an area where launching of saboteurs and terrorists into Israel was relatively easy. During the period January 1965 to February 1967, a total of 53 incidents of sabotage and mining activity took place along this border. These activities resulted in three killed, 35 wounded, and damage to houses, roads, bridges, railroads, and water and electric power installations in Israel. Instances of exchange of small arms fire occurred quite frequently. The majority of these events took place from the Mount Hebron and Aravah areas where the Jordanian authorities did not take sufficient measures to protect against line crosses and saboteurs. The high ground running north-south through the middle of West Jordan overlooks Israel's narrow midsection and offers a route for a thrust to the sea which would split the country in two parts.
    b. Requirements. A boundary along the commanding terrain overlooking the Jordan River from the west could provide a shorter defense line. However, as a minimum, Israel would need a defense line generally along the axis Bardala-Tubas-Nablus-Bira-Jerusalem and then to the northern part of the Dead Sea. This line would widen the narrow portion of Israel and provide additional terrain for the defense of Tel Aviv. It would provide additional buffer for the air base at Bersheeba. In addition, this line would give a portion of the foothills to Israel and avoid interdiction by artillery in

N

LEBANON

UN ZONE

SYRIA

GOLAN
HEIGHTS

MEDITERRANEAN
SEA

SEA OF GALILEE

Bardala

Tubas

Herzliyya

Nablus

X'

WEST
BANK

JORDAN RIVER

Tel Aviv

Bira

DEAD SEA

Jerusalem

GAZA
STRIP

•Bersheeba

JORDAN

ISRAEL

EGYPT

0   20   40   60

Km

CROSS SECTION

X

X'

1000

Nablus

600

JORDAN
RIVER

Herzliyya

200

M

WEST BANK

0   10   20   30   40   50   60   70   80   Km

Israel and the West Bank Territories of Judea and Samaria

the Israeli villages in the lowlands. This line would also provide a shorter defense line than the border of 4 June 1967 and would reduce the Jordanian salient into Israel. It also provides adequate lines of communications for lateral movement.[6]

In the immediate aftermath of the Six Day War, both American and Israeli analysts recognized the security assets of the West Bank. Since then, though the scope of settlement envisioned as necessary for Israel's acquisition of those assets has differed, there has been a high degree of consensus among the Israeli leadership regarding the need for some kind of military presence in the West Bank region. Moshe Dayan and Ezer Weizman broke with Menachem Begin over what they considered to be a not so subtle attempt to undermine the Camp David promises of Arab autonomy on the West Bank, denouncing the enactment of "provocative settlement programs and unnecessary land confiscations" that included the establishment of the Eilon Moreh settlement by members of the militant Jewish Gush Emunim religious group.[7] Nevertheless, both men agreed that a direct Israeli role on the West Bank was vital to Israel's security. During the 1977 talks that paved the way to Camp David, Moshe Dayan, then Begin's foreign minister, met President Carter in Washington and decided to boldly express his assessment of Israel's security needs to the new president: "One thing he should know immediately: in my view, if the West Bank were annexed to Jordan, it would lead to the destruction of the State of Israel. It would mean our return to the pre-1967 borders; the dismantling of our military installations on the mountain ridges; and the pull-back of our armed forces from the Jordan Valley. The territory would be ruled by the PLO, and would serve as a base for a devastating attack on Israel."[8]

Shmuel Katz—a political rival of Dayan's who served as Begin's spokesman in the United States and represented those Israelis who felt that Jews had a right to total sovereignty on the West Bank—insisted that the West Bank lands of Judea and Samaria had been part of the Jewish historic homeland in Palestine and that they had been unjustly cut off by the United Nations and later held by Jordan, a nation created by the British and likewise established on land rightfully owed to the Jews. However, in a conversation with Carter's national security adviser, Zbigniew Brzezinski, Katz left the Biblical arguments over ancient Israeli claims to scholars and theologians and made a point of emphasizing modern Israel's security needs and political rights in the West Bank. He had just assured the Americans that the new Begin government would honor U.N. Resolution 242, which called for an Israeli withdrawal from territories occupied in 1967 in exchange for a peace settlement with the Arabs. "I do not want a withdrawal," Katz told Brzezinski, "but it is feasible under Resolution 242." Brzezinski then asked if this also pertained to the West Bank:

> I [*Katz*]: Correct, but I hope it will not come to a withdrawal, because the whole of Judea and Samaria, apart from the question of our rights, are necessary for our security.
>
> B [*Brzezinski*]: Does the use of the names Judea and Samaria indicate your firm resolve not to make concessions?
>
> I [*Katz*]: Judea and Samaria have been the names of those areas since ancient times. No political significance actually attaches to the use of them. It is the use of the name "the West Bank" that has a negative political connotation. To change the names of the areas is tantamount to changing the legal status quo.
>
> B [*Brzezinski*]: In any case, if you do contemplate the possibility of withdrawal, what will become of the settlements beyond the line of retreat?
>
> I [*Katz*]: Nothing. What should happen to them?
>
> B [*Brzezinski*]: Well, you'll have to dismantle them.
>
> I [*Katz*]: Why? Regardless of my view of the solution, or any other view, what you say has grave moral implications. Why can Jews not live in an area ruled by Arabs, just as Arabs live in the State of Israel? You are, after all, speaking of peacetime conditions. Or am I to assume that you are not talking about peace, but only about withdrawal?[9]

Previously, when Yigal Allon met with King Hussein in London in 1968, he was eager to talk peace *and* withdrawal. Under his proposal, though it appeared faithful to Israel's security needs as later articulated by Weizmann, Dayan, and the U.S. Joint Chiefs of Staff, and was cognizant of the rights of Jewish settlement as expressed by Katz, Begin, and others, the establishment of military outposts in the unpopulated areas of Judea and Samaria would be accompanied by a call for "immediate negotiations with Arab leaders of the West Bank with the idea of forming an Arab autonomous district in all the area not included in the Jewish territory that would be linked economically with Israel and buttressed by a mutual security pact".[10]

Hussein heeded the plan's call for negotiations, though still insisting they be held in secret, yet in his meeting with its author Allon in London the king rejected any arrangement that might leave Israeli forces on the West Bank. Assurances that the Israeli presence would be a limited one, confined to unpopulated areas away from Arab towns and villages, were not enough. The king wanted the entire region returned to him, including east Jerusalem.

What seemed like a maximalist position to the Israelis perhaps seemed like the minimum route acceptable to Hussein, given the radicalized nature of the Arab world. According to Mideast researcher Rosemary Sayigh, the PLO, led by Arafat's Fateh faction, still refused to accept Jewish sovereignty over any parcel of Palestine, however small, be it the West Bank of the Jordan River or the coastal plain along the Mediterranean coast. "For Fateh's leaders," wrote Sayigh, "the urgent need created by the 1967 defeat was to prevent the Arab governments from negotiating, from a position of weakness, an end to the Palestinian liberation struggle in return for Israeli withdrawal from the territories occupied in the June War."[11] The PLO appeared to succeed when Arab leaders adopted the three "no's," vowing "no peace with Israel, no negotiations with Israel, no recognition of Israel" at the Khartoum conference of August 1967.[12] Hussein may have been willing to secretly violate the second "no" prohibiting negotiations with the Jewish state, but he was bent on recovering east Jerusalem and the West Bank territories before making the slightest move toward an abandonment of the injunctions against peace and recognition.

Allon pressed on, trying to sell the king on a political settlement. Hussein repeated the line: he had to regain the territories lost in the Six Day War. At one point, Allon asked, Why did you go to war with us in 1967 when we warned you to stay out? It was your fault, Hussein answered, Israel's behavior in the weeks leading up to the 1967 fighting gave the impression that it was so weak that the king had no choice but to run to Cairo, meet Nasser, and join in the war. The remark in part contradicted reports that Hussein was pushed into the fight, that his decision was simply an attempt to avert civil unrest by disgruntled Palestinians and to avoid alienation from fellow Arab leaders, rather than an aggressive move designed to exploit Israeli weakness.

Indeed, in the days prior to the Six Day War, Israel did seem to offer Hussein a tempting target. As Nasser was mobilizing his forces, Israel's leaders had hesitated. The public and the army began to lose confidence in the government. On 28 May, Prime Minister Eshkol gave a radio address to rally the nation. "The speech was awaited with expectancy," Dayan recalled. "In every house throughout the country, in every tent and tank in the field, ears were glued to the radio set. At last there would be a clear analysis of the crisis, a lucid presentation of government thinking. But the prime minister faltered and bumbled through his address, stumbling over the words."[13]

The day after the speech, on 29 May, the Israeli public felt itself increasingly imperiled as Nasser continued his tough talk while Arab armies continued their threatening moves against the Jewish state. The editorial in the Israeli daily *Haaretz* added to the growing chorus of concern surrounding Prime Minister Eshkol, who was also serving as Minister of Defense: "As long as Mr. Eshkol continues as Prime Minister and Minister of Defense, what good are traditional advisors? If we had confidence in Mr. Eshkol's ability to steer the ship of state in these troubled times we would willingly follow him; but this certainly is lacking, and more and more people feel this. Mr. Eshkol's address last night over Kol Israel has served to enlarge their number. He is not cut out to be Prime Minister and Minister of Defense in the present situation."[14]

The Israelis were not the only ones listening to Kol Israel and reading *Haaretz*. The next day, 30 May, King Hussein flew to Cairo. He signed a military pact aligning himself with Nasser in the upcoming war. It was Israel's fault, Hussein told Allon. Its apparent weakness left him no choice but to attack.

In his meeting with the king, Allon put forward his government's position regarding the need for security outposts along the West Bank. The Allon Plan was not rooted in chauvinistic ideas of conquest, he explained, but practical concerns essential to the survival of the Jewish state. If I were you, I would suggest the same thing, Hussein said. But I cannot accept it and remain on my throne. The king continued his refrain: the return of the West Bank, free of Jews, and the return of Arab Jerusalem.

By the time of Allon's 1968 meeting with Hussein, the Israelis had already decided the fate of Jerusalem. They would allow for Arab jurisdiction over the Islamic holy places, but they would not agree to re-divide the city. Realizing that a political breakthrough with the king was unlikely, the Israelis reconciled themselves to a unilateral implementation of the Allon Plan, parceling off strategic areas and erecting fences on the West Bank in preparation for the construction of a line of military outposts. But although he was forced to temporarily abandon hopes for achieving a political settlement, Allon nevertheless stressed to the king the importance of continuing the practical arrangements concerning security along the Israeli-Jordanian border. Hussein was sympathetic, but the disillusionment with his regime that followed in the wake of the 1967 defeat led him to believe that unless he gave the Palestinians an outlet for their anger, they would soon turn on him. That outlet, of course, was Israel. Not only was the political dialogue between Hussein and the Israelis at a stalemate, but now even the fruits of the practical dialogue begun with Yaacov Herzog in 1963 were in jeopardy.

20

All the King's Men

FOLLOWING Yigal Allon's discussion with Hussein, Israeli Foreign Minister Abba Eban held his own meeting with the king in London. The results were more or less the same as with Allon. This time, however, the Israelis wanted to let Washington in on the dealings. The United States had been pressuring Israel to give up the occupied territories in exchange for a peace agreement with Hussein. The Israelis wanted the United States to know that it was sincere in its search for a negotiated settlement, and as proof would inform them of the secret contacts with Hussein. The king did not object. He too saw the benefit in telling Washington. His meetings with the Israelis would testify to his commitment to a moderate course. The White House would probably consent to a request for increased financial and military aid from the head of a pro-Western Arab regime willing to at least work with Israel in private.

After Abba Eban's London talk with the king in 1968, the Americans were informed of Israel's undercover diplomacy with Hussein. Eban flew to Washington and reported directly to President Johnson. Secrecy remained a priority. During the session with Johnson, Eban even asked the Israeli Ambassador, Yitzak Rabin, to excuse himself from the meeting. It was then that he gave Johnson the details of Israel's encounters with the king.

A review of Israeli-Jordanian relations in 1968 would have had to include a bleak assessment of possible breakthroughs on the diplomatic front. The Israelis, especially those in the Labor Party of Prime Minister Eshkol, were bent on continuing the secret talks. Menachem Begin, then a cabinet minister from the opposition serving in the National Unity coalition, rejected the territorial concessions on the West Bank envisioned under the Allon Plan and opposed any direct contacts between the prime minister and Hussein. Later, as prime minister himself, one of Begin's first moves would be to request his own meeting with Hussein to discuss peace. But in 1968,

Begin would go only so far as to consent to the Allon and Eban meetings with the king to explore the minimum conditions for a political settlement with Jordan. Eban told one interviewer that the report of the King's "total rejection" of the Allon Plan elicited a satisfied chuckle from Begin.[1]

In 1968, the deadlock in the political discussions with Hussein was not the only setback. The king's ambivalence toward the PLO was undermining the delicate policing arrangements with Israel that had been designed to keep the Israeli-Jordanian frontier quiet.

The debacle of 1967 had brought King Hussein's prestige to a low, but his subsequent decision to indulge the Palestinian guerrillas in hopes of deflecting their violence away from his regime and onto Israeli was a strategic mistake nearly as disastrous as the one that brought him into the Six Day War.

In 1967, Israel had urged the king without success to stay out of the fighting; the result was the breakup of his kingdom. In 1968, the Israelis implored Hussein to continue to apply the coordinated security agreement that had been worked out with Prime Minister Eshkol's emissary in 1963. Again, the king rebuffed the Israelis, and instead gave comfort to the Palestinian commandos whose frustration over the 1967 defeat had primed them for a renewed terrorist onslaught. The decision was a boon to the PLO. Arafat's lieutenant, Abu Iyad, who harbored a deep resentment toward Hussein, nevertheless admitted that the king's actions helped swell the ranks of the Palestinian resistance and contributed to the Fateh faction's takeover of the guerrilla movement: "The Six Day War opened new prospects for our development. The Jordanian regime was too weak to oppose us. King Hussein released the Palestinian patriots he had locked up in the years preceding the conflict. More importantly, he closed his eyes to the bases we were establishing along the Jordan River to serve as launching points for the fedayeen. We also got help from the local population and the Jordanian armed forces, with which we established excellent relations."[2]

Arafat and Iyad's operational headquarters in Jordan were established at Karameh, a village in the highlands about five miles north of the Allenby Bridge and two miles from the Jordan River, where Israeli troops were stationed on the other side throughout the West Bank region. Karameh was the reason Moshe Dayan ordered his air force into action on 15 February, 1968, the first Israeli air strike since the Six Day War. Towns along the Jordan Valley had come under increasing attack from Palestinian terrorists. Explosives had been planted at Kibbutz Gesher, a resident was ambushed and killed at Kibbutz Maoz Chaim, and, on the night of 15 February, two farming settlements plus Kibbutz Kfar Ruppin were raked by heavy shelling pouring in from across the Jordanian border, striking silos, stables, and a children's dormitory that had been evacuated just prior to the attack. Moshe Dayan had been touring the region and witnessed the artillery barrage firsthand. He ordered Israeli pilots to launch retaliatory strikes against the PLO's gun emplacements on the other side of the Jordan. The bombing at Karameh triggered a mass exodus from the area, leaving behind only one thousand villagers out of a population of fifteen thousand.[3] The Jordanian village all but deserted, Karameh's sole function became that of a military headquarters for PLO terrorists.

A month later, on 18 March, 1968, a mine exploded on a road twenty-five miles north of Eilat. A bus carrying students from the Herzliya school in Tel Aviv had been on a trip through the Negev. Two children were killed in the explosion, seven others wounded. The same day, Yassir Arafat and Abu Iyad held a meeting in Amman with the Jordanian chief of staff, General Amer Khammash. The general reiterated what the Jordanian intelligence officer al-Hajj Arabiyat had told them ten days earlier: the Israelis were planning a large-scale ground assault against Karameh. The information had been uncovered by the CIA and passed along to Jordanian officials. General Khammash advised Arafat and Iyad to take the necessary precautions.[4]

Three days later, the Israeli Air Force dropped pamphlets over Karameh, warning the remaining residents that they would be attacking in two hours and that all noncombatants should flee the area.[5] An armored force then set out for the Allenby Bridge, crossed the Jordan River, and headed north into Karameh. The column consisted of tanks and half-tracks carrying paratroop commandos. One unit broke away to intercept the Jordanian army along the eastern perimeter at Es Salt; the other advanced on the Palestinian stronghold. Assault helicopters dropped another contingent of Israeli paratroopers behind enemy lines along the northern hills surrounding the village in an attempt to block the PLO escape route. A third force moved across the Damiyah Bridge to complete the pincer movement against the guerrilla fighters deployed nineteen miles to the south.[6]

Israeli leaders speculated that Hussein would not commit his forces in defense of Karameh unless his army came under direct attack by Israel. To assure the king that the invading force had no intention of striking Amman, the Israeli Air Force dropped leaflets stating that the action was directed solely against the terrorist base at Karameh. Kol Israel, the Israeli radio service, announced that Israeli troops were not to engage regular Jordanian forces.[7]

Despite Israel's intention to avoid a fight with Jordan, Hussein decided to throw his army into the battle. Under the command of General Mashur Haditha, Jordanian artillery opened up from fortified posts along the East

Bank. Jordanian units, equipped with seventy U.S.-made Patton tanks, advanced on the Israeli armored force while artillery deployed along the high ground pummeled Israeli infantry operating in the lowlands around Karameh. The Israeli forces remained static, under orders not to move too deeply into Jordanian territory, in order to prevent an all-out war with Hussein.[8]

The battle at Karameh lasted twelve hours. Israeli soldiers were instructed to be on the lookout for Yassir Arafat, and his photograph was distributed to the troops by unit commanders. Another assault against Palestinian guerrilla training camps south of the Dead Sea at Safi had also been launched that morning, but by 8:00 P.M., all Israeli forces had been withdrawn from the East Bank. The base at Karameh had been destroyed, three-quarters of the buildings lying in ruins. The operation left approximately 200 PLO and 40 Jordanian soldiers dead. About 150 Palestinians were taken into custody for interrogation in Israel. The Israelis lost four tanks, two armored carriers, and one aircraft. Twenty-eight Israelis were killed, 69 wounded.[9]

Poor visibility delayed the landing of the paratroop unit that was to block the escape route in the northern sector of the village. Yassir Arafat, the Fateh leader, fled eastward to Es Salt on a motorcycle.[10]

The Israelis admitted that the fighting had been tougher than expected and that they had made several tactical mistakes, though the operation was still viewed as a victory. It demolished the PLO stronghold and demonstrated that the villages along the East Bank of the Jordan River would no longer provide a safe haven for Palestinian guerrillas.

For the Palestinians, the battle of Karameh quickly assumed mythic proportions. *Karameh* is the Arabic word for "honor." The PLO promoted the battle of Karameh as a victory over the Jews that restored Arab honor in the wake of the humiliating defeat in the Six Day War the previous year. The Palestinians were the only ones vigorous enough to continue the battle against the Zionists, the PLO spokesmen declared, the outnumbered Palestinian guerrilla *fedayeen* proved capable of warding off the might of the Israeli army for nearly twelve hours. Yassir Arafat's Fateh stood heroically to the last man, the Palestinians boasted, inflicting numerous casualties on the enemy. The PLO triumphantly displayed one of the damaged tanks that had been left behind by the Israelis, and they told the jubilant spectators that their fighters, not Hussein's, had been the ones who kept Israeli forces from advancing on Amman.

Funeral processions for the Palestinian victims of Karameh erupted into mass celebrations hailing the slain martyrs and extolling the centrality of a reinvigorated PLO. Abu Iyad's assessment of Karameh revealed that the

Palestinian leadership's main message to the Arabs in the aftermath of the Six Day War was that the destiny of Arab liberation rested upon PLO terrorism against Jews.

> For the Palestinian masses, jeered at and humiliated for decades, the Karameh victory gave rise to an immense pride and hope, marking what they saw as the beginning of their liberation. By the thousands, by the tens of thousands, young and old flocked to join Fatah. High school and university students abandoned their studies to swell our ranks. Our absorption capacity was limited, however, and we were obliged to make a strict selection. Out of the 5,000 candidates who tried to enlist in the forty-eight hours following the battle of Karameh, for instance, we recruited only 900.
>
> The fedayeen movement witnessed an unprecedented growth. With the active sympathy of the population in the occupied territories, our comrades stepped up their operations. These increased from a monthly average of 12 in 1967 to 52 in 1968, 199 in 1969, and 279 in the first eight months of 1970. Fatah militants gave no respite to the occupying authorities, placing bombs in Israeli supermarkets and at bus stops, firing rockets on border settlements, engaging in skirmishes along the cease-fire lines, attacking Jewish army barracks.[11]

Hussein had given the PLO commandos free rein to attack Israel from bases along the Jordan River. When Israel retaliated against Karameh, the king sent his army in to protect them, providing the decisive element that contributed to the tough fighting and high casualty rate suffered by the Israeli forces.

"What should I do to a people who have lost everything," the king asked in the midst of the elation over Karameh, "who were driven out of their country? Shoot them? I think we have come to the point where we are all *fedayeen*."[12] Hussein's identification with the Palestinian guerrillas in the weeks following Karameh only hastened the day when he would indeed decide to "shoot them."

Four months after the Israeli incursion into Jordan, the fourth meeting of the Palestine National Council met in Cairo. The PLO, still riding the crest of Karameh, amended its charter to include the following point:

> Article 9: Armed struggle is the only way to liberate Palestine. Thus it is the overall strategy, not merely a tactical phase. The Palestinian Arab people assert their absolute determination and firm resolution to continue their armed struggle and to work for an armed popular revolution for the liberation of their country and their return to it. They also assert their right to normal life in Palestine and to exercise their right to self-determination and sovereignty over it.[13]

The primacy of a protracted guerrilla war upheld, the PLO leadership moved to preclude any moves toward a political settlement under the "territory for peace" formula. With the West Bank and Gaza in Israeli hands, a significant portion of Arab opinion lobbied for an arrangement that would return the occupied territories even if it meant ending the twenty-year-old war against the Jewish state. The PLO was well aware that in those first twenty years, the West Bank had been in Arab hands anyway, yet the struggle against Israel had still been relentlessly pursued. To abandon that struggle for a return to the pre-1967 status quo would appear to make a mockery of the previous two decades of Arab resistance to Israel and a capitulation that represented abject surrender to the Jews. The PLO militants demanded the "liberation" of *all* of Palestine, from Nablus and Hebron on the West Bank to Haifa and Tel Aviv on the Mediterranean Sea. Spurred on by the glory of Karameh and their entrenched attachment to the war with Israel, the Palestinian leadership in Cairo added another article to their National Covenant, pledging to block any territorial compromise with the Jewish state: "Article 21. The Arab Palestinian people, expressing themselves by the armed Palestinian revolution, reject all solutions which are substitutes for the total liberation of Palestine and reject all proposals aiming at the liquidation of the Palestinian problem, or its internationalization."[14]

In February 1969, Yassir Arafat, fresh from his newfound prestige as leader of the Karameh fighters, took over as chairman of the PLO. The Fateh commandos, no longer safe in the villages along the Jordan River despite the "victory" at Karameh, retreated eastward to Es Salt and established their military headquarters on the outskirts of the city. They moved through the population of thirty thousand, flaunting their arms, training new recruits, and either ignoring or openly challenging Jordanian jurisdiction. When the Israelis retaliated for a series of cross-border assaults by PLO guerrillas by bombing Es Salt in July 1968, the *fedayeen* withdrew into the refugee camps of Amman. "By the autumn of 1968, Hussein's capital was the commando stronghold that Karameh had been a year earlier," journalist Peter Snow reported. "They drove with loaded weapons through the streets of Amman and looked more like a second army within Jordan."[15]

By rejecting Israel's appeal to clamp down on the PLO guerrillas, and instead granting them sanctuary, logistical support, and political independence, the king helped set the stage for Karameh and the subsequent Israeli raids that drove the militants to his doorstep in Amman. Heartened by the Arab world's new respect for the resistance movement and the swelling grass-roots support among the refugees, the PLO commandos pressed their fight against Israel and consolidated their power in Jordan, flouting the king's authority as they maneuvered themselves into the position of preeminent spokesmen for the Arab cause and rightful rulers of the Palestinian homeland, which they increasingly spoke of as including Hussein's Hashemite Kingdom in eastern Palestine.

According to Moshe Dayan, between the end of the 1967 Six Day War and the 1970 Black September civil war in Jordan, nearly 5,840 terrorist acts were launched against Israel from Jordanian bases, killing 141 Israelis and wounding 800.[16] The budding military might of the Palestinian guerrillas had not only brought death and destruction to Israel, but loomed ominously in the heart of Hussein's kingdom. After the PFLP's Waddieh Haddad carried out a daring multiple hijacking operation in September 1970, ordering three civilian passenger planes to land at Jordan's Dawson Field and keeping them on the ground for days while threatening to blow them up if the terrorists' demands were not met, the king finally decided to move decisively against the PLO in his midst. For more than a week, the king had been forced to stand helpless while world attention focused on the innocent passengers sweltering on the desert airstrip surrounded by PLO commandos. Hussein's own army winced at their inability to control the Palestinian guerrillas. The king told one correspondent from *Le Figaro* that his army was "not accustomed to being so vilified, denigrated and provoked endlessly without being able to react."[17]

During what was later to become known as Black September, the king did react, but after four days of fighting the PLO commandos, Jordanian troops became bogged down in Amman. Syria seized the opportunity to topple the Hashemites and sent one hundred of its Soviet-built T-55 tanks across the northern border into Jordan. On 20 September, another one hundred tanks crossed into Jordanian territory and headed toward Irbid. Hussein panicked, calling on the U.S. State Department's Middle East chief, Joseph Sisco, for help.

The Americans could not intervene directly, having already received a warning from the Russians two days earlier that they would not tolerate U.S. involvement in the Jordanian-Palestinian dispute.[18] The Soviets were patrons of both the PLO and the Syrians, and did not intend to stand by while American forces crushed their Middle Eastern clients. Hussein knew this, but bet that the Israelis, despite his previous rejection of a joint effort to combat Palestinian terrorism and his aid to the guerrillas at Karameh, would agree to help protect his throne from a Syrian takeover and thereby allow Jordan to press its attack against the PLO. Feeling too threatened to make a direct appeal through covert channels, the king called in Sisco and asked him to pass the word along to the Israelis.

Sisco immediately notified Henry Kissinger. After consulting with the president, Nixon gave his national security adviser the go-ahead to contact the Israelis, and Kissinger telephoned the Israeli ambassador, Yitzak Rabin. The ambassador was attending a reception for Prime Minister Golda Meir at the Hilton Hotel in New York. Kissinger told Rabin that Washington wanted Israel to come to Hussein's aid and stop the advance of Syria's tanks on Jordan's northern border. Israel must use its air force to deter the Syrians, Kissinger said. With Washington aware of the secret Israeli contacts with the king, the State Department wanted to ensure that Hussein would be around long enough for these behind-the-scenes talks to bear fruit. Moreover, according to Kissinger, Syria was behind the PLO, and behind Syria was the Soviet Union. The U.S. backing for Hussein served as a shield against Soviet penetration in the Middle East.

Rabin responded to Kissinger's call for Israeli intervention by asking if the request was being made on behalf of the king. Was Hussein aware of it? Was he behind it? Kissinger hesitated before responding. The answer will come in due course, he said. But Rabin persisted: Would Israel be acting as America's policeman, or in the interests of Jordan? Would the dividends from the action on behalf of Hussein fall only to the United States, or to Israel as well? Kissinger was still noncommittal.

While still at the Hilton, meeting in a private area off the grand ballroom, Rabin consulted with Prime Minister Meir, Foreign Minister Abba Eban, and their advisers. Golda called Israel to speak with her Deputy Prime Minister, Yigal Allon. At 3:00 A.M., Rabin received a callback from Kissinger: the request for Israeli intervention had been made with the full knowledge of King Hussein. Kissinger was dispatching an air force jet to New York to bring Rabin to Washington for further talks.

At general headquarters in Israel, Defense Minister Moshe Dayan was presiding over a debate that included Allon, Chief of Staff Haim Bar-Lev, and Ariel Sharon, head of the Southern Command. Allon, who had been a key player in the secret contacts with the king, was strongly in favor of intervention on his behalf. After all, Israel had protected Hussein in the past. Mossad operatives working within the refugee camps of Jordan had gathered not only intelligence concerning planned attacks against Israel but also information concerning Palestinian moves against the king; such information was then turned over to Hussein. Sylvia Raphael—a key Mossad intelligence agent later arrested in Norway for her participation in a bungled assassination attempt against PLO leader Ali Hasan Salameh—had already established an espionage network in the kingdom, working undercover in Amman as a journalist from Paris. "Through her charm, hard work, and through contacts already in place, she soon gained entry to the ruling groups in Amman," British journalist John Bulloch later reported. "On one occasion she was invited to a party at which King Hussein was the guest of honor."[19] The Mossad operative had been able to amass valuable information on the PLO's clandestine commando structure in Jordan. "She once showed me her engagement book, crammed with dates for lunches, drinks and dinner parties with the elite of Amman," Bulloch wrote. Raphael's reports on Palestinian activities in Jordan had already enabled Israel to pass along warnings to Hussein that helped protect his throne from PLO guerrillas. Allon was in favor of continuing the policy of tacit support for the king.

Defense Minister Dayan was more reserved. Dayan harbored doubts about Hussein's ability to retain power over the long run. Six months earlier, in March 1970, Dayan had met personally with the king aboard a ship anchored off the port of Eilat. The Israeli army had occupied the area around Safi, south of the Dead Sea, in response to PLO guerrillas who had established a base there and were firing Soviet-made Katuysha rockets at Israel's Potash Works across the border. Dayan agreed to pull back his troops only after Hussein pledged to station a Jordanian force around Safi to prevent future PLO attacks.[20] Despite the agreement brokered off the coast of Eilat, Dayan was dismayed by Hussein's insistence that Israel return the entire West Bank to Jordan. The Israelis were flexible on the issue of Arab control in the Gaza Strip, but the defense minister felt that the strategic value of Judea and Samaria precluded a return to the pre-1967 armistice lines. Hussein had shown an unwillingness to compromise. Dayan's slogan had become, "I am waiting for a telephone call from Hussein." The ball was in the king's court, Dayan had reasoned. If Jordan wanted a permanent peace with Israel, then it was up to Hussein to take the inititiative.

Dayan had other reasons for his wariness over the proposed involvement in the Black September fighting in Jordan. Israeli moves against a Soviet-backed Syria might spur Moscow into digging in its heels in Egypt. Should Israel face hostilities on the Suez Canal, the Soviets, after having stood idly by while Syria was weakened by combined American-Jordanian-Israeli intervention, might decide that they could not risk the demise of another Mideast client and would have to introduce their own forces on behalf of Cairo.

The officers under Haim Bar-Lev, however, were itching for a fight with the PLO and their Syrian backers. They saw the American-Jordanian request as a golden opportunity for Israel to hand the PLO a decisive defeat. Those in favor of saving the king for the most part feared a takeover in Amman by Palestinian extremists. A Jordanian kingdom that provided lax control over the fedayeen militants had already resulted in repeated shelling of Israeli towns and cross-border raids by Arab terrorists. A PLO government in Amman would surely represent an exponential increase in the threat to the Jewish state, and an evasive Hussein vacillating between war and peace with Israel was preferable to a forthright Arafat fixated on armed struggle.

The Southern Region's commander, Ariel Sharon, disagreed. He was adamant about the need to retain the West Bank territories of Judea and Samaria, and the Americans were using their influence with Hussein to press for acceptance of Secretary of State William Rogers's peace plan of 9 December 1969, which called for the "withdrawal from occupied territories, the nonacquisition of territory by war, and the establishment of secure and recognized boundaries."[21] To many political observers, Washington's appeal for Israel's "withdrawal from occupied territories" was quickly taking precedence over its commitment to work for the establishment of "secure" borders. Though the Rogers Plan acknowledged that the pre-1967 boundaries were "armistice lines, not final political borders," the proposal allowed for only "insubstantial alterations required for mutual security."[22] Sharon feared that under this formula, even the West Bank military outposts that were a prerequisite for the Allon Plan—which Sharon believed did not go far enough in meeting Israel's security needs—would be challenged. Hussein's own rejection of a limited Israeli presence on the West Bank meant that fruitful negotiations with the king were unlikely, if not impossible. Hussein's answer to Dayan's remark about waiting for a call from the king had been, "I am now waiting for a phone call from Washington." Encouraged by the Rogers Plan, Hussein speculated that the United States might deliver what the Israelis would not: the near complete return of the West Bank. Sharon saw no reason to perpetuate Hussein's rule and contribute to a situation whereby the king might indeed one day succeed in tapping America's clout in an attempt to force Israel to cede strategic West Bank lands.

Sharon also cautioned his colleagues to be mindful of the need to come to terms with PLO demands. "The thickening of the Palestinian cloud above our heads will keep the problem with us for some time," Sharon said. Palestinian militants were steadily expanding their influence in the region. "Why not give them a political expression in Jordan?" the general suggested. "It will take the wind out of their sails." To persist in the hope that Hussein was capable of reaching a negotiated settlement was merely to submit Israel to a mirage of diplomacy fashioned by an Arab king too timid and/or too powerless to make real peace. "We tried to persuade the king to end his war against us," Sharon said. "Our ministers were running to him day and night." The results were private peace talks and public belligerence. "Let the *fedayeen* have their Palestinian state," Sharon advised. "Then we will negotiate with them state to state, or, if they want war, then we will fight with them state to state."[23] Even if the PLO state in Jordan received the backing of the Soviet Union, Sharon explained, it would still pose less of a problem for Israel than the frustrating, complicated search for a political outlet that could satisfy Palestinian nationalism.

Golda Meir contended that there was no need to recognize a separate Palestinian identity. Even the Arab leaders themselves at the end of World War I insisted that Palestine was not a distinct entity, but just a part of the greater Arab nation that had been colonized and subjected to Ottoman rule for four hundred years. For the founders of modern Arab nationalism, the liberation from the Turks had not meant the liberation of the "nation" of Palestine. At the very least, they argued, Palestine was a province of Syria, and its emergence as an independent state would go against Arab history and culture. Many Arab leaders, however, were willing to see Palestine granted separate status as an Arab nation if that would prevent its settlement as a Jewish homeland. It was just this preference that helped give rise to Palestinian nationalism. The drive for Palestinian nationhood had only been born with the arrival of the Jews, Meir reasoned, invented as a bulwark against Zionism rather than emerging as the natural expression of an oppressed people. Israel was under no obligation to acquiesce in the establishment of an independent Palestinian state.

Regardless of the merits of the argument regarding the origins of Palestinian nationalism, Sharon believed there was a need to recognize its existence. But that recognition should come in the context of Jordan, not on the West Bank, or in Jerusalem or Jaffa.

Sharon asserted that if the Hashemites were dislodged from Amman, and Palestinian nationalists could build their state in what was once accurately dubbed "eastern Palestine," the dispute between Israel and the Arabs might be reduced to a question of fixing mutually agreed upon borders between two independent nations: the Jewish State of Israel west of the Jordan River, and the Arab State of Palestine to the east.[24] The conflict would no longer appear to revolve around a Jewish nationalism that had succeeded and a Palestinian one that had failed. A PLO-led state headed by Yassir Arafat might still covet all of Palestine, but the experience of governing an independent nation ruled by the Arabs of Palestine rather than Hashemites from the Arabian Peninsula might temper the fervor for expansionist wars with Israel. The day-to-day rewards of a Palestinian state might lead PLO officials into accepting a compromise over territory just as Ben-Gurion and Begin did when they decided to honor the 1947 U.N. Partition Resolution, relinquishing their dream of a Jewish homeland in all of Palestine in favor of a concrete, albeit greatly reduced, State of Israel.

Sharon's argument did not prevail. Israeli leaders were gravely alarmed by the prospect of a PLO state on their eastern border. Many were offended by the injustice of pitting legitimate Zionist national aspirations against an historically unsound Palestinian nationalism conjured up solely to block Jewish settlement in the region. They saw no moral imperative or practical benefit in accommodating PLO demands. In Sharon's view, the decisive factor in their rejection of his call to let the *fedayeen* have their way with Hussein was that American pressure to support the king was simply too great to resist. The Israeli leaders were not willing to say no to Richard Nixon and Henry Kissinger.

When Rabin flew to Washington to meet with Kissinger on the morning of 21 September, he took with him Prime Minister Meir's reply to Hussein's appeal for help. If the Syrians moved past the Jordanian city of Irbid, Israeli troops would block their advance. If they sent in their air force, Israeli jets would intervene. In the meantime, Israel would mobilize its forces along the Syrian border to signal its intentions to Damascus. Should the Soviets enter the fighting against Israel in response to Jerusalem's introduction of forces, the United States would have to agree to deter them, militarily if necessary.[25]

Israeli troops massed along the region near the Beit Shean Kibbutz in the Jordan Valley, southeast of Irbid. Israeli tanks openly rolled northward along the Golan Heights at the Syrian frontier. Israeli aircraft flew across Syrian positions in Jordan. An American reconnaissance plane took off from the U.S. aircraft carrier *Saratoga*, operating off the Lebanese coast, and landed in Tel Aviv. By the following day, twenty thousand American troops were on alert, additional U.S. fighters and transport planes were being flown to Europe for possible action in the Middle East, two battalions of the U.S. 82nd Airborne Division were on special six-hour alert, and a naval fleet that included two aircraft carriers, twelve destroyers, and an amphibious task force of twelve hundred marines was operating along the eastern Mediterranean.[26]

The naval officers from the *Saratoga* had been sent to coordinate U.S. air cover for Israeli troops should it be needed. Their arrival in Tel Aviv was kept secret, but was done in such a way as to allow their movements to be picked up by Soviet surveillance. It was a clear signal to Moscow that the United States was prepared to back Israel's defense of Jordan.

Hussein sent in Hunter Mark-9 fighter planes to stop the Syrian tank units operating around Irbid. Hafez Assad, then Syria's defense minister, had opposed his president's decision to attack Jordan, fearful that it would embroil Syria in a war with Israel that it was unprepared to wage, and that an Arafat victory in Amman might one day threaten Syria's own interests in the area. As Jordanian fighter planes moved against Syrian tanks, spurred on by the active cooperation of Israel and the United States, Assad held back from committing the full weight of his superior forces against Hussein. On the evening of 23 September, Syrian forces began their pullback from Jordan, three days after Rabin received Kissinger's urgent call.[27] The joint

United States-Israeli action had succeeded in helping the king retain his throne. Hussein began rounding up Palestinian dissidents, relying in part on a list of names and the subversive actions associated with them that had been gathered by Mossad operative Sylvia Raphael.

21

Playing the Wild Card

AFTER Black September, King Hussein and his Israeli partners decided to dispense with the London rendezvous and instead meet closer to home. An Israeli ship would set sail from Eilat while Hussein would board a motor boat at Aqaba. Under the cover of darkness, the king would climb aboard the Israeli vessel for talks with Allon and his associates. The negotiations soon moved south to the tiny island of Fa'run, occupied by Israel during its 1967 conquest of the Sinai. A tent was erected for the meetings, and the secret discussions would go on for hours at a time.

Israeli participants in the talks included Prime Minister Golda Meir, Deputy Prime Minister Yigal Allon, Defense Minister Moshe Dayan, and Foreign Minister Abba Eban. According to Moshe Zak, former editor of the Israeli daily *Ma'ariv*, in the months following Black September, Israel's negotiating team began expanding on the Allon Plan. They offered to give the king total jurisdiction over the Gaza Strip, to initiate joint Jordanian-Israeli economic projects, including the construction of a railroad line from the Eilat-Aqaba ports to the Dead Sea, and to build permanent housing for the Palestinian refugees living on the West Bank. In Jerusalem, the Jordanian government would be granted the right to appoint the head of the Moslem Supreme Council, with the ultimate question regarding sovereignty over the eastern sector of city to be left open until all other outstanding issues between the two nations were settled. In return, Israel requested that Jews be allowed to settle in the West Bank, provided that the local Arab inhabitants were not displaced, and that Israeli security bases be established in the area, away from population centers so as to avoid disrupting civilian life. As a further inducement, Dayan offered to permit the Jordanian army to install bases along the Gaza Strip to offset the presence of Israeli forces on the West Bank. In five years, should the border remain peaceful, Israel would consider removing its troops along the Jordan River. The king rejected the Israeli proposals.[1] Hussein told the negotiators that the complete withdrawal of their forces and the return of the entire West Bank to Jordan was the only acceptable basis for a peace agreement between the two nations.

On 15 March, 1972, the king announced his own plan to a conference of Jordanian cabinet ministers, Parliament members, army officers, political leaders, tribal representatives, journalists, and Palestinian refugee officials, held at the Basmah Royal Palace in Amman:

> The Hashemite Kingdom of Jordan shall become a United Arab Kingdom and shall be thus named.
> The United Arab Kingdom shall consist of two regions:
> A. The region of Palestine and shall consist of the West Bank and any other Palestinian territories to be liberated and where the population opt to join it.
> B. The region of Jordan, and shall consist of the East Bank.
> Amman shall be the central capital of the kingdom and at the same time shall be the capital of the region of Jordan.
> Jerusalem shall become the capital of the region of Palestine.
> The King shall be the head of the state and shall assume the central executive authority assisted by a central council of ministers. The central legislative authority shall be vested in the King and the national assembly, whose members shall be elected by direct and secret ballot.
> It shall have an equal number of members from each of the two regions.[2]

Because Hussein's proposal for a United Arab Kingdom ruled out an independent Palestinian state on the West Bank and Gaza, some observers speculated that the plan had been "pre-cooked" with Israel.

The Iraqi government charged that the king's proposal was "a defeatist idea advanced by a hireling regime," labeling it an "American-Zionist surrender document" seeking to block the "armed struggle waged by the Palestinian people against the Zionist-Imperialist occupation."[3]

The government of South Yemen condemned Hussein's scheme as "a link in a chain of imperialist-Zionist conspiracies against the Arab national liberation movement."[4]

Syria's President Assad charged that "the plan aims at the establishment of a Palestinian entity under the control and influence of Israel," and Syrian demonstrators took to the streets to rally against the plan and demonstrate their support for the PLO.[5]

President Sadat declared, "The plan is an attempt to liquidate the Palestine problem, and we have defined our attitude to it on this basis. We were not carried away by emotion but acted out of our adherence to our declared principles: We shall not accept any solution that forsakes Arab Land or jeopardizes the Palestinian people's rights.''[6] Egypt severed diplomatic relations with Jordan.

Algeria's government-controlled daily in Oran, *La Republique*, wrote that ''The king of Amman has become an enemy, just like Israel.''[7]

The Central Committee of Arafat's Fateh faction of the PLO issued a statement ''to confirm its decisive and absolute rejection of the King's plan and to condemn any Palestinian individual or group attempting to take part in the plan. These will be regarded as dissenters from the will of the Palestinian people and traitors to the people's national aspirations. Our people will treat them as traitors and conspirators.'' The Fateh announcement went on to assert that ''there is no dispute between the Palestinian and Jordanian people. However, the core of the dispute is the king, the Hashemite family, and the regime. The source of the dispute is the Hashemite family in Jordan, its history of conspiracy against our people and cause, and its role in serving imperialist ends in the area. To oppose this family and overthrow the royal regime in Jordan has now become the short-term requirement for normalizing the situation and placing the relations between the Palestinian and Jordanian peoples in their true context.''[8]

Reaction by the West Bank Arabs—the people who would be directly affected by Hussein's plan—was mixed, and the comments of those rejecting the king's proposal were more restrained. One Palestinian resident remarked that the creation of a semi-autonomous West Bank state in union with Jordan would be ''too little and too late.'' The mayor of Hebron, Sheik Mohammed Ali Jaabari, advised West Bank leaders to discuss the United Arab Kingdom scheme and ''decide what to accept and what has to be changed,'' adding that it was the most promising solution to the Palestinian problem ever offered.[9]

On 29 March, 1972, the first elections to be held in the West Bank under Israeli occupation yielded five new mayors who were critics of Hussein and advocates of a Palestinian state independent of Jordan. The other five West Bank seats that were being contested were won by Palestinian leaders in favor of the more traditional pro-Jordanian position. The lack of an overwhelming endorsement for Hussein's scheme in the mayoral elections was seen as a setback for the plan.[10]

The king's stand against an independent Palestinian state on the West Bank left him open to a barrage of criticism from fellow Arab leaders, and rumors persisted that he was acting in secret tandem with the Israelis. On 21 March, six days after the king publicly unveiled his United Arab Kingdom proposal, Yassir Arafat told a gathering of Palestinian residents in Kuwait that a Jordanian army officer who had defected to Egypt reported that he had accompanied King Hussein to the Jordanian port of Aqaba for a secret meeting with Israeli Prime Minister Golda Meir. According to Arafat, the soldier claimed that Hussein had reached an agreement with the Israelis whereby a portion of the West Bank would be returned to Jordan and that the Jordanian flag would be allowed to fly over Al Aqsa Mosque in Jerusalem, with the Vatican flying its flag over the Church of the Holy Sepulcher. Arafat denounced the purported agreement, declaring that "Hussein wants to give us a mutilated part of Palestine." The PLO chief accused the king of being an "agent of Zionism and imperialism," vowing that "the new agents shall have the same fate as that of Wasfi Tal," the Jordanian prime minister who had been assassinated the year before by commandos from Arafat's clandestine strike force, Black September.[11]

Prime Minister Golda Meir responded to reports of Arafat's charge by telling foreign journalists in Jerusalem, "If there were any meetings such as you describe, I would not tell you about them."

King Hussein reacted to questions regarding the meeting with Meir by telling reporters in Amman, "It is immaterial whether I deny it, for the simple reason these rumors will continue," adding that "Mrs. Meir has answered this question. No such contacts."[12]

The following week, the controversy over Hussein's secret talks with Israel escalated with the publication in the French newsmagazine *L'Express* of letters allegedly written by Jordanian officials documenting the existence of a private dialogue between the king and Israeli officials. One of the letters was purportedly sent by the former Jordanian prime minister Bahjat Talhouni to the Jordanian ambassador in Rome, four months after the 1967 Six Day War. Talhouni supposedly instructed the ambassador to urge the Italian press to refrain "from publishing anything on the secret meetings between the king of Jordan and representatives of the Israeli authorities." In a second letter to the Jordanian ambassador in Washington, Talhouni asked him to inform the United States that Jordan would "cancel the secret and nonsecret agreements linking us with Israel" if the Israelis did not bow to Jordanian demands. The next week, in a follow-up interview by *L'Express*, the former prime minister denied ever having written such letters and claimed no knowledge of any secret contacts with Israel. The French magazine wrote that a government spokesman in Amman said the letters had been printed at the request of Israel. Talhouni, however, accused the PLO of having forged the documents as part of a campaign to discredit the king.[13]

As the charges and countercharges continued, Hussein found himself

forced to issue more forthright denials. "There has been no meeting with Israeli leaders," he said flatly in an interview held at Washington's Blair House, "nor, unfortunately, has there been a meeting of the minds."[14] The king was on a visit to the United States to drum up American support for his United Arab Kingdom proposal.

If, as his Arab critics suggested, King Hussein's plan for the West Bank had been developed in collusion with Israel, then the Israeli response to it could only be viewed as a remarkable piece of Machiavellian deception hatched in order to shore up Arab support for the scheme by demonstrating Jewish opposition to it. Hussein and Meir's strategy for promoting the United Arab Kingdom proposal would have had to rest on the kind of logic that says that if Israel is against something, it must be in the interest of the Arabs to support it. Reports from Jerusalem, however, talked of a "furious" Golda Meir totally at odds with Hussein's plan. The day after the king outlined his proposal to the conference at the Basmah Royal Palace, the prime minister issued a series of denunciations of it in front of the Israeli Knesset:

> The King is treating as his own property territories which are not his and are not under his control.
>
> He crowns himself king of Jerusalem and envisions himself as the ruler of larger territories than were under his control prior to the rout of June, 1967 [Hussein's United Arab Kingdom would include the Gaza Strip, which had been under Egyptian control prior to 1967].
>
> In all this detailed plan the term 'peace' is not even mentioned, and it is not based on the concept of agreement.
>
> The whole of King Hussein's proposal is based on the assumption that he is capable of reaching a solution of controversial problems at issue without an agreement between our states, as if he could dictate to Israel the plan he has put forward.
>
> No unilateral declarations of actions whatsoever will bring Jordan one inch nearer to peace. No sophistry, even if it wins banner headlines, will lead to any constructive change.
>
> There is only one way which has any prospects, namely, serious negotiations for a peaceful solution, a bold and realistic effort to reach understanding and agreement.
>
> Pretentiousness is a pervading characteristic of Hussein's address. The King defines the results of Jordan's participation in the six-day war as a disaster, but unfortunately five years later he puts forward a plan which goes to show that he has failed to learn the lesson from his disaster.[15]

One journalist wrote that Meir had labeled charges that she had struck a a secret deal with Hussein "ridiculous," and that political analysts had "found nothing in the King's proposal to suggest that he was trying to make it palatable or conciliatory to the Israelis."[16]

Abba Eban told Knesset members that Hussein's plan for the West Bank was akin to "moving furniture in a house that is not your own."[17]

Yigal Allon told an interviewer from *Ma'ariv* that although the "constitutional structure of the Arab, Jordanian-Palestinian entity" did not conflict with his own plan for an autonomous government by the Arab inhabitants of the West Bank, there was "an absolute contrast on the territorial concept or the proposed boundaries." According to Allon, the lines mapping out the borders of Hussein's United Arab Kingdom constituted a "maximalist" position. "This map should be rejected before new allusions grow in Amman or Nablos [*sic*]," he said. "Naming Jerusalem as a possible capital of the Palestinian province in the United Arab Kingdom sounded [like] more of a joke than a challenge," Allon went on. "His statement proves that he has not yet reached the crucial conclusion without which there can be no (constructive) change."[18]

Allon, who had held numerous secret meetings with the king, clocking more "Hussein hours" than any other Israeli, flatly denied that the United Arab Kingdom scheme was a viable alternative to his own plan for the West Bank.

If Hussein's proposal had been pre-arranged with the Israelis, the vigorous condemnations by Golda Meir, Abba Eban, and Yigal Allon, and the subsequent failure by both sides to take concrete steps to implement the plan, revealed a startling combination of diplomatic deception and political incompetence. Its rejection by PLO militants and its unpopularity among Arab governments wary of Jordanian hegemony in Palestine would not have required a particularly astute mind to predict. Had Hussein and the Israelis agreed on a joint strategy to sell the plan to the Arabs, they would have had to acknowledge the necessity of embarking on a lengthy campaign to garner Palestinian support, while at the same time taking practical steps to alter the realities on the ground, such as a unilateral redeployment of Israeli troops along the Jordan River, the setting up of a provisional Jordanian authority in the West Bank, and a public declaration by Hussein recognizing the right of 'Israel to exist, coupled with a statement that he intended to sign a peace agreement with the Jewish state.

The harsh rebuff by Israel and the widespread Arab hostility directed against the United Arab Kingdom proposal suggested that Hussein had played a card on his own, gambling that U.S. backing and the support of moderate Palestinians would enable him to successfully challenge both the PLO hardliners and his Israeli negotiating partners. The payoff for Hussein was suspicion from the Israelis and a call by Arafat's Fateh for the over-throw of the Hashemite regime in Amman.

Though disappointed with Hussein, Israel was still willing to continue the secret dialogue with the king. *Time* magazine reported in September that Allon had held two other meetings with Hussein to try to reconcile the Allon Plan with the United Arab Kingdom proposal, and in December, the Israeli newspaper *Ha'aretz* reported that Golda Meir had again met with the Jordanian monarch in an effort to hammer out an agreement.[19] But the deadlock over the West Bank brought overall progress toward a peace treaty to a near standstill.

Despite the grim outlook, the secret dialogue between the king and the Israelis continued into the following year, and hopes for a breakthrough remained. On 6 October 1973, when Anwar Sadat launched his surprise Yom Kippur attack, Hussein, still engaged in the secret diplomacy with Israel and not wanting to repeat the fiasco of 1967, hesitated before joining Egypt and Syria in the battle. Only on the eighth day of fighting did the king reluctantly send his crack 40th Armored Brigade to join Iraqi forces in a coordinated attack behind Syrian lines.[20] But the Yom Kippur War was not a rerun of the six-day Israeli blitz of 1967. Israel suffered enormous losses. Sadat's move sent the prestige of the Arabs soaring. When the cease-fire took effect on 23 October, Hussein found himself without a share of the Arab glory. Ezer Weizman was to later remark that the king had made two mistakes in his dealings with Israel: he joined the war in 1967, and he didn't join the war in 1973. Weizman then added a third mistake to the list: Hussein didn't join Anwar Sadat in Jerusalem in 1977.

22

Clocking the Hussein Hours

ON 3 June 1974, Yitzak Rabin succeeded Golda Meir as Prime Minister of Israel. Shimon Peres then took over the defense ministry from Moshe Dayan, and Yigal Allon replaced Abba Eban as minister of foreign affairs. Four months later, Rabin, Allon, and Peres met with King Hussein. The secret contacts were to continue under the newly installed Israeli government.

By 1977, Yigal Allon had held fifteen meetings with Hussein. Abba Eban met with the king ten times. Between 1974 and 1977, the powerful high-level triumvirate of Rabin, Peres, and Allon went together to talk peace with Hussein seven times. These secret encounters were not impulsive, hit-or-miss affairs. Although they had failed to produce a peace agreement, the meetings had become institutionalized over the years, a cherished outlet for Israeli diplomacy reaffirming the mutual security interests between the two nations while holding out the hope that a larger political breakthrough might one day emerge. After Rabin came to power, the sessions shifted from the island of Fa'run in the Gulf of Aqaba to Israeli territory. Hussein would helicopter to the site accompanied only by his loyal pilot. In the past, at the sessions outside Israel, he had on occasion brought his close advisor and foreign minister, Zeid al-Rafai. For his meetings inside Israel, the king traveled with only his pilot.

Hussein's helicopter would touch down just across the border in the southern part of the Negev Desert where it would be met by a caravan of Israeli vehicles. Moving to a secluded area, negotiations between the Jordanian king and the Israeli leaders would be conducted inside a parked car. At other times, the king's helicopter would land on top of the ancient Israeli fortress of Masada, the towering thirteen hundred-foot plateau near the Dead Sea where nearly one thousand men, women, and children of the Jewish resistance group known as the Zealots had held out against a two year siege

198

before taking their own lives in A.D. 73 rather than submit to defeat by the Romans. At Masada, an Israeli helicopter would be standing by to take Hussein to Tel Aviv.

In April 1977, Hussein's pilot was killed in a helicopter accident that also took the life of his wife, Queen Alia. The king continued the secret contacts, flying alone, personally piloting the helicopter into Israel. Hussein's hosts worked diligently to satisfy the king's insistence on absolute secrecy while maneuvering to make the necessary arrangements with ground personnel to ensure that the Jordanian aircraft would not be shot down after penetrating Israeli air space.

The discussions were held in English, though Allon spoke fluent Arabic. The Israelis were charmed by the king's small talk. Hussein was a good storyteller, describing his exploits as a parachutist and pilot and the thrill of water skiing along the Gulf of Aqaba. The Jewish leaders liked Hussein. They were impressed by his royalty, and moved by the gloominess of his spirit and the sadness in his eyes that had set in after the defeat of 1967.

Before the fatal helicopter accident, the Israelis asked Hussein's pilot if the king could accept a gift from Israel without jeopardizing security. The pilot said, "Of course," and Hussein was given an Israeli-made Galili rifle. "To His Royal Highness, King Hussein," read the inscription on the wooden case, "from Yitzhak Rabin, the Prime Minister of Israel."[1] Hussein gave Allon a sword, and he presented Eban with a fountain pen bearing the emblem of the Hashemite Kingdom, telling the Israeli, "I hope you will use it one day to sign a peace treaty with Jordan."

Some of the talks in the immediate aftermath of the 1973 Yom Kippur War were conducted in conjunction with Henry Kissinger's shuttle diplomacy. Kissinger wanted to integrate Hussein into the Israeli-Egyptian-Syrian peace process being brokered by the United States. He requested that he be kept informed of the secret dialogue between the Israelis and Hussein, and, when he received a report from one side, he would quickly ask the other party why its was late. Kissinger was eager for a settlement and advised the Israelis to take a soft line with the king.

Kissinger presented the Israeli leaders with the argument that despite the fact that Sadat and Assad had waged an aggressive war against Israel in 1973, the Israelis were willing to make concessions in the Sinai and the Golan Heights in order to reach a disengagement agreement. Since King Hussein had chosen not to go to war, Kissinger argued, the Israelis must not appear to be penalizing him for it by refusing to offer concessions on the West Bank. Kissinger managed to win some Israeli officials over to this line of reasoning. One Israeli observer noted with a hint of self-deprecation that some Israeli politicians felt they were being hoodwinked by the cleverness of Kissinger's Jewish logic, the kind that had kept the Jewish people enslaved for centuries. Only the Jews should sacrifice; only the Jews should carry the burden of peace; only the Jews should be held accountable. According to Kissinger, the Jews had to avoid humiliating the Arabs who had waged war upon them and suffered defeat. The enemy's honor had to be upheld in order for real peace to prevail. It would be the Jews who would have to make the concessions if they wished to arrive at a negotiated settlement. The result was an Israeli pullback from the 1973 cease-fire lines and the Kissinger disengagement agreements with Syria and Egypt. The Jews also had to avoid punishing Arabs who were willing to break with their brethren and refrain from going to war against Israel. The result was Kissinger's push for an Israeli withdrawal from the West Bank as a prelude to coming to terms with Jordan. Such logic always seemed to lead the Jews to the same place: Jewish concessions to the aggressor, the vanquished, and the neutral; Israeli concessions to all as a prerequisite for peace.

On 18 January, 1974—after Israeli forces had pushed across the Egyptian frontier on the west bank of the Suez Canal during the Yom Kippur War and encircled the Egyptian Third Army trapped on the east bank—the first Israeli-Egyptian disengagement agreement was signed. Israeli troops withdrew to a line back across the eastern side of the canal. On 31 May, 1974—after Israeli troops had advanced deep into Syrian territory during the previous October's fighting to threaten the capital of Damascus a mere thirty miles away—an Israeli-Syrian disengagement agreement was signed. Israel's army pulled back to positions along the Golan Heights. Hussein had previously demanded a similar disengagement agreement for the West Bank, insisting that Israel retreat to a line approximately five miles from the Jordan River. With Henry Kissinger likewise pressing for an Israeli gesture toward Jordan, Allon came up with the Jericho Plan, which he offered as "a token withdrawal" to satisfy Hussein and Kissinger, perhaps enticing them both into accepting a permanent settlement based on the original Allon Plan.[2]

Under the Jericho Plan, Israel's security forces would remain in the area, but the civil administration of the city would be turned over to Hussein. Kissinger said this did not go far enough, that Israeli troops would have to withdraw completely from the region, but that U.N. troops could be stationed there instead of Jordanian soldiers. Allon was open to Kissinger's alteration. Hussein said he would consider the plan. But the other two members of the Israeli triumvirate, Rabin and Peres, were opposed to both Allon's initial version of the Jericho Plan and Kissinger's amendment of it.

Rabin had pledged to call for new elections to approve any proposals for an Israeli withdrawal from the West Bank. Aside from their own assessment that only an Israeli military presence in Judea and Samaria could guarantee Israel's security, Rabin and Peres did not believe that implementation of the Jericho Plan was feasible given the mood of the electorate. Israel had just managed to avoid a disastrous defeat in the surprise attack the previous October, and many believed that Israel's buffer zones in the Sinai, the West Bank, and the Golan had played a key part in forestalling a devastating raid on Israeli population centers by the invading Arab forces. The Israeli public was not prepared to relinquish the strategic depth it had won in 1967, given the losses it had suffered in 1973. In addition, many felt that Israel was under no moral obligation to return the captured territory, and indeed that relinquishing land might serve only to convince the Arabs that they could attack Jews with impunity. Golda Meir had explained this to Kissinger when he was pressing her for concessions in the Golan Heights. "If you strangle me, I don't know how to go to the people and explain to them that, after all, never mind, there was a war, there was another war, more dead, more wounded, but we have to give up Syrian territory," Meir said. "I can never accept that there is no difference between the attacker and the attacked," she explained. "Isn't it an encouragement for our neighbors to go on fighting when the fighting does not lose anything?"[3]

Meir eventually acceded to a partial withdrawal from Syria that not only removed Israel from lands occupied during the 1973 Yom Kippur War but also from territory it had already captured in the 1967 Six Day War. There was widespread feeling that the security risks were too great to allow such gestures on the West Bank, which lay across the heart of Israel. Rabin ordered Allon to go back to Kissinger and explain that his Jericho disengagement plan was unacceptable to the Israeli leadership.

Kissinger was adamant that only an Israeli concession on the West Bank could keep Hussein afloat as a partner in the peace process. As in 1970, when PLO and Syrian forces were converging on the Jordanian army, Kissinger feared that Yassir Arafat would push aside Hussein and emerge as a key player in the region. "The question is who represents the Palestinians," the king told Kissinger in Amman a month after the Yom Kippur fighting ended. "Our position is that the West Bank is Jordanian-Palestinian territory occupied by Israel. It is Jordan's duty to recover that territory with minor changes on a reciprocal basis."[4] Kissinger agreed that it should remain Jordan's responsibility to negotiate the future of the West Bank, not the PLO's.

Two weeks later, King Hussein barely managed to block a draft resolution at the Arab Summit Conference in Algiers that, for the first time, would have designated the PLO as the sole spokesman for the Palestinian Arabs. On 8 February, 1974, Kissinger spoke before a group of American

Jewish leaders: "I predict that if the Israelis don't make some sort of arrangement with Hussein on the West Bank in six months, Arafat will become internationally recognized and the world will be in a chaos. . . . If I were an adviser to the Israeli government, I would tell the Prime Minister: 'For God's sake do something with Hussein while he is still one of the players.'"[5]

Less than a year later, on 28 October 1974, the Seventh Arab Summit was held in Rabat, Morocco. This time, King Hussein was forced to give way, and a resolution was passed affirming "the right of the Palestinian people to establish an independent national authority under the command of the Palestine Liberation Organization, the sole legitimate representative of the Palestinian people, in any Palestinian territory that is liberated."[6] The resolution not only attempted to pound the last nail into the coffin bearing Hussein's plan for a United Arab Kingdom incorporating the West Bank and Gaza, it also stripped the Hashemites of their historical role as spokesman for the Arabs of Palestine, bestowing it instead on the PLO as their "sole legitimate representative".

On 13 November 1974, Yassir Arafat was invited to address the United Nations General Assembly as the representative of the Palestinian people. "The difference between the revolutionary and the terrorist lies in the reason for which he fights," Arafat told the United Nations, in the year in which PLO gunmen attacked Israeli civilians at Qiryat Shemona and Ma'alot, slaughtering unarmed men, women, and children.[7]

Journalist David Hirst wrote that Arafat's U.N. speech constituted "a diplomatic victory that avenged the military defeat of Black September 1970."[8] It also bore out Kissinger's prophecy of 8 February. For the Israelis, a diplomatic victory by Arafat was still preferable to a military one by Arab soldiers based on the West Bank, be they Jordanian or PLO. Israel had been willing to risk a confrontation with Syria in 1970 in order to satisfy the American request to save Hussein. In 1974, sacrificing the strategic West Bank for the same purpose appeared to be too great a gamble. If the cost of keeping Jews in the West Bank was the emergence of Arafat in New York, or Cairo, Baghdad, Beirut, Damascus, or even Amman, then Israel would pay it.

In the years that followed, Hussein elected to continue his secret talks with Israel. After the 4 July, 1976, rescue of the hostages at Entebbe, the king even told the Israelis that although he could not endorse the political implications of the operation, he admired its military aspects.

One of Menachem Begin's first acts as prime minister was to instruct Moshe Dayan to make contact with Hussein. Begin had earlier sent word to the king stating that he would like to meet him personally, but Hussein had flatly rejected the offer. Begin then sent Dayan in his place.[9] Dayan was no longer representing the Labor Party government of Golda Meir and Yitzak Rabin, serving instead as foreign minister in Begin's Likud-dominated cabinet. Dayan had two meetings with Hussein in August 1977, one on the 22nd and another on the 23rd.

Dayan saw how much the Rabat decision had demoralized Hussein. The king vented his frustration by telling Dayan to speak to the PLO about the West Bank; he would only concern himself with the security of his kingdom on the east bank.[10]

Instead of turning to the PLO, Begin and Dayan sought out Anwar Sadat. The king was left on the sidelines.

23

The Jordanian Option

THE Begin years marked a dormant period as far as Israeli-Jordanian relations were concerned. Anwar Sadat's public diplomacy had pushed Hussein onto the sidelines. Sadat's assassination and the 1982 Israeli invasion of Lebanon appeared to end any movement toward peace: Hussein was not about to risk his life by duplicating Sadat's journey to Jerusalem, nor was he about to break ranks with his fellow Arab leaders by entering into open negotiations with an Israel that had besieged an Arab capital for weeks in its drive to evict the PLO from Beirut. As for hidden diplomacy, that too seemed fruitless: if years of secret discussions with various members of Israel's Labor Party had failed to produce a settlement, what chance would there be that the king could reach agreement with Begin's hard-line Likud faction? Begin himself had trouble convincing some of his supporters that the peace treaty with Egypt was worth trading territory for, and Likud's connection to the West Bank territories of Judea and Samaria far outstripped any attachment to the Sinai. "These are not *occupied* territories," Begin declared during a press conference held on the West Bank shortly after his election as prime minister. "You've used this expression for ten years, but from May 1977, you'll start using the word *liberated* territories. A Jew has every right to settle these liberated territories of the Jewish land." As for the possibility that he would officially annex the West Bank, Begin replied: "We don't use the word annexation. You annex foreign land, not your own country."[1] The deadlock with the Labor Party had centered on Hussein's insistence on regaining the entire West Bank region including east Jerusalem, while Peres, Rabin, Allon, and the others were willing to offer only a partial withdrawal, leaving behind limited Israeli security outposts. To Hussein, if the Labor position was unworkable, the Likud approach was hopeless.

Following Begin's resignation from office in 1983, his handpicked successor Yitzhak Shamir took over, a man held to be even more extremist than Begin, having opposed the Camp David Accords because he believed they granted dangerous concessions to the Egyptians. After the 1984 general elections ended in stalemate, with neither Likud nor Labor winning a majority in the Knesset, a National Unity Government was formed with Shimon Peres as prime minister, Shamir as foreign minister, and Yitzak Rabin as minister of defense (Peres and Shamir would exchange jobs two years later in accordance with the "rotation" agreement that formed the basis of the 1984 coalition).

Early in 1985, Prime Minister Peres tried to push beyond his previous private diplomacy with Hussein to create a similar Sadat-like breakthrough, frequently alluding to the superior power of public action over that of covert communication. "You know the speech of Sadat to the Knesset of Jerusalem was not necessarily a Zionist Speech," Peres told reporters during a visit to Rome. "Sadat pointed out exactly what he had on his mind, and all of us were listening very carefully."[2] For Peres, it was not the content of the Egyptian president's speech that was of utmost significance, but the fact that he had been publicly welcomed on Israeli soil, embraced by former enemies and saluted by an Israeli band playing an Arab national anthem, had prayed at the al-Aqsa Mosque in Jerusalem, had paid his respects at the Yad Vashem Holocaust memorial, and had addressed the Israeli Knesset. At his press conference in Rome on 20 February 1985, Shimon Peres was signalling the Jordanian leader to move beyond the two decades of secret talks with Israel, transcend the rhetoric and take the bold step that could break the psychological barriers to peace. "I am ready to go to Amman. I am sure Israelis would like to see it if King Hussein would come to Jerusalem and announce whatever he has in mind," Peres said.[3]

The king did not take up Peres's call for face-to-face public talks, and so another round of hidden diplomacy began.

At the time, Shimon Peres refused to admit publicly that he had embarked on another series of secret meetings with the king, but in 1985, the Israeli prime minister did initiate behind-the-scenes talks by sending a private message to Amman: no more Allon Plan, no more autonomy plan, Israel had something totally new to offer. Hussein was ready to listen. Two meetings were held between Peres and the king: one in Europe, reportedly in Paris; the other in Israel, reportedly in the south along the Jordanian-Israeli border.

Joining Peres at the secret encounters with Hussein was his close adviser, Dr. Yossi Balin, and Avraham Tamir, the director general of the prime minister's office and chief of military planning under the Begin government. In his account of the diplomatic breakthrough with Anwar Sadat, Ezer Weizman had singled out Tamir as a key force in keeping the negotiations on track:

General Tamir had clear views on the peace process. He regarded it as part of a broad overall strategic concept that would make Israel part of a defense alliance embracing the entire region. In effect, Tamir belonged to the third echelon of the constellation built up around the negotiations. This constellation was headed by Menachem Begin, at the peak of the pyramid, where the decisions were taken. Below Begin was the second echelon, taking the initiative in proffering advice and recommendations: it consisted of the ministers of defense and foreign affairs. The third echelon—made up of senior officers and civilian experts—put forward ideas, prepared alternatives, and submitted recommendations, but was not required to take any initiatives. General Tamir was an exception. In view of his experience in the talks that preceded the disengagement agreements of 1973 and his preparatory work well before anyone dreamed that peace was on the horizon, he became part of the echelon entrusted with launching initiatives. He proposed ideas, examined them, analyzed the intentions of the other side, and suggested gambits. His contribution to peace was weighty. When the time comes for the historians to rummage through the heaps of documents in an attempt to sketch out the process with the perspective of distant events, General Tamir will emerge as one of the architects of the Israeli-Egyptian peace treaty.[4]

Peres appeared to have shared Weizman's assessment of Tamir's abilities. The prime minister's meetings with the king in 1985 had been one of the most secret operations ever conducted by the Israeli leadership. Though leaks surrounding the Hussein meetings in the late 1960s and the 1970s had become almost routine, the 1985 encounters returned to the airtight climate of the early 1960s, though this time the Israeli participants not only kept them secret from the outside world but also withheld knowledge of them from senior members of their own ruling government and inner cabinet. The one noticeable exception was Avraham Tamir, who was invited to play a direct role in the Peres-Hussein negotiations.

In the summer of 1985, less than four months before press accounts about the Peres meetings with Hussein surfaced as a result of criticism leveled against the prime minister by Ariel Sharon and other Likud Party members serving in the Labor-Likud ruling coalition, a senior U.S. Pentagon official said that Peres was, even at that time, conducting behind-the-scenes talks with the king, if not in person then at the very least over the telephone.[5]

Still, some veteran Middle East analysts were skeptical of the reports of Peres's hidden diplomacy with Hussein, despite his history of talks with the previous Labor governments of Levi Eshkol and Golda Meir. The Likud leaders would not serve as the hapless opposition, observers noted, a role to which they had been relegated in the years prior to Menachem Begin's election as prime minster in 1977. Labor no longer had such a free hand, and any secret deals struck with Hussein on such a sensitive issue as the future of the West Bank would risk tearing the government apart. Labor and Likud had agreed to form a national unity coalition in order to combat the rapidly deteriorating Israeli economy, but they had agreed to disagree about the terms for a future peace agreement with Jordan. New elections would have to be called to approve any government action designed to alter the status of Judea and Samaria. Yet, despite the risk that the public disclosure of a secret Israeli-Jordanian deal would bring the government down, many American and Israeli sources both assumed that Peres was engaging in hidden diplomacy with the king throughout 1985.

Speculation on the outcome of the prime minister's talks with Hussein, however, whether they remained private or became public, was another matter: reaching an Israeli-Jordanian accord would prove to be much more difficult than the treaty signed with Sadat. The Sinai was not the same as the West Bank, which straddled the heart of Israel, and El-Arish was not Jerusalem, the time-honored capital of the Jewish people. Even the peace treaty with Egypt had involved torturous negotiations that nearly broke down at several points. Striking a deal with Hussein over the West Bank and Jerusalem would require unusual foresight, inventiveness, and courage, and for Peres, absolute secrecy.

The rationale for the unusual security surrounding the Hussein-Peres talks was not only that any undue publicity would jeopardize the king's life, or at the least his future political standing in the Arab world, but that premature publicity would likewise threaten Peres's own position in the fragile ruling coalition before he had a chance to obtain an agreement that might get him safely through new elections. Under the National Unity Government, Begin's successor, Yitzhak Shamir, was serving as foreign minister, and the cabinet included Likud leaders David Levy, Ariel Sharon, and Moshe Arens, all of whom were committed to a strong Israeli presence on the West Bank. For Peres, Hussein had become a partner in diplomacy, but members of his own cabinet were seen as potential adversaries who could derail his budding peace plan. Only when an agreement with Hussein was locked into place, Peres reasoned, could he reveal the substance of his secret talks with the king, at which time he would call an election and ask for a "mandate for peace." With the promise of a treaty with Jordan dangled before an Israeli public eager for an accommodation with their Arab neighbors, the electorate would be unlikely to unseat the prime minister who had managed to negotiate a possible solution with Hussein. Peres would still be challenged by Shamir, Sharon, Levy, Arens, and other members of the opposition, but with a peace agreement with King Hussein—however imperfect—in hand, surviving an Israeli re-election campaign would be practically a given. Should the details of the Peres position emerge prior to his reaching a final settlement with Hussein, however, the Israeli leader would be put on the defensive by his Likud challengers, with charges of appeasement and betrayal falling upon more receptive ears, the public not yet convinced that the Peres approach would do anything other than weaken the Israeli negotiating position and whet the Arab appetite for further concessions. If the Peres peace plan was to work, it had to be held under wraps until an agreement in principle had been worked out with the king, the negotiations kept secret not only from the world at large but from the key members of the Peres ruling coalition with Likud.

An "agreement in principle" between Peres and Hussein might have contained little more than a formula allowing for the start of public peace talks between Israel and Jordan. Though many observers might have concluded that a preliminary agreement on the outlines of a final settlement would likely prove as difficult to attain as it did during all the previous secret talks among Labor leaders and the king in the pre-Begin period, there was hope among Peres supporters that the latest round with Hussein might at a minimum yield agreement on the venue for formal discussions, a list of approved participants, and an agenda to be followed. "Once launched, the [public] negotiating process might produce a dramatic challenge to Israel and an ensuing coalition crisis," wrote Samuel Lewis, who served as American ambassador to Israel from 1977 to 1985. "This, in turn, could ignite an active debate over the price of peace, which could provide Peres with an opportunity to go to the electorate with some chance of gaining a workable Labor majority government. Such a government could then proceed unfettered to hammer out a peace agreement with Jordan. This was the Peres strategy."[6]

Though several prominent Israeli officials remained uninformed of Peres's hidden diplomacy with the king throughout most of 1985, senior members of the Reagan administration and Egypt's President Mubarak were made privy to the secret negotiations, along with Hussein's prime minister, Zeid al-Rafai. The terms of Israel's National Unity Government called for Yitzhak Shamir to take over from Peres as prime minister the following year, in October 1986. Reagan and Mubarak had a mutual interest in seeing to it that Peres succeeded in his talks with Hussein: they believed that an Israeli government under Shamir's Likud leadership would accelerate Jewish settlement of the West Bank and make progress toward a peace agreement much more difficult.

Geula Cohen, the former LEHI (Stern Gang) member who broke with Begin over her opposition to the Camp David accords, hoped to sabotage any Jordanian-United States-Israeli pact necessitating an Israeli withdrawal from Judea and Samaria. Speaking in the Israeli Knesset, Cohen attacked the Peres peace initiative and publicly accused him of holding a secret Paris meeting with Hussein sometime in October 1985, prior to his visit to the United States.

Peres had traveled to Paris on an private executive jet, meeting with President Francois Mitterand for a discussion of a French offer to assist in the emigration of Soviet Jews to Israel. After Paris, Peres flew to New York. On 21 October, he delivered an address to the United Nations calling for the immediate termination of war between Israel and Jordan and the beginning of direct peace talks. "This gathering can take place before the end of the year, in Jordan, Israel or any location, as mutually agreed upon," the Israeli prime minister said. "We will be pleased to attend an opening meeting in Amman."[7] Peres also announced his willingness to allow for some kind of international sponsorship, saying that the five permanent members of the U.N. Security Council could be involved in the "initiation of these negotiations," a formula whereby the talks would ostensibly begin under international or U.N. auspices and then break up into a series of direct one-on-one meetings between Israeli and Jordanian negotiators.

Israeli leaders had long been opposed to outside participation in peace talks with Jordan. They regarded few nations outside of the U.S. as capable of acting as honest brokers in the dispute with the Arabs. They were especially wary of the Soviet Union, a country that broke diplomatic relations with Israel in 1967 and openly sided with Israel's enemies, from Nasser's Egypt to Assad's Syria to Arafat's PLO. Peres's concession regarding an international setting for Israeli-Jordanian talks was viewed as an outright invitation to the Soviets, handing them an implicit veto power over any agreement worked out between Jerusalem and Amman. Peres's newfound receptivity toward the Soviets reportedly stemmed from a softening in Moscow's attitude to Israel, exhibited in Poland's agreement with Israel to open diplomatic interest sections in each other's countries and indications that large-scale immigration of Soviet Jews to Israel might be resumed via France.

Former defense minister Ariel Sharon, serving as minister of industry and commerce in the National Unity Government, accused the prime minister of not informing the cabinet of the secret dealings with Hussein, which he said consisted of such unacceptable Israeli concessions as granting the Soviets a seat at the negotiating table, pulling back in Judea and Samaria, and a political formula allowing for PLO participation in the peace process. A prominent and popular Likud member, Sharon declared that "Peres, with unequalled cynicism, totally contemptuous of proper Government procedure, is leading the Government down a crooked path without its ministers having any idea what is going on.''[8]

After repeated criticisms of his overtures to Hussein, Peres threatened to fire Sharon from the cabinet, thereby threatening the fragile Labor-Likud coalition. The prime minister demanded an apology and Sharon complied. Shortly thereafter, a close associate of Sharon said that if Peres continued on the same path, Sharon would continue his attacks, and the cycle of criticism-apology-criticism would persist if that was what it took to alter the prime minster's approach.

Despite the political attacks against Peres within Israel, King Hussein welcomed the prime minister's call at the United Nations calling for direct Jordanian-Israeli peace talks under international sponsorship:

> I feel that the spirit is what I had anticipated it to be, having watched his [Peres's] political actions over a period of time and having listened to his statements.
>
> I believe he is a man of vision and a man who is acting with very strong feelings regarding the rights of future generations in our area and their right to live under conditions different from those we have known.
>
> I realize he has enormous difficulties. One can only see him as a bright light in an area of darkness.[9]

Sharon was not impressed by the king's praise of Peres. In 1974, after quitting the army to enter politics, Sharon had told a reporter, ''I've just entered the political arena, and it already looks more dangerous than the battlefield. There, at least, you're fighting the enemy. In politics, you have to fight all sides—including your own.'' With his prime minister moving toward an accommodation with Hussein, Sharon found himself in the familiar position of fighting his fellow Jews as well as the Arabs.

At the secret Paris meeting with Peres in October 1985, Hussein was said to have lobbied for an interim agreement on the West Bank, harking back to the shuttle diplomacy days of Henry Kissinger and Yigal Allon's disengagement scheme under the Jericho Plan. If Israel made an attempt to reach a final settlement in any future peace talks, the king said he would enter formal negotiations by demanding a complete return of the entire West Bank, including east Jerusalem. In addition to the interim agreement formula, Hussein was also said to have insisted on the international forum for the Jordanian-Israeli talks in order to avoid accusations that he was seeking a separate peace with Israel at the expense of the Arab world—especially Syria and the PLO—a charge leveled against Sadat and which had led to Egypt's ostracism.

The private diplomacy between Peres and Hussein brought about some movement on the issues of a partial Israeli withdrawal on the West Bank and possible third party—that is Soviet—involvement in the peace process. The aim of the Reagan administration and Egypt's President Mubarak was to break the impasse over Palestinian representation in the proposed Jordanian-Israeli peace talks. Hussein insisted on giving the PLO a place at the negotiating table. The Israelis had been consistently opposed to any PLO representation. In an interview with an American reporter, Peres explained his government's position:

What is wrong is that it is not at all clear that the PLO is seeking a peaceful solution to the issue. There is a real suspicion here that the PLO seeks U.S. recognition against a promise to change but without really changing anything, as they did in Europe. They kept promising many countries they would change their policies, but they remained unchanged.

Then again, we don't feel very easy about PLO intentions toward Jordan. We believe in the basic sincerity of King Hussein. But what is really on the minds of the PLO is neither clear nor trustworthy. While the PLO has ostensibly declared a change in its direction, they are continuing with acts of terror to this very day. We cannot just keep our ears open, we have to keep our eyes open. And when we open our eyes, we get the same old dark picture.[10]

As of 3 September 1985, the "same old dark picture" was the fact that thirteen Israelis had been killed by PLO guerrilla attacks in the previous ten months. There had been a dramatic increase in terrorist incidents occurring on the West Bank. Israeli analysts reported that the outbreak of violence had been traced to Hussein's reconciliation with Arafat. The PLO had opened offices in Amman following the 11 February 1985 agreement between Hussein and Arafat, pledging cooperation in future peace negotiations. Hundreds of key guerrilla officials entered Jordan to take up their positions in Hussein's capital. The new arrivals included fighters from the PLO's Western Sector Office, which supervises terrorist operations on the West Bank, and fighters from Force 17, an elite commando unit whose name reportedly stemmed from the telephone extension number at a former PLO office in Beirut. The members of Arafat's personal bodyguard were hand-picked from Force 17, and the group's first commander was Ali Hasan Salameh, the man assassinated by the Israelis for his role in masterminding the Munich Olympic Massacre.[11] "Arafat and his friends feel they can maintain a double policy," Peres charged. "Talk peace in Jordan, kill people in Israel."[12]

Although Israeli sources admitted that Hussein was not allowing the Palestinian guerrillas to launch direct armed attacks into Israel from bases in Jordan, the establishment of a PLO military administrative office in Amman shortened the lines of communication with Fateh agents on the West Bank, enabling Arafat's commando leaders to funnel logistical support and planning to local fighters. Moreover, the "open bridges" policy in effect between Jordan and Israel allowed for a relatively free flow of people between the two countries; thus the large numbers of PLO operatives converging on Amman also increased the likelihood of direct PLO infiltration into Israel.

In August 1985, Israeli Defense Minister Yitzak Rabin told a gathering at the northern border town of Nahariya—the site of two deadly terrorist attacks and repeated PLO shelling from bases in southern Lebanon—that despite the Israeli invasion of Lebanon in 1982 and the summer siege of Beirut, "All the terrorist mechanisms of all the key terror organizations escaped from Lebanon. None of the key terrorists were hurt or liquidated. The key systems were not damaged or eliminated. Today, most of these systems are located in Amman rather than Beirut or Damascus." The following month, Rabin pointed to the "open bridges" policy and charged that the PLO had taken advantage of the easy access between Amman and Jerusalem. As a result, "enlistment operations, sending of orders, giving money to individuals" had become "unbelievably active" and was a cause of grave concern to Israel. If Hussein "does not put an end to this activity," Rabin warned, "as much as we would like to maintain a fabric of good neighborly relations, the terrorist headquarters and commands will not enjoy immunity just on account of their being located in Jordan."[13]

In the second half of 1985, as the political process advanced, the military situation escalated along with it: Peres engaged in secret diplomacy with Hussein while his defense minister threatened to carry out military reprisals in retaliation for the king's tacit approval of Arafat's clandestine warfare against Israel. Rabin's warning was all the more ominous because of his position as a member of the moderate Labor faction in the National Unity coalition. As a spokesman for the hard-line Likud, Ariel Sharon completed the spectrum of opinion, adding his voice to the chorus denouncing Hussein's entente with Arafat's commandos. "Israel under no circumstances can tolerate the presence of terrorist organization commandos so close to its borders," Sharon told reporters.[14] Many observers, especially in the U.S. State Department, concluded that despite the behind-the-scenes Peres-Hussein peace talks, a consensus was emerging in Jerusalem regarding the need to stamp out Palestinian terrorism organized from Amman. They feared that the Israelis were not bluffing about taking military action against the PLO bases in Jordan. On 1 October, 1985, Israeli warplanes had flown thirteen hundred miles across the Mediterranean to destroy the PLO head-quarters in Tunisia. The raid was in retaliation for the murder the previous month of three Israelis aboard a yacht moored at Larnaca harbor in Cyprus, one of whom was reported in the press to have been Sylvia Raphael, the Mossad agent who had helped secure Hussein's throne from PLO attacks during her undercover operations in Amman. Raphael was purportedly on a surveillance mission to ferret out PLO agents in Cyprus.[15] Six months after her supposed assassination by the PLO, Raphael wrote of her upcoming travel plans in a letter to the author.[16] The press accounts of the former Mossad agent's death in Cyprus were obviously wrong, apparently part of a deliberate disinformation campaign designed to quell the outcry over the PLO's murder of three Israeli tourists.[17] Ironically, the Norwegian newspaper that originally broke the story of Raphael's death falsely named an adviser to Ariel Sharon as the source of the report.

Israel "had nothing against Tunisia," the Israeli ambassador to France, Ovadia Sofer, told reporters following Israel's reprisal for the terrorist attack in Cyprus, but "the P.L.O. headquarters are protected by Tunisia, and the country bears some responsibility for the raid." Israel felt it could not stand by while Arafat's political headquarters in Tunis turned into a full-fledged operational center orchestrating terrorist assaults against Jews.

Tunisian President Habib Bourguiba, however, was a friend of the United States and was widely viewed as a constructive voice in the Arab-Israeli dialogue for peace. Bourguiba had accepted the Palestinian comman-dos in 1982 at the urging of the United States, when American officials were seeking to end the Israeli siege of Beirut by arranging an evacuation of the PLO fighters. Complicating matters further for Bourguiba was the view that the Israelis could not have carried out an air strike involving a thirteen hundred mile, seven hour flight across the Mediterranean by eight F-15 fighter-bombers without being detected by American surveillance equip-ment, which monitors the region heavily. Furthermore, the Israelis had managed to aim their bombs with pinpoint accuracy, demolishing PLO of-fices at Arafat's seven-acre complex, located in the Haman Shatt suburb just twelve miles southeast of Tunis, while leaving private Tunisian homes just a few feet away virtually untouched. "I am amazed how they were able to select these buildings as a target and not hurt any others," said one East European diplomat at the scene. "It was 100% precision."[18] There were numerous charges among the Arabs and their supporters that the United States had provided direct support for the strike. American officials vigorously denied any complicity in or foreknowledge of the attack. U.S. ships in the Mediterranean had not been in position to detect the flight of the fighter-jets and the tanker that refueled them in mid-flight during their return to Israel, said one senior administration official.[19] While the PLO, Cuba, Libya, and others accused the United States of "complicity" in the bombing, America's United Nations Ambassador Vernon Walters condemned such charges as "false," telling assembled delegates that "the United States had no knowledge of nor did it participate in this operation in any way."[20]

A somewhat different kind of American link to the Tunis raid did arise shortly after the attack however, when U.S. Navy analyst Jonathan Pollard was arrested the following month in November 1985 and charged with spying for Israel. Among the documents that Pollard allegedly passed along to Israeli intelligence were American reports on U.S. reconnaissance flights over Tunisia that included descriptions of the PLO complex outside Tunis, data on Libyan air defenses in the region, and details concerning the movements of U.S., French, and Soviet ships in the Mediterranean. *Jerusalem Post* reporter Wolf Blitzer quoted one Israeli official as saying that Pollard's disclosures "made our life much easier" in the strike against the PLO headquarters in Tunis.[21] Pollard himself was found guilty of espionage in 1987 and was given a life-sentence.

Foreign Minister Yitzhak Shamir said at the time of the bombing that the Tunis raid was "a warning that Israel will retaliate and fight against terrorist acts against its citizens."[22] Defense Minister Rabin declared, "We have shown terrorist groups and the world that there is no place where terrorist organizations can be immune to blows from our forces."[23] Rabin also reiterated that his government had "nothing against Tunisia," but that it could not tolerate "immunity for the PLO because they are located in countries which are not active against Israel."[24]

A few weeks after the attack against the PLO headquarters, Ariel Sharon told reporters that the lesson of the Tunis raid should not be lost on Hussein.[25]

The consensus among both the more moderate Peres-Rabin Labor faction of the Israeli leadership and the more extreme Shamir-Sharon Likud wing regarding the determination to check PLO power in the region, underscored by the Tunis attack carried out under Peres's premiership, led many to question the wisdom of Hussein's new flirtation with the PLO. Why would the king risk aborting the peace process with Peres by allowing Arafat's commando leaders to operate inside Jordan?

Hussein may have concluded that the Israeli public was growing increasingly impatient with the status quo, that it had been left divided and debilitated by the controversial 1982 invasion of Lebanon, and that its growing frustration over Israel's inability to thwart PLO terrorism might put pressure on the Israeli leadership to come to terms with Hussein and Arafat, even if it meant agreeing to significant concessions on the West Bank.

The upsurge in Fateh violence might have also served to demonstrate that the king was still a player to be reckoned with: that, far from the popular wisdom that it was the powerful President Assad of Syria who held the key to any Middle East settlement, Hussein of Jordan still retained geopolitical assets capable of disrupting Israeli society—a long frontier with Israel, and a highly motivated restless Palestinian refugee population eager for battle, composed of would-be fighters enjoying close ties to relatives and friends on the West Bank.

Hussein's rapprochement with the Palestinian guerrillas also undoubtedly enhanced his image in the Arab world, his readiness to provide an operational headquarters for attacks against Israel clearly displaying his fidelity to the "liberation" of Palestine. The willingness to employ terror in the war against Israel had become a virtual litmus test among Arab patriots. When Khaled Hassan was asked why the Fateh leadership had not condemned the use of terror from the outset of its operations and had not moved to block it in subsequent years, the PLO official replied: "We would have lost our credibility as leaders; nobody in the rank and file of our movement would have listened to us; and the terror operations would still have taken place. And some of us would have been assassinated."[26]

Whether or not this was the only reason for his sanction of terrorism, Khaled Hassan had nevertheless learned that his status as an authentic Palestinian leader would be severely weakened by the rejection of guerrilla raids against Israeli civilians. Conversely, Hussein may have figured that his own stature would be bolstered by his willingness to lend support, albeit indirectly, to the PLO's commando attacks against Israel. It would undoubtedly enable him to at least ingratiate himself with Yassir Arafat to some extent, for as Ambassador Lewis observed, Hussein "remained convinced that his reign would be endangered were he to meet or negotiate openly with Israeli leaders about the West Bank and Gaza without the legitimacy conveyed by Arafat's seal of approval."[27] Providing Fateh with an operational headquarters in Jordan to facilitate PLO raids into Israel could only help the king in his effort to garner the Arafat seal.

There were some who believed that the monarch's renewed effort to win the hearts of the Palestinian masses through such means as a periodic readiness to support terrorist attacks inside the West Bank and Gaza was consistent with Hussein's long-term goal of securing his own power base within Jordan, and that whatever risks it engendered for a Jordanian-Israeli peace accord were worth it because the king was not serious about seeking an agreement with Peres.

According to former Haig assistant Harvey Sicherman, Hussein was interested in the appearance of movement in the peace process in order to convince Washington that he was a reliable moderate who deserved increased military support from the United States. Prime Minister Peres, said Sicherman, was aware that Hussein was not ready to make real peace with Israel, but he too wanted to contribute to the illusion of movement in order to woo the Israeli electorate and successfully challenge his Likud rivals in the wake of a break-up of the National Unity Government coalition.

For Arafat, the alignment with Hussein not only rescued him from obscurity in the aftermath of the PLO's exile from Beirut, but also served notice to Syria's President Assad, whose support for the anti-Arafat Fateh rebels had forced the PLO chief from his base in Tripoli, Lebanon, on 20 December, 1983. Arafat's first stop after his expulsion from Tripoli was Ismailia, Egypt. He was then taken by helicopter to Cairo for an audience with President Mubarak, a gesture breaking the PLO's ban against official contacts with Egypt, taken at the Baghdad summit of 1979 in response to Sadat's "traitorous" peace with Israel. With Mubarak embracing him in front of the cameras, and Hussein welcoming him back to Amman, Arafat sent a signal to his arch-rival Assad that he had alternative allies in the Arab world. Sicherman reasoned that the PLO chief's reconciliation with Cairo and Amman might prompt Damascus into seeking an accommodation with Arafat in order to undercut Egyptian-Jordanian influence and reassert the Syrian role in the Middle East peace process.[28]

Hirsh Goodman, the military correspondent for the *Jerusalem Post*, also saw the Hussein overtures to Peres as an exercise in propaganda rather than as a sincere effort for peace. Hussein was seeking to buy nearly $1.9 billion in arms from the United States, a package that included advanced F-16 fighter aircraft and other sophisticated weaponry. Israel's supporters in Congress had long been in favor of linking such purchases to progress on the diplomatic front, making them conditional on Hussein's willingness to accept Israel's right. to exist and enter public, face-to-face talks with the country's leadership. Senator Edward Kennedy (D-Mass.) explained that "opposing the attempt to arm the enemies of Israel is no partisan issue—but a national commitment." Despite his moderate pose, Hussein's refusal to recognize the Jewish state and sign a peace agreement with Jerusalem meant that Jordan still numbered among the list of Israel's Arab enemies. Senator John Heinz (R-Pa.) said that "selling advanced weapons" to Hussein "prior to direct negotiations between Israel and Jordan, is premature and unwarranted."[29] According to Goodman, the king was going through the motions of peace, demanding PLO involvement and Soviet sponsorship while praising Peres as a "man of vision," all in a calculated effort to win Congressional approval for the billion dollar weapons sale. "Despite the king's platitudes, formulas, and convoluted prescriptions for proceeding with the peace process, he has no intention of acting upon them," Goodman wrote:

> Hussein and the PLO are competitors for the allegiance of the Palestinians, and any ostensible alliance between them now is tactical, not strategic. The PLO is currently using Hussein to help itself gain de facto American recognition, and Hussein is using the PLO to perpetuate the impression of moderation and movement while the Reagan administration discusses more weapons sales for his army. These maneuvers are not designed to change the status quo in the Middle East, but to preserve it through an illusion of progress.[30]

Hussein claimed that he needed U.S. weaponry not to challenge Israel but to confront the Syrians, whose leadership has had a history of hostility toward the Jordanian monarchy. The Syrians had challenged Hashemite rule by backing PLO guerrillas during the Black September uprising of 1970, and in 1984, when there were indications that the king might engage in a dialogue with the newly-elected Prime Minister Peres, Syria's Vice President Zuheir Masharka issued a death threat against Hussein and his colleagues, warning that "Jordanian leaders should not expect their fate will not be different from that of the late Anwar Sadat."[31] Supporters of the American arms sale to Jordan noted that, unlike other radical Arab states such as Syria and Libya, Hussein held moderate views regarding the conflict with Israel, as shown by the monarch's willingness to engage in secret negotiations with Peres. Furthermore, they contended, he alone could bring Arafat and his recalcitrant PLO followers to the negotiating table, as demonstrated by the February 11th Agreement. But in order for the king's peace initiatives to continue, he would have to get U.S. arms to protect him from the ever-present threats from rejectionist regimes in Damascus, Baghdad, and Tripoli. If, as Sicherman, Goodman, and others proclaimed, Hussein's secret diplomacy with Peres was in fact a ruse to seduce American policymakers, it nevertheless yielded results. In a defense of the Jordanian arms sale, the U.S. assistant secretary of defense for international security affairs, Richard Armitage, noted that "King Hussein has been working assiduously during the past year to steer the Palestinian movement toward a negotiated peace settlement," and he warned that "every step Jordan takes toward peace with Israel will virtually guarantee greater tension with Syria."[32] The apparent corollary was that an increase in military supplies to the Hashemite Kingdom would strengthen his defense against an extremist Syria, freeing him to pursue the peace process with Israel, bringing the PLO with him.

The Israelis, including Peres, were adamantly against the sale, whether or not Hussein's peace initiative was sincere. "Is not the greatest threat to Hussein, and the other moderates, insurgency—not tanks and missiles?" Goodman wrote. "Did Phantoms save Sadat, and did F-14s save the shah? And perhaps, most significantly, did not President Sadat make his journey to Jerusalem in 1978 [*sic*] only when he realized that Israel could not be dealt with by military means?"[33] To the Israeli leadership, it was a willingness to conduct direct negotiations, not the possession of American weapons, that was the prerequisite for peace.

President Reagan strongly advocated the need for a safe Israel, but he was also convinced of the need to safeguard Hussein's throne with U.S. armaments, which might serve to deter Syrian aggression and build confidence in Hussein's drive for a peace agreement with Israel. The Reagan team lobbied for the arms transfer to Jordan, and pressed Peres to come up with a political formula that could satisfy the Hussein-Mubarak-Arafat axis. Despite the Israeli abhorrence of the PLO, the U.S. assistant secretary of state for Near Eastern and South Asian affairs, Richard Murphy, privately worked with Fateh's Khaled al-Hassan, reportedly using intermediaries, in an effort to formulate a list of Palestinian leaders who would be acceptable to the PLO as participants in preparatory Jordanian-Palestinian peace talks with the United States

On 17 July 1985, the U.S. charge d'affaires in Jerusalem, Robert Flaten, handed Prime Minister Peres a list of seven Palestinians that had been compiled by Yassir Arafat the previous week and forwarded to King Hussein for delivery to the Americans and the Israelis.[34] The proposed Palestinian team was composed of the following people:

Hatem Hussaini, the former PLO spokesman in Washington who in 1982 told "Nightline's" ABC reporter Sam Donaldson that there had indeed been direct ongoing political contacts between American officials and PLO members;

Saleh al-Taamri, a pro-Arafat member of Fateh who served as a PLO commando in southern Lebanon. Taamri, who married King Hussein's first wife, Dina, was released from Ansar detention camp in a 1983 prisoner exchange after serving more than a year in the Israeli jail;

Nabil Shaath, an Arafat adviser and prominent member of the Palestine National Council, the PLO's parliamentary body, and the PLO's former liaison in Cairo;

Faiz Abu Rahmeh, a pro-Arafat lawyer from the Gaza Strip who served as head of the Gaza Chamber of Advocates and a traditional leader among the Palestinians living within the Israeli-occupied territories;

Hanna Seniora, editor of the Palestinian East Jerusalem daily, *Al-Fajr*, an American-educated pro-Arafat leader who is viewed as a moderate who supports the establishment of a PLO state alongside Israel;

Henry Kattan, a Paris-based lawyer and historian with special expertise in Palestinian affairs, and Fayez Sayigh, a Palestinian economist and scholar, the two men proposed as alternate members of the delegation;

Khaled al-Hassan, a co-founder of the Fateh faction and member of the PLO's Central Committee.

The inclusion of people like Hatem Hussaini, Saleh al-Taamri, and Khaled Hassan might have been an attempt by Arafat to make the other proposed members more palatable to Israel when compared to these outright PLO functionaries.

The Israelis, both those in Shimon Peres's Labor Party and Yitzhak Shamir's Likud, however, quickly rejected the proposed Palestinian delegation. "Basically this list is P.L.O.," said a Peres official. "You don't need to be a hawk to oppose it. Even the super doves here see it as an attempt to legitimize the P.L.O. in American eyes." Yitzhak Shamir asked a group of followers, "How is it possible that this terrorist organization [the PLO] should suddenly be a dialogue partner for the United States, which stands at the forefront of the war against world terrorism?"[35]

The Israelis saw any future negotiations between American officials and those included in the Arafat list as a clear violation of the Kissinger statement pledging to withhold U.S. recognition of the PLO until the guerrilla group accepted Israeli's right to exist and agreed to abide by U.N. Resolutions 242 and 338.

The inclusion of Khaled Hassan was a particularly brazen attempt to subvert the Kissinger ban. Khaled had been a key operative since Fateh's inception. He had not only been named by Palestinians like Fawaz Turki as the PLO contact in secret talks with American officials, but his ties to terrorist operations had surfaced frequently over the years, as they did during the Achille Lauro hijacking when he ostensibly acted as a go-between in the negotiations for the ship's release. Israeli sources dismissed his professed role as intermediary, claiming to have evidence pointing to Khaled's collusion in the Palestinian commando takeover of the Italian cruise liner. Khaled Hassan's political views were also suspect: in August 1985, he told a Kuwaiti newspaper that U.S. recognition of the PLO and the subsequent establishment of a Palestinian entity on the West Bank and Gaza were only "stages in a struggle," the "final objective" being the destruction of the Israeli nation and its replacement by an expanded PLO state.[36]

Hassan's brother, Hani, had also played a prominent role in PLO politics for years, having established an effective underground recruiting center in West Germany for would-be Fateh commandos. "By 1963, Hani was what Arafat had been—the most powerful Palestinian leader of his generation,'' wrote Arafat's British biographer, Alan Hart.[37]

Following the Six Day War in 1967, Arafat and the two Hassan brothers had decided to step up the guerrilla campaign against Israel. The Mossad, however, had managed to infiltrate deeply into the ranks of the PLO. When Fateh decided to launch its first large-scale operation by sending ten commandos across the Jordanian border, Israeli forces were waiting. The entire terrorist squad was captured, and according to Israeli intelligence, so was Hani Hassan.

The Mossad reportedly told Hani that Israel wanted to reach a settlement with the Palestinians. According to the Israelis, the hands of the PLO were still relatively clean of Jewish blood at that time, so the leadership was still open to an accord with the Palestinian group. Prime Minister Eshkol and Mossad Chief Meir Amit decided to try and turn Hani Hassan into a goodwill ambassador who could convey their sentiments to Arafat. Hani was taken on a tour of Israeli kibbutzim and introduced to the residents of Jewish towns and villages, hoping to give him a picture of daily life in Israel that might soften his attitude and instill a desire for peaceful coexistence with the Jewish state.

The Six Day War had overwhelmed the Arabs like a flood, the Israelis reasoned, and with their crushing defeat might come the realization that the moment had arrived to start anew and put a final stop to the war against the Jews. After seeing Israel firsthand, it was thought that Hani Hassan might agree to serve as a messenger of peace, like the dove sent out from Noah's ark after the flood:

> And the dove came in to him in the evening; and lo, in her mouth *was* an olive leaf pluckt off: so Noah knew that the waters were abated from the earth.[38]
>
> Gen. 8:11

Eshkol and Amit ordered Hani Hassan's release, and the PLO militant was told to inform his brother Khaled and Arafat that Israel was eager to arrive at a solution to the conflict with the Palestinians. But Hani did not return with an olive leaf. The Israelis never heard from him again. Hani remained with Khaled and Arafat and continued the assault against the Jewish state. Khaled Hassan explained the reasons for the decision to keep fighting in the aftermath of the 1967 war, when there were signs that Israel was willing to withdraw from the captured territories in exchange for a peace agreement with the Arabs:

We became dominated, I can even say obsessed, by the idea that Israel might withdraw from the West Bank. At the time this was really a horrifying idea to us in Fateh. And that's why we began to think that we should resume our military activities. If the Israelis withdrew from the West Bank for peace, they would continue to enjoy the support of world opinion and we Palestinians would not be allowed to fight. We would have nowhere to fight. So we had to begin confrontation with Israel before there was any Israeli withdrawal. To keep the possibility of struggle alive, and also to keep the Arabs on our side, we needed a situation in which we could say that we were not defeated, that we had raised the banner of struggle and that it was as a result of our actions that the Israelis had been forced to withdraw![39]

For Arafat and the Hassan brothers, it was not enough that the West Bank be placed under Arab (Jordanian) rule; the territories had to fall within the PLO's jurisdiction. So the guerrilla assault against Israel following the Six Day War was not only a struggle to "liberate Arab lands from the Jews," as was frequently proclaimed, but also a PLO war against the Arab world, fought under the banner of anti-Zionism, a political / military / propaganda battle to secure PLO dominance in Palestine. As Arafat later explained, "From the very beginning I was saying that it was only by fighting that we could fix our identity." Apparently, recognition, or at least acceptance, by fellow Arabs of the reality of a "culturally and politically distinct Palestinian people that had inhabited Palestine from time immemorial" required a prolonged guerrilla struggle against the Jews.

The precariousness of the Palestinian national identity had long been an issue in the Arab-Israeli dispute. Pressing the point even further were people like Golda Meir, who asserted that the establishment of Israel by the Jews did not threaten Palestinian nationalism, it created it. Without the Jews, there would have been no fight through which to "fix" the Palestinian identity among fellow Arabs. The Palestinian identity would have naturally been subsumed by the Syrian one, perhaps the Jordanian one, or some larger pan-Arab political association. But the adamant refusal to accept Jewish sovereignty in any portion of the Middle East unleashed a century-old conflict that eventually engendered a separate Arab Palestinian political identity which was used to match Zionist claims that the Jews are a distinct people and thus have a right to their own national homeland. The war against Jewish rule in Palestine could then be said to be that of an indigenous Arab population with a unique national, political, and cultural identity locked in battle against the Zionist usurpers, struggling for their very survival as a people. "The Arab movement is not one of revival, and its moral value is dubious. But in a political sense, this is a national movement," David Ben-

Gurion had written in 1929. "The obvious characteristic of a political movement is that it knows how to mobilize the masses. From this perspective there is no doubt that we are facing a political movement, and we should not underestimate it."[40] To those who shared this view, the Palestinian movement was not a revival simply because there was no historical Palestinian national identity to revive, and therefore its moral claims to statehood were dubious. But for Ben-Gurion, the very fact that the Palestinians were sufficiently motivated and adequately organized in their resistance to Jewish settlement gave them status, at least in political terms, as a legitimate national movement. For Golda Meir, the motivation of Palestine's Arabs stemmed more from this rejection of the Jews than from any ambition to reconstruct a lost Palestinian nation.

The centrality of the conflict with Zionism in the evolution of the contemporary Palestinian identity has been widely accepted on both sides of the Arab-Israeli conflict. Even the official PLO historians readily attest to this, though of course for them, unlike Ben-Gurion and Meir, the fact in no way delegitimizes or mars the moral worth of that identity. "It was the particularity of the oppression and resistance [to British rule and Jewish settlement] which determined that the Palestinians would develop a special national identity, distinct from that of neighboring Arab peoples — Jordanian, Lebanese, Syrian, and others," journalist Sheila Ryan wrote in a publication put out by the Association of Arab-American University Graduates, an organization sympathetic to PLO aims.[41] Citing the Israeli historian Yehoshua Porath, the author points out that the Arabs of Palestine decided to concentrate their efforts on the political future of Palestine as a distinct entity because "the ambitions of the Jews were also concentrated in that country alone."[42]

Of course, the authenticity of a five thousand-year-old Jewish national heritage has also been challenged by Arab thinkers and their supporters. They have, indeed, insisted that the Hebrew legacy is purely a religious one, and that the Jews therefore could not be said to possess a shared sense of national destiny. Jewish claims of nationhood had ceased two thousand years ago, they explain, when the Kingdom of Israel was destroyed by the Roman legions, and thus there is no legitimate legal basis for the modern day creation of the Jewish state. The nation of Canaan, the country which Palestinian activists cite as the historical basis for their own national identity, had ceased as an independent political entity not two thousand, but more than three thousand years ago. But in making the case for Arab Palestine, the statute of limitations governing a people's right to nationhood was to be selectively applied: the descendants of a Canaanite nation that dated back nearly three thousand years still retained the right to an independent state in Palestine; the Jews of an Israeli kingdom that disappeared two thousand years ago did not.

Descending from the Arab-Israeli dispute's ideological plane to a more immediate level, Yassir Arafat's Fateh, in the months following the 1967 Six Day War, was horrified by the prospect of a voluntary Israeli withdrawal from the West Bank and Gaza because it would have robbed the PLO of the opportunity to claim that it had spearheaded the liberation of Arab land by forcing the Israelis out, thus weakening PLO leverage in any subsequent fashioning of an Arab-Israeli peace agreement.[43] Another unspoken concern might have been that such an exchange of land for peace might have left the Arab world with the belief that the conflict with the Jews had come to a close. For many PLO members, including the "moderate" Fateh faction, the West Bank and Gaza was not enough: the complete eradication of the Israeli state and the installation of an Arab regime ruling all of Palestine were the only acceptable terms for ending the conflict. Blocking a settlement that would have called for an Israeli retreat from the West Bank and Gaza might help to ensure that the Arab battle against all of Israel continued, the Palestinian militants might have reasoned, the distinction between the pre-1967 borders and the post-1967 frontiers blurred by the persistent Arab struggle against Jewish rule.

In 1985, Arafat and the Hassan brothers were being touted as PLO moderates whose only aim was to secure a Palestinian "mini-state" on the West Bank and Gaza Strip that would exist in quiescent harmony with their Jewish neighbors in a pre-1967 Israel. Apparently, the bloodshed over the eighteen year period since 1967 had enabled them to "fix" the Palestinian identity. Their leverage in any negotiated agreement with the Israelis, however, did not stem from any ability to claim that the PLO had forced the Israelis to withdraw from the West Bank and Gaza, but from a joint decision by Egypt and Jordan to co-opt the Palestinian militants by including Arafat in the peace process.

The question of ultimate sovereignty over the proposed Palestinian mini-state in the West Bank and Gaza was given a temporary answer by Ronald Reagan, Hosni Mubarak, and King Hussein: Arafat and Hussein would agree to set up a federation encompassing the newly-created Palestinian entity west of the Jordan River and the Hashemite Kingdom to the east. The missing element in the United States-Egyptian-Jordanian scheme was the acquiescence of the Israelis and the approval of the Palestinian Arabs on the West Bank and Gaza. Securing Jerusalem's approval for a Palestinian-Jordanian federation would require direct, detailed discussions between Israel and Jordan, leading to concrete arrangements satisfying the security needs that would arise for Israel following its withdrawal from the West Bank territories of Judea and Samaria.

For Reagan, Hussein, and Mubarak, the first step toward federation had to be the development of a procedure that would ultimately lead to face-to-face talks between Jordan and Israel. Hussein demanded an international forum that included the Russians, and the Americans relented despite their antagonism toward Moscow. The king also demanded PLO participation. The American effort to engage in preparatory talks with a Jordanian-Palestinian delegation turned up the pressure on Israel to consent to the inclusion of PLO-sanctioned participants in the peace process. Peres was not necessarily expected to accept Arafat loyalists like Khaled Hassan, Hatem Hussaini, and Saleh al-Taamri as negotiating partners, but the United States was intent on breaking the impasse over the issue of Palestinian representation in the proposed Jordanian-Israeli talks.

In his secret meetings with Peres, the king pressed his demand for the inclusion of PLO-sponsored delegates. Avraham Tamir, the tough-minded adviser who had previously served as an aide to Ariel Sharon, was reportedly ready to deal with the PLO directly, but Peres was not prepared to go that far. The prime minister told Hussein that he would be willing to accept political representatives belonging to the PLO's Palestine National Council as long as they were not members of any of the various PLO military factions. Peres even was said to have initially hesitated before rejecting Khaled Hassan's name as a possible participant, though he eventually settled on his narrower criteria barring guerrilla members from the talks. Meanwhile, Peres's foreign minister, Yitzhak Shamir, told American Secretary of State George Shultz that his Likud Party rejected participation by Palestine National Council members regardless of their particular affiliation. "There is no good or bad PLO," Shamir reportedly told Shultz.[44]

On 4 September 1985, Tamir held a meeting in Cairo with President Mubarak and his adviser, Osama el-Baz, to discuss the subject of Palestinian participation in Israeli-Jordanian peace talks. At the same time, el-Baz also held discussions with Yassir Arafat, briefing him on the progress of the meetings with Tamir. The deliberations among Mubarak, el-Baz, and Tamir were an attempt to come up with a list of Palestinians that would be mutually acceptable to Peres and Arafat.

In addition to the demand for a PLO role in any Israeli-Jordanian settlement, Hussein stuck to his refusal to hold public negotiations without an international endorsement. He was not ready to follow the Egyptians into Arab exile for having made a separate peace with the Jews. Yet any meaningful United Nations involvement or other international participation required the support of the Soviet Union. The United States was not eager to invite the Soviets into the peace process after Henry Kissinger's shuttle diplomacy and Jimmy Carter's Camp David accords had managed to effectively shut them out. Yet the United States had dropped its objection in the face of Hussein's continuing demand for Soviet involvement. Peres conditioned his approval on a reestablishment of diplomatic relations between Israel and the USSR and an easing of restrictions blocking the immigration of Soviet Jews. The Israelis, said Peres, could not be expected to allow a country that did not even have diplomatic relations with one of the parties to play the role of mediator, nor could they accept Soviet participation when the leaders in Moscow were still enforcing draconian measures against their own nation's two million Jews. In 1984, emigration of Soviet Jews had dwindled to 896, down from the 1979 peak when 51,000 Jews were permitted to leave the USSR. The New York-based National Council of Soviet Jewry reported that as of October 1985, 400,000 Jews had taken steps to apply for the hard-to-obtain exit visas required for emigration from the Soviet state.[45]

The Mideast players—Mubarak, Hussein, and Peres—hoped that satisfactory terms for meeting the Israeli conditions could be hammered out during the November 1985 Geneva summit between President Reagan and Soviet leader Mikhail Gorbachev. But with arms control and Reagan's controversial Strategic Defense Initiative dominating the Geneva agenda, there were no immediate. breakthroughs regarding the normalization of Soviet relations with Israel, the lessening of restrictions against Soviet Jewry, or the prospects for a United States-Soviet sponsored forum for Middle East peace talks.

The secret Hussein-Peres talks of 1985 did not bring a dramatic Sadat-like breakthrough, but they did result in a new Israeli proposal for a peace agreement with Jordan. The plan, presented to Hussein by Prime Minister Peres, had been formulated in consultation with Secretary of State George Shultz, the American ambassador to Israel, Thomas Pickering, the Ambassador to Egypt, Nicholas Veliotes, and the assistant secretary of state, Richard Murphy. The two key phrases of the Peres plan were "power sharing" and "interim."

Power sharing: Peres proposed that Israel and Jordan engage in joint administration of the West Bank and Gaza Strip for an indefinite period, though this was eventually reduced to a three-year period. There would be a total freeze on new Jewish settlement on the West Bank, and a transfer of a five hundred thousand acres of government land to Hashemite control, effectively blocking expansion by the existing settlements into undeveloped areas. An Arab flag would fly over the Moslem holy places in Jerusalem, possibly the Saudi flag.

Interim agreement. The three-year joint Jordanian-Israeli arrangement would not constitute a final peace agreement. Thus, Hussein would retain the right to demand the return of east Jerusalem to Jordanian control. He would not have to relinquish the position he had presented to Israeli leaders for the last two decades: the total withdrawal of Israeli forces from lands captured during the 1967 Six Day War. Just as Allon's Jericho Plan was to serve as an interim "disengagement" agreement on the way to a complete pullback of Israeli forces, the Peres plan could likewise be viewed by Hussein as a temporary arrangement, established in lieu of an eventual reassertion of Jordanian authority over all of the kingdom's pre-1967 territories, with the likely addition of the formerly Egyptian-controlled Gaza Strip. This interim stage might very well lead to the settlement envisioned under Hussein's 1972 United Arab Kingdom Plan: a Palestinian entity on the West Bank and Gaza, federated with Jordan and under the leadership of the Hashemite monarchy.

In the mid-1980s, the dominant view among Middle East experts ostensibly ruled out the "Jordan is Palestine" formula that saw Palestinian nationalism expressing itself in Amman rather than the West Bank. There was increasing talk of a federation linking the territories on the West Bank and Gaza with the state of Jordan, with various demilitarized zones and military arrangements designed to safeguard the security of Israel. Hussein had patiently maneuvered to win the backing of Arafat as well as that of Mubarak's Egypt, and the federation scheme promulgated by the king was in essence little more than a thinly disguised version of the Reagan Middle East peace plan issued in September 1982, so the Hussein peace process enjoyed the support of the United States as well.

Is federation just a temporary stopover on the road to a "Jordan is Palestine" solution? It is unlikely that the Palestinians on the West Bank would willingly remain under the rule of a Hashemite monarchy in Amman for any prolonged length of time. Their own West Bank entity would have a degree of self-government, yet it would inevitably be hemmed in by the two powers on either side of it, Jordan and Israel. It would be a state lacking an independent foreign policy and a standing army, and its population would contain a large segment whose roots lay outside the West Bank, refugees who still longed to return to their homes in pre-1967 Israel. The PLO leadership would probably resent efforts to trim their powers in the Palestinian portion of the federation, especially if the constraints were imposed by the "alien" Hashemite regime from the Hejaz, a government that had nearly annihilated the Palestinian militants during the Black September civil war in 1970 .

Any attempt by West Bank and Gaza Palestinians in league with the PLO to break out of their predicament by launching an outright attack against Israel would be suicidal. Subverting the Jordanian monarchy from within would be the safer way to expand PLO power, and there would be no shortage of help from the Soviets and their allies who could only benefit from the overthrow of Hussein's pro-Western regime. An Israeli-Jordanian settlement that guaranteed the continued military strength of the Jews, while at the same time placing hundreds of thousands of Palestinian Arabs under the indefinite autocratic rule of Hussein's Hashemite regime, could indeed block Palestinian nationalism from turning west toward Israel, but might prompt the PLO to move eastward toward Amman.

A demilitarized, dependent West Bank entity under Hussein's thumb could press the PLO into revolt, and should their rebellion succeed in toppling the Hashemites, then the "Jordan is Palestine" formula would come to fruition, except that the new "Arab Republic of Palestine" would consist of an expanded Jordan that included the formerly Israeli-held lands in the West Bank and Gaza. To avoid such an eventuality might require an ongoing United States-Israeli effort to bolster repressive measures in the newly-constituted "Federation of Jordan and Arab Palestine" in order to keep Hussein on his throne in Amman. Federation might yield peace in the short term; the long run could see the establishment of a pro-Western, oppressive, forty-year shah-like reign by the Hashemite dynasty—or a PLO state run by pro-Soviet radicals like those in Marxist South Yemen.

Writing in 1970, Shimon Peres was moved to comment on the injudiciousness of forging a peace that relied on the continued rule of the Hashemites:

> King Hussein is almost certainly one of the few Arabs who has sincerely tried to learn the lesson of war, and there have been indications that he is prepared to conduct negotiations with Israel for a permanent peace settlement. But he is a weak candidate for peace—because of the weakness of his position. There are basic domestic obstacles which he must overcome, and it is doubtful whether he is able to do this. His first problem is that of status and authority. A king is not a president or a prime minister. His authority does not spring from popular elections or from an appointment backed by force, but from a title inherited from his father. Monarchs today are few and rare, and they are fast disappearing from the world's landscape. Even a courageous king is not a representative leader, as is the rule in most modern countries, but is born to the title, as in olden times, and most of his thoughts and energies are inevitably concerned with how to preserve it.
>
> Hussein's second problem is the very isolation of both his monarchy and his dynasty within his own kingdom. His is a non-indigenous dynasty, a foreign plant from the Hedjaz [*sic*], enthroned in Jordan by the grace of outsiders. There are numerous signs that opposition to it, both open and

concealed, is widely supported in Jordan. Hussein is thus forced to rely on Bedouin tribes, who are in the minority. He cannot count on the backing of the bulk of his population.[46]

The precarious nature of Hussein's government was singled out by Peres as an important factor in Israel's reluctance to place the West Bank under Jordanian rule:

> The return of the West Bank to Jordan, for example, would mean the siting of Jordanian artillery along the whole of Israel's Mediterranean coastal strip, the most densely populated in the country. These guns could again try to do what they did before—shell Israel's cities and villages from short range whenever the Jordanians felt like it. Even if there were an agreement to demilitarize the West Bank, the value of such an agreement would depend upon the power of the signatory—or indeed upon his very existence. Kingship may be a life job, but monarchs are not immortal. Jordan may be able to base her security on the words of a document, but Israel cannot base hers on a king.[47]

Fifteen years after his statements elaborating on the king's vulnerability, Peres privately and publicly demonstrated a readiness to accept Hussein as a willing, though perhaps still "weak candidate for peace." The king had indeed proved that he was a survivor, though Israeli analysts still predicted a precarious future for the Jordanian monarch. The consensus remained among both Peres's Labor Party supporters and Ariel Sharon's Likud followers that the security issues on the West Bank had to take precedence over the political opportunities presented by a Hussein peace initiative. The choice of the "Jordanian option" for an Arab-ruled West Bank federated with Amman over a "Jordan is Palestine" solution had to ensure that the region would not become a base for infiltration by disgruntled Palestinians and PLO extremists operating with or without Hussein's tacit approval.

The Israeli leadership agreed that protection from West Bank PLO extremism could not be entrusted to Hussein and the uncertainties of his continued reign. For Peres, the answer was a three-year joint administration between Israeli and Jordanian forces, with security arrangements to be developed in an atmosphere of trust as the peace process unfolded. For Sharon, only Jewish soldiers, not Jordanian Legionnaires, would be willing to vigorously pursue the fight against Arab terrorist attacks on Jews. "Never shall a Jordanian soldier or policeman or official be able to have any role in conducting or administering Samaria, Judea, or Gaza," Sharon declared.[48]

Indeed, in the spring of 1987, the extremist factions within the PLO that would surely produce Palestinians neither loyal to a Jordanian regime on the West Bank nor faithful to any peace with Israel showed their continuing strength: Arafat, in a desperate bid to salvage his leadership, gave in to their demands by both formally renouncing his 11 February, 1985 cooperation agreement with King Hussein and acceding to a PLO resolution criticizing Egypt for its peace treaty with Israel. The moves were part of the price Arafat decided to pay for convening the 18th session of the Palestine National Council, a gathering which had previously been blocked twice by radicals opposed to any reconciliation with Egypt or an accord with Jordan. A reaffirmation of the centrality of "armed struggle" was another price exacted by the PLO's extremist wing, many of them still adherents of the radical line laid out more than two decades earlier by Frantz Fanon, whose writings on the Algerian war against France stirred revolutionaries from Ireland to Uruguay:

> At the level of individuals, violence is a cleansing force. It frees the native from his inferiority complex and from despair and inaction; it makes him fearless and restores his self-respect.[49]
>
> Violence alone, violence committed by the people, violence organized and educated by its leaders, makes it possible for the masses to understand social truths and gives the key to them. Without that struggle, without that knowledge of the practice of action, there's nothing but a fancy-dress parade and the blare of the trumpets. There's nothing save a minimum of readaptation, a few reforms at the top, a flag waving: and down there at the bottom an undivided mass, still living in the middle ages, endlessly marking time.[50]

In April 1987, with the Palestinian leadership holding their Palestine National Council gathering in Algiers, the chairman of the meeting, Abdel-Hamid Sayeh, felt compelled to assure the crowd that Arafat would not attempt to unify the PLO with mere flag-waving and a few reforms at the top, for Sayeh was quick to hail a recent upsurge in guerrilla attacks against Israeli targets, telling delegates that just a few days earlier Fateh fighters had infiltrated into Israel from southern Lebanon. According to Israeli spokesmen, the terrorists were intent on taking hostages inside Israel and then hoped to trade them for Palestinian prisoners being held in Israeli jails. Two Israeli soldiers were killed before Arafat's three-man guerrilla unit was slain by supporting troops. The timing of the Fateh attack was apparently orchestrated to bolster Arafat's credentials as a faithful follower of armed struggle, a fearless leader still mindful of the "cleansing force" of violence, ever ready to use it as a "key" in the restoration of "self-respect."[51] At the council's opening meeting, Arafat told the audience: "We will maintain our armed struggle against Israel, not because we seek war but because we want peace, a just and comprehensive peace on the basis of the Palestinian right to self-determination and to an independent state with Jerusalem as its capital."[52] Arafat went on to say, "This Arab nation was created to stay and this Arab land will continue to speak Arabic; our forebears' bones were buried there and our children's bones will be buried there. This land, including Jerusalem—headed by Jerusalem—will remain Arab, Arab, Arab." He concluded his speech with the promise of "fire and destruction on the occupiers until we regain Palestine and until the Palestine flag is raised and we build the Palestine state on these Palestinian territories, on Palestine national soil."[53]

While in Algiers, in addition to giving the Achille Lauro hijacking mastermind Mohammad Abbas a place on the PLO executive committee, Arafat also met secretly with Abu Nidal, the notorious terrorist whose organization had murdered and maimed both Arab adversaries as well as Israeli opponents, assassinating moderate PLO leaders Said Hamami and Issam Sartawi, attempting to kill Shlomo Argov, Israel's ambassador to London, and in Bucharest fatally shooting Azmi al-Mufti, the Circassian diplomat who had served as Hussein's emissary. Abu Nidal, who had broken away from Arafat to form the more militant Fateh Revolutionary Council, had reportedly been under a death sentence from the mainstream Fateh for his violent challenges to Arafat's rule. Yet it was purportedly at Abu Nidal's urging that Arafat backed the move to elect Abbas to the PLO executive during the PLO National Council gathering. In an interview with Kuwait's *Al-Anba* newspaper a month after the meeting in Algiers, Abu Nidal's spokesman Atif Abu Bakr made it clear that despite his group's apparent reconciliation with Arafat, it would not desist from attacking targets both within Israel and in other places around the world, particularly those associated with the United States. "We say firmly that this entity of imperialism and Zionism is sustained by world-wide channels of support, and constitutes a threat to Palestinian existence. As such, we have to destroy it and to do so we have to sever and destroy the channels that feed it, starting with the U.S., the world-wide Zionist movement and the dens which inject this entity with its daily sustenance." International terrorism would continue, Abu Bakr assured: "We shall soon provide tangible evidence that we regard our enemy as a single network stretching from the occupied Palestinian territory to the farthest den of evil in the world."[54]

It was a threat by Abu Nidal to kill Lt. Col. Oliver North—the man who helped bring part of the Achille Lauro terrorist team to justice by using

Israeli intelligence to help arrange for American fighter planes to intercept the Egyptian airliner that was spiriting them out of Cairo—that prompted the former National Security Council staffer to install an expensive and elaborate security fence around his home.

The return to the violence embodied by Mohammad Abbas and Abu Nidal and the reassertion by Arafat of the goal of taking control of Jerusalem and creating an independent state may have helped win over the hard-line PLO factions, but it undermined the tireless efforts by President Mubarak and King Hussein to devise a compromise formula that would enable Arafat to participate in negotiations for a peaceful settlement with Israel. In Cairo, the rebuff by the PLO leadership was met with bitterness and disdain: "We have had enough suffering on account of the Palestinian cause," read an editorial in the semi-official Egyptian newspaper, *Akhbar el Yom.* "The losses [during Egypt's four wars with Israel] have turned us from a rich country helping others into a poor one mocked by our brothers. Enough wasted efforts and resources. Enough deprivation of our masses for the sake of a people who insult us."[55] In Israel, the response to the standard PLO rhetoric of "armed struggle" and "independent state" merely solidified the opposition to any compromise with the PLO chairman. "Today our enemies are meeting to harm us and, heaven forbid, rob Jerusalem from us," said Yitzhak Shamir, the hawkish Likud leader (Shamir had assumed the prime ministership the previous October under the rotation agreement worked out with the Labor party in the summer of 1984). "But the people of Israel are strong and united and this plot will not be carried out," Shamir said. "We will overcome all of our enemies. Jerusalem will remain Israel's capital forever." Defense Minister Yitzak Rabin quickly denounced "Arafat and his murderous henchmen."[56] Peres, serving as foreign minister, warned: "Whoever wants war will turn to Arafat. Whoever wants [peace] talks will turn to Jordan. Whoever wants to live in eternal terror will turn to the PLO. Whoever wants to find another road, the way is in the direction of Hussein." Peres, the more moderate member of the ruling coalition, concluded that the militant position taken at the PLO council session was "a disaster to Palestinians. They will pay the price, and we will continue on our way." As for Arafat's pledge to press the fight against Israel, Peres said: "The return to terror will only unite us and strengthen us. He will bring disaster on the Palestinian people."[57]

Israeli sensitivity to the persistence of PLO militarism, and the concern over a future settlement with Jordan that would require the complete removal of Jewish forces from the occupied territories—forces which could otherwise curtail PLO terrorism—was highlighted during the author's visit to the West Bank while accompanied by a Sharon aide. "From here, you have a clear target to Israel's population centers in the flatlands,'' the Israeli said as the car climbed along the rolling hills that overlooked the Mediterranean. "If a Palestinian state is established on the West Bank, the guerrillas will be free to fire at us almost at will." But Israel is a military superpower, the driver was told: surely a group of fanatical Palestinians operating illegally from bases on the West Bank would not pose much of a threat to the Jewish state. "Officially, the government of the newly formed Palestinian entity would declare that the terrorists were operating illegally," the Israeli predicted, "but the Palestinian people would not be satisfied with the boundaries of their new state, so the authorities would give their unofficial blessing to the actions of the guerrillas."

The high ground of the West Bank was a strategic necessity, Sharon's aide insisted. He was then asked about Arab rights in the area. Was Israel destined to turn the West Bank into the South Africa of the Middle East, with a Jewish minority lording over the Palestinian majority? "The Palestinians can have autonomy, or even a federation with Jordan," the Israeli said, "but there must always be Jews living in the area who could help keep PLO fighters from firing shells into Israeli towns. Rockets and missiles cannot stop terrorists from operating in a small area filled with civilians," he explained. "If the government of Israel ever had to move against an independent Palestinian state on the West Bank, it would take a worse siege than the one at Beirut to get the terrorists out. It would be the bloodiest of all the Arab-Israeli wars."[58]

American Dreams

The initiative for peace talks must come from the United States . . .
Jimmy Carter

24

A Key Player

THE United States has held an influential role in the Arab-Israeli conflict for more than half a century: Woodrow Wilson gave his endorsement to the Balfour Declaration promising a Jewish homeland in Palestine; Harry Truman granted U.S. diplomatic recognition to Israel just eleven minutes after the United Nations General Assembly voted in favor of partition; Dwight Eisenhower brought the full weight of American leverage to bear in pressuring the British, the French, and the Israelis to withdraw from Arab territory following their combined attack on Suez; Richard Nixon ordered a massive airlift of arms supplies to Israel during the Yom Kippur War; Jimmy Carter brokered the first Arab-Israeli peace treaty between Egypt and Israel.

The broad historical outlines of America's Mideast policy can be seen as one looks back at the major events that have unfolded over the past decades. What may lie ahead is difficult to predict, given the shifting alliances in the region and the volatile events that seem to alter the political landscape without warning: Sadat's visit to Jerusalem, the fall of the Shah and the rise of militant Khomeinist Islam, the lingering Iran-Iraq war, the Israeli invasion of Lebanon, the spread of Syrian-sponsored state terrorism, the United States air strike against Libya and it's adoption of a counterterrorist reprisal policy, the secret American arms deal with Iran and the attempt to buy hostages in Lebanon and influence in Teheran with weaponry and cash.

In recent years, U.S. Middle East policy has had to grapple with three significant goals in its search to bring peace and stability to the region: 1) the desire to satisfy the demands of the Palestinian refugees while meeting Israel's need for security guarantees; 2) the need to block Soviet influence and secure pro-Western Arab regimes in the region; 3) the drive to combat international terrorism.

America's back-channel relationship with the PLO reveals how various administrations struggled to come to terms with the first element concerning the Palestinian question; U.S. behind-the-scenes involvement with Israel's Christian Phalangist allies in Lebanon highlights an approach to the second factor regarding pro-Western moderate Arab governments; the sharing of intelligence information with the Mossad demonstrates America's dedication to the third aim of fighting international terror.

25

The U.S. Shadow in Lebanon

AFTER the 1970 Black September uprising in Jordan, the PLO moved its headquarters to Lebanon, eventually turning Beirut into the center of international terrorism. The PLO's armed presence created enormous pressures on the Lebanese populace. In addition, the hundreds of thousands of Palestinian refugees that had settled in the country following the various Arab-Israeli wars upset the delicate political balance that had been painstakingly worked out among Lebanon's various religious groups. (The Lebanese National Pact, adopted in 1943, stipulated that the president of the republic would always be a Maronite Christian, the prime minister a Sunni Moslem, and the speaker of the parliament a Shiite Moslem.) The Lebanese Christians, a group including Greek Orthodox, Maronite, and Greek Catholic Christians, and the mainstream Sunni establishment were traditional holders of wealth, education, and power in the nation, but by the early 1970s the Christians were facing increasing challenges from their Moslem countrymen, many from the poorer Shiite classes teaming up with leftist Sunnis, Druze activists (the Druze had been relegated to second-rate cabinet posts under the National Pact), and the disgruntled Palestinians in a demand for greater political power and expanded economic opportunity. The Christians, many of them oriented more toward the capitals of Europe and America in the West than the Arab nations of the East—due in part to their isolation in the Islamic Arab world and their ties to the Vatican and the other larger Christian communities across the Mediterranean—smarted under the growing threat of Moslem dominance and Palestinian radicalism. Furthermore, the terrorist operations staged by PLO guerrillas operating throughout Lebanon brought inevitable Israeli military reprisals staged on Lebanese soil, all for a cause somewhat distant from the Christian Lebanese bankers and merchants of Beirut.

Following an Israeli nighttime retaliatory raid on the Beirut airport in 1968 (when helicopter-borne troops led by Rafael Eitan blew up fourteen parked aircraft belonging to Lebanon's Mideast Airlines and other Arab airline companies while fifteen hundred onlookers stood idly by under Israeli guard in the airport terminal), tensions within Lebanon reached the boiling point. The bulk of the Christians lobbied for greater restrictions on Palestinian guerrilla activity while the majority of Moslems urged increased support for their war against Israel. After sporadic fighting between Lebanese government troops and armed PLO forces and a flurry of violent street demonstrations by Palestinians and their supporters, the Lebanese government appealed to the Arab League to mediate in the dispute. The result was the Cairo Agreement, signed on 3 November 1969, which in effect granted the PLO extraordinary powers to bear arms, police the refugee camps, and carry out guerrilla raids from bases in southern Lebanon, ostensibly in coordination with the official Lebanese authorities but in practice providing for the emergence of an autonomous PLO "mini-state" in Lebanon. In 1975, civil war broke out, pitting the various Christian factions against an alliance of PLO guerrilla groups, leftist and pan-Arab Nasserite Sunnis, and Druze and Shiite Moslems.

The fragile coalition that had held Lebanon together began to break up: Moslem soldiers from the Lebanese Army, which was dominated by a largely Christian officer corps, broke away to form their own factional fighting units: Lieutenant Ahmed al-Khatib, a Sunni Moslem, formed the Lebanese Arab Army to fight alongside the Druze and the PLO; Brigadier General Aziz al-Ahdab, also a Sunni, attempted a coup d'etat, seizing control of the television station and demanding that President Sulemein Franjieh, a Maronite Christian, resign (Ahdab was assisted by a Fateh unit commanded by Ali Hasan Salameh). The diverse ethnic groups meanwhile consolidated their power through the build-up of their own respective militias. The PLO, allied with leftist Sunni Moslems, was already an independent armed force deployed throughout the Palestinian refugee camps; the Druze fighters, led by Kamal Joumblatt's Progressive Socialist Party, operated from their power base in the Shouf Mountains; the Shiites, under the leadership of Imam Musa al-Sadr, head of the Supreme Islamic Shia Council and founder of the Shiite militia, Amal (Hope), organized their forces in South Lebanon and West Beirut.

The Christians were represented by several factions: the Lebanese Kataeb Social Democratic Party (*kataeb* is Arabic for "battalions, regiments, or squadrons"—the party is commonly known as the Phalangists), led by its founder, Pierre Gemayel, a pharmacist from Mount Lebanon who launched the group as a youth movement in 1936 to fight for Lebanese independence and soon transformed it into a paramilitary unit protecting Maronite interests in Lebanon; the Tiger (Numr) military wing of the National Liberal Party, a Maronite group led by former president Camille Chamoun, formed shortly after Chamoun's presidency was saved from a leftist overthrow by Eisenhower's dispatch of Marines to Lebanon in 1958; the Zugharta Liberation Army, based in northern Lebanon, established in 1969, and run largely by Tony Franjieh, the younger son of President Sulemein Franjieh; the Maronite League, headed by Shaker Abu Seleiman, a follower of Father Sharbal Qassis, a militant Maronite monk and chairman of the Association of Lebanese Monastic Orders; the Tanzim (Arabic for "organization"), a small Maronite fighting force commanded by George Adwan that functioned independently of any political party; the South Lebanon Army, created by Major Sa'ad Haddad, a Greek Catholic who broke from the Lebanese Army to form his own militia in the south; and the Guardian of the Cedars, the most extreme of the Maronite groups, led by Etienne Saqr and dedicated to the revival of Lebanon's ancient Phoenician identity while minimizing the country's historic and contemporary links to Islam and Arabism.

During the fight against their Moslem rivals, the Christian factions coordinated efforts under the banner of the Lebanese Forces, an alliance eventually dominated by the young Phalangist militia leader, Bashir Gemayel. The Moslems fought under the collective name of the Lebanese National Movement, spearheaded by Kamal Joumblatt and backed by Yassir Arafat's PLO.

With the approval of the Americans and the acquiescence of the Israelis, Syria intervened in 1976 to impose a settlement in Lebanon, initially sending in fighters from the Syrian-backed Palestine Liberation Army to side with the Moslems, then dispatching regular Syrian army troops in support of the beleaguered Christians in an attempt to both avoid a partition of Lebanon that would leave an Israel-backed independent Christian Maronite state on its southern border and to prevent the emergence of a radicalized Moslem Lebanon capable of challenging Syrian power in the region. The Damascus regime had long considered Lebanon a part of "Greater Syria," refusing to recognize the dismemberment of the former Ottoman-ruled territory by the European powers following World War I. The Syrians also considered Palestine part of southern Syria, and thus sought to control the PLO militants with an aim toward eventual Syrian hegemony over both the Israeli and Jordanian portions of historic Palestine.

In entering the Lebanese conflict, Syria's President Hafez Assad deftly played one faction against the other, tilting his support and applying the might of his army in various directions to achieve an equilibrium that left all parties dependent on the dictates of Damascus. Assad, a member of Syria's tiny Alawite Moslem minority, was used to manipulating one side against another as a means of preserving Alawite rule over his nation's Sunni majority. Lebanese President Elias Sarkis, who came to power in 1976, sanctioned Syria's presence in Lebanon by inviting the mostly Syrian-manned Arab Deterrent Force into the country to police a cease-fire, yet Sarkis was keenly aware of Assad's cunning: "Assad made and unmade alliances with disturbing virtuosity," Sarkis's adviser Karim Pakradouni observed; "he would take 180-degree turns and no sooner had he gained an ally, he would be looking for an alternative, a tactic perfectly suited to the divisions of the Arab world. Assad was careful to strike an enemy without destroying him, and when he came to an ally's help he would hold back from saving him entirely; the enemy might one day be a friend and vice versa."[1]

As for the Americans, after the quagmire of Vietnam and the trauma of Watergate, the Ford administration was not about to dispatch marines to Lebanon as Eisenhower had in 1958 to quash Assad's plans and guarantee U.S. interests in the region. Furthermore, the bewildering shift of internal alliances and the myriad factions vying for power in Beirut made it difficult for Washington to formulate a quick fix to the Lebanese crisis. When Syria entered the fighting, there was at least the hope that the situation would be stabilized, blocking the further break-up of the country or the even more worrisome possibility that PLO-leftist Moslem forces would triumph. Such a triumph would inevitably invite an Israeli military response to the newly-fashioned Palestinian stronghold on its northern border, thus bringing an even deeper Syrian involvement seeking to offset Israeli aims in Lebanon and in turn harboring a potential confrontation between Syria's patron, the USSR, and Israel's ally, the United States. The importance of avoiding a superpower clash in the region and the desire for a stable, albeit Syrian-imposed peace in war-torn Beirut prompted Secretary of State Henry Kissinger to offer an American passive acceptance of Assad's role in Lebanon.

For the Israelis, the prospect of a Soviet-equipped Syrian army entrenched in Lebanon not only posed a strategic threat to its territory, opening up yet another hostile front (Lebanon had previously played only a minor role in the Arab-Israeli wars), but also promised to provide a safe haven for PLO terrorists. Israel's counterterrorist policy of military reprisals, including air strikes and commando raids, could be jeopardized by well-guarded Palestinian military bases freely functioning within the refugee camps protected by Syrian ground troops and missile defenses. The solution was an American-brokered arrangement carving up Israeli and Syrian spheres of influence in Lebanon, much the way the United States and the

Soviet Union had in Eastern and Western Europe. Known as the ''red line'' agreements, the Israelis agreed to accept Syria's presence in Lebanon (nearly thirty thousand troops) provided that it not move its soldiers beyond a line running across the Litani River in South Lebanon and that it not use its air force over Lebanese territory. Syria was also precluded from install-ing ground-to-air missiles that could threaten Israeli reconnaissance flights and aerial strikes against PLO positions, and it pledged not to attempt to close the Christian port of Jounieh.[2] Despite the tacit agreement, Syria con-tinued to maneuver to solidify its hold on Lebanese affairs and expand its control over the country's political future, arming terrorists and various militia factions to prevent the emergence of any one group, Christian or Moslem, that could one day become capable of ruling the country and or-dering the Syrians out. The Israelis, for their part, also sought to exert their influence, working mainly through the Christian forces opposing both the Syrian and Palestinian presence in Lebanon. As minority groups living in the Arab Islamic world, the Jews and the Christians shared mutual aims in securing Western interests in the region and blocking the unchecked dominance of radical Moslem regimes. Syria, often in tandem with Qaddafi's Libya and Khomeini's Iran, backed hard-line PLO factions, Shiite militants, and leftist Druze and Sunnis, while Israel openly backed the Christians, providing arms and training to Sa'ad Haddad's South Lebanon Army, to Camille Chamoun's Tigers (led by his younger son Dany), and to Pierre Gemayel's Phalangists (commanded by his youngest son, Bashir).

A spate of internecine warfare among the rival Christian militias led to the wounding and exile of the prominent politician Raymond Edde by Phalangist forces, and the group's subsequent attack on the Franjieh head-quarters in Zugharta left the former president's thirty-six-year-old son Tony, his thirty-two-year-old wife Vera, and three-year-old daughter Jehane sprawled dead along with thirty-one other Franjieh loyalists. A reprisal in-tended to kill Bashir Gemayel resulted instead in the death of his young daughter along with two bodyguards and four other people. By the begin-ning of 1980, twelve months of bitter factional fighting within the Lebanese Christian camp had left more than a hundred people dead.

In the summer of 1980, Bashir Gemayel launched a decisive strike to end the infighting, code-named ''LENA.'' The Phalangist leader sent his commandos into the strongholds of the Chamouns' National Liberal Party, simultaneously raiding their offices and military barracks in Ashrafieh, the Metn, the Kesrouan, and Jbeil, leaving scores of dead and wounded, seizing arsenals, disarming Tiger militiamen, eventually forcing Dany Chamoun to flee to Paris, the military and political infrastructure of his organization completely destroyed. Lasting only hours, the operation of 7 July, 1980 enabled Bashir Gemayel, still in his early thirties, to emerge as the Christian strongman in Lebanon.

Though condemned as a madman and brutal warlord by some while hailed by others as a military genius and charismatic political leader destined to become the savior of Christian Lebanon, it soon became obvious to many that Bashir Gemayel was determined to play the primary role in shaping his country's future. "The Lebanese Forces had needed a unified structure since 1977," Bashir said a month after the LENA operation. "They were no more than a coordination organisation and we failed to integrate all the militias into a single, homogeneous military body. We should have carried out the July 7 operation three years earlier."[3]

During this time, Jimmy Carter assumed the U.S. presidency, hammered out an agreement between Anwar Sadat and Menachem Begin at Camp David, and helped forge the Egyptian-Israeli peace treaty. In his administration's view, Lebanon was a sideshow, the militia leaders thugs. The official U.S. policy was simply to keep Lebanon on hold, hoping to prevent an eruption of violence that might derail the Egyptian-Israeli peace process. Washington would back the official Lebanese government and use its influence to keep the "red line" agreements between Israel and Syria intact. Dealings with the militia leaders were supposedly off-limits; the Carter administration would not take sides in what was viewed as a power struggle among rival Christian and Moslem gangs in Beirut. Bashir Gemayel was no exception. According to Karim Pakradouni, a top Phalangist official, the Americans regarded him "as a trouble-maker, a gang leader, a terrorist, even as—the phrase had been used—'a non-clandestine Carlos.'"[4] As for Israel's support of the Phalange, many in the State Department took a dim view of it, with some charging that Bashir's militia had been responsible for the summer 1980 assassination attempt against the U.S. ambassador to Lebanon, John Gunther Dean, who had been highly critical of Israeli-Christian actions against PLO positions in the south.[5] According to William Quandt, who served as Jimmy Carter's Middle East expert on the National Security Council, Ambassador Dean's predecessor, Richard Parker, was particularly opposed to the Israeli-Christian alliance and relayed his position to the President: "Summing up his long experience, he [Parker] warned that the Maronites were bringing great trouble on themselves by refusing to show respect for the Muslim majority in Lebanon. 'They have insisted on affirmative action carried to its ultimate extreme, i.e., preservation of a dominant position for themselves.' After criticizing the Israelis for undermining the authority of the Lebanese government by supporting various Lebanese militias, he [Parker] warned, prophetically, 'Those who think the Lebanese infection can be isolated do not understand the nature of social diseases.'"[6]

For Carter, a cure for the Lebanese infection was elusive. On a State Department memo reviewing the options for U.S. policy in Lebanon, the president simply noted, "There don't seem to be any really good ideas."[7] Yet, according to Emile Khoury [a pseudonym], a former Lebanese journalist and diplomat with ties to both the Christian leadership in Lebanon and members of the U.S. government, including Senator Edward Kennedy who helped push for increased humanitarian aide to embattled Beirut, the Carter administration did not remain idle. In fact, it had struck a secret bargain with Bashir Gemayel's Phalange despite the official U.S. boycott of the militias. According to Khoury, who had become an American citizen and worked for a U.S. multinational company based in the United States, the CIA supplied arms to Bashir as early as 1977, with Israel facilitating delivery.[8]

It is not unlikely that the U.S. would have wanted to nurture ties to the various parties involved in the Lebanese conflict, especially those among the pro-Western Christians, and that limited aid to the influential Phalangist militia might have been authorized despite Preisdent Carter's general reluctance to continue the practice of previous administrations, which frequently used American weapons and military training as tools in the construction of foreign alliances.

Nicholas Veliotes, who served as deputy assistant secretary of state during the Carter presidency, admitted meeting with Bashir in 1977 and 1978, but explained that the administration's policy was not to boycott the militia leaders in the sense that American officials would not hold talks with them.[9] Abdallah Bouhabib, an associate of Bashir's who became the Lebanese ambassador to the United States in 1983 after serving as an economist at the World Bank in Washington, said that true, American officials did hold discussions with Bashir on several occasions during the Carter administration, but such talks were restricted to State Department personnel. In 1977, Bashir had met with the State Department's Middle East expert Alfred Atherton during a Washington visit, Bouhabib recalled. In 1979, Bashir was again in Washington and met with Morris Draper, another Mideast specialist at State. But during the same 1979 visit, William Quandt had in fact refused to meet with Bashir. According to Bouhabib, though the State Department may have been simply carrying out its natural function of establishing diplomatic contacts with foreign leaders when it chose to hold talks with Bashir, neither members of the National Security Council nor White House officials were to meet with the militia leader, imposing a kind of limited boycott by the administration's inner circle that would underscore America's firm support for Lebanon's central government.[10] High-level discussions were to be reserved for Lebanon's President Sarkis and representatives of his legally elected cabinet.

Still, according to Khoury, in 1980 the CIA personally trained half a dozen Maronite militiamen. Alfred Maady, Bashir's handpicked director of the Washington-based American Lebanese League and later chief of the Phalangist foreign relations department in Beirut, confirmed that transfers of U.S. arms to Bashir's militia did occur during the Carter presidency, indicating that the weapons pipeline opened signficantly in 1980, sometime around St. Patrick's Day, rather than in 1977, as reported by Khoury.[11] In either case, the military aid would have pre-dated the LENA operation of 7 July 1980, which was viewed by many as the turning point in the Carter administration's attitude toward the Phalange, when Washington was forced to recognize Bashir as the most powerful leader of Christian Lebanon.

The Phalangists had been struggling for years to convince the Carter White House that Bashir was indeed its best hope, apparently with limited success. Bashir, who was educated in the United States at Southern Methodist University in Dallas, Texas, had directed a public relations campaign to convince the American administration of the value of a Phalangist-dominated regime in Lebanon. In Beirut, he sought to make amends with Ambassador Dean, telling him over lunch to relay a message to Washington: "We wish to be part of America's strategy in the Middle East. We want to be part of the free world. We want to become the legal authority by legal means."[12] In addition, Bashir had brought his case personally to the United States, appearing annually since 1977 at Lebanese-American gatherings to raise money and explain his plans for Lebanon's future, setting up the American Lebanese League in Washington to help garner support, the organization supervised by Alfred Maady and given limited assistance by members of the American Israel Public Affairs Committee (AIPAC), Israel's own Jewish lobby in the United States.[13] Despite the effort, however, the Carter administration was still unwilling to go public with its support of the Phalange, which in any case was most likely not exclusive, the United States probably also supplying weapons and training to the other Christian factions fighting to contain PLO-leftist influence and / or block a total Soviet-backed Syrian takeover of the country. Quandt acknowledged that the Phalangists did attempt to bring the U.S. connection out from the shadows, with Maady meeting with members of the State Department in an unsuccessful effort to win broader administration support for Bashir's efforts. Quandt also noted that the U.S. was not yet aware of the full extent of Israel's support for the Phalangists, and that appeals by Bashir for a meeting with Quandt were turned down. The Phalangists, apparently hoping to break out of its dependence on the Israelis, continued the campaign to win stronger backing from Washington. Meanwhile, said

Quandt, American intelligence detected that Bashir was purchasing arms on the open market.[14]

As the Carter administration came to a close, with the Phalangists having been rebuffed by the White House and the National Security Council, received by the State Department, refused open support from the Pentagon, and reportedly supplied in secret by the CIA, the exact nature of America's position toward the militant Lebanese Christian factions in general and Bashir Gemayel in particular remained clouded. The ambiguity in the U.S. position was not new: at the outset of the Carter presidency, during a visit to Beirut by Secretary of State Cyrus Vance in February 1977, President Sarkis's foreign minister Fouad Boutros had voiced his concern that Washington was "openly supporting the President but backing the Lebanese Front [Forces] and its ideas behind the scenes."[15] But by the end of 1980, one thing had certainly changed: the devastating Phalangist strike against its rivals on 7 July made it obvious that if the United States was going to work for a solution to the Lebanese crisis, it would have to deal directly with Bashir Gemayel. Even President Sarkis himself began urging closer contacts between Washington and the Phalange. And it was only after the July operation that Ambassador Dean, a longtime foe of Bashir's, consented to meet with the Phalangist leader in Beirut.

In 1981, Ronald Reagan became president, and the Phalangist position in Washington improved even more dramatically. The Lebanese lobby had been busy during the 1980 presidential race, with several prominent conservative Lebanese-American Christians donating money and their good offices to the Reagan campaign. Their staunch anti-communist views and pro-Israeli sympathies fell on receptive ears. In his analysis of the Reagan administration's Lebanon policy, which he helped fashion during his brief eighteen-month tenure as Secretary of State in 1981-82, General Alexander Haig outlined the view which saw Lebanon as the latest battleground in the struggle to block Soviet expansionism: "Quite simply, the Soviet Union wants to displace the United States as the most influential foreign power between the Caspian Sea and the Indian Ocean. From her point of view, the prizes are enormous—population, wealth, energy, the strategic position of the Middle East as a bridge linking three continents. But in the last decade, following its banishment from Sadat's Egypt, the Soviet Union has been on the periphery of events in the Middle East. Throughout that period, Moscow has been trying, with little success, to recapture the center. It was only natural that the Soviets would see Lebanon as an opportunity to advance their interests through her ally, Syria, and her ofttime agent, the PLO."[16]

While the need to rid Lebanon of Soviet-backed Syrian and PLO forces was being emphasized by Haig at State, the administration's new CIA

Director, William Casey, formerly a Wall Street lawyer, had ties to associates in Beirut—once the capital of Middle East banking—and many of these conservative Lebanese attorneys reportedly began a correspondence with him promoting Bashir Gemayel as the man to back in Lebanon. Given the necessary support, they explained, Bashir could unite the Christians, reconcile with the Moslems, crush the PLO, drive out the Syrians, and keep the Soviets at bay. As the Reagan team began to construct its foreign policy, Casey, Haig, Deputy Secretary of State William Clark, and Defense Secretary Weinberger were either positively disposed or at worst neutral to Bashir's proposal that the Phalangists become "part of America's strategy in the Middle East." The complimentary Israeli view, spearheaded by Defense Minister Ariel Sharon, gave additional impetus for an expanded U.S. relationship with the Phalange. Sharon, like his military colleague Haig, viewed the Soviet threat as an ominous cloud hovering over the Arab-Israeli conflict. Speaking before an audience at Tel Aviv University's Center for Strategic Studies, Sharon said that Israel's main security problems in the 1980s stemmed from two main factors: the confrontation with the Arabs, and "the Soviet expansion which both builds on the Arab confrontation and at the same time provides it with its main political and military tools."[17] Syria and the PLO were the obvious beneficiaries of Soviet expansionism and thus posed immediate dangers not only to Israel but to overall Western interests in the region as well: "Today, as in the past two decades, the Soviet strategy of expansion in the area continues to build on: Arab regimes which Soviet political and military support enables them to survive, to carry out their own ambitions and to maintain military confrontations—including the confrontation with Israel; radical elements and terrorist organizations, which Soviet political and military support enables to create upheavals threatening to shift the region towards Soviet political-strategic patronage. The shadow of Soviet presence in the Middle East and Africa endangers the stability of the region and vital interests of the free world."[18]

With the Camp David peace process between Egypt and Israel stalled, Lebanon could once again be brought forward from the back burner, becoming the immediate focus of America's Mideast policy. And what emerged was a seemingly natural confluence among the geopolitical ideas of Alexander Haig, Ariel Sharon, and Bashir Gemayel, all of whom shared the view that Soviet-backed regimes like Syria and Soviet-supported terrorist organizations like the PLO endangered the security of America's Christian and Jewish allies in the region, at the same time providing Moscow with a foothold to further its expansionist goals. And so, the Carter administration's general aversion to Bashir was replaced by the Reagan embrace.

"The Lebanese situation needed a change," recalled Haig's assistant

Harvey Sicherman. The Carter "patchwork" approach was no longer sufficient; a major step had to be taken to stop the PLO and its radical Moslem allies in Beirut from tearing Lebanon apart and blocking further progress toward a settlement of the Arab-Israeli dispute. "Bashir had control of the strongest militia," Sicherman observed. "Whether fellow Lebanese liked him or not, he had the power."[19] The United States however, did not yet regard him as a possible candidate for the Lebanese presidency, for tradition had usually disqualified militia leaders from the post. Sicherman said the administration viewed him largely as a "kingmaker," like the late Mayor Daley of Chicago, a local power broker whose support was vital in any presidential contest. Whether Bashir was to be a kingmaker or a presidential candidate, the Reagan White House saw him as the man who could bring about the major change called for in Lebanon.

Despite the harmony of views held among the various Lebanese-American lobbyists, AIPAC activists, Beirut lawyers, Israeli strategists, and Reaganite conservatives who were all working to fashion a new American policy of support for a united Lebanon ruled by the Phalange, Raymond Tanter, the man in charge of Lebanon policy at the National Security Council, saw less ideological reasons for Washington's new preoccupation with Bashir Gemayel. A vigorous anti-communism, the building of a grand NATO-like alliance among pro-Western Arab regimes, these notions did not drive the Reagan administration's interest in forging closer links to the militia leader. What had changed since the days of the Carter presidency, said Tanter, was the fact that the strategic situation on the ground had changed: in the spring of 1981, Bashir had attempted to expand Phalangist control by establishing a road that would link the Maronite heartland in Mount Lebanon to the Greek Orthodox town of Zahle in the east. Syria, however, felt its links to Lebanon threatened by the move, for Phalangist control of the corridor might enable it to block the Beirut-Damascus highway at will. The Mount Lebanon-Zahle road might also enable Phalangist militiamen to one day meet up with Israeli troops mounting a thrust toward Zahle from the south, giving the Christian and Jewish allies a foothold in the Bekka Valley and thereby effectively blocking future Syrian moves into Lebanon.[20] Syria reacted to the challenge by shelling Phalangist units in Zahle and landing helicopter-borne commando troops on Mount Sanin, a key position that dominated the village of 200,000. The Israelis saw the introduction of the helicopters as a violation of the "red line" agreements, and Prime Minister Begin was moved to answer the Syrians and relieve the beleaguered Christians by having the Israeli Air Force shoot down two Syrian helicopter transports on 28 April, 1981. Syrian President Assad then moved Soviet-built SAM 6 anti-aircraft missile batteries into the Bekka, and tensions quickly escalated to the point where Begin appeared determined to make good his threat to launch another air strike to knock out the SAMs within days. A major Syrian-Israeli clash seemed imminent. President Reagan dispatched Middle East trouble-shooter Philip Habib to the region to put further Israeli actions on hold while attempting to structure an Israeli-Syrian accord that would allow for the voluntary removal of the SAM missiles.

By provoking the Syrians in a drive to expand Phalangist influence in Lebanon, Bashir Gemayel's actions had undermined the U.S.-brokered "red line" agreements and sparked a missile crisis in the Bekka Valley, destabilizing the status quo and bringing the region's major powers, Israel and Syria, to the brink of war. The Reagan administration's eyes became glued on Bashir not for ideological reasons, said Tanter, but for strategic ones: Carter was able to place Lebanon and the Phalange on the back burner, but by May 1981, barely five months into his presidency, Reagan was already facing the prospect of a full-scale confrontation between an American ally, Israel, and a Soviet client, Syria. The Reagan administration had little choice but to focus its diplomatic efforts on Bashir Gemayel, a man capable of radically altering events in the area, someone who was bound to be a key factor in any effort to defuse tensions.[21] As Ambassador Bouhabib put it, the events surrounding Zahle opened the U.S. eyes to what Bashir could do.[22]

Whether out of ideological considerations, strategic necessity, or more likely a mixture of both, by the spring of 1981 the Reagan administration had shifted to a more intimate alliance with the Phalangist forces in Lebanon. According to Robert Basil, former deputy assistant to the director of research and development at the U.S. Department of Defense and a senior executive of the American Lebanese League, Elie Hobeika, the chief of the Phalangist intelligence network and Bashir's personal bodyguard (later implicated in the massacre of Palestinian civilians at Sabra and Shatilla), was brought to the United States in 1981 to receive CIA training. Hobeika had already received similar training at the Staff and Command College in Israel. Basil also confirmed Khoury's claim that the Reagan administration secretly supplied arms to the Phalangists.[23] William Clark, who took over as national security adviser in 1982, and another former senior level American diplomat who did not wish to be identified by name, likewise indicated that the Reagan White House had furnished military supplies to the Phalange.[24]

In contrast to the Carter policy, these shipments were apparently not part of a simple effort to thwart the Syrians and the PLO, but rather the basis of a concerted plan to influence a particular faction which the United

States hoped would one day take power in Beirut. As was revealed during the disclosures about secret American arms sales to "moderate" factions in Iran (an operation in which Israeli intelligence agents served as middlemen by using their clandestine contacts in Teheran), the Reagan administration was in part attempting to employ military shipments as a means of gaining political leverage in pursuit of its foreign policy objectives. In his testimony before the House Foreign Affairs Committee investigating the secret Iranian arms deal, Reagan's former NSC advisor Robert McFarlane actually invoked the case of Bashir Gemayel as evidence that factional leaders could one day prove capable of governing and that in some instances military support for non-governmental forces was therefore justified. The way to approach the wisdom of providing weapons to certain groups in Iran, said McFarlane, "is to examine at some length history in the Middle East, and what it has taken for leaders who ultimately took charge and governed sensibly to get where they got, and you find time and time again that people have risen to power relying centrally upon military support and subsequently for them to get it in the first place, the currency of getting that military support has very often been—from Lebanon to Egypt to the Gulf States and to Iran—building that support by the ability to deliver arms to people they need to help, but it doesn't mean that those people turn around and use those arms in a particular way over time. They develop a coalition which over time governs."[25] Apparently, the logic used to justify weapons shipments to "moderate" factions in Ayatollah Khomeini's Iran had been applied earlier when the Reagan administration decided to step up its military support for the Phalange militia in Lebanon.

Early on in the Reagan presidency, at a forum sponsored by the American Enterprise Institute, a conservative Washington think-tank, former ABC news chief John Charles Daly had taken note of the increased reliance on weapons shipments as a foreign policy tool: "In mid-1981, the Reagan administration announced its arms transfer policy, emphasizing that the 'basic thrust is to recognize that arms transfers properly considered and employed represent an indispensable instrument of American policy that both complements and supplements the role of our own military forces.' This is a marked change of direction from the policy of the Carter administration, which emphasized restraint and consideration of a recipient's human rights policies in approving arms sales."[26]

By 1981, Israel's vigorous support for the Phalangists was an open secret, which made the effort to forge a Washington arms connection seemingly redundant when such supplies could be had much more easily from Lebanon's southern neighbor just across the border. But both Reagan and Bashir had their own purposes in structuring an arms channel independent of the Israelis. For Bashir, an American connection would add significant prestige to his drive for the Lebanese presidency. It might help him achieve what Robert McFarlane—a former Marine colonel who had originally been brought in as State Department counselor by Secretary Haig—saw as a prerequisite for leadership in the Middle East: Bashir could further demonstrate the ability of the Phalangists to "deliver arms to people they need to help" which would in turn help him to "develop a coalition over time that governs." In addition, the U.S. connection would afford him greater maneuverability with Israel, for the Christian and Jewish interests in the region were parallel but not identical. "Bashir wanted a major U.S. relationship to balance the Israeli one," said one former State Department diplomat.[27] For the Reagan team, successful U.S. Middle East policy required a consensus of conservative Arab regimes lined up against the Soviets and their allies, willing to offer tacit support to an American-led coalition implicitly in league with Israel but falling well short of outright cooperation with the Jewish state. Arab political realities as well as deep religious and ideological convictions would not allow Saudi Arabia and the other Gulf Sheikdoms to fall behind Egypt in an open embrace of Israel and the United States, nor was King Hussein ready to accept such a tie without first settling the West Bank issue. According to Basil, the owner of an international trading company dealing in high technology products who encouraged the overseas arms transfers to the Phalangists, the administration believed that if Haig's "strategic consensus" was to work, the Arab regimes, including Bashir's should he attain power in Lebanon, could not openly identify with Israel. Policymakers inside the NSC and State agreed with Basil's assessment: Lebanon in particular, already fraught with competing domestic allegiances and subject to powerful external forces (Syrians, Iranians, Saudis, Iraqis, Libyans), could not afford to break with the Arab world. Apparently, in part to counteract Israeli influence over Bashir, the Reagan administration had decided to widen the U.S. arms pipeline to the Phalangists.

During his Beirut discussion with Bashir, Ambassador Dean had in fact already foreshadowed the policy that would attempt to wean the Phalangists away from their Israeli patrons: "Beware of them [the Israelis], they are never satisfied. You can given them everything, but they will always find something else they want. Do you have any aircraft to offer? We do. We provide them with our best models and they are not satisfied. Do not count on Israel, Sheik Bashir, count on yourself!"[28]

The Israelis, hoping to create a Lebanese regime that would be an extension of Israeli foreign policy, found itself in conflict with the United States, which was maneuvering to bring Bashir into its orbit and make

Beirut an extension of American foreign policy. There was even talk of a future U.S. navy base in Lebanon. The Israelis, however, did not want the Americans to serve as both broker and guarantor of an agreement between Lebanon and Israel. As understood by Basil—whose ongoing intimate involvement with the administration's weapons shipments to the Phalange led many Washington observers to conclude that he was operating an illegal arms ring—the Israelis feared that the United States did not have staying power, and should their grand "strategic consensus" one day collapse America would turn its attention to other interests, leaving the Middle Eastern antagonists to slug it out on their own. "I want to emphasize that in spite of our deep friendship with the U.S., we have never once relied on them," Sharon was to later tell Pierre Gemayel. "We have never once believed that somebody else would fight our battles for us. Assistance, cooperation, coordination, yes! But nobody can defend us except ourselves. And this is the same for you, for the Lebanese." Sharon recalled the warning he had issued during his secret meeting in January 1982 with Sheik Pierre, Bashir, and Camille Chamoun, six months before Israel's thrust to Beirut: "Don't expect the United States to solve your problems. It will solve only its own."[29] The Israeli approach was to help Bashir's forces prevail, with the alliance eventually leading to a formal treaty with Israel, making Lebanon the second Arab nation to make peace with the Jewish state and perhaps prompting Hussein into coming to terms as well. Thus, the pieces of Haig's pro-Western "strategic consensus" would be in place, but with firm, bilateral relationships between Israel and its neighbors holding it together rather than the unsteady diplomatic hand of Washington. Thus the Israelis, not wishing to rely on America, were applying their own version of Ambassador Dean's wisdom: do not count on the United States, count on yourself.

As the American-Israeli competition for influence over the Phalangists intensified, Bashir continued to make advances into Washington. On 11 August 1981, Bashir was officially welcomed at the State Department by deputy secretary of state William Clark, Middle East envoy Morris Draper, and Nicholas Veliotes, then serving as assistant secretary of state. "Before, they regarded us as an outlaw militia," Karim Pakradouni, then working as an aide to Bashir, told a Washington reporter prior to the talks. "Under the Reagan Administration, this has changed, and Washington now regards the party as a main party to the Lebanese formula."[30] But according to Geoffrey Kemp, a Middle East specialist at the National Security Council who attended the gathering in Washington, the meeting was simply "just handholding," an exercise in public diplomacy that would put a positive political gloss on the bridge between Bashir and the U.S. without exchanging anything of substance.[31] Veliotes similarly stated that the August meeting brought no marked change in U.S. policy toward the Phalange. "Bashir didn't need to lecture us on the need for a Lebanon policy," Veliotes quipped, and "we didn't need to lecture him on the need for Lebanese unity."[32] The militia leader had long sought recognition from Washington that a coherent U.S. policy toward Lebanon aimed at the solution of the civil war in that country was essential to an overall Middle East peace settlement. Lebanon was no sideshow, Bashir insisted. The post-Camp David period seemed to bolster his position, for the Israeli-Egyptian peace treaty did not stop the Palestinians, the Syrians, or the Israelis from simply carrying out their battles on Lebanese soil. A Department of Defense study also seemed to underscore this view:

> It [Lebanon] is a country beset with virtually every unresolved dispute afflicting the peoples of the Middle East. Lebanon has become a battleground where armed Lebanese factions simultaneously manipulate and are manipulated by the foreign forces surrounding them. If Syrians and Iraqis wish to kill one another, they do so in Lebanon. If Israelis and Palestinians wish to fight over the land they both claim, they do so in Lebanon. If terrorists of any political persuasion wish to kill and maim American citizens, it is convenient for them to do so in Lebanon. In a country where criminals involved in indiscriminate killing, armed robbery, extortion, and kidnapping issue political manifestos and hold press conferences, there has been no shortage of indigenous surrogates willing to do the bidding of foreign governments seeking to exploit the opportunities presented by anarchy in Lebanon.[33]

The report, though issued in 1983, more than a year after Bashir's death, still held tragic relevance for the conditions that prevailed in Lebanon in the summer of 1981. For the Reagan administration, however, the abiding need was to show Bashir that Phalangist dominance in Lebanon would not solve the crisis. "The only hope for Moslem-Christian reconciliation is if no one faction imposes its will on the others," was the American message, said a State Department officer who had been stationed in Beirut at the time. As the embassy officer understood it, during the August 1981 meeting in Washington, the U.S. team attempted "to impress on Bashir that America's interest in him was a direct function of his support for his own government; he should not work against the legal authority. Our interest in him was dependent on his not opposing President Sarkis."[34]

The August 1981 meeting in Washington brought the U.S.-Phalangist relationship further out from the shadows, and thus strengthened Bashir's hand back home. According to a former senior staffer at the National Security Council, to the Lebanese, the fact that Bashir was able to attend such a meeting with high-level officials in Washington served as a major symbol of political power.[35] A former American ambassador to the region added that for the Arabs, personal contact is paramount, which is why a Lebanese politician like Pakradouni might have promoted as a breakthrough the mere fact that the Washington talks took place at all while Americans officials like Kemp could see them as little more than "hand-holding." Assurances of support for Bashir would not have been sufficient coming through American emissaries in Beirut; direct contact with State Department officials in Washington would be the true litmus test of the U.S.-Phalangist alliance. "In the West, institutions are important, not people," the former ambassador said. "For the Arabs, people are important, the institutions aren't trusted. Eye to eye meetings are vital."[36]

According to Wadi Haddad, a Lebanese scholar who later was to serve as President Amin Gemayel's national security adviser, what enabled Amin's brother Bashir finally to gain the U.S. public blessing was that he had already demonstrated that he was moving in the same direction as Washington regarding Lebanon's future. Unlike the mainstream Phalangists, Bashir was not working to carve out an autonomous Christian enclave in the country. His goal was to form a government that would guarantee the rights of Christians living in a unified Lebanon alongside their Moslem countrymen. As the leader of the Lebanese Forces, Bashir enjoyed a broad base of support that went beyond the Phalange itself to include a majority of Lebanese Christians whose allegiance cut across party lines. According to Haddad, his political platform departed somewhat from that pushed by the Phalangists, and his power did not rest solely on the support of the Phalange; it lay with the bulk of Lebanese Christians whose primary loyalty was to Bashir himself. For Haddad, although it was Phalangist muscle that enabled Bashir to come to prominence, it was his emergence as the leader of the Lebanese Forces, a group more politically compatible with the U.S., rather than his role within the hard-line Phalange, that helped pave the way for a more intimate relationship with Washington.[37] The attempt by the Lebanese Forces in 1981 to "build bridges to the other Lebanese communities" had naturally dovetailed with Washington's own aims in the region, for it required a distancing from Israel and a move toward a power that could serve as Bashir's new patron. As Haddad observed, "Once he decided he wanted to be the president of a united Lebanon—not a Christian mini-state—through the constitutional process, he could not afford to be tainted in the view of the Lebanese Muslims or the other Arabs." The stain, of course, was relations with Israel. Haddad thus claimed that "the

Lebanese Forces refused to be directly involved or even associated with the Israelis.''[38]

Bashir's message to the Americans during the face to face encounters in the summer of 1981 seemed to fit neatly into the anti-communist East-West framework of the Reagan ideologues: a Phalangist-led coalition of Lebanese Christians and moderate Moslems, working through a legally-elected central government, could serve as a bulwark against Soviet expansionism and provide a stable influence in the region. Upon his return to Beirut, Bashir gave an upbeat account of his talks in Washington:

> The Americans have now started to realize that Lebanon is a basic element of stability, an important "stabilizer". After all that has happened, whether in Iran or Afghanistan, the countries of the area are threatened, and there is a feeling that the Palestine problem must be solved. There is a tendency to realize that there are two occupations, and that there is an oppressive occupation that must be got rid of—the Syrian occupation.
>
> The Lebanese state that is established after the recovery of sovereignty will be responsible for regulating the situation and providing the element of stability. There is a feeling that, should Syria "swallow up" part of Lebanon, what is to prevent Iraq from doing the same thing with Kuwait and other states tomorrow? What is to prevent the desires of the Arabs from being realized?
>
> If a Babrak Karmal [the Soviet-backed Marxist leader in Afghanistan] took over from President Sarkis, what would there be to prevent the moderate states from adopting a Babrak-like regime? When Lebanon collapses while the world looks on, the contagion spreads rapidly and it is no wonder that every day a cache of arms should be discovered and there should be explosions in one country after another. All these are indicators.
>
> The Americans have a feeling that the Lebanese crisis has been kept on ice long enough. President Reagan and his administration are ready to understand this fact and to start seeking the implementation of solutions. The solutions are clear enough, but courage is needed to implement them.[39]

The solution looming on the horizon was evidently a coordinated Israeli-Phalangist push that would bring Ariel Sharon's troops to Beirut, evicting the PLO and setting the stage for a takeover by Bashir's militia and his election as President of Lebanon. The military strike would enjoy the material and political backing of the Reagan administration. The scheme was eventually set in motion through a series of secret meetings between Ariel Sharon and Bashir Gemayel, with the Israeli general actually traveling undercover to the mountains of Beirut to survey the terrain and plan his invasion. According to an aide that accompanied him there, Sharon quickly concluding that the urban layout would make a frontal Israeli assault unacceptably bloody and would thus require instead either a prolonged siege or the assistance of Bashir's militiamen who could carry out the street fighting from their bases within the city.[40] Israel's cabinet was reportedly only partially informed of the plan, with the Israeli commitment to drive all the way to Beirut said to be Sharon's unilateral innovation.[41] The Americans were later to claim that they too had been unaware of the plan to encircle Beirut, and that in fact they had warned Israel against launching a major incursion into Lebanon.[42] Israeli journalist Ze'ev Schiff reported that in reality Sharon had been given a "green light" for the invasion by Secretary of State Haig.[43] Others subsequently amended the Schiff version, saying that the light had been "amber", with the Reagan team truly ambivalent about the Israeli plan and at best only cautiously acquiescing to it.[44] In any case, most observers concluded that the absence of a "red light" from Washington was all Sharon needed to proceed.

On 29 November 1981, Bashir delivered an historic speech in Beirut at the forty-fifth anniversary celebration of the Phalangist Party, outlining his platform for the settlement of the Lebanese crisis:

1. The restoration of Lebanese sovereignty over all of its territory

2. The withdrawal of all Syrian forces

3. The regulation and control of all PLO factions by the Lebanese authorities

4. The adherence to the basic tenets of the confessional system guaranteeing Moslem and Christian rights as structured under the National Pact of 1943

In presenting his proposals, Bashir signalled his intention to run for the presidency, a step that would at the very least satisfy the American demand that he work through the legal, political apparatus of the state rather than through the guns of his private militia:

> We declare as of now that the country needs a strong president and that it rejects a weak president. It is better for the persons who do not have the qualities of the man of salvation not to sneak their names on the candidates' list because the rise of such a weak person to the seat of the presidency would mean the destruction of what remains of the Lebanese people's ambitions and dream. We want a president whom the Lebanese resistance can trust with its achievements. We want a president whom the Lebanese resistance can trust with its achievements and gains and who will not exploit them for bargains but for confrontation. We want a president who will establish cohesive relations among the various parts of the homeland and who will have a national vision reaching the extent of a

dream, and not a man with a political lust which does not exceed the limits of ruling.[45]

But as a precondition for the selection of such a president, the elections would first have to be held free from Syrian and PLO influence. "How can the Lebanese freely elect a strong person with the presence of 30,000 Syrian soldiers and thousands of intelligence men and 600,000 Palestinians on our land?" Bashir asked. "The withdrawal of the Syrian Army from Lebanon is a necessity and [a] condition for holding honest presidential elections." And how would such a condition come about? According to Bashir, the task would obviously be better suited to the Phalange than to the Lebanese army: "Why doesn't the Lebanese Army enter the occupied Lebanese areas? If 23,000 Lebanese soldiers cannot be deployed in [Moslem-dominated] western Beirut and its suburbs to restore security and freedom to all their inhabitants, then how many soldiers are needed for such an operation? A total of 90 fighters of the [Phalangist] Lebanese forces and the inhabitants of Zahlah [*sic*] confronted the Syrian Army for 3 months in defense of the city. Cannot the Lebanese Army, with its thousands of soldiers, restore dignity to western Beirut, particularly since the Muslim leaders are demanding this?"[46]

But despite the apparent heroism of the ninety fighters defending Zahle, it would take more than a Phalangist militia to dislodge the Syrian and Palestinian forces in Lebanon, and Bashir of course knew it. He was wasting no time in putting the pieces of the Israeli-Phalangist plan into place: Sharon's troops would crush the PLO and push the Syrians out of the country; the Lebanese people would elect Bashir president as the man possessing the prescribed "national vision," and the nation's sovereignty would be restored under a government ruled according to the provisions of the original National Pact. Meanwhile, the Americans would provide the necessary diplomatic, perhaps even military, backing for the newly-drawn political map of Lebanon.

Indeed, by the end of 1981, a consensus for stronger U.S. action in Lebanon had already emerged. In a speech before the American Lebanese League in June, Senator Edward Kennedy charged that "Syrian 'peacekeeping' is a mockery of the name; it now constitutes the primary obstacle to peace and to the establishment of a strong central government." Kennedy, an avowed liberal, went on to give what appeared to be an implicit endorsement of the Phalangist struggle: "We hear much of 'Christian rightists' in the news. But what is rightist about wanting to survive? What is reactionary about wanting to live in one's ancient homeland? Christian civilization in Lebanon is almost as old as Christianity itself."[47] Kennedy seemed to echo Bashir's line regarding the upcoming presidential contest in Lebanon, warning that "if the election takes place under the domination of Syrian occupation, or if the PLO is permitted to intrude, then a splendid opportunity could be lost, and peace will be set back."[48] Even the Vatican had entered the fray, working in conjunction with New York's Cardinal Terence Cooke, who had traveled to Lebanon at the end of 1979. In an unpublished report on his visit, Cooke had already called on the United States to help "persuade" Syria to withdraw its troops from Lebanon. The regional director of the Pontifical Mission in Lebanon, Monsignor John Meaney, reported that Cooke's assessment "had great influence in getting the State Department perspective on the right track. It shaped their policy to a great extent and the policy of Congress."[49] Cooke reportedly urged Kennedy, himself a Roman Catholic, to persist in the effort to protect the Christians of Lebanon.

By Alfred Maady's account, the Reagan administration stepped up American support for the Christians by furnishing the Phalange with small shipments of light weapons, though they were valued more for their political than military significance. Robert Kupperman, a Middle East expert at the Center for Strategic and International Studies in Washington who studied low-intensity warfare while under contract for the Department of Defense, was familiar with the Reagan policy of using weapons to buy allegiances. The administration might have supplied Bashir's men with M-16 rifles, mortars, rocket-propelled grenade launchers, and other small arms, while holding back on major systems like TOW anti-tank missiles, as part of a calculated strategy to cement ties with the Phalange.[50] A less exotic, and less lethal, type of military hardware that is known to have been sent to the Phalange was sophisticated communications gear that enabled militia commandos to coordinate maneuvers throughout country without fear of their transmissions being monitored by hostile forces. "It also gave us the ability to communicate with Bashir during times of trouble," former ambassador Veliotes pointed out. Getting a White House message to the top during the Phalangist drive toward Zahle might have helped avoid the escalation that culminated in the missile crisis of May 1981. Setting up the Phalangists with an American-made communications network may also have yielded more subtle fruits than the mere presence of a "hot line" to Bashir: while Phalangist transmissions might have been secure from others, U.S. intelligence was in a unique position do some eavesdropping of its own, tapping into equipment that their own specialists had built. Warning the Israelis, or even the Syrians, about an impending Phalangist assault could bring a prompt countermove that might deny Bashir the ability to manipulate the regional powers through Zahle-like brinkmanship.

The CIA's training of Bashir's personal bodyguard and intelligence chief Elie Hobeika afforded Washington an additional opportunity to bring the Phalangist militia closer into America's orbit. Charles Waterman, a veteran Middle East expert at the CIA who served as the agency's national intelligence officer at the time, said that the purpose of such training would not be to simply increase the efficiency of the Phalangist militiamen, but also to gain influence over them.[51] (Due to security regulations, Waterman could not comment directly on Hobeika's CIA connections, though Basil's claim about the militiman's U.S. training was confirmed by a former American State Department official and a senior Lebanese diplomat.[52]) Bringing Hobeika and his men to the United States and exposing them to American advisers over a period of weeks would hopefully establish a rapport and an identification of interests that could prove vital once the militiamen returned to Beirut. Personal relationships and an understanding of the psychology of each individual, established during the coursework in the U.S., might enable American officials to more effectively persuade, cajole, seduce, or intimidate the Phalangist trainees into following a line more acceptable to Washington.

In January 1982, William Clark took over as U.S. national security advisor, replacing Richard Allen, whom Secretary Haig had earlier charged with undermining his policies. The following month, Israel's chief of Military Intelligence, Maj. Gen. Yehoshua Saguy, arrived in Washington to confer with Haig, reportedly bringing maps to review the upcoming Israeli-Phalangist operation in detail. In May, Sharon himself arrived and further discussed the Israeli plan to invade with Haig. The following month, on 6 June, 1982, Sharon's troops rolled into Lebanon, the government offering a transparent official description of the operation as a reprisal action for the PLO's attempted assassination of Shlomo Argov, the Israeli ambassador in London. Within three days, Sharon's forces were on the outskirts of Beirut, and Syria's Soviet-built SAM missile batteries in the Bekka had been destroyed. Bashir, however, refused to send his Phalangists into battle against the PLO. As one military analyst observed, the militia leader chose to avoid an open collaboration with the Israeli forces in order to secure the eventual allegiance of his Moslem countrymen: "The Christian forces gambled that the Israelis could not leave the job unfinished and would sooner or later, with or without Christian help, deal with the PLO trapped in Beirut."[53]

As with his desire for an independent American arms connection to supplement the one in Jerusalem, Bashir did not want to find himself totally reliant on his Israeli allies. He was in basic agreement with the Begin government's position that the Phalangists had many mutual interests with

Israel, but believed that once in power they were likely to have fewer options domestically and greater ones externally. The Christian Phalangists would have to placate both the leftist and the fundamentalist Moslems of Lebanon, which would entail maintaining a reasonable distance from Israel, but as rulers of an Arab state they would also be in a position to enjoy the benefits of open relations with the entire Arab world. Israeli leaders primarily needed to serve only the interests of the country's Jewish majority, and hence were free to ally themselves with whatever nation helped serve that interest. But as a Jewish state, the nation had been frozen out of the region by all its neighbors, except Egypt, with whom it held a rather cold if not fragile peace. For the Phalangists, although they were Christians, they were still Arabs, a claim Israel's Jewish leaders could never make, and therein lay the line that separated Bashir from Sharon. As long as the Lebanese Christians were faced by Syrian troops, besieged by the Palestinians, threatened by the Shiites, challenged by the Druze, and opposed by the Sunnis, the gap between Israeli and Phalangist interests in Lebanon appeared quite small and easily bridged. But should Sharon's master plan succeed, leaving the guns silent and Bashir at the helm of a stable, unified Lebanon, the gulf between Arab and Jew could once again make itself felt. With Sharon's troops at the gates of Beirut and victory nearly certain, Bashir decided to avoid making a clean break with the Arabs, a position repeatedly advocated by various State Department envoys as well as by Ambassador Habib, himself of Lebanese Christian ancestry.

Bashir's failure to confront the Palestinians as planned came as no surprise to some members of the Israeli intelligence community. In its review of the country's relations with the Christian forces in Lebanon, the Israeli government noted that while the "Mossad, to a not inconsiderable extent under the influence of constant and close contact with the Phalangist elite, felt positively about strengthening relations with that organization," the members of the Military Intelligence branch emphasized "the danger in the link with the Phalangists, primarily because of this organization's lack of reliability" and "its military weakness."[54] The result was the siege of Beirut that Sharon had predicted would occur in the absence of Phalangist participation. The subsequent bloodshed turned world opinion against the Israelis and saw the beginnings of America's disassociation from the entire scheme. What began as a lightning strike designed to bring Lebanon back into the Western fold had turned into a pitched battle laboriously waged against a guerrilla force entrenched among the houses and neighborhoods of defenseless civilians.

On 25 June, Alexander Haig, Sharon's advocate in Washington, resigned as secretary of state, and the shift away from Israel accelerated.

After nearly six weeks of massive Israeli shelling and the blockading of food, water, and electricity, the PLO fighters trapped in Moslem West Beirut eventually agreed to an evacuation agreement mediated by Philip Habib. On 21 August, under the protection of a multinational peacekeeping force that included the French Foreign Legion and U.S. Marines from the Sixth Fleet, the first contingent of nearly eight thousand PLO guerrillas began to depart Beirut. On 23 August, Bashir Gemayel was elected President of Lebanon. The Syrians, however, having retreated from Beirut, were still deployed in the Bekka Valley, and Assad's agents were still operating within the city. On 14 September, they succeeded in planting seventy-five pounds of TNT inside the Phalangist headquarters in East Beirut. The explosion killed the thirty-four-year-old president-elect and several of his supporters. Sharon's forces quickly moved into West Beirut to secure the city. With the multinational force gone, the Israelis decided to allow Phalangist militiamen into the Sabra and Shatilla refugee camps to ferret out remaining PLO terrorists. This time, the Phalangists were eager to join the fight, ready to exact their revenge, to administer the final dose of terror that might spark a mass Palestinian exodus from the country. What followed was a massacre of hundreds of defenseless men, women, and children. The killing went on for thirty-six straight hours. "We begged him, 'Please, for God's sake, don't shoot us,'" a sixty-five year-old woman later recalled, speaking from her hospital bed. "'For God's sake, we are women and children.'"[55] The Phalangist gunman then tossed a hand grenade into the room. The woman, hit in the eye with shrapnel, somehow managed to escape.

The tragedy at Sabra and Shatilla, with the bitter memories of Israel's six-week siege of West Beirut still fresh, brought an outcry from around the world, including the three hundred thousand Israelis who took to the Tel Aviv streets to protest their government's actions in Beirut. The American peacekeeping force that had earlier left the country following the PLO evacuation was ordered back to Lebanon, and the newly installed secretary of state, George Shultz, turned his sights on creating another possible "red line" agreement with Assad, aiming for a modus vivendi that would guarantee Syrian and Israeli security interests in Lebanon while allowing for the total withdrawal of both nations' forces and the establishment of a government led by the slain Bashir's brother Amin, who was known to have somewhat better ties with Damascus and the Lebanese Moslems than Bashir. For the time being, the Syrians were back in, Bashir's hard-core followers out. As the months unfolded, the American position appeared to confirm the prevalent view that the dead Phalangist militia leader had presided over a band of cut-throat fascists, capable of committing the kind of atrocities visited upon the Sabra and Shatilla refugee camps, while Sharon was pegged as a mad military genius run amuck, an uncontrolled Jewish Patton who had barreled headlong into the Lebanese quagmire in defiance of Prime Minister Begin and the political echelon back home as well as of his patron Secretary Haig and the American allies abroad.

Much was made of the fact that Elie Hobeika, the Israeli-trained Phalangist commander, had led the Christian troops into the Sabra and Shatilla camps, a clear attempt to further smear Jerusalem with the crime against the refugees. Hobeika had attended the Staff and Command College in Israel, wrote *Time* magazine in its report on the massacre. "A man who always carries a pistol, a knife and a hand grenade on his belt, Hobeika was the most feared Phalangist in Lebanon," the article said. "He had taken part in the Tel Zaatar massacre and in attacks on the rivals of Bashir Gemayel. The Israelis knew Hobeika and his followers as ruthless, brutal security men, and knew they did not constitute a disciplined military force."[56]

During Ariel Sharon's libel suit against *Time* magazine, which ran another cover story on the massacres four months later falsely accusing the Israeli general of "discuss[ing] with the Gemayels the need for the Phalangists to take revenge for the assassination of Bashir" during a condolence call at the Gemayel family residence at Bikfaya the day after the murder, the newsweekly's attorney Thomas Barr delivered to the jury a widely shared characterization of Hobeika and the Phalange:

> Elie Hobeika was the head of a very special group of Phalange. He had a reputation throughout the Middle East as a killer, a murderer, a person who had participated in a number of massacres with this special unit of troops. This was well known. Everybody in the Middle East knew it. And Hobeika was the man, and that special unit was the group, that was sent into those camps on the night of the 16th. Mr. Gould [Sharon's attorney], in his opening, suggested that the Phalange were sort of gentlemanly soldiers, doctors, lawyers who picked up the sword when it was necessary. Our evidence will suggest something quite different. Our evidence will suggest that the Phalange were really a gang, a gang of murderers, rapists, who destroyed as a way of life, who were well known to destroy as a way of life, who massacred civilian populations routinely.
>
> It was common. It was repeated. It was well known. Revenge, blood for blood, is as common to this group, as ordinary and as expected as that the sun will rise.[57]

What was apparently not well known was that America had been supplying the Phalange with military equipment for more than a year prior to Israel's 1982 invasion of Lebanon and that Hobeika and members of his special unit had been brought to the United States for personal training by the CIA.

Hobeika was to later agree to a Syrian-sponsored plan to alter the Lebanese political system and thus found himself on the losing end of a bloody civil war with his fellow Christian militiamen, ousted in January 1986 from his role as commander of the Lebanese Forces by troops fighting under Bashir loyalist Samir Geaega and Lebanese Army units allied with President Amin Gemayel. Hobeika was forced to flee to Damascus. The Syrian plan was viewed by its critics as a virtual surrender of Lebanese sovereignty to Damascus, and Hobeika's consent to it further confirmed suspicions that he had indeed been a Syrian operative from the beginning. Hobeika was Bashir's bodyguard, Robert Basil explained, he never left his side, except for the afternoon when the bomb exploded inside his head-quarters in West Beirut. In May 1986, during testimony before the Senate Subcommittee on Foreign Relations, Basil was to further insinuate that Hobeika had acted without authorization in taking the Phalange into the camps, and that the action may indeed have been another of Hafez Assad's cruel Machiavellian ploys to destroy the credibility of Israel and undermine international support for the Phalangists. "Mr. Hobeika, one of the prime suspects in the assassination of President elect Bachir [sic] Gemayel, and who subsequently launched the vicious attacks against civilians in Sabra and Chatilla [sic], tried to sign away Lebanon's sovereignty," Basil declared.[58] Other observers subscribed to Basil's view that Hobeika had been a Syrian agent, including a former high-level national security council staff member deeply involved in Middle East policy during the Reagan administration.[59] Using Hobeika to kill Bashir and wreak havoc in the Palestinian camps would have certainly been the kind of devious maneuver that had earned the Syrian strongman his reputation for brilliance and brutality. The murders would send a dual signal to Assad's adversaries: One, the assassination of Bashir would demonstrate to the world that neither the Phalangists nor the Israelis would be able to install a government in Lebanon without the consent of Syria. Two, since the Syrian president had no use for the Palestinians, having long ago developed a hatred for Arafat and his PLO loyalists, the Sabra and Shatilla slaughters would show that Arafat was weak, incapable of protecting his people, abandoning them in the face of Israeli guns, leaving them to the mercy of their enemies in Beirut. With Arafat's leadership undermined, the way would be cleared for a new PLO more conducive to Syrian aims in the region. As it happened, Arafat's own Fateh would soon split into rival factions as Syrian-supported rebels battled openly for control of the guerrilla group, violently splitting the entire PLO along Arafat and anti-Arafat lines.

If Hobeika was indeed a Syrian agent, then he was undoubtedly one of the most intriguing intelligence operatives ever to come out of the region. For here was a man who had managed to rise to the top of the most powerful Christian militia in Lebanon; then penetrate the Israeli Mossad, reputedly one of the best intelligence organizations in the world, attending training courses at a war college in the midst of Israel itself; and then penetrate the CIA, traveling to the United States under the agency's own sponsorship, availing himself of American intelligence know-how firsthand—all of this while secretly working for Syrian intelligence, an organization advised and supplied by the Soviet KGB. The question, of course, remains: Was Hobeika a Syrian agent or not? The CIA's Charles Waterman explains that the key element is "control." Was Hobeika close to the Syrians? Perhaps. But was he *controlled* by them?[60] Did Hobeika do their bidding, or his own? It is one thing for Syria or the CIA or the Mossad to introduce agents into Beirut and establish ties with militia leaders like Hobeika, exchanging information, offering cash and military supplies, coordinating strikes against mutual enemies. But such agents are operating on foreign soil, and it is their clients who are surrounded by well-armed loyalists. American, Israeli, or Syrian power is limited in such situations; intelligence agents, operating virtually alone with limited protection, are often at the mercy of their foreign contacts, dependent on them not only for information and cooperation but for their own safety as well. Unlike Brad Kirkland, the ex-British officer who lacked an independent power base, free-lancing for Qaddafi before being compelled to work as a double agent for the Mossad, Elie Hobeika was an established, recognized force operating on native terrain. Was Hobeika—a commander of a well-equipped Phalangist unit that did not shrink from confronting either the Syrian army or PLO guerrillas on the battlefield—simply forced to carry out orders by Syrian intelligence agents operating undercover in Beirut? Or was the Mossad capable of directing Hobeika's moves, ordering him at will to either attack PLO terrorists in West Beirut or refrain from such strikes? Was he an agent of the CIA, moving through the Lebanese labyrinth while the strings were being pulled from Washington? Perhaps Elie Hobeika had connections with one or all of the parties involved, taking from each that which would strengthen his own position, giving to each that which would earn him enough just leverage to operate freely of any one of them. Elie Hobeika may indeed have been an agent of Syria, the Mossad, the KGB, or the CIA, or maybe instead just an agent of Elie Hobeika.

Hobeika, the Christian militia commander trained and armed by both the Mossad and the CIA, seemed to symbolize the baffling conspiracies and bewildering fate that had befallen Lebanon: the rise and fall of the Phalangists, at once scorned and embraced by the United States, encouraged by Israel only to later betray it; secret arms deals with a young and ambitious Bashir Gemayel and a deft jockeying for position as Washington sought to gain the upper hand against its closest ally in the Middle East, Israel; a covert plan to reshape the Lebanese map using Israeli troops and American political clout, only to end in the resignation of a beleaguered secretary of state, an embattled Israeli defense minister, a tarred Israel, and a discredited U.S. policy, leaving a bloodied Lebanon still tragically torn between warring factions, tottering under the watchful eyes of Syrian troops in the north and Israeli proxies in the south, a sad and shattered Beirut, still the terrorist center of the Middle East.

26

The Kissinger Ban

FOR more than a decade, while Israel was carrying out its counterterrorist reprisal raids, Sadat was carrying out his peace initiative, King Hussein was conducting his secret diplomacy, and the United States was attempting to contain the chaos in Lebanon, the Palestinian guerrilla leadership was vigilantly pursuing its aim of gaining international approval and American support. The Israelis, however, were adamant about freezing them out of any negotiated settlement. "Of all of Israel's nightmares," Henry Kissinger once wrote, "none was more elemental than the PLO." Kissinger was characterizing the climate surrounding his mid-1970s shuttle diplomacy. "The possibility that a group claiming all of Palestine for itself might gain any legitimacy whatever was considered a basic threat to Israel's survival." A key to gaining such legitimacy would be U.S. recognition of the PLO and acceptance of the organization as a partner in the Middle East peace process.

According to Kissinger, the PLO's first significant overture to the United States came in a message delivered by an Arafat associate to an assistant of Richard Helms, the American ambassador to Iran. It was late July 1973, and Yassir Arafat was interested in establishing diplomatic contacts with Washington. The PLO chief implied that he was ready to accept the reality of Israel, but Jordan should be turned into a Palestinian state. On 1 August, Kissinger instructed Helms to send back word to Arafat that although the United States was interested in hearing Palestinian ideas for a peace settlement, it was firmly committed to the security of Hussein's throne in Amman.

I considered King Hussein a valued friend of the United States and a principal hope for diplomatic progress in the region. Our aim should be to strengthen his position, not to encourage a group that avowed its determination to overthrow him in its very first communication with us. A Palestinian state run by the PLO was certain to be irredentist. Even should it change its professed aims, it would not likely remain moderate for long; its many extremist factions would see to that. Its Soviet ties, too, would lead it in the direction of becoming a radical state like Libya or South Yemen. Any Palestinian structure on the West Bank had every incentive to turn to Jordan—if only to gain a secure base for later operations against Israel and to avoid the provisions of a peace accord that would inevitably demilitarize the West Bank.[1]

Ten days later, Morocco's King Hassan gave Vernon Walters, deputy director of the CIA, the same message that had been delivered to Helms's assistant. Two months later, on 10 October, 1973, the fourth day of the Yom Kippur War, Arafat sent another message to the United States, this time imploring the Americans to refrain from assisting Israel. It further stated that when the fighting ceased, the PLO would be willing to join the Arab states in subsequent peace negotiations. Again, Arafat emphasized, his immediate target was Hashemite Jordan, not the Jewish state.

On 23 October, Arafat signaled his interest in meeting with an American representative. On 3 November, General Walters flew to Rabat, Morocco, to hear the PLO's proposals, but he was to avoid substantive negotiations with the guerrilla group. In the interim, the PLO's representative in Cairo, Said Kamel, was holding discussions with U.S. diplomat Arthur Holten. The newly-appointed American ambassador, Hermann Eilts, then received word from Washington that such contacts should cease and the talks with Kamel were broken off.[2] Another meeting between General Walters and an Arafat official took place on 7 March, 1974.[3]

The spotty encounters between U.S. representatives and PLO members did not lead to any diplomatic breakthroughs: the PLO was committed to Hussein's overthrow in the short term and Israel's ultimate destruction in the long run. What did emerge from the meetings with General Walters was an arrangement similar to the one that had been secretly struck between Yigal Allon and King Hussein: in the absence of a political dialogue, a practical dialogue would be maintained involving cooperation on security matters. Arafat offered to grant immunity from terrorist attack to U.S. diplomats in an attempt to win gradual American recognition of the PLO.[4]

The previous year, on 1 March, eight Fateh commandos had taken over the Saudi Arabian embassy in Khartoum where a farewell reception was being held for the American charge d'affaires, Curtis Moore. They demanded the release of Fateh leader Abou Doud and sixteen other PLO guerrillas imprisoned in Jordan. When their demands were rejected, the PLO terrorists ordered Moore, the American ambassador to the Sudan, Cleo Noel, and the Belgian charge d'affaires, Guy Eid, into the basement, where they were machine-gunned to death.[5] Arafat's emissary told Walters that Fateh was ready to see to it that such incidents were not repeated. For the Americans, Fateh's ability to deliver on such a pledge could be a test of its sincerity and would be a factor in any future re-evaluation of the PLO's place in the United States-sponsored Middle East peace process. The security arrangement with the PLO was put into place. (Ironically, reports later surfaced alleging that American intelligence officers at the time managed to monitor a phone call in which Arafat personally gave the order to kill the hostages in Khartoum.)

In his autobiography, Walters offered an oblique reference to his meeting with the Arafat lieutenant: "On one occasion the U.S. government sent me to talk to a most hostile group of terrorists. I saw them alone and unarmed in a part of the world sympathetic to their cause. My position made me a major target. I had studied their past, their hopes, their dreams, even their poetry. I was able to convey to them the message that I had been ordered to deliver. We were able to communicate and there were no further acts of blood between us."[6]

American journalist David Ignatius reported that the key man behind the tacit United States-PLO security agreement was Ali Hasan Salameh, the mastermind behind the Munich Massacre, the number two man in Abu Iyad's Black September commando squad, a PLO commander during the Moslem-Christian fighting in Lebanon, and the chief of Force 17, Yassir Arafat's personal security unit. Regardless of his purported role in protecting American diplomats, the Israelis sent an assassination team after Salameh to avenge the deaths at Munich, killing him in a car bomb blast in Beirut on 22 January, 1979. Hermann Eilts later commented that as U.S. ambassador to Egypt he had indeed become acquainted with Salameh's activities. "I know that on a good many occasions, in a nonpublic fashion, he was extraordinarily helpful—as was Fatah—in assisting in security for American citizens and officials. I regard his assassination as a loss."[7]

Theoretically, the loss of Salameh would impact solely on U.S. security procedures in the region, not on its political interests. Washington had already pledged four years earlier not to enter into a diplomatic dialogue with the PLO.

On 1 September 1975, the Sinai II disengagement agreement between Israel and Egypt had been made public. "The Parties shall hereby undertake not to resort to threat or use of force or military blockade against each other," the accord stated.[8] Israel agreed to withdraw from the Milta and Gidi passes in the eastern Sinai and the Abu Rodeis oil fields in the peninsula's southern region. Many observers cited the references to the renunciation of force as evidence of a major breakthrough in the Middle East conflict. Israel's leaders were more circumspect. They had traded concrete strategic lands for the vague promise of peace. In fact, Ismail Fahmy, Egypt's foreign minister at the time of the Sinai agreement, went to great lengths to undermine any attempt to view the accord as a milestone on the road toward a peaceful settlement:

> They [political commentators] argued that this document contained explicit references to the renunciation of force, and that this must surely imply the end of belligerency. My answer to these people is that they should compare the language of the second disengagement agreement with that of the Egyptian-Israeli General Armistice Agreement signed on 24 February 1949 at Rhodes, Greece: they will find identical expressions there. Yet, three major wars between Egypt and Israel had taken place since then, in 1956, 1967 and 1973. The 1949 Armistice Agreement repeatedly committed the parties to renouncing the use of force. Article 1, for example, stated that "the injunction of the Security Council against resort to military force in the settlement of the Palestinian question shall henceforth be scrupulously respected by both parties." The same Article again repeated that "no aggressive action by the Armed Forces—land, sea or air—of either party shall be undertaken, planned or threatened." The article finally concluded that the establishment of the armistice was "an indispensable step toward the liquidation of armed conflict and the restoration of peace in Palestine." Although many similar quotes could be extracted from the 1949 Armistice Agreement, this is sufficient to show that the 1975 disengagement did not introduce any new language or concepts. This is not accidental, I must point out. In dictating the Egyptian proposal for disengagement to a line east of the passes, I had consulted the Armistice Agreement and was most careful to use the same wording.[9]

The Israelis were acutely aware of the viewpoint espoused by Fahmy and embraced by much of the Arab world. Despite the peaceful rhetoric of previous agreements, three major wars had indeed taken place with Egypt since the first one in 1948. Israel wanted more than paper in exchange for its withdrawal from Egyptian soil. What Kissinger offered was increased American economic and military assistance, and a political commitment that would have a significant impact on future diplomacy in the region: the United States formally pledged to refrain from negotiating with the PLO, the organization Kissinger was later to describe as one of the most "elemental" of "Israel's nightmares." The promise was spelled out in a secret memorandum to Israel which accompanied the terms of the Sinai II disengagement agreement: ''The United States will continue to adhere to its present policy with respect to the Palestine Liberation Organization, whereby it will not recognize or negotiate with the P.L.O. so long as the P.L.O. does not recognize Israel's right to exist and does not accept Security Council Resolutions 242 and 338.''[10]

For the PLO, the key section of U.N. resolution 242, formulated in the aftermath of the Six Day War and passed on 22 November, 1967, was Article 1, section 1: ''Termination of all claims or states of belligerency and respect for and acknowledgement of the sovereignty, territorial integrity and political independence of every State in the area and their right to live in peace within secure and recognized boundaries free from threats or acts of force.''[11]

Resolution 338, passed in the wake of the Yom Kippur fighting on 22 October, 1973, reaffirmed the United Nation's call for ''implementation of Security Council Resolution 242 (1967) in all of its parts.''[12] To the PLO leaders, acceptance of 242 and 338 clearly meant that the Palestinian guerrillas would be adopting the path of negotiation over that of ''armed struggle'' in their dispute with the Jews. If the PLO wanted to establish a political dialogue with the United States, the terms Kissinger set forth in 1975 required not only that it accept 242 and 338, but also that it publicly and unambiguously acknowledge Israel's right to exist as a nation. For Arafat and his associates, Kissinger's conditions proved too exacting. The relationship with the Americans would instead have to be confined to what Kissinger described as ''low-level technical contacts'' involving security guarantees for U.S. diplomatic personnel.[13]

At times, Arafat attempted to mitigate the impact of his hard-line stand against Israel by offering gestures of moderation such as his periodic interventions aimed at saving Americans from terrorist assaults by other Palestinian guerrillas. U.S. Ambassador Dean Brown reported that Kissinger once instructed American officials to arrange PLO protection for Brown during his March 1976 peacekeeping mission to Beirut at the height of the Lebanese Civil War, and there were reports that Arafat indeed complied with the U.S. request for security assistance.

However, Arafat's inclination, or perhaps his ability, to control the PLO factions under his command was not great enough to prevent the attack of 17 June, 1976, when unidentified gunmen in Moslem West Beirut kidnapped the newly-appointed American ambassador to Lebanon, Francis Meloy, Jr., his economics counselor Robert O. Waring, and the U.S. embassy chauffeur, Zuhair Moghrabi, as they were driving to a meeting with Lebanese President-elect, Elias Sarkis. All three bodies were found hours later in a garbage dump near the ocean. There was speculation that the murders had been carried out by a group allied with George Habash's PFLP faction.[14] Habash had previously demonstrated his opposition to PLO secret dealings with the United States by resigning from the PLO Executive Committee in October 1974, a move that was partly a response to a dispute with Arafat arising after Habash learned of the chairman's private contacts with the Americans in 1973.[15]

Three days after Ambassador Meloy's murder, the U.S. Sixth Fleet evacuated 263 Westerners from Beirut. This time, troops from Arafat's own Fateh faction were out in full force, reportedly under the direct supervision of Hasan Salameh. According to West German journalist Harold Vocke, "The surrounding coastal area was guarded by Palestinian Fatah guerrillas with tanks and infantry weapons to safeguard the embarkation."[16] Ignatius reported that "Mr. Salameh was in regular contact with U.S. embassy personnel during the evacuation."[17]

The secret talks between representatives of PLO Chairman Arafat and U.S. government officials continued after the Beirut evacuation of 1976, though compliance with Kissinger's 1975 pledge to Israel required that no political discussions take place until the PLO accepted Israel's right to live in peace. This policy prohibiting diplomatic contact with the PLO was not always followed.

In June and July of 1979, the U.S. ambassador to Austria, Milton Wolf, held three meetings with the PLO's Isam Sartawi, an associate of Arafat and an advocate of Palestinian recognition of Israel. Sartawi reportedly wanted to elaborate on Arafat's latest position regarding the Middle East peace process. State Department spokesman Thomas Reston disclosed that Ambassador Wolf was "reminded by the department on July 2 and again on July 7 of the official policy against substantitive discussions with the P.L.O."[18] Sartawi was assassinated on 10 April, 1983 by Palestinian terrorists opposed to his peace overtures to Israel.

On 26 July, 1979, less than three weeks after the State Department "reminder" to Ambassador Wolf, U.S. Ambassador to the United Nations Andrew Young went to the apartment of the Kuwaiti ambassador and held a secret meeting with the PLO's envoy to the United Nations, Zehdi Labib Terzi. The PLO had long objected to Resolution 242's reference to the Palestinians as refugees, rather than as legitimate claimants to a state of their own. Kuwait had been working to amend the U.N. resolution to include a call for the establishment of an independent Palestinian state to be inserted along with the existing guarantees for the right of Israel to exist within secure boundaries. The Kuwaiti ambassador hoped to pre-arrange American and Palestinian approval of the new resolution prior to its introduction in the United Nations.[19] Israeli intelligence in New York reportedly monitored the meeting and sent word of the encounter to the Americans. Other accounts had it that Young informed the Israelis himself, naively believing that they would support his attempt to broker an agreement. At the time, the State Department disclosed that Young had in any case failed to notify his superiors about his talk with Terzi and that after news of the incident was disclosed by the Israelis he tried to mislead Carter administration officials about the content of the discussion. Secretary of State Vance was said to have criticized Young's actions as "intolerable," with a close associate telling one reporter that Vance had found himself in the awkward position of having to "learn from the Israelis the truth about what his man at the United Nations has been up to."[20] Young was forced to resign his U.N. post. The Carter administration, however, insisted that restricted contacts with the PLO, short of actual negotiation, were essential to the peace process and would therefore continue.

The exact nature of the restrictions imposed by the 1975 Kissinger pledge to Israel remains a source of controversy. Some U.S. observers, like Hermann Eilts, have taken it to mean that even the most inconsequential contacts between American officials and PLO representatives are banned by the Kissinger memorandum.[21] Such a total boycott is essential if the U.S. is to avoid giving the appearance that it is endorsing, recognizing, or negotiating with the Palestinian guerrilla group prior to its acceptance of Kissinger's conditions. Others, like Harvey Sicherman, the policy analyst who served as an assistant to Alexander Haig for Mideast affairs during his term as secretary of state, have argued that the Kissinger ban was never meant to preclude the everyday human contacts that are inevitable in international politics, especially given the fact that for years the American embassy in Lebanon was situated in the heart of PLO-controlled West Beirut. "A U.S. diplomat couldn't work in Beirut without bumping into the PLO," Sicherman explained. Young's problem was not that he "talked" to the PLO, Sicherman said, but that he *negotiated* with them. The standing U.S. policy was that American officials would not grant the PLO a place at the negotiating table until it accepted the ground rules, which meant acceptance of Israel. Sicherman asserted that Young had tried to circumvent the policy by cutting a deal on the proposed Kuwaiti U.N. resolution in the hope that he might bring all of the parties closer together. But the strategy required the acknowledgement of PLO claims as legitimate and a U.S. willingness to accommodate them. Young and others insisted that "talking" to the PLO was harmless, but conversation wasn't the point: negotiations, which implied an endorsement of the PLO's right to have its demands addressed by the United States government, were opposed to America's interests, unless the Palestinian guerrillas demonstrated their readiness to renounce their pledge to dismantle the State of Israel.[22]

Donald McHenry, who succeeded Andrew Young as U.N. ambassador under President Carter, insisted that the confusion over the Kissinger ban stemmed from a mix-up between the concept of formal recognition, which is a diplomatic term that can be applied only to organizations of legal character, and communication. The United States has not granted the PLO any legal standing as a governmental body and American diplomatic recognition is not necessarily conferred on it merely through the act of communicating with its members. For McHenry, the cocktail party encounters proscribed by Eilts—the polite exchanges among PLO members and U.S. officials that might occur in the halls of the United Nations or the living rooms of foreign diplomats—were not only permissible under the Kissinger memorandum, but should actually be compelled by the dictates of simple "human courtesy".[23]

Alfred Atherton, the Middle East specialist who served as a key adviser under Presidents Nixon, Ford, and Carter, asserted that the Kissinger ban was in fact a ploy to keep the PLO out of the subsequent Geneva peace conference that followed the shuttle disengagement agreements, and that it was not intended to bar the possibility of working level contacts between American officials and PLO representatives. Furthermore, according to Atherton, the imposition of the tight restrictions governing PLO-U.S. talks was simply an attempt by Kissinger to centralize the American negotiating process. By elevating the mere act of discussion to the policy level— thus requiring U.S. envoys to get prior authorization from senior officials in Washington before any PLO encounters could take place—Kissinger hoped to avoid the false signals and misinformation that would probably result from uncoordinated PLO-U.S. meetings that might be held by any number of State Department analysts and political officers stationed across Europe and the Middle East. The strict guidelines limiting official American contact with the PLO was later misinterpreted by State Department members and others as a restriction dictated under the terms of the Kissinger memorandum.[24]

Atherton also added that Kissinger had purposely limited his commitment to Israel so as to keep open the necessary options that might be needed in maneuvering toward a future Mideast settlement. Formal recognition of and negotiations with the PLO would be withheld by the United States until the Palestinian organization accepted Israel and U.N resolutions 242 and 338, but the United States would retain the right to hold informal exploratory talks in an effort to move the guerrilla group toward such acceptance. The fact that Kissinger himself later decided to expand the ban to cover all political contact with the PLO did not reflect the nature of the commitment to Israel, being rather an attempt by the secretary of state to use the leverage of U.S. recognition as a means of pressing the PLO leadership into making concessions that would allow for a peaceful solution to the conflict.

Journalists and diplomats have frequently attempted to portray the Kissinger ban as an example of Israel's inordinate political power, which, in conjunction with its allies in the the American Jewish lobby, limits the ability of the United States to conduct an independent foreign policy. If Atherton's depiction of the Nixon administration's application of the Kissinger ban is correct, then the decade-old U.S. refusal to consult with the PLO on political matters initially stemmed from an internal policy decision by the American government, acting in its own interest, and not on a decision compelled by any agreement with a foreign power.

That the U.S. ban on talks with the PLO is the product of an independent American foreign policy and not the result of coercion by Israel and the Jewish lobby has also been underscored by Harold Saunders, a former high-ranking State Department official and a veteran of both Kissinger's shuttle diplomacy and Carter's Camp David peace process. Saunders reported that at the time of the Kissinger memorandum, the Israelis in fact submitted a draft that precluded all talks between U.S. officials and the PLO, but the restriction was removed by the American negotiators. It was U.S. policy, not an Israeli fiat, that subsequently prevailed in the American attitude toward the Palestinians:

> What has precluded our talking to the PLO have been policy decisions since 1975 that we would not talk to the PLO at given times. That policy prohibition continued in the Carter administration, but President Carter added something to it. He said positively that if the PLO accepts Israel's right to exist and resolutions 242 and 338, we talk to the PLO. There is a commitment to talk if the PLO takes that step. He did not just say that their acceptance of those resolutions would remove the obstacles to negotiating; he said if they did that, we would talk. And that is the position of the Reagan administration. So it's a matter of policy that has precluded us from talking to the PLO, not the Kissinger agreement.[25]

But the public's apparent misinterpretation of the Kissinger memorandum indeed continued into the Reagan administration. Harvey Sicherman recalled one occasion when a group of West Bank Palestinians held a meeting with Nicholas Veliotes, then serving as the assistant secretary for Near Eastern and South Asian Affairs, and as they got up to leave one of the Arab participants turned to the State Department official and announced, "He's PLO," pointing to another member of the West Bank delegation.

The incident brought to mind the time when a PLO official slipped into the receiving line during a presidential visit to the United Nations in 1977 to shake Carter's hand. These gestures were meaningless, Sicherman explained, merely PLO tricks designed to make "contact" with the United States as if the slightest association with the guerrillas constituted a significant challenge to America's Middle East policy. A polite exchange at a diplomatic function or a conversation with someone who had failed to disclose his or her PLO connection would not lay the groundwork for a fundamental change in U.S. interests. Serious, direct, above-board negotiations with the PLO would come about only if the Kissinger criteria were met. If that came to pass, America would make the appropriate adjustments to its policy.

As former Undersecretary of State Joseph Sisco explained, the United States was simply unwilling to sit down and hammer out a Mideast agreement with a PLO that did not accept Israel's right to exist. Casual contacts or informal talks had no bearing on this position. "I wrote the Kissinger ban," Sisco said. "Kissinger made sense." The problem had not been a lack of communication between the Palestinian and American leaders, said Sisco, the messages were getting through. At the time of the Kissinger agreement, the United States knew what Arafat wanted: he wanted to be president of a West Bank Palestinian state. But Sisco did not see Arafat as a reliable partner in the peace process. There was no need to pursue in-depth discussions with a leader that remained unwilling to grant Israel a place in the Middle East. That was the essential rationale of the Kissinger memorandum, Sisco explained, and a decade later it still made sense for American foreign policy.[26] Indeed, the chairman's continuous waffling on resolutions 242 and 338 over the years, and the 1983 violent split in PLO ranks triggered by rebel Palestinian forces backed by Syria, revealed that Arafat's grip on the PLO mainstream was tenuous and his determination to announce unequivocally his acceptance of Israel questionable.

27

Dealing the PLO In

As noted in the incidents involving Ambassadors Wolf and Young, efforts to quietly depart from the Kissinger ban on political contacts with the PLO were made by U.S. policymakers who believed that the guerrilla organization's rejection of Israel's legitimacy should not disqualify it as a negotiating partner, and that discussions with PLO leaders were a vital ingredient for Middle East peace.

Sometimes the U.S.-PLO contacts consisted of impromptu talks which were neither perceived nor intended to serve as concrete negotiating sessions. For instance, former ambassador Hermann Eilts admitted that although American officials insisted on confining the discussions of the 1970s with Hasan Salameh and other PLO members to consular security issues, the Palestinian guerrilla leaders might have naturally added a "political dimension" to the talks.[1] But the inclusion of such a political dimension, even in the context of a dialogue on the implementation of security measures for U.S. diplomats, was in conflict with the stated American position on the PLO. Therefore, any deliberate pursuit of this political realm would have had to have fallen to the U.S. clandestine services if the public contours of America's Middle East foreign policy were to remain intact.

In 1981, George Habash's Popular Front for the Liberation of Palestine published charges in its English language magazine that an employee at the American Center in Cairo—a cultural exchange institution—and a senior U.S. diplomat attached to the American embassy in that city were both working undercover in Egypt as CIA officers. The embassy official, whose real identity will remain anonymous for security reasons but who will be referred to as Mr. Morgan, became part of the U.S. team involved in the West Bank autonomy negotiations between Egypt and Israel following the signing of the 1979 peace treaty. He was later shifted back to Washington for a senior-level post at the Bureau of Near East and South Asian Affairs.

"Soviet disinformation," was Morgan's reaction when confronted with the story in his State Department office.[2] He laughingly dismissed the PFLP piece as a bit of routine Middle East mischief, then asked if he could photocopy the article. The Soviets are always trying to drive a wedge between America and the Arabs, Morgan explained, such propaganda asserting CIA activities in Egypt is aimed directly at the Arab world. Morgan cited as another instance of Soviet disinformation a memo purportedly circulated by Ambassador Eilts advising that the United States "dump Sadat" and move away from further alliances with his regime. The memo was a forgery, Morgan explained, an attempt by the Russians to undermine Sadat's confidence in his U.S. supporters.

Eilts, who was the American ambassador during Morgan's tenure at the U.S. embassy in Cairo, had the identical reaction to the PFLP piece alleging that his former staff member was actually in the employ of the CIA. It was clearly a product of Soviet disinformation, he said, emphasizing that such disinformation was dangerous, because it could virtually end an American diplomat's career in the Middle East. There is already wide suspicion that American intelligence agents have a stranglehold on events in the region. U.S. diplomats linked to the CIA make tempting targets for Arab radical gunmen.[3]

In Mr. Morgan's case, if the charges of CIA involvement are true, then it appears that Arab guerrillas were drawn to him for the purpose of negotiation, not assassination. Hamdi Fuad, the Washington correspondent for Egypt's respected *Al Ahram* newspaper, remembered Morgan from his days at the American embassy in Cairo. On one particular occasion, during the celebration of an Egyptian national holiday at the Nile Hilton in 1975, Fuad recalled having been approached by Morgan and being asked if he would introduce him to Said Kamel, the PLO representative to Egypt. Fuad obliged, and escorted Morgan over to Kamel, where the two men struck up a conversation. Fuad said that Eilts later accused him of tricking Morgan into the discussion with Kamel, an attempt to subvert Kissinger's ban against contact with the PLO.[4]

When questioned about the secret diplomatic channel between the United States and the PLO, Eilts sought to refute its existence by demonstrating how sensitive the issue was during his term of office in Cairo. Without any prompting, Eilts brought up a story about a CIA official who had a talk with Said Kamel while attending a cocktail party. Eilts reported that he was forced to reprimand the CIA man. Such contact, however casual, was a breach of U.S. policy. The parallel with Fuad's story about the Nile Hilton reception seemed strikingly coincidental. When asked directly if Morgan was the CIA man in question, Eilts quickly responded with a forceful no.

The exact nature of Mr. Morgan's role in Egypt may never be known, but Israeli sources contend that the CIA carried on extensive contacts with the PLO that went beyond security matters to include substantive consultations on U.S. policy in the region, especially in the years prior to Israel's 1982 invasion of Lebanon. Haig assistant Harvey Sicherman downplayed the existence of a political dialogue with the PLO: the stories by David Ignatius and *Los Angeles Times* reporter Doyle McManus detailing the history of secret contacts between PLO members and American diplomats were an attempt by the CIA to cover up for the intelligence failure in Lebanon that resulted in the bombing of the Marine barracks by Shiite guerrillas on 23 October, 1983. According to Sicherman, the CIA tried to pass the buck by claiming that it had excellent undercover sources throughout Beirut but that the Israeli invasion of 1982 destroyed the PLO infrastructure and with it the American intelligence network in Lebanon. To substantiate the claim, the CIA leaked stories to Ignatius, McManus, and others, providing information about the Salameh-United States security link. CIA operatives didn't know what was happening in Lebanon before or after the Israeli invasion, said Sicherman. One widely held exception was Robert C. Ames, the CIA station chief in Beirut. Even Sicherman agreed that Ames knew more about the PLO than any other American official.[5]

Bob Ames had a distinguished record with the CIA, having served in South Yemen, Lebanon, Kuwait, and Iran. He replaced Charles Waterman as national intelligence officer for the Middle East, and later became the agency's chief of operations for the area. He was subsequently promoted to the position of CIA director of assessment and analysis for the Near East and South Asia. He was fluent in Arabic and had experience in all levels of intelligence work. In an unusual departure from precedent for a CIA officer, Ames was given a direct role in the formulation of U.S. policy at the State Department, sitting in on National Security Council sessions as an adviser to Secretary of State George Shultz. He also became part of an inter-agency task force on the Middle East led by assistant secretary Veliotes. Intelligence officials commenting on Ames's role explained that even high-level analysts "normally work on the periphery of policymaking"; however, in this instance, Ames "played a more central role because he impressed Mr. Shultz and other officials with his grasp of Middle East Affairs."[6]

Ames, the CIA's key man in the development of the Reagan Plan, was a professional, Harvey Sicherman emphasized; his job was to gather intelligence. He worked his contacts, used intermediaries to reach adversaries, and never masked opinion as fact or distorted information in order to pursue a particular policy. In addition, according to Charles Waterman, the U.S. system nevertheless made it difficult for intelligence agents to conduct diplomacy. The level at which discussions would have to take place (exploratory talks involving possible concessions, give-and-take negotiations, economic and military commitments) required that at a minimum a senior State Department assistant be brought in to deal with such fundamental policy questions. The Israelis were different, Waterman observed. There was often a crossover between the political echelon and the intelligence apparatus. Waterman's point is well taken. Prime Minister Yitzhak Shamir had been a senior-level officer for the Israeli secret service; President Chaim Herzog had served as the chief of military intelligence;[7] David Kimche, Begin's director-general of the foreign ministry, had been a Mossad operative in West Africa;[8] Uri Lubrani, the coordinator for Lebanese affairs, was an intelligence agent who played a key diplomatic role during the days of the shah as Israel's "unofficial ambassador to Iran," helping to shape Israel's policy toward Teheran.[9]

A confidential CIA report prepared in March 1979 detailed the prominent role played by Israeli intelligence in the formulation and execution of state diplomacy:

> The intelligence and security community enjoys a strong position in the government, and their affairs are well integrated into more general operations. Members of the generation which worked for the establishment of the state were companions of longstanding and joint veterans of such enterprises as illegal immigration and arms-running. Many of the current leaders came up through the ranks of the military in a series of wars with the Arabs and entered politics through affiliation with one of the major political parties. All of them had some experience in clandestine matters and have been personally convinced by stern lessons of the value of good intelligence and security.
>
> The intelligence and security services receive excellent support from the Ministry for Foreign Affairs. Many senior diplomats are former intelligence officers and therefore conversant with intelligence problems and operations. With their experienced observations and manifold talents, they serve as valuable auxiliaries to their covert colleagues, whose diplomatic cover is diligently sustained by the Ministry for Foreign Affairs.
>
> The Israeli intelligence and security services play an important role throughout the government and private sector. Many leaders in both the civil service and industry have at some time in their careers been directly or indirectly involved with the intelligence community. Service assignments are not regarded as the end of a career, as persons with intelligence and security backgrounds frequently are selected for other jobs in government. Thus the services are supplemented by persons who know and continue to relate their missions to intelligence and security responsibilities, in senior posts in both the public and private sectors.[10]

Though in the United States there had traditionally been a much wider separation between the intelligence arm of the government and its political echelon than that which existed in Israel, certain Israelis saw Bob Ames as a distasteful exception to the American approach. To them, Ames was the PLO's advocate. He thought the guerrilla group could become a viable partner in the peace process, that the PLO would renounce violence if Israel offered the proper concessions in the West Bank and Gaza.

Ames may have also reckoned that the Palestinian organization had become an unshakeable symbol to the Arabs, and therefore was destined to be a party to any comprehensive settlement of the Arab-Israeli conflict. But the PLO was a highly diverse mixture of various factions often at odds with one another—independent Marxists, pan-Arab Nasserists, Palestinian nationalists, pro-Syrian socialists, Islamic fundamentalists, Christian capitalists—some radically anti-American, others more conservative, even pro-Western. By developing ties with the PLO's "moderate" wing, i.e. Arafat's Fateh, Ames might have reasoned that the United States could avoid a repeat of what he had witnessed first-hand as a CIA agent stationed in the former British colony of South Yemen: a Soviet-backed revolutionary group, known as the National Liberation Front, had managed to establish a Marxist-Leninist regime following the country's independence in 1967. In a talk with CIA director Casey in 1981, Ames described how the Yemenite leader Abd'al Fatah had "captured and subverted a legitimate war of liberation," how he "killed or drove into exile those members of the movement who believed in democracy and then went about the work of consolidating a communist regime."[11] Ames was no doubt aware that Abd'al Fatah's National Liberation Front had its roots in the Arab Nationalist Movement (ANM), formed by George Habash in the 1950s. The ANM was a precursor to the Popular Front for the Liberation of Palestine, the hardline, pro-Soviet faction of the PLO founded by Habash.[12] South Yemen owed "a special debt to the PFLP," observed British journalists Christopher Dobson and Ronald Payne, and had expressed its solidarity with its Marxist colleagues by allowing Habash's terror chief Waddieh Haddad "absolute freedom to plot and plan. Hijacked planes landed there and the hijackers were given sanctuary."[13]

Anti-colonial national liberation movements in Africa and the Middle East were indeed subject to communist influence, and their ascension to power could produce an axis of radical states ready to follow South Yemen's lead in providing bases, materiel, and training not only for guerrillas struggling to throw off foreign rule but for revolutionary terrorists working to destabilize legitimate capitalist regimes in their own countries as well. "The Middle East is at the crossroads of the European socialist countries and the vast regions where the national-liberation struggle is going on,'' wrote Yevgeni Primakov, one of the Soviet Union's pre-eminent Middle East specialists. ''The Arab peoples' struggle against imperialism and feudalism has made the Middle East a centre of the national-liberation movement. In the 1960s the anti-imperialist struggle developed into an anti-capitalist struggle to a greater extent in the Arab world than it did in many other parts of Asia and Africa. Quite a few of the developing countries which have chosen to base their social and economic progress on socialist orientation are in the Middle East and North Africa, and the changes in these countries are particularly important for the progress of the world revolutionary process.''[14]

Ames's support for Arafat may have stemmed in part from a recognition that anti-imperialist struggles in the Middle East could indeed turn into anti-capitalist ones, a phenomenon he had witnessed personally during his experience in South Yemen. By siding with Fateh, a faction that enjoyed the support of friendly pro-Western Arab regimes like Saudi Arabia, Kuwait, and Egypt, the United States might help block the more radical PLO factions like the PFLP, which were backed by states like Cuba, Libya, Iran, Syria, the USSR, and South Yemen, thereby preventing Habash or other extremist elements from ''capturing and subverting a legitimate war of liberation'' and establishing either a communist-led or Khomeni-like anti-American Palestinian state in the region. The rationale for selecting Arafat as a bulwark against communist expansion in the region may have been reinforced by the persistence of Fateh founders like Khaled al-Hassan who claimed that their organization had no intention of becoming the puppet of any foreign power, least of all the Soviet Union. Arafat's British biographer Alan Hart quotes Khaled as assuring Kissinger's emissary Vernon Walters during their March 1974 meeting that ''Fatah was of and on the right'' and that ''our leadership was the only one in the Arab world which believed in and was practicising democracy.'' As for communist influences within the guerrilla group, ''Yes, you are right,'' Khaled confessed. ''We have some so-called Marxists, some so-called radicals and some so-called leftists in our ranks,'' he told Walters. ''But do you know why some Palestinians and Arabs are looking to Moscow?'' the PLO leader asked. ''Because the U.S. had left them with no choice.''[15] Bob Ames may have been hoping to give them a choice: American support might keep Arafat's Fateh loyal to the Western camp.

Ames's position in the Reagan administration was fairly unique—for a CIA analyst he carried quite a bit of weight in the formulation of Middle East policy. George Shultz had brought him in as part of an advisory group that included former Secretary of State Henry Kissinger, assistant secretary

Veliotes, Lawrence Silberman, a former Ambassador to Yugoslavia, and Irving Shapiro, the former Chairman of the Board of Dupont. Silberman had been the leader of the Reagan transition team in late 1980, charged with assessing the CIA's status under the Carter administration.[16] He recalled meeting with Ames and Kissinger in Palo Alto, California to discuss Middle East policy just a day or two after Shultz took over from Haig.

Ames's dual role as both a policy consultant and a clandestine operative did not fit the traditional mold that usually kept CIA personnel away from diplomatic activity. CIA operatives were ordinarily restricted to intelligence gathering and reporting in an attempt to ensure that their assessments remained without bias and did not serve particular policy interests. A president needing a CIA evaluation of Soviet compliance with arms control agreements must not feel that the data is being colored by a CIA policy that either favors the continuation of SALT II, supports the "Star Wars" SDI space-based weapons program, or advocates any other specific policy related to America's nuclear strategy toward the Russians. The intelligence apparatus is ostensibly there to provide objective information to members of the executive and legislative branches, who are charged with the task of setting U.S. foreign policy.

Admiral Stansfield Turner, the CIA director under President Carter and a former military career officer who no doubt brought his own built-in biases toward national security issues to the job of intelligence chief, nevertheless insisted that the CIA does not have a political role to play.[17] Yet, under President Reagan, it appears that one of its more respected agents found himself engaged in a key foreign policy role in Secretary of State Shultz's inner circle, much to the displeasure of some Israelis. In his memoirs, Turner wrote that the new Reagan team, led by Lawrence Silberman, had hoped to "unleash" the CIA upon coming into office.[18] While not directly confirming the existence of secret U.S.-PLO talks, Silberman did remark that "every country uses its intelligence agency to conduct prediplomacy," and that "if the CIA is doing its job, direct contact [with adversaries like the PLO] is indispensable."[19]

It appears that the newly "unleashed" CIA was in fact doing the job Silberman expected. According to an Israeli source privy to Mossad reports at the time, Bob Ames was the architect of ongoing secret political talks worked out between himself and Yassir Arafat, Abu Jihad, and Hasan Salameh. Ames knew these men personally, having held direct meetings with each of them.[20] According to Israeli journalist Ze'ev Schiff, "knowledge of these contacts was kept from even the U.S. embassy in Beirut," and it was the Lebanese intelligence chief Johnny Abdo who helped arrange for the secret rendezvous with Arafat and Jihad.[21] Karim

Pakradouni confirmed Abdo's role, relating a discussion between Abdo and President Sarkis in which he heard Abdo disclose his knowledge of the secret U.S.-PLO talks: "Ultra-secret contacts had been made, Abdo went on, between a representative in Beirut of Alexander Haig and Arafat and Khalil Wazir (Abou Jihad). Since neither Syria nor Israel must know that the talks were taking place, the envoy had come from Washington without his embassy's knowledge; not even the CIA had been aware of his mission. For their part, the Palestinians did not tell any other member of the PLO."[22]

In addition, Ames was reportedly instrumental in formulating the Reagan Middle East peace plan announced on 1 September, 1982. According to William Quandt, the Middle East specialist who sat on President Carter's National Security Council during the heyday of the Camp David peace process, it was Bob Ames who put an advance copy of the Reagan Plan into Yassir Arafat's hands.[23] Reagan's position paper was formulated while Arafat was still trapped in Beirut during the Israeli encirclement of the city that summer, so it is unlikely that Ames literally slipped into Arafat's besieged refugee camp headquarters to personally deliver the document. More likely, the broad outlines of the policy had been discussed with Arafat prior to Israel's invasion, perhaps during the meetings referred to by Johnny Abdo. When the decision was made for President Reagan to float an Arab-Israeli peace plan later that summer, Ames may have used his contacts to smuggle a draft of the initiative to Arafat's people.

The Reagan Plan was quickly denounced by Prime Minister Begin, and Jordan's King Hussein and the PLO followed suit. On the face of things, it would seem that the effort by Ames to formulate a policy acceptable to Arafat backfired with Reagan's still-born initiative. However, although it rejected an independent Palestinian state on the West Bank, the plan put the United States firmly on record as being opposed to continued Jewish sovereignty in the occupied territories. It envisioned an eventual West Bank association with Jordan, and it moved the U.S. position beyond the terms worked out under the Camp David framework, which for the PLO had become a virtual synonym for capitulation and betrayal.

In the Camp David talks thus far, both Israel and Egypt have felt free to express openly their views as to what the outcome should be. Understandably, their views have differed on many points.

The United States has thus far sought to play the role of mediator; we have avoided public comment on the key issues. We have always recognized—and continue to recognize—that only the voluntary agreement of those parties most directly involved in the conflict can provide an enduring solution. But it has become evident to me [Reagan] that some clearer sense of America's position on the key issues is necessary to encourage wider support for the peace process.

First, as outlined in the Camp David accords, there must be a period of time during which the Palestinian inhabitants of the West Bank and Gaza will have full autonomy over their own affairs. Due consideration must be given to the principle of self-government by the inhabitants of the territories and to the legitimate security concerns of the parties involved.

The purpose of the 5-year period of transition, which would begin after free elections for a self-governing Palestinian authority, is to prove to the Palestinians that they can run their own affairs and that such Palestinian autonomy poses no threat to Israel's security.

The United States will not support the use of any additional land for the purpose of [Jewish] settlements during the transition period. Indeed, the immediate adoption of a settlement freeze by Israel, more than any other action, could create the confidence needed for wider participation in these talks. Further settlement activity is in no way necessary for the security of Israel and only diminishes the confidence of the Arabs that a final outcome can be freely and fairly negotiated.

I want to make the American position well understood: The purpose of this transition period is the peaceful and orderly transfer of authority from Israel to the Palestinian inhabitants of the West Bank and Gaza. At the same time, such a transfer must not interfere with Israel's security requirements.

Beyond the transition period, as we look to the future of the West Bank and Gaza, it is clear to me that peace cannot be achieved by the formation of an independent Palestinian state in those territories. Nor is it achievable on the basis of Israeli sovereignty or permanent control over the West Bank and Gaza.

So the United States will not support the establishment of an independent Palestinian state in the West Bank and Gaza, and we will not support annexation, or permanent control by Israel.

There is, however, another way to peace. The final status of these lands must, of course, be reached through the give-and-take of negotiations. But it is the firm view of the United States that self-government by the Palestinians of the West Bank and Gaza in association with Jordan offers the best chance for a durable, just and lasting peace.[24]

Begin charged that the Reagan Plan was prejudging the outcome of the autonomy plan devised at Camp David: that by eliminating some form of Israeli political control ahead of time, it undermined Israel's position in any future give-and-take of negotiations. Given its decades-old demand for sovereignty in Palestine, the PLO leadership was not about to publicly embrace a plan that eliminated the creation of a Palestinian state, but the fact that Reagan was calling for Jordanian jurisdiction over the West Bank and Gaza at least meant that the territories might be taken out of Israeli hands and placed under Arab control. This would free the PLO to establish itself in the West Bank and Gaza, perhaps eventually turning its sights on Amman in eastern Palestine and Tel Aviv in western Palestine, which would be in keeping with the PLO strategy of gaining a foothold in the occupied territories in order to liberate all of historic Palestine.

To the Begin government, the invasion of June 1982 and the summer siege of Beirut had managed to break the back of the PLO as a political and military force in the region. Even the CIA veterans in the region were reportedly impressed by what the Israelis were able to accomplish in destroying the center of international terrorism in Beirut. They had long thought it impossible to take on the various paramilitary guerrilla factions in the country. Through the Reagan Plan, Bob Ames was able to resurrect the PLO, bringing Yassir Arafat to the political forefront once again, providing him with the opportunity to strike a temporary alliance with Jordan in pursuit of an Israeli withdrawal from the West Bank and Gaza. His talks with Arafat and Jihad, however, could have simply been for appearances only: a gesture to the Arab world offered to offset U.S. support for Israel's invasion of Lebanon, a subtle demonstration that Washington was willing to deal with the Palestinian question by engaging in a dialogue with the PLO, yet in actuality lacking any serious American effort to make progress on issues of substance. Or the discussions with Arafat and Jihad may have involved sincere give-and-take encounters, with the U.S. adjusting its position to accommodate PLO demands, the Reagan administration offering to go on record publicly and unequivocally that it would not endorse an Israeli de facto annexation of the West Bank and Gaza in exchange for a muted Arafat response to the Reagan initiative and a willingness to consider an arrangement that would at least for the near term leave the PLO vulnerable to Jordanian dominance.

But to certain members of the Israeli leadership, Ames's flirtation with the PLO was to be taken quite seriously, and there was an irony in that Bob Ames had lost his life in the car bomb blast that demolished the American embassy in Beirut on 18 April, 1983. The CIA officer had been one of the most sympathetic spokesmen for the PLO ever to serve in a high-level policymaking position in the U.S. government. Yet Ames was killed by Syrian-backed Lebanese Moslem terrorists while engaged in consultations that could have led to a pro-Palestinian shift in U.S. policy. The blindness of Arab terrorism wound up destroying a friend of the Arabs.

America's secret talks with the PLO, however, were not confined to the liaisons with Bob Ames. As the Middle East Institute's executive director Philip Stoddard observed, the United States does not need to hold direct talks with the PLO to know what they are thinking; there are plenty of intermediaries.[25] True, the Israeli government has likewise made use of intermediaries, even availing itself of the services offered by the country's dissident "Peace Now" group that advocates mutual recognition between Israel and the PLO. According to Landrum Bolling—himself an intermediary between the United States government and Arafat during the Carter administration—in the 1970s, when certain members of Peace Now met directly with PLO representatives, the Israeli activists kept Prime Minister Rabin closely informed of the progress of their talks.[26] In 1976, after Reserve-General Matti Peled met with Arafat's adviser Issam Sartawi, the Israeli reportedly briefed Rabin personally on the discussions.[27] As for the Reagan White House, in 1981, Secretary of State Haig was contacted by John Edwin Mroz, head of a New York-based think-tank, The Center for East-West Security Studies. Mroz had been in touch with Arafat and indicated that the PLO was ready to take the necessary steps to enable it to receive diplomatic recognition from the United States. Similar claims were being made by other PLO intermediaries, such as the Saudis. Haig instructed Assistant Secretary Nicholas Veliotes to look into the Mroz matter. Over the next year, Mroz said that he held more than fifty meetings with Arafat. Discussions were also held with two of Arafat's advisers, the brothers Khaled and Hani Hassan. The plan was for Mroz to act as a go between in an effort to persuade Arafat to agree to a formal acceptance of Israel's right to exist in exchange for American recognition of the PLO.

Mroz reportedly kept assuring Veliotes that the PLO was about to meet the conditions stipulated in the Kissinger memorandum, but by June 1982, the concessions had not been forthcoming and the discussions broke off in the wake of the Israeli invasion of Lebanon. "A lot of people in the PLO were skeptical about the whole thing, but they figured it couldn't hurt to go ahead with it," said Rashid Khalidi, a former PLO official. "Even if it turned out that Washington wasn't serious about the idea, getting into negotiations would help to show that the PLO was. A lot of the (PLO) leadership felt that the Israeli invasion was intended to derail the whole process."[28] Khalidi's account was echoed in Johnny Abdo's report to President Sarkis on the secret U.S.-PLO talks in Beirut: "According to Abdo, these preliminary talks were about to yield fruit when Israel invaded Lebanon," Pakradouni wrote. " 'I am convinced that one of the objectives of the operation which have not been admitted was to frustrate these American-Palestinian contacts,' Abdo said."[29]

Khalidi's comment about the extremes to which Israel might go in blocking a U.S.-PLO dialogue found parallels in such statements as the one that appeared in the Paris-based monthly *Israel & Palestine*, which advocates the establishment of a PLO-led Palestinian state alongside Israel, frequently condemns Israeli policies, and is often dismissed by mainstream American and Israeli observers as a discredited voice on the fringes of serious thought. In its October-November 1983 issue, the journal stated that the bombing of the American embassy in Beirut was considered by Western intelligence services to be the work of the Mossad.[30] In a confidential letter from one of the publication's associates, the charge was reiterated: "After the embassy bombing, US intelligence circles and State Department circles were mad as hell at the Israelis. Policy from above precluded this being made known officially; but certain observations were made behind the scenes to certain Israelis. And Western circles knew about this quite freely."[31] The rationale for such a daring—if not reckless and chillingly brutal—terrorist attack was not given, but one might surmise that according to this view, the embassy attack was designed to rid Lebanon of the American presence so the Israelis and the Phalangists could have their way with the country unimpeded by the more restrained approaches of Secretary Shultz and his staff. Or, the Israelis may have been so alarmed by Ames's secret contacts with Arafat that they were actually willing to attack the embassy of its most important ally, a nation without whose support the Jewish state might virtually cease to exist.

The charge that the Mossad was responsible for the bombing of the American embassy on 18 April, 1983 was reminiscent of the accusation that Israel had deliberately attacked the *USS Liberty*, an American navy vessel that was operating in the Mediterranean off the coast of the Sinai peninsula in the midst of the Six Day War. Three days into its war with the Arabs, on 8 June, 1967, Israeli aircraft and torpedo boats opened fire on the surveillance craft, killing thirty-four American crewmen and wounding over a hundred others. The U.S. vessel had been classified AGTR-5, an "electronic intelligence-collection platform," or Technical Research Ship, assigned to monitor communications and other military movements in the region. Israel claimed that the United States failed to notify Jerusalem of the vessel's presence in the war zone, and thus its commanders had mistaken it for an Egyptian navy ship that was reportedly shelling Israeli troops at El Arish.[32] Other observers, including Lieutenant James Ennes, the officer in charge of the *Liberty's* electronic maintenance technicians, claimed that the Israelis purposely chose to sink the intelligence ship, possibly to avoid having their efforts to launch an imminent retaliatory strike into Syria's Golan Heights detected by Washington. Such a discovery might have prompted an American administration eager to bring a halt to the fighting at all costs to put premature pressure on the Israeli government to show restraint, even if it meant leaving Israel short of its aim of capturing the strategic high ground that had been the site of Syrian artillery attacks against the Jewish settlements below for the previous nineteen years.[33] "I cannot accept the claim by the Israelis that this was a case of mistaken identity, " wrote retired U.S. Admiral Thomas Moorer.[34]

During the 1982 war in Lebanon the Israelis were accused of carrying out yet another attack against its foremost ally, that of bombing the American embassy in Beirut—a ploy supposedly designed to either destabilize Lebanon and allow for Israeli hegemony or simply sabotage the growing Ames-Arafat dialogue. The associate of the Paris-based *Israel & Palestine* emphasized the importance the Israelis had placed on blocking U.S.-PLO talks:

> According to both PLO and Israeli oral sources, Ali Hassan [*sic*] Salameh was chief of intelligence for the PLO and as such, in charge of contacts with the United States which agreed only to communicate with that organization at CIA level. Although Hassan Salameh was known to have been one of the "Black September" chiefs, the Mossad left him alone for a long while, and specifically from the Scandinavian mess [in which Sylvia Raphael and her Israeli hit team in Lillehammer, Norway mistakenly killed a Moroccan waiter thinking he was Salameh] till his assassination—until it became clear that he was opening a "back channel" to Washington. In my view, he was killed for that reason rather than for "romantic vengeance" grounds [arising out of the Black September massacre of the Israeli Olympic athletes at Munich].
>
> Ali Hassan Salameh was replaced, by the CIA chief of station in Beirut, as responsible for the ongoing dialogue with the PLO. This station chief was Robert Ames, the case officer of the man who first talked to Salameh.[35]

With regard to Salameh's assassination, intelligence agencies in the world's democracies have long been plagued by the moral questions involved in such paramilitary operations. It has been difficult to draw the line between justified operations and criminal acts. All intelligence gathering and covert activities are illegal under international law, so a government must set its own private moral guidelines when initiating a clandestine operation. For Israel, the ideal is that a covert act sanctioned by the government must be viewed as just by the political leadership, the intelligence commanders, and the agents assigned to carry it out. During the organization of the Mossad "hit team" that executed the Black September leaders in Beirut in 1973, Israeli intelligence officials felt it was not enough for the agents involved to have a general knowledge of PLO terrorist attacks against Jews. The Israeli commandos were given detailed dossiers about each of their targets. They were provided with documentation describing each victim's responsibility for specific raids against unarmed civilians, complete with a thorough accounting that included meeting times with fellow guerrilla members, the planning behind each terrorist attack, and the political orientation of the Palestinian commando leader slated for execution. The link between the assassination of a PLO member and his tie to a particular terrorist incident had to be absolute. The evidence had to be there: a gun traced to the PLO member; surveillance revealing a direct involvement in the planning.

"You just don't send in some 'hit-man' to murder someone," an Israeli intelligence specialist explained. "When the Mossad recruits an Israeli citizen for a special operation, it is mindful of the fact that he or she will eventually return to civilian society. You don't want to recruit criminals, nor do you want to make criminals. You will be asking a fellow citizen to take the law into his or her own hands, but you must first establish a moral basis for the act if you are to safeguard the national ideal and avoid corrupting the honor of the individual agent."[36]

This very concern about the line between criminality and legitimate covert warfare came to the fore in 1984, when an Israeli military commission revealed that two captured Palestinian terrorists who had hijacked a civilian bus near Ashkelon were led away, interrogated, and pistol-whipped to death by members of Shin Bet, Israel's military intelligence. In an attempt to block further investigations and thus protect the security of Shin Bet and its effectiveness as a clandestine force, President Chaim Herzog, himself a former intelligence chief, granted a pardon to the organization's director, Avraham Shalom. The Israeli press, however, continued to protest governmental moves aimed at sabotaging efforts to bring the killers of the Palestinian hijackers to justice, claiming that intelligence agencies are not exempt from the law. "When an institution as sensitive and powerful as the one headed by the official [Avraham Shalom] is so flawed, it must be a warning to the entire Israeli public," Israeli TV reported.[37] If the Israeli public was prone to outrage over the killing of two PLO terrorists caught red-handed in the act of hijacking a civilian bus on its own soil, then Hasan Salameh's consultations with Bob Ames and other CIA members in Beirut would surely have been viewed as possessing an even more dubious moral basis for murder. More likely, it was indeed Salameh's role in the slaying of nine defenseless Israeli athletes at the 1972 Munich Olympics that had prompted the Mossad into sending in its hit team, though agreeably the execution might not have been based on "romantic vengeance" but instead designed to both undermine the PLO infrastructure and serve as a warning to other terrorist leaders that there would be a price for their attacks against Jews. Regarding the bombing of the U.S. embassy in Beirut, in which

Dealing the PLO In   289

seventeen Americans were killed along with forty-six others, aside from the moral reprehensibility of staging such an attack against a civilian diplomatic facility, and that of a close ally no less, the sheer enormity of the risk entailed in being discovered and Israel's subsequent alienation of a nation that provides it with billions of dollars in aid annually and consistent political support within the international community would makes such an operation by the Mossad appear incredulous. Furthermore, the CIA itself, along with other West European intelligence organizations, reportedly concluded that Syrian-backed Iranian militants and their followers within the Shiite Hezbollah, or Party of God, faction in Beirut carried out both the embassy bombing and the 23 October, 1983 attack against the U.S. marine barracks that killed 241 servicemen.[38]

As ludicrous as the charge regarding Israeli complicity in the U.S. embassy bombing may seem, it must nevertheless be weighed against the allegation, given credence by such prominent Middle East observers as Rashid Khalidi, a professor at Columbia University, and Johnny Abdo, a one-time aide to President Sarkis and chief of Lebanese intelligence, that Israel launched a full-scale invasion into Lebanon in 1982 to derail secret talks between America and the PLO. The reasons given for Israel's invasion of Lebanon do indeed vary. Some have claimed that it was necessary to eliminate the PLO threat in order to induce King Hussein to enter the peace process; some say the blow against the Palestinian resistance was designed to crush the guerrillas' hold on the loyalties of West Bank Arabs; others insist that it was an effort to reshape the political map in the region by assisting in the takeover of Lebanon by Bashir Gemayel's pro-Israeli Maronite Christian Phalangist Party; while still others assert that it was primarily a pre-emptive strike against Syria: that Israeli intelligence had predicted a combined Syrian-PLO attack against Israel and the 1982 operation was necessary to thwart the military build-up on Israel's northern border. More than likely, it was some combination of these factors. It remains difficult to imagine, however, that the political damage to Israel caused by John Mroz's mediation between Nicholas Veliotes and Yassir Arafat could have been great enough to prompt Israel to launch a major war in order to stop it.

Moreover, neither the execution of Salameh nor the abandonment of the Mroz mission in the aftermath of Israel's invasion of Lebanon brought to a halt the secret U.S.-PLO connection. In mid-July 1982, during the Israeli siege of Beirut, Saudi Arabia's foreign minister Saud al-Faisal and Syria's foreign minister Abdel Halim Khaddam traveled to Washington to discuss the Middle East crisis with President Reagan and Secretary of State Shultz. Press reports stated that Khaled al-Hassan, a longtime Arafat associate and co-founder of Fateh, also visited Washington and kept in touch by telephone with the Arab ministers during their deliberations with the Americans. The application of the Kissinger memorandum by successive administrations precluded open, face-to-face meetings between Khaled al-Hassan and Reagan administration officials. Yet PLO activist and author Fawaz Turki stated that he knew for a fact that Khaled had held a series of private meetings with State Department representatives during his stay in Washington. After his resignation, Haig later wrote that indeed, many in the State Department had viewed the Israeli siege of Beirut as an opportunity for the United States to engage in direct talks with the PLO.[39] Middle East scholar Steven Spiegel also reported that by July, "the PLO was demanding American recognition as the price for its departure. This position had strong support in the U.S. bureaucracy."[40] According to Turki, by the summer of 1982, Khaled had succeeded in establishing a direct relationship with U.S. officials, but the contacts ended when Hatem Hussaini, director of the PLO's Information Office in Washington, revealed the existence of the secret "back-channel" relationship with the United States on the ABC News broadcast, "Nightline."[41] Hussaini made the remarks during his response to a question by newsman Sam Donaldson about whether or not the PLO had discussed with Washington the plight of the Palestinian guerrillas trapped in West Beirut by the Israelis:

> *Dr. Hussaini*: Well, as you know, the U.S. government does not recognize the PLO or talk to it, although it has talked to the PLO leaders on different matters. I have had one or two meetings with some American officials, but I think there is this hurdle of direct talks. Our leadership—
>
> *Donaldson*: Just a moment, sir. You have had one or two meetings with some American officials. Who? When?
>
> *Dr. Hussaini*: Well, I've had one meeting with one American official. I've met with Congressman Zablocki, chairman of the Foreign Relations Committee in the House; I've had some communication with—
>
> *Donaldson*: I'm talking about a member of the executive branch, a member of the State Department or President Reagan's executive branch.
>
> *Dr. Hussaini*: Well, the legislature, executive, these are the bodies that make policy. But I think the most important thing here is for the U.S. government, it's about time for the U.S. government, to talk directly with the PLO—
>
> *Donaldson*: Well, let me press you on this, let me press you on this, because as you know, former U.N. Ambassador Andrew Young had to resign because he simply had an informal, casual conversation with Ambassador Terzi in New York some years ago. Our position is, the U.S. position is, we do not talk to the PLO officially, as you yourself said. Now you tell me you've had a meeting with a U.S. official? Have you?

Dr. Hussaini: Well, as I told you, I've met and talked to officials, whether in the legislative branch or maybe one or two in the executive branch—

Donaldson: One or two in the executive branch.

Dr. Hussaini: There is nothing wrong in talking. It doesn't mean that you fully agree with the other party. Actually, as you know, the U.S. government talked to the government in North Vietnam for arriving at peace. I think—

Donaldson: I'm not saying there's anything wrong with it; I'm saying it's against our current policy and could you tell us the name of the official that you talked to?

Dr. Hussaini: No, I don't think it is against the policy; I think on the contrary American foreign policy should talk to all sides, including the PLO; and our chairman, Arafat, said he would like to talk to Philip Habib and other American officials. This is—it's surely a reflection of the feelings of the American people. The American people have been talking to us in Washington, daily. Even American Jews, distinguished American Jewish leaders have talked to us. Why not have the government talk to us so that we can move for peace, for—

Donaldson: Well, our position is, sir, that we will talk to you if you will recognize the state of Israel, recognize its right to exist peacefully.

Dr. Hussaini: Well, I think, Mr. Donaldson, if there is a Security Council resolution, a new resolution, that emphasizes the right of the Palestinian people to self-determination and to establishing an independent state, then obviously we would have jumped over the hurdle and we would have begun to move forward towards a comprehensive and real and lasting peace in the area.

Donaldson: Well, now, that's an old idea—that is, to rewrite U.N. Resolution 242 to include some reference to Palestinian rights. Do you have any reason to believe that the United States government might support the idea?

Dr. Hussaini: Yes, I think it should, because we've had—

Donaldson: No, do you have any reason to believe it will?

Dr. Hussaini: Yes, yes, because we've had a war for 47 days now, one of the longest wars in the area, and the PLO stood fast, strong, heroic struggle; it has proven that it is a force, a military-political force in the area, so let us recognize realities, adopt a new resolution at the Security Council and work through the U.N., through the international community, for some kind of a political solution to this very acute and difficult problem.

Donaldson: Well, forgive me, Dr. Hussaini, I said earlier in this broadcast that something's happening, but clearly I don't know what it is. So I'm going to go over some of this ground again with you, if I may. You say you've talked to a U.S. official in the executive branch. Is that correct?

Dr. Hussaini: I've had meetings with many people in the U.S. government—the legislative branch, one or two in the executive branch.

Donaldson: And you are an official of the PLO, are you not?

Dr. Hussaini: I am a member of the Palestine National Council and I am head of the PLO information offices.[42]

According to Turki, Hussaini, after his talk with Donaldson, was demoted from his position as information director and the secret contacts between Khaled al-Hassan and United States officials ceased.

A year and a half later, on 22 February, 1984, following press disclosures of the Mroz mediation effort between Veliotes and Arafat, Secretary of State Shultz offered a summation of his position regarding the history of U.S. relations with the PLO. "Practically every Arab leader who comes to the United States, or you run into, has a message and wants to carry a message and so on," Shultz said. Echoing sentiments of Joseph Sisco, author of the Kissinger memorandum barring direct negotiations with the PLO, the secretary said: "The problem is not with the communications system. The problem is with the content."[43]

The Mysterious Middle East

When historical truth is involved, the more anyone claims to possess it the more he lies.

Albert Camus

28

Conspiracy at the Top

MOST of what is happening in the Middle East is either leaked or told to the press, a State Department official once said. There is no secret warfare or hidden diplomacy. The more simple the explanation, often the more truthful.

Many people, especially those living in the Middle East, do not subscribe to this point of view. More importantly, many of the Middle East's leaders do not either. Arabs and Jews both harbor their own complex conspiracy theories to explain their tragic history.

In his book, *The Hollow Peace*, Menachem Begin's former aide Shmuel Katz accused the USSR of violating the detente agreement with the U.S., which called for a joint effort to decrease international tensions. According to Katz, the violation stemmed from the Soviet Union's involvement in a carefully scripted subterfuge with Egypt:

> How did the Soviets proceed? They concluded a secret agreement with Egypt to facilitate that country's preparations for war against Israel. They staged a noisy rift between themselves and the Egyptians with much mutual recrimination. Most dramatically, in July 1972 Egypt expelled thousands of Soviet "advisers" who until then had been operating in Egypt (some of them secretly returned to Egypt in early 1973); and for more than a year after the signing of the detente agreement, the Soviet Union supplied Egypt with all the weapons she needed for launching what came to be the Yom Kippur War (6 October 1973).[1]

Katz published his charge in 1981, eight years after the Yom Kippur War and the subsequent United States-Egyptian alliance that took hold following Henry Kissinger's shuttle diplomacy and Jimmy Carter's talks at

Camp David. The dominant historical view remains that Sadat's move to oust the Soviets was no keen act of deception designed to lull the West into complacency on the eve of his attack against Israel. Sadat's expulsion of the advisers was a real loss for the Soviets, forcing them to throw their full weight behind Hafez Assad's Syria in order to retain a measure of influence in the region. Katz rejects the prevailing view, characterizing Sadat's realignment with the West in 1972 as a tactical maneuver in a strategic conspiracy against Israel.

Certain Egyptians have likewise made their own case for the conspiratorial version of history. In his book, *Negotiating for Peace in the Middle East*, Sadat's former foreign minister Ismail Fahmy asserted that Egypt's losses in the Yom Kippur War resulted from the United States' clandestine intervention on behalf of Israel. The U.S. airlift of military equipment to Israel has been well documented (706 flights between the United States and Israel, carrying tanks, ammunition, helicopters, and missiles—a total of 22,985 tons of equipment), but Fahmy insisted that American assistance went far beyond a resupply of war materièl:

> I will add here that in my opinion the possibility that American personnel also were sent to Israel cannot be dismissed. My conclusion is based on the fact that all the new equipment which was suddenly included in the battle—the TOW [anti-tank missiles], the laser-guided bombs, the "smart" bombs—cannot have been used by the Israelis alone, because they had never had it before and thus could not have known how to operate it. Such training takes a long time, and the Israelis had only a few days in which to score their victory. According to Dupuy [Trevor N. Dupuy, *Elusive Victory, The Arab-Israeli Wars 1947-1974* (New York: Harper and Row, 1978)]:
>
> > *A number of Israeli students attending colleges in the United States were mobilized on 6 October, and ordered to the US Army Infantry School at Fort Benning, Georgia, to take a crash course in the use and maintenance of the TOW. But by the time these eager young students were able to bring their new training and knowledge back to Israel, and to teach Israeli soldiers how to use the new weapons, it was October 24, and a cease-fire was finally setting over the fighting front.*
>
> However, Dupuy also concludes that there is evidence that the Israelis had TOWs and trained crews for these weapons, available for employment by October 14 and 15. Dupuy does not dare draw the obvious conclusion, and he leaves the question open where the crews came from. But the obvious conclusion is that the Americans provided not only the weapons, but also the personnel to operate them.[2]

For Fahmy, the participation of American ground troops fighting alongside Israel in the Yom Kippur War was obvious. This assertion, published in 1983, was made despite the fact that no direct evidence to substantiate the charge ever appeared in the United States, this in a period that saw the public exposure of Nixon's secret war in Cambodia, the Pentagon Papers, the Watergate scandal, unauthorized wiretaps, FBI dirty tricks, CIA involvement in the coup against Allende in Chile, undercover arms shipments to Iran, hidden diversions of funds to the *contra* rebels in Nicaragua, and a score of other revelations documenting the hidden workings of the United States government and its officials.

With the Watergate crisis heating up, the cease-fire in Vietnam barely ten months old, and the notion of direct military intervention by U.S. ground forces still under attack from anti-war groups, the clandestine introduction of American troops in the Middle East during the October 1973 Yom Kippur War could have had disastrous consequences for the Nixon White House. If such troops were in fact introduced, and the government was then able to keep the fact so well hidden from the American public that two decades later it was still being dismissed by former officials, journalists, and political analysts as a bit of Middle East fantasy, it would demonstrate a remarkable feat of security unique in recent U.S. history.

When Ambassador Eilts was asked if in fact Egyptian leaders believed Fahmy's charge or if the accusation was just the usual play of propaganda aimed at the Arab populace to justify Egypt's defeat in 1973, Eilts said that Sadat himself was convinced that U.S. troops had played a direct role in the fighting. Rather than landing its transport planes in Israel proper, Sadat claimed, U.S. aircraft touched down in the battle zone at El-Arish on the Mediterranean coast of Israeli-occupied Sinai. The evidence? The odometer readings on captured Israeli tanks were too low for them to have made the trip from Israel.[3] Kissinger's assistant at the time of the airlift, Lawrence Eagleburger, categorically dismissed the suggestion that U.S. troops played an active part in the Yom Kippur War. The Israelis probably turned the odometer back, Eagleburger joked.[4] Perhaps they were hoping for a higher resale value on the used-tank market.

The fact that claims of U.S. involvement in the Yom Kippur fighting were almost universally rejected by American officials, including staunch "Arabist" State Department members, did not deter men like Sadat and Fahmy. As with Katz's charge of Egyptian-Soviet collusion on the eve of the 1973 war, conspiracy theories have fallen on fertile soil in the Middle East.

And not just *in* the Middle East. Conspiracy theories *about* the Middle East are also prevalent among the uppermost echelons of governments respected and trusted by America and its allies, as illustrated by the case of Nezar Hindawi. On 17 April, 1986, Hindawi, a thirty-two year old Palestinian with Jordanian citizenship, gave a good-bye kiss to his pregnant, Irish-born girlfriend, Ann-Marie Murphy, also thirty-two, as she boarded an El Al flight in London for a trip to Israel, where she would supposedly meet Hindawi's family in preparation for their upcoming marriage in "the holy land." They would have to travel separately, Hindawi explained, but he would meet her shortly in Tel Aviv upon his arrival on another flight. During the taxi ride to Heathrow Airport, Hindawi had placed what appeared to be a battery in a pocket calculator, stuffing it deep down into her carry-on flight bag, telling his fiancée that it was a gift for a friend. Inside the calculator was a timing device set to go off at 1:04 P.M., which would trigger three and a quarter pounds of Czechoslovakian plastic explosives that had also been hidden at the bottom of the hand luggage, the bomb rigged to explode when the El Al jetliner was scheduled to be flying over Austria at an altitude of 39,000 feet with 375 people aboard, including the unsuspecting Ann-Marie and her unborn child.[5] As the young woman passed through the elaborate screening checks at El Al, the calculator successfully performed routine mathematical functions when tested by an Israeli security, and the metal-free explosives passed through the X-ray detector without a hitch. But when El Al guards took a closer look, reportedly as part of a random secondary hand-search of carry-on luggage, the bag seemed much too heavy though it had been completely emptied.[6] Another account given by a terrorist expert had it that an alert El Al security agent had actually detected a slight wetness on the outside of the bag, which could result from the natural condensation that occurs when packing a plastic explosive.[7] In any case, a thorough, final check of the luggage revealed the existence of a concealed bomb that would have ripped through the Israeli aircraft with the force of thirty grenades. It quickly became apparent to the authorities that Ann-Marie had been duped: she was no would-be suicide bomber like the Shiite Moslem driver that drove an explosive-laden vehicle into the United States embassy in Beirut.

On 24 October 1986, Hindawi was convicted in a British court and sentenced to forty-five years in prison. "A more callous and cruel deception and a more horrendous massacre it is difficult to imagine," the judge told Hindawi shortly before he was led away from the courtroom.[8] The British government immediately broke off diplomatic relations with Syria, charging that the trial had produced conclusive evidence linking Damascus to the plot. Hindawi was acting on the orders of Syrian intelligence, the British insisted; they provided him with a Syrian passport issued in a false name, and the terrorist was granted refuge through the Syrian ambassador in London once the explosives were detected at Heathrow Airport. Condemning the bombing attempt as a "monstrous and inhumane" plot to destroy a civilian aircraft filled with passengers on their way to Israel for the Passover holiday, British Foreign Secretary Geoffrey Howe told the House of Commons that the government's decision to break ties with Syria was made "in order to make plain our repudiation of the wicked involvement of the Syrian government in terrorism of this kind."[9]

On 3 November 1986, French Premier Jacques Chirac gave an interview to Arnaud de Borchgrave, editor of the *Washington Times*. In it they discussed the plot to blow up the El Al airliner:

Chirac: Let's take the Syrian affair. I spoke to both [West German Chancellor Helmut] Kohl and [Foreign Minister] Hans-Dietrich Genscher about it. I don't go as far as they do, but their thesis is that the [Nizar] Hindawi plot was a provocation designed to embarrass Syria and destabilize the Assad regime. Who was behind it? Probably people connected with the Israeli Mossad in conjunction with certain Syrian elements close to Assad who seek his overthrow. Things of this nature can be infinitely complex.

de Borchgrave: But [Syrian President Hafez] Assad is in complete control of his own secret services.

Chirac: Yes, but it's also a real can of worms. Nobody really knows what role his brother Rifaat is playing. Is Rifaat manipulating Assad? And who is manipulating Rifaat? The experts who know the Syrian ambassador, who was alleged to have been part of the plot and who was expelled from Britain, say it is utterly implausible, nay impossible, that he had contact with Hindawi. That Hindawi had contacts with certain members of a Syrian service is another matter.

de Borchgrave: But the British are pretty good with electronic surveillance, and they know what happened between Hindawi and the Syrian ambassador.

Chirac: Nothing is easier than to fake that kind of evidence without government leaders knowing about the real plot.

de Borchgrave: I know the British service chief. He's a straight shooter, and such diabolical schemes to entrap his own prime minister are definitely not his cup of tea.

Chirac: Be that as it may, I am always suspicious of this sort of affair, especially when it fits into a certain policy.

de Borchgrave: In other words, the evidence that came out of a British court of law is phony in your judgment?

Chirac: No, I did not say that. I have not been given the complete file and, therefore, I am not rendering judgment. I merely told you what West Germany's leaders believe and which I tend to share. [10]

As the interview shows, when it comes to the Middle East, the possibilities for duplicity seem limitless, or as Premier Chirac put it, "things of this nature can be infinitely complex." In just a single discussion with one of France's most influential political leaders, allegations arose that 1) the Israelis had staged an elaborate fraud, planting a passenger with a flight bag stuffed with explosives at Heathrow Airport only to have her later apprehended by their own security forces, thereby implicating the Damascus regime in terrorism, discrediting both Syria and the Palestinian cause; 2) British intelligence had doctored evidence in order to either protect Israel by keeping the Mossad connection from surfacing or to generate increased antagonism toward Syria as part of a foreign policy inititiative launched by conservative factions within the British government; 3) dissident factions within the Damascus regime had hooked up with the Arab nation's archenemy, Israel, to orchestrate an operation that would embarrass the Syrian president and strengthen the hands of his opponents, the scheme possibly involving Hafez Assad's own brother Rifaat. (The Syrian ambassador implicated in the plot, Loutof Allah Haydar, offered his own version of the conspiracy, agreeing that the incident had indeed been staged for propaganda purposes, but not by the Mossad acting alone or in collusion with some rival Syrian group, but by "the Americans and Israeli intelligence.")[11]

A few weeks after Chirac's interview, Nezar Hindawi's thirty-five-year old brother Ahmed Hazi was sentenced to fourteen years in prison by a West German court for his role in the 29 March, 1986 terrorist bombing of the headquarters for the German-Arab Friendship Society, a blast which severely injured nine people, all Arabs. Hazi testified that his brother Nezar had suggested the attack to punish the society for being too moderate in its views on the Arab-Israeli dispute. As in the Nezar case, the West German judge concluded that Syria was behind the bombing.[12] The day after Hazi's conviction, which included the imposition of a thirteen-year sentence on his accomplice, the Bonn government ordered the expulsion of five Syrian embassy officials and downgraded its diplomatic ties with Damascus. "West Germany considers the involvement of Syrian agencies as found in the Berlin court's decision of Nov. 26 to be in contempt of fundamental rules governing relations between states," the official statement said. "The Syrian government must accept that the behavior of its agencies will be attributed to it."[13]

Like Ismail Fahmy's claims about secret American troop deployments in the Sinai during the Yom Kippur War, and Shmuel Katz's assertion that Sadat's break with the Soviets in 1972 was a ruse designed to mask the Egyptian president's preparations to launch a surprise attack against Israel the following year, the view making the rounds in France and West Germany that it was Israeli intelligence, working either alone or in tandem with dissident Syrian agents, who staged the El Al bomb attempt of April 1986 may have been dismissed by many veteran observers as sheer folly. But such conspiratorial approaches to Middle Eastern events are frequently embraced by Middle East leaders and their colleagues in the West, the facts often shrouded by the flurry of allegations that range from the simple and the sensible to the convenient and the fanciful.

29

The Hundred Years War

WHEN Anwar Sadat signed his peace treaty with Israel on 26 March, 1979, there was hope that at last an end to the Arab-Israeli wars was near. The way might now be open for a grand pro-Western, NATO-like alliance of Israel and its Arab neighbors that could integrate America's democratic values, Israeli technology, and Arab wealth and manpower, forging a powerful, progressive economic center that would benefit the peoples of the area as well as the interests of the United States and its European and Asian allies.

The reality proved to be more somber. President Sadat was assassinated. Terrorist assaults by Palestinian guerrillas continued. Israel invaded Lebanon and expelled the PLO from Beirut. A cold peace settled over Egyptian-Israeli relations. Lebanon continued to rattle in a whirlpool of terror. Arafat struggled vainly with sterile, aborted moves toward a settlement with Israel. And it took eight years from Sadat's journey to Jerusalem and more than twenty years from his own first secret meeting with Levi Eshkol's emissary in London for King Hussein to take the first real steps toward establishing a public dialogue with Israel.

And yet, even in the wake of a possible peace treaty between Israel and Jordan, the ideological conflict between Zionism and Arab nationalism will remain. "Ideological conflict is not the right phrase," said one State Department official. "Hate is the proper term. The Arabs *hate* the Israelis." In his office at Cairo's *Al Ahram* newspaper, Dr. Abd el Moniem Said remarked matter-of-factly, "Israel will always be viewed as an historical sin in the Arab world."[1] In *Al Ahram's* Washington bureau, Hamdi Fuad gleefully predicted that the United States would one day abandon its support for Israel.[2] These comments did not come from Syrian, Libyan, Iraqi, or PLO extremists, but from moderate Egyptians, prominent spokesmen from the only Arab country ever to make peace with the Jewish state.

Instead of a grand NATO-like alliance or "strategic consensus" of moderate, pro-Western Middle Eastern regimes, a comprehensive Arab-Israeli peace would seem to augur a cold-war type of coexistence between two intractable foes who could be deterred from fighting only by the threat of mutual destruction. In such a world, Arabs and Jews in the Middle East would mirror the American-Soviet standoff, with both parties poised to exploit the other side's slightest weakness. An escalating arms race and an aversion to any relaxation of military readiness would be the prerequisites for peace between Arab and Jew. As with the superpowers, the dangerous clash between two competing belief systems, Zionism and pan-Arabism, could raise tensions to the point where an unexpected spark could set off a major confrontation.

One need not necessarily despair at such a scenario, provided that the Arab-Israeli standoff could be successfully managed. Seasoned diplomats have often noted that a man need not love his neighbor to refrain from killing him. The same applies to nations: Middle Eastern states do not require ideological compatibility, merely a mutual investment in peace. Hermann Eilts often cautioned the Israelis and their supporters not to harbor unrealistic expectations about the implications of peace. A realistic assessment of the Arab threat was preferable to a naive view about Arab acceptance of Israel's legitimacy. The Arabs might choose to abandon their armed struggle, but for the foreseeable future it is unlikely that they will renounce their anti-Zionism. Even at the height of detente, no one expected Moscow to discard its anti-capitalist ideology. Likewise, no one should anticipate an Arab embrace of Zionism, whatever the terms of a negotiated settlement.

An Israeli peace with its neighbors should be based on the realization that the Arabs are deeply opposed to Jewish nationalism (Zionism) in the Middle East. Such a peace would enable Israeli leaders to fashion military and defense policies that might seek a minimum of stridency and a maximum of compromise, while at the same time rejecting any moves toward appeasement. The alternative would be a utopian attitude toward the Arab threat that would lead only to disillusionment, resentment, and a subsequent anti-Arab radical backlash.

Hermann Eilts pointed out that there were indeed signs of unrealistic expectations in Israel in the wake of the peace treaty with Egypt. Israelis, who had been isolated in the region for years and restricted to the borders of their tiny state, were eager to travel abroad: visit an Arab capital, bathe from its beaches, tour its pyramids, and establish cultural ties with their neighbors. The Egyptians did not reciprocate.[3] First, there was the practical reality that those who could afford to vacation saw no reason to visit the Negev and tour another Middle Eastern desert, or travel to Tel Aviv to swim in the same Mediterranean waters that hit Egypt's own shores. They would much rather visit the cities of Europe, enjoying the nightlife of Paris, the museums of Florence, the beaches of the Riviera, the ski runs of Switzerland. Secondly, many Egyptians, influenced by the Islamic revival sweeping the region, found it difficult to reconcile themselves to a Jewish-ruled Jerusalem and a Palestine governed by Zionists. They were not eager to bestow an implied sanction of the Jewish state by volunteering to close the personal and cultural gap between Egyptians and Israelis.

Harvard professor Herbert Kelman also addressed the impact of unrealistic expectations on the Arab-Israeli peace process. Kelman, an American Jewish supporter of Israel who has interviewed Arafat and attended sessions of the PLO's National Congress, pressed for a U.S.-PLO-Israeli dialogue attuned to the deep-seated ideological issues that separate Arabs and Jews.

> Egyptians accept the reality of the state of Israel and they often express friendly sentiments toward Jews as a religious group that has lived in the Arab world for generations. They find it difficult, however, to conceive of Jews as a nation with a right to a state of its own. Now that this religious group has—inappropriately, in their view—managed to acquire a state, they are prepared to come to terms with it, but they do not regard it as a realization of historically based Jewish national rights. Thus, they do not accept the Zionist foundation of the state and their image of Israel's eventual integration in the region implies a dezionized Israel.[4]

Inventive diplomacy, territorial compromise, economic interdependency might help keep the guns silent, but they will not guarantee the disappearance of Arab antagonism toward Jewish nationalism. Arab antipathy to Zionism cannot be discounted in any agreement designed to secure the survival of Israel. The Reagan administration's former U.N. Ambassador, Jeanne Kirkpatrick, expressed the degree to which someone might underestimate the problem:

> As for Israel, I was not really aware until I came to the United Nations of the extent or the intensity of hostility to that nation: It's just extraordinary. I had no idea, frankly, of the extent to which so-called "moderate" Arabs are willing to say, for example, scornful things about Israeli honor and Israeli legitimacy.
>
> The analogies drawn between Nazis and Israelis are practically a daily affair at the United Nations. It happens all the time—accusations against Israel of genocide, contempt for the notion that there is a rule of law in Is-

rael, or that there is honor in Israel, or that there is *any kind of legitimacy* about Israel. There is a readiness to believe anything about Israel, no matter how outrageous.[5]

Jews who have been cognizant of such ingrained hostility have nevertheless welcomed the fact that Arab and Jewish blood is no longer being shed along the Israeli-Egyptian frontier (notwithstanding the isolated though popular acts of terrorism like the 1984 wounding of an Israeli official by an Islamic militant organization, the group's 1985 assassination of an Israeli diplomat in Cairo, the subsequent machine-gunning of seven Israeli tourists playing along a Sinai beach by an Egyptian policemen, and the 1986 terrorist attack on an Israeli Embassy official that left a twenty-four-year-old female secretary dead and three other people injured). In the afterglow of Camp David, those who anticipated a warm stable alliance rather than a cold, rocky peace may have discovered that their disappointment overshadowed their ability to appreciate the immediate benefits of secure borders and an absence of war. Disillusioned, formerly utopian, dovish Jewish Zionists, especially among the younger generation, might be prone to seize on the anti-Israeli attitudes of their erstwhile partners in peace rather than on Arab adherence, however grudging, to the terms of a negotiated settlement. Arabs reconciled to Israel's existence might very well rail against Jewish ideals, as exhibited in the frequent, blatantly anti-Semitic tracts appearing in the official and semi-official Egyptian press. Jews looking toward their Arab partners with unrealistic expectations run the risk of finding betrayal where they should detect toleration.

It is Arab tolerance of Israel, not Arab love of Israel, that is to be hoped for in the short term. That tolerance will be based on a combination of creative compromise, mature political analysis, realistic expectations, and military power. As in the American-Soviet superpower rivalry, the deterrent effect of a strong military base is crucial if a commitment to peaceful coexistence is to be upheld by parties whose respective belief systems would otherwise prompt them to hurl themselves at each other's throats.

In 1983, at the Baqaa Palestinian refugee camp northwest of Amman, an aging *mukhtar* who spoke on behalf of his people demanded to know why the United States continued to supply Israel with advanced F-15 and F-16 fighter aircraft when all the Arab countries combined were not strong enough to threaten the Jewish state. The answer he was given was that perhaps they were not strong enough *because* of the F-15s and F-16s.[6]

The ideological compatibility of a Japan, a Canada, an Australia, a Spain, and a Norway might make the maintenance of a powerful military arsenal aimed at one another ludicrous, but for Israel, a strong armed force is essential if Arab governments and Palestinian refugees are ever to decide that the peaceful coexistence of a cold war is preferable to heated exchanges on the battlefield.

Almost from the moment the Jewish return to Zion began in the late 1800s, violence between Arab and Jew has been an overriding feature of the Middle Eastern landscape, though it took several decades for anti-Zionist sentiment to fully organize itself into an armed political resistance. At the opening session of the Geneva Peace Conference on 22 December 1973, Henry Kissinger addressed this tragic fate of modern-day Palestine: "When the history of our era is written, it will speak not of a series of Arab-Israeli wars but of one war broken by periods of uneasy armistices and temporary cease-fires. That war has already lasted 25 years. Whether future histories will call this the era of the 25-year-Arab-Israeli war, or the 30-year war, or the 50-year war, rests in large measure in our hands."[7]

Perhaps the history of Palestine has already reached the stage where one must speak of a hundred-year war, if one starts with the Zionist pioneers of the first Aliya immigration in the 1880s and their clashes with the local Arab peasantry. This hundred-year war has been fought with the primitive rifles and pistols of the old Ottoman and British empires as well as with the most advanced jetfighter aircraft of the modern world's two great superpowers, the United States and the USSR. It has witnessed subversion, assassination, terrorism, and guerrilla warfare by both sides, and it has seen daring and courageous statesmanship by both Arabs and Jews. Battles have been fought in the open and in secret, peace has been sought in the shadows of barren deserts and under the glare of internationally televised forums.

The clash between Arab and Jew in the Middle East has covered nearly the full range of human conflict: religious, cultural, political, emotional, historical, psychological, national, ideological, racial, geographical. And history's three great spiritual movements—Judaism, Christianity, Islam—have all looked to the Middle East as the source of salvation. In recent times, a combination of powerful sacred and profane elements in the region have exerted their pull on international consciousness: due partly to the hunger for oil, partly to moral, cultural, and religious bonds to the area, nearly three-quarters of the world has found itself riveted by the ebb and flow of Middle Eastern events. It may be no accident that the great prophets felt impelled to walk the streets of Jerusalem, a center of power, a scene of battle, an opportunity for reconciliation.

At times, it appears as if the entire spectrum of human conflict in all its diversity and intensity has concentrated itself into the clash between Arab and Jew over a tiny land called Palestine. Rarely has such a localized struggle had relevance for so many millions. Perhaps its peaceful conclusion will generate the wisdom needed to end conflict everywhere, revealing the path to salvation that is believed to be rooted in the Holy Land.

May the need for secret warfare and hidden diplomacy cease, and the blessings of peace prevail.

Notes

1   The Merciless Sword

1. Jonathan Randall, *Going All The Way: Christian Warlords, Israeli Adventurers, and the War In Lebanon* (New York: Vintage, 1984), 12.

2. Jillian Becker, *The PLO: The Rise and Fall of the Palestine Liberation Organization* (London: Weidenfeld & Nicolson, 1984), 124.

3. Ibid., 118.

4. *Los Angeles Times*, 12 October 1982; *The Commission Of Inquiry Into The Events At The Refugee Camps In Beirut* (Israel: Government Authorized Translation, 1983), 21.

5. *Los Angeles Times*, 28 May 1985; *The New York Times*, 27 May 1985.

6. *Los Angeles Times*, 24 June 1985.

7. "The Camps," *Palestine Refugees Today*, No.112 (Vienna: UNRWA, October 1985), 4.

8. *The New York Times*, 29 May 1985.

9. *The New York Times*, 25 November 1986; 2 December 1986.

10. *Los Angeles Times*, 11 February 1987.

11. Itamar Rabinovich, *The War For Lebanon* (Ithaca: Cornell University Press, 1985), 58.

12. Lawrence Meyer, *Israel Now* (New York: Delacorte Press, 1982), 37.

13. Kamal Joumblatt, *I Speak For Lebanon* (London: Zed Press, 1982), 44.

14. Deut. 20:17–18.

15. Deut. 20:13–14.

16. Joshua 6:20–21.

17. Eric Silver, *Begin* (New York: Random House 1984), 94.

18. Ibid., 93.

19. Menachem Begin, *The Revolt* (New York: Dell Publishing Co., 1978), 226.

20. Larry Collins & Dominique Lapierre, *O Jerusalem!* (New York: Pocket Books, 1972), 306.

21. Rosemary Sayigh, *Palestinians: From Peasants to Revolutionaries* (London: Zed Press, 1979), 75.

22. *The Commission Of Inquiry Into The Events At The Refugee Camps In Beirut*, 29.

23. Ibid., 49.

24. Joumblatt, *I Speak For Lebanon*, 58.

25. Jillian Becker, *The PLO* (London: Weidenfeld & Nicolson, 1984), 124.

2   Caucasia's Legacy

1. Leonard J. Davis and Moshe Decter, *Myths and Facts 1982* (Washington, D.C.: American Israel Public Affairs Committee, 1982), 199.

2. Ibid., 200.

3. *Los Angeles Times*, 26 May 1985.

4. Dr. Jamal Shurdom, letter to the author dated 18 June 1987.

5. Interview with author; the source requested anonymity. Due to the sensitivity of Circassian-Palestinian relations in Jordan, I have either honored the requests for anonymity from members of the Circassian community or in the absence of such requests have nevertheless chosen not to reveal their true identities when discussing the role of Dina al-Asan.

6. Kadir I. Natho, comments on the thesis "The Circassians In Jordan" (New York: 1980, unpublished), 7, forwarded to the author by Bruce Mackey in a letter dated 30 August 1985.

7. I. Abu-Lughod and B. Abu-Laban, *Settler Regimes in Africa and the Arab World*, 1974; K. H. Karpart, "Ottoman Immigration, Politics and Settlement in Palestine," 64, cited in Bruce Douglas Mackey, "The Circassians in Jordan" (M.A. thesis, Naval Postgraduate School, 1979), 35.

8. Kadir Natho, *Circassian Star* (New York) 3, nos. 5,7 (January–June 1980).

9. Jombolet, *Circassian Star* (New York) 3, no. 5 (January–June 1980): 38.

10. Ibid.

11. Jamal A. Shurdom, "What About Circassians' Human Rights" (Paramus, N.J.: 1986, unpublished).

12. Dr. John Colarusso, Professor of Anthropology, McMaster University, Hamilton, Ontario, letter to the author dated 14 June 1985.

13. Shurdom, letter to the author, 18 June 1987.

14. Shai Franklin, "Keeping the Balance," *Near East Report* (Washington, D.C.) 31, no. 26 (29 June 1987): 104.

15. George Weightman, "The Circassians," *Middle East Forum* (Beirut) 37, no. 10 (December 1961): 29.

16. Jan Bazell (a pseudonym), interview with author; the source requested anonymity.

17. Mackey, "The Circassians in Jordan," 4. Circassian historian Mohammed Haghandouqa—author of *Al-Sharkass* (The Circassians) (Amman: Rafidi Press, 1982)—estimates that there are 65,000 Circassians in Jordan, 100,000 in Syria, and 1 million in Turkey (*Los Angeles Times*, 17 May 1987); Dr. Jamal Shurdom set the Circassian population of Jordan at 45,000; according to *The Jerusalem Post International Edition*, 16 May 1987, there are approximately 3,000 Circassians in Israel.

18. Shurdom, letter to the author, 18 June 1987.

19. Jacques Derogy and Hesi Carmel, *The Untold History of Israel* (New York: Grove Press, 1979), 259–60.

20. Shurdom, letter to the author, 18 June 1987.

21. The Marine officer's assessment was conveyed to the author during an interview with a member of the U.S. Department of Defense's political-military office who requested anonymity.

22. Shurdom, letter to the author, 18 June 1987.

23. Mackey, "The Circassians in Jordan," 101.

24. Bazell, interview with author.

25. Jan Bazell. Comments intended for Bruce Mackey contained in a letter to Kadir Natho, dated 27 March 1980. Forwarded to the author by Mackey in a letter dated 30 August 1985.

26. Shurdom, letter to the author, 18 June 1987.

27. Mackey, "The Circassians in Jordan," 101.

28. Lesley Blanch, *The Sabres of Paradise* (New York: Viking Press, 1960), 6.

29. Jamal Shurdom, interview with author, quoted from "King Hussein and the Palestinians—Jordan's Civil War 1970" by Jamal Shurdom (Miami: University of Miami, Graduate School for International Studies, 1978, unpublished).

30. Richard Gabriel, *Operation Peace for Galilee* (New York: Hill and Wang, 1984), 34.

31. *International Documents on Palestine* (Beirut: Institute for Palestine Studies, 1970), 932.

32. *The Guardian*, 20 July 1971, 11.

33. *Palestine Perspectives* (Washington, D.C.) 14 (March 1985): 6.

3   The Human Factor

1. Seteney Khalid Shami, " Ethnicity and Leadership: The Circassians in Jordan" (Ph.D. thesis, University of California, Berkeley, 1982), 96, published on demand by University Microfilms International, Ann Arbor, Michigan.

2. Davis and Decter, *Myths and Facts 1982*, 200.

3. Interview with author; the source requested anonymity.

4. Interview with author; the source shall remain anonymous.

5. Jan Bazell, interview with author.

6. Dr. Jamal Shurdom, interview with author.

7. Shami, " Ethnicity and Leadership: The Circassians in Jordan," 111.

8. Ibid., 108.

9. Ibid., 111–12, 110, 112.

10. Ibid., 112–113.

11. Elaine Ruth Fletcher, "The Circassians: a cohesive, loyal community," *The Jerusalem Post International Edition*, 23 May 1987.

12. *Los Angeles Times*, 17 May 1987.

13. *The New York Times*, 26 May 1987.

14. *Los Angeles Times*, 18, 25, 26 May 1987; *The New York Times*, 26 May 1987.

15. Interview with author; the source shall remain anonymous.

16. Dr. Jamal Shurdom, letter to the author, dated 18 June 1987.

17. Fletcher, "The Circassians: a cohesive, loyal community."

18. Interview with author; the source shall remain anonymous.

19. *The New York Times*, 1 December 1974.

20. Becker, *The PLO*, 188.

21. *The New York Times*, 5 December 1985.

22. Interview with author; the source shall remain anonymous.

23. Interviews with author; the sources requested anonymity.

24. *The New York Times*, 6 November 1986.

25. Inspector Kolvarnik, interview with author.

26. Dina's landlord in Vienna, interview with author; though not a Circassian, for security reasons the source shall remain anonymous.

27. Ibid.; Dina's neighbor in Vienna, interview with author; though not a Circassian, for security reasons the source shall remain anonymous.

28. Frank Snepp, interview with author.

4   Retribution

1. Michael Jansen, *The Battle of Beirut* (Boston: South End Press, 1983), 52.

2. Gabriel, *Operation Peace for Galilee*, 123, 173.

3. Matti Shavitt, *On The Wings of Eagles* (Tel Aviv: Olive Books, 1972), 49–50

4. Ibid., 50.

5. Moshe Dayan, *Story of My Life* (New York: William Morrow & Co., 1976), 189.

6. Uzi Benziman, *Sharon: An Israeli Caesar* (Tel Aviv: Adama Books, 1985), 55.

7. Becker, *The PLO*, 45.

8. Peter Snow, *Hussein* (New York: Robert B. Luce, Inc., 1972), 164.

9. Abu Iyad, *My Home, My Land* (New York: Times Books, 1981), 49.

10. Dayan, *Story of My Life*, 431.

11. Ibid.

12. *Los Angeles Times*, 28 May 1985.

13. George P. Shultz, *Terrorism: The Challenge to the Democracies* (Washington, D.C.: Jonathan Institute), 24 June 1984, Address delivered to the Jonathan Institute's Second Conference on Terrorism, 15.

14. Wilbur Crane Eveland, *Ropes of Sand* (New York: W. W. Norton & Co., 1980), 95.

5   The Camps

1. Bassam Sirhan, "Palestinian Refugee Camp Life in Lebanon," *Journal of Palestine Studies* (Beirut) (Winter 1975): 93.

2. *The Washington Post*, 5 December 1976.

3. *UNRWA: A Survey of United Nations Assistance to Palestine Refugees* (New York: United Nations, 1972), inside cover.

4. *Health for Palestine Refugees* (Beirut: United Nations, 1972), UNRWA Report, 13.

5. Ibid., 5.

6. *Arab Report and Record*, (London), 1–15 April 1974, 138–139.

7. *New York Times*, 16 May 1974; *Newsweek*, 26 May 1974.

8. *Daily Star* (Beirut), 17 May 1974, 3; *International Herald Tribune*, 21 May 1974, 1.

9. Matti Golan, *The Secret Conversations of Henry Kissinger* (New York: Bantam Books, 1976), 259–263.

10. Helena Cobban, *The Palestinian Liberation Organisation* (Cambridge: Cambridge University Press, 1984), 17.

11. Aaron David Miller, *The PLO and the Politics of Survival* (New York: Praeger Publishers, 1983), 62.

12. *PFLP Bulletin* (Beirut), 52 (July 1982): 7.

13. Fawaz Turki, *The Disinherited* (New York: Monthly Review Press, 1974), 8.

14. *The New York Times*, 25 June 1974.

15. Yossi Klein, "Journeys into the New Israel," *The Village Voice* (New York), 26 October 1982, 14.

16. Ibid.,15.

17. *The New York Times*, 13 October 1985.

18. *Los Angeles Times*, 22, 23, 26 April 1987.

19. *The New York Times*, 9 July 1974.

20. Ibid., 10 July 1974.

6 Fellow Travelers

1. Derogy and Carmel, *The Untold History of Israel*, 230; Uri Dan, *The Face of Terror* (New York: Leisure Books, 1978), 190–204.

2. Abdullah Schleifer, *The Fall of Jerusalem* (New York: Monthly Review Press, 1972), 67–68; Riad el-Rayyes and Dunia Nahas, *Guerrillas for Palestine* (New York: St. Martin's Press, 1976), 138–141; Zeev Schiff and Raphael Rothstein, *Fedayeen* (New York: David McKay Co., 1972), 108; Albert Parry, *Terrorism: From Robespierre to Arafat* (New York: Vanguard Press, 1976), 460; Becker, *The PLO*, 70–71; Cobban, *The Palestinian Liberation Organisation*, 140–143; Miller, *The PLO and the Politics of Survival*, 48–49.

3. Dan, *The Face of Terror*, 33; Peter Snow, *Hussein* (New York: Robert B. Luce, Inc., 1972), 102–103, 113.

4. Snow, *Hussein*, 115.

5. William J. Pomeroy, *Guerrilla Warfare and Marxism* (New York: International Publishers, New World Paperbacks, 1968), 291.

6. Ibid., 290.

7. Cobban, *The Palestinian Liberation Organisation*, 143.

8. Ibid., 145–146; Stewart Steven, *The Spymasters of Israel* (New York: Macmillan Publishing Co., 1980), 242; Schiff and Rothstein, *Fedayeen*, 130–135.

9. Leila Khaled, *My People Shall Live* (Toronto: NC Press, 1973), 110.

10. Steven, *The Spymasters of Israel*, 243.

11. Khaled, *My People Shall Live*, 130.

12. Steven, *The Spymasters of Israel*, 244–245.

13. Ibid., 245–247; Becker, *The PLO*, 74–75.

14. *PFLP Bulletin* (Beirut), 56 (November 1981); *PFLP Bulletin* (Beirut), 50–51 (May–June 1981).

15. Dan, *The Face of Terror*, 203.

16. Christopher Dobson, *Black September: Its Short, Violent History* (New York: Macmillan Publishing Co., 1974), 128–129.

17. Carlos Marighella, *Minimanual of the Urban Guerrilla* (Boulder: Paladin Press, 1978), 20, 33, 37.

7 The Circle Closes

1. Iyad, *My Home, My Land*, 12.

2. Ibid., 25.

3. Ibid., 25–27; Schiff and Rothstein, *Fedayeen*, 58; Cobban, *The Palestinian Liberation Organisation*, 21–24

4. Iyad, *My Home, My Land*, 98; Michael Bar-Zohar and Eitan Haber, *The Quest for the Red Prince* (London: Weidenfeld & Nicolson, 1983), 97, 111.

5. Iyad, *My Home, My Land*, xi.

6. Oriana Fallaci, "We Want a War Like the Vietnam War," interview with George Habash, *Life*, 12 June 1970, 32–34.

7. Turki, *The Disinherited*, 105.

8. David Hirst, *The Gun and the Olive Branch* (London: Futura Publications, 1977), 302–303.

9. Raphael Israeli, *PLO In Lebanon: Selected Documents* (London: Weidenfeld & Nicolson, 1983), 31.

8   The Flesh of the Usurper

1. Khaled, *My People Shall Live*, 219.

2. Derogy and Carmel, *The Untold History of Israel*, 225–226.

3. Ibid., 187–188; Colin Smith, *Carlos: Portrait of a Terrorist* (New York: Holt, Rinehart and Winston, 1976), 49–50; Christopher Dobson and Ronald Payne, *The Carlos Complex* (London: Coronet Books, 1977), 21; Derogy and Carmel, *The Untold History of Israel*, 229.

4. Khaled, *My People Shall Live*, 187.

5. David Tinnin, *Hit Team* (London: Futura Publications Limited, 1976), 32; Derogy and Carmel, *The Untold History of Israel*, 229; Bar-Zohar and Haber, *The Quest for the Red Prince*, 115–116.

6. Smith, *Carlos: Portrait of a Terrorist*, 74–75; Dobson and Payne, *The Carlos Complex*, 21, 30.

7. Dobson and Payne, *The Carlos Complex*, 191; Bar-Zohar and Haber, *The Quest for the Red Prince*, 116–117; Steven, *The Spymasters of Israel*, 261.

8. *Arab Report and Record* (London) 1–15 May 1972, 245.

9. Mahmoud Darwish, *The Music of Human Flesh* (Washington D.C.: Three Continents Press, 1980), 11–12.

10. Iyad, *My Home, My Land*, 34.

11. Khaled, *My People Shall Live*, 58.

12. Becker, *The PLO*, 43.

13. Cobban, *The Palestine Liberation Organisation*, 14.

14. S. H. Behbehani, *China's Foreign Policy in the Arab World 1955–1975: Three Case Studies* (London and Boston: Kegan Paul International Ltd., 1981), 34–35.

15. Ibid., 38, 40.

16. Lillian Craig Harris, "China's Relations With The PLO," *Journal of Palestine Studies* (Beirut: Institute for Palestine Studies and Kuwait University) (Autumn 1977): 136.

17. Aryeh Yodfat and Yuval Arnon-Ohanna, *PLO Strategy and Tactics* (London: Croom Helm, 1981), 79.

18. Iyad, *My Home, My Land*, 67–70.

19. Mohammed Heikal, *The Road to Ramadan* (New York: Quadrangle Books, 1975), 64–65.

20. Ibid., 65, 82.

21. Israeli, *PLO In Lebanon*, 96, 100.

9   Palestinian Prison

1. Interview with author.

2. *The Jerusalem Post Magazine*, Associated Press, 24 February–1 March 1980.

3. Schiff and Rothstein, *Fedayeen*, 187–188, 190.

10   "Magnoun"

1. John Cooley, *Libyan Sandstorm* (New York: Holt, Rinehart and Winston, 1982), 11–12.

2. Anwar el-Sadat, *In Search of Identity* (New York: Harper Colophon Books, 1979), 201.

3. Hamdi Fuad, interview with author.

4. Ismail Fahmy, *Negotiating for Peace in the Middle East* (Baltimore: Johns Hopkins University Press, 1983), 134.

5. "Qaddafi's Italian Evacuation Anniversary," Libyan Radio, 7 October 1972; Jebran Chamieh, ed., *Record of the Arab World* (Beirut: The Research and Publishing House) 2, no. 206 (1972): 1584–1585.

6. Alfred Lilienthal, *The Zionist Connection II* (New Jersey: North American, Inc., 1982), 374–379; Cooley, *Libyan Sandstorm*, 106–107.

7. Anwar El-Sadat, *Those I Have Known* (New York: Continuum Publishing Company, 1984), 48–49.

8. Ibid., 107; Derogy and Carmel, *The Untold History of Israel*, 237–238.

9. Sadat, *Those I Have Known*, 49–50.

10. Cooley, *Libyan Sandstorm*, 108.

11. Amos Elon, *Flight Into Egypt* (New York: Pinnacle Books, 1981), 55–56.

12. Muammar Al Qathafi, "The Social Basis of the Third Universal Theory," *The Green Book*, Part Three (Tripoli: Public Establishment for Publishing, Advertising and Distribution), 38–39.

13. Cooley, *Libyan Sandstorm*, 108–109.

14. Hamdi Fuad, interview with author.

15. Cooley, *Libyan Sandstorm*, 230.

16. R. Michael Burrell and Abbas R. Kelidar, *Egypt* (Beverly Hills and London: SAGE Publications, 1977), 64–66; *The New York Times*, 22 July 1977.

17. Hermann Eilts, interview with author.

18. Cooley, *Libyan Sandstorm*, 106.

19. Sadat, *Those I Have Known*, 42.

11   Begin's Ploy

1. Eric Silver, *Begin* (New York: Random House, 1984), 2–3.

2. Mustafa Tlas, *The Matzoh of Zion* (Los Angeles: Simon Wiesenthal Center, 1986), translated excerpts, 17.

3. Silver, *Begin*, 4.

4. Ibid., 7–8.

5. Ibid., 4.

6. Ibid., 10.

7. Shlomo Avineri, *The Roots of Modern Zionism* (New York: Basic Books, 1981), 164.

8. Menachem Begin, *The Revolt* (New York: Dell Publishing Co., 1978), 80–81.

9. Ibid., 63–64.

10. Ibid., 63; Silver, *Begin*, 65–66.

11. Thurston Clarke, *By Blood and Fire* (London: Arrow Books, 1982), 31–33.

12. Ibid., 252, 293; Silver, *Begin*, 70.

13. Silver, *Begin*, 73; Clarke, *By Blood and Fire*, 298–299.

14. Abd el Moniem Said, interview with author.

15. Moshe Dayan, *Breakthrough* (New York: Alfred A. Knopf, 1981), 197.

16. Elon, *Flight Into Egypt*, 40.

17. Begin, *The Revolt*, 46.

12   Second Thoughts

1. Al Qathafi, *The Green Book*, Part Three, 10.

2. John Laffin, *The Dagger of Islam* (London: Sphere Books Limited, 1979), 89; Davis and Decter, *Myths and Facts* 1982, 135.

3. Cooley, *Libyan Sandstorm*, 100.

4. Hamdi Fuad, interview with author.

5. Shmuel Katz, *The Hollow Peace* (Jerusalem: DVIR and *The Jerusalem Post*, 1981), 186.

6. Walter Laqueur and Barry Rubin, *The Israel-Arab Reader* (New York: Penguin Books, 1984), "Prime Minister Menachem Begin: The Wars of No Alternative and Operation Peace for Galilee," 653.

7. Chaim Herzog, *The Arab-Israeli Wars* (New York: Vintage Books, 1984), 317.

8. Laqueur and Rubin, *The Israel-Arab Reader*, "Address to the People's Assembly, October 16, 1973," 470, 467.

9. Herzog, *The Arab-Israeli Wars*, 316.

10. Katz, *The Hollow Peace*, 306.

11. Derogy and Carmel, *The Untold History of Israel*, 318.

12. Paul Eidelberg, *Sadat's Strategy* (Dollard des Ormeaux, Quebec: Dawn Books, 1979), 78–79.

13. Laqueur and Rubin, *The Israel-Arab Reader*, "Speech (October 16, 1973) By Anwar Sadat," Address to the People's Assembly, Cairo, 467.

14. "President Anwar al Sadat's Speech on the Occasion of the Prophet's Birthday," April 24, 1972, Jebran Chamieh, ed. *Record of the Arab World* 2, no.108, 1423–1424.

13   Sadat's Initiative

1. "The Untold Story of the Mideast Talks," by Sidney Zion and Uri Dan, *The New York Times Magazine*, 21 January 1979, 22.

2. Ibid., 22; Steven, *The Spymasters of Israel*, xvi.

3. Dayan, *Breakthrough*, 38.

4. "The Untold Story of the Mideast Talks," *The New York Times Magazine*, 21 January 1979, 22; Steven, *The Spymasters of Israel*, xvi

5. Derogy and Carmel, *The Untold History of Israel*, 315; Dr. Mohammad Said, *Al Ahram*, Center for Strategic Political Studies, interview with author.

6. *The New York Times*, 18, 26, 30 April, 1 May 1984; *Los Angeles Times*, 18, 19, 21, 23 April 1984.

7. Ibid., 314.

8. Stefan T. Possony and Francis L. Bouchey, "Moscow's Support of International Terrorism," *The Ukrainian Quarterly* 34, no. 4, 386–387.

9. Mohamed Heikal, *Autumn of Fury* (New York: Random House, 1983), 94–95.

10. Wolfgang Lotz, *The Champagne Spy* (London: Vallentine, Mitchell, 1972), 20–21.

11. *The New York Times*, 22, 23, July 1977; Time, 1 August 1977, 20; *Newsweek*, 1 August 1977, 29; Heikal, *Autumn of Fury*, 131.

12. "The Untold Story of the Mideast Talks," *The New York Times Magazine*, 21 January 1979, 21; Derogy and Carmel, *The Untold History of Israel*, 314.

13. *The New York Times*, 23 July 1977.

14. Hermann Eilts, interview with author.

15. Cooley, *Libyan Sandstorm*, 166–168.

16. Ibid., 34, 38.

17. Michael Austrian, Director, Office of Public Affairs, Bureau of Near East and South Asian Affairs, U.S. Department of State, interview with author.

18. *The New York Times*, 22, 23 July 1977; *Time*, 1 August 1977, 20; *Newsweek*, 1 August 1977, 29.

19. *The New York Times*, 24, 25, 1977.

20. Ibid., 24, 26 July 1977.

21. Cooley, *Libyan Sandstorm*, 38.

22. Dayan, *Breakthrough*, 42–43; Fahmy, *Negotiating for Peace in the Middle East*, 240.

23. Philip Stoddard, interview with author.

24. Fahmy, *Negotiating for Peace in the Middle East*, 257.

25. Ibid., 257–258.

26. Sadat, *In Search of Identity*, 306.

27. Dayan, *Breakthrough*, 47.

28. Sadat, *In Search of Identity*, 302.

29. Ibid., 303–304.

30. Sadat, *Those I Have Known*, 105.

14   The Price of Peace

1. *The Jerusalem Post*, 8 July 1981.

2. Heikal, *Autumn of Fury*, 95.

3. *Jamahiriya Journal*, (Washington, D.C.) 2, no.4, cited in excerpts from an address by Muammar Qaddafi at a public rally in Benghazi on 1 September 1979, celebrating the tenth anniversary of his revolution.

4. Ibid., cited in "Qadhafi Attends Palestine Day Rally," 18.

5. *The New York Times*, 4 October 1984.

6. Interview with author.

7. Fadwa El Guindi, "The Killing of Sadat and After, A Current Assessment of Egypt's Islamic Movement," *Middle East Insight* (Washington, D.C.) 2, no. 5, (January/February 1983): 19–20.

8. Saad Eddin Ibrahim, "Egypt's Islamic Militants," *MERIP Reports* (Washington, D.C.) 12, no. 2, (February 1982): 14, no. 2; Marie-Christine Aulas, "Sadat's Egypt: A Balance Sheet," *MERIP Reports* 12, no. 6, (July–August 1982): 8–9.

9. Aulas, "Sadat's Egypt," 230–231, 246.

10. Sadat, *In Search of Identity*, 343.

11. *The Koran*, N. J. Dawood, translator (New York: Penguin Books, 1980).

12. Ibid.

13. Gilles Kepel, *Muslim Extremism in Egypt* (Berkeley: University of California Press, 1985), 112–113.

14. Ibid., 195, 202–203.

15. Heikal, *Autumn of Fury*, 242–243, 246, 249, 251.

16. *Time*, 19 October 1981, 23.

17. *Nightline* (Washington, D.C.), November 20, 1984, ABC News transcript, Show #912, 3–4.

318   *Notes*

18. Sadat, *Those I Have Known*, 50.
19. Seymour M. Hersh, "Target Qaddafi," *The New York Times Magazine,* 22 February 1987, 24.
20. *The New York Times*, 1 October 1984.
21. *Time*, 19 October 1981, 22.
22. Heikal, *Autumn of Fury*, 250, 252.
23. Michael Austrian, interview with author.
24. *Time*, 19 October 1981, 32.
25. Ibid., 24; Elon, *Flight Into Egypt*, 2.
26. *The New York Times*, 22 November 1981.
27. *Los Angeles Times*, 16 April 1982; *The New York Times*, 1 October 1984.
28. Ibid.
29. *Time*, 19 October 1981, 26.
30. *The New York Times*, 17 July 1985.
31. *Los Angeles Times*, 5 December 1986.

16   King of the Arabs, Guardian of Islam

1. George Antonius, *The Arab Awakening* (Beirut: Khayat's College Book Cooperative, 1955), 328–329.
2. Snow, *Hussein*, 252.
3. Antonius, *The Arab Awakening*, 414.
4. Laqueur and Rubin, *The Israel-Arab Reader*,"The McMahon Letter," 16.
5. Antonius, *The Arab Awakening*, 169.
6. Laqueur and Rubin, *The Israel-Arab Reader*, "The Sykes-Picot Agreement," 13.
7. Ibid.
8. Ibid., 256.
9. Antonius, *The Arab Awakening*, 257.
10. Ibid., 432.
11. Ibid., 352–353.
12. Joumblatt, *I Speak for Lebanon*, 78.
13. British Public Records Office, Foreign Office, Kew Gardens, London, 371/6342, 23 March 1921, cited in Joan Peters, *From Time Immemorial* (New York: Perennial Library, 1984), 238.
14. Paul A. Jureidini and William E. Hazen, *The Palestinian Movement in Politics* (Lexington, Massachusetts: Lexington Books, 1976), 45.
15. Ibid., 238.
16. Philip Knightley and Colin Simpson, *The Secret Lives of Lawrence of Arabia* (New York: McGraw-Hill Book Company, 1970), from Feisal's diary, cited on 164–165.
17. Laqueur and Rubin, *The Israel-Arab Reader* "The Balfour Declaration," 18.
18. Knightley and Simpson, *The Secret Lives of Lawrence of Arabia*, 121.
19. "Appendix of Previous Commitments of His Majesty's Government in the Middle East to the Memorandum on British Commitments to King Hussein," cited in Lilienthal, *The Zionist Connection II*, 812, n. 16
20. Laqueur and Rubin, *The Israel-Arab Reader*, "The Churchill White Paper—1922," 48.
21. *The Times of London*, 23 July 1937.
22. Laqueur and Rubin, *The Israel-Arab Reader*, "Agreement Between Emir Feisal and Dr. Weizmann January 3, 1919," 19.

23. Knightley and Simpson, *The Secret Lives of Lawrence of Arabia*, 134.

24. Laqueur and Rubin, *The Israel-Arab Reader*, "Feisal-Frankfurter Correspondence," 21.

25. Sami Hadawi, *Bitter Harvest* (New York: Caravan Books, 1979), 16–17.

26. Laqueur and Rubin, *The Israel-Arab Reader*, "Recommendations of the King-Crane Commission," 29, 31.

27. Lilienthal, *The Zionist Connection II*, 22, 24.

28. Antonius, *The Arab Awakening*, "Resolutions of the General Syrian Congress," 440–441.

29. Knightley and Simpson, *The Secret Lives of Lawrence of Arabia*, 134.

30. Antonius, *The Arab Awakening*, 412.

31. Hadawi, *Bitter Harvest*, 75.

32. Bernard Lewis, *Semites & Anti-Semites* (New York: W.W. Norton & Co., 1986), 121–122.

33. Ibid., 169.

34. Ibid., 174.

35. Antonius, *The Arab Awakening*, 450.

36. Hadawi, *Bitter Harvest*, 284.

37. Dayan, *Story of My Life*, 133–143.

38. Golda Meir, *My Life* (New York: Dell Publishing Company, 1975), 206.

39. Ibid., 206–207.

17 Cloak and Dagger Diplomacy

1. Snow, *Hussein*, 114.

2. Ibid., 154–155.

3. David Ben-Gurion, *Israel: A Personal Story* (New York: Herzl Press, 1972), 688–89.

4. Moshe Zak, "Israeli-Jordanian Negotiations," *The Washington Quarterly* (Winter 1985): 167–168.

5. Eveland, *Ropes of Sand*, 130.

6. Dayan, *Story of My Life*, 144.

7. Shimon Peres, *David's Sling* (London:Weidenfeld and Nicolson, 1970), 222.

8. Khaled, *My People Shall Live*, 62.

9. Schiff and Rothstein, *Fedayeen*, 63.

18 Talking Peace, Making War

1. Miles Copeland, *The Game of Nations* (New York: Simon and Schuster, 1969), 110.

2. Cobban, *The Palestinian Liberation Organisation*, 29.

3. Paul Riebenfeld, "The Integrity of Palestine," *Midstream* (August–September 1975): 22.

4. Cobban, *The Palestinian Liberation Organisation*, 30–31.

5. *Near East Report* (Washington, D.C.) 3, no. 20 (15 March 1960): 80.

6. *The New York Times*, 22 August 1960.

7. Ibid., 29 August 1980.

8. Dov Eppel, "Arab League Fiasco," *New Outlook* (April 1960): 9.

9. Snow, *Hussein*, 172–173.

10. Copeland, *The Game of Nations*, 110.

11. Donald Neff, *Warriors for Jerusalem* (New York: Linden Press, 1984), 204.

12. Schleifer, *The Fall of Jerusalem*, 147.

13. Derogy and Carmel, *The Untold History of Israel*, 206.

14. Snow, *Hussein*, 182–183; also Herzog, *The Arab-Israeli Wars*, 169; Dayan, *Story of My Life*, 366; Neff, *Warriors for Jerusalem*, 205.

15. Hadawi, *Bitter Harvest*, 233–234; Steven, *The Spymasters of Israel*, 193.

19   All or Nothing

1. *The New York Times*, 25 December 1968.

2. *The New York Times*, 6 January 1969.

3. Snow, *Hussein*, 207.

4. Ezer Weizman, *The Battle For Peace* (New York: Bantam Books, 1981), 83.

5. Schleifer, *The Fall of Jerusalem*, 214–215.

6. "Memorandum for the Secretary of Defense," *Journal of Palestine Studies*, (Beirut: Institute for Palestine Studies and Kuwait University) 13, no. 2 (Winter 1984): 123–124.

7. Weizman, *The Battle for Peace*, 383; Dayan, *Breakthrough*, 313.

8. Ibid., 61.

9. Katz, *The Hollow Peace*, 112–113.

10. Amos Perlmutter, "Unilateral Withdrawal: Israel's Security Option," *Foreign Affairs* (New York) 64, no. 1 (Fall 1985): 147–148.

11. Sayigh, *Palestinians: From Peasants to Revolutionaries*, 145.

12. Davis and Decter, *Myths and Facts* 1982, 37.

13. Dayan, *Story of My Life*, 333.

14. Ben-Gurion, *Israel*, 764.

20   All the King's Men

1. *Jerusalem Post*, 4 June 1982.

2. Iyad, *My Home, My Land*, 57.

3. Becker, *The PLO*, 62.

4. Iyad, *My Home, My Land*, 57–58.

5. Becker, *The PLO*, 62–63.

6. Herzog, *The Arab-Israeli Wars*, 205; Schiff and Rothstein, *Fedayeen*, 82–83.

7. Schiff and Rothstein, *Fedayeen*, 82; Snow, *Hussein*, 204; Becker, *The PLO*, 62–63.

8. Schiff and Rothstein, *Fedayeen*, 82–83; Herzog, *The Arab-Israeli Wars*, 205.

9. Herzog, *The Arab-Israeli Wars*, 205.

10. Dayan, *Story of My Life*, 415.

11. Iyad, *My Home, My Land*, 60.

12. Snow, *Hussein*, 205.

13. Cobban, *The Palestinian Liberation Organisation*, 43.

14. Laqueur and Rubin, *The Israel-Arab Reader*, "The Palestinian National Charter: Resolutions of the Palestine National Council," 369.

15. Snow, *Hussein*, 205.

16. Dayan, *Story of My Life*, 413.

17. Christopher Dobson, *Black September: Its Short, Violent History*, (New York: Macmillan Publishing Co., 1974) 33.

18. Derogy and Carmel, *The Untold History of Israel*, 261, 263; Snow, *Hussein*, 228–229.

19. *Daily Telegraph*, 3 October 1985, cited in *Palestine Perspectives* (Washington, D.C.), 20 (November / December 1985): 6.

20. Zak, "Israeli-Jordanian Negotiations," *The Washington Quarterly*, (Winter 1985): 170.

21. United States Department of State, *The Quest for Peace* (Washington D.C.: U.S. Government Printing Office, 1984), "The Rogers Plan, December 1969," 27.

22. Ibid., 26, 27.

23. Interview with author; the source requested anonymity.

24. Derogy and Carmel, *The Untold History of Israel*, 257.

25. Ibid., 264.

26. Ibid., 265; Snow, *Hussein*, 230–231; Henry Kissinger, *White House Years* (Boston: Little, Brown and Company, 1979), 614, 622; Richard Nixon, *RN* (New York: Grosset and Dunlap, 1978), 485.

27. Nixon, *RN*, 232, 235; Derogy and Carmel, *The Untold History of Israel*, 263, 265–266.

21   Playing the Wild Card

1. Zak, "Israeli-Jordanian Negotiations," 172.

2. *The New York Times*, 16 March 1972.

3. *The New York Times*, 16 March 1972; Chamieh, *Record of the Arab World*, Vol. 1, 280.

4. Chamieh, *Record of the Arab World*, 281.

5. Ibid., 282.

6. Ibid., Vol. II, 1417.

7. Ibid., Vol. I, 278.

8. Ibid., 275.

9. Ibid., 278; *The New York Times*, 16 March 1972.

10. *The New York Times*, 30 March 1972.

11. *The New York Times*, 22 March 1972.

12. Ibid.

13. Chamieh, *Record of the Arab World*, Vol. 1, 283.

14. *The New York Times*, 30 March 1972.

15. *The New York Times*, 17 March 1972.

16. Ibid.

17. Chamieh, *Record of the Arab World*, Vol. 1, 276.

18. Ibid., 276–277.

19. Ibid., Vol. II, 1193; *Time*, 11 September 1972;

20. Herzog, *The Arab-Israeli Wars*, 302.

22   Clocking the Hussein Hours

1. Zak, "Israeli-Jordanian Negotiations," 167.

2. Matti Golan, *The Secret Conversations of Henry Kissinger* (New York: Bantam Books, 1976), 222–223.

3. Henry Kissinger, *Years of Upheaval* (Boston: Little, Brown and Company, 1982), 1054.

4. Ibid., 655.
5. Ibid., 976.
6. Cobban, *The Palestinian Liberation Organisation*, 60.
7. Hatem Hussaini, *Toward Peace In Palestine* (Washington, D.C.: Palestine Information Office, 1975), "The United Nations Appeal For Peace" by Yasser Arafat, 10.
8. Hirst, *The Gun and the Olive Branch*, 333.
9. Silver, *Begin*, 168–169.
10. Dayan, *Breakthrough*, 35–37.

23   The Jordanian Option

1. Silver, *Begin*, 160.
2. *The New York Times*, 21 February 1985.
3. *Los Angeles Times*, 21 February 1985.
4. Weizman, *The Battle For Peace*, 149–150.
5. Interview with author; the source requested anonymity.
6. Samuel W. Lewis, "Israel: The Peres Era And Its Legacy," *Foreign Affairs* 65, no. 3 (1986): 598–599.
7. *Des Moines Register*, 22 October 1985.
8. *The New York Times*, 14 November 1985.
9. *The New York Times*, 24 October 1985.
10. *U.S. News & World Report*, 7 October 1985.
11. *Los Angeles Times*, 3 September 1985; 29 September 1985.
12. *Near East Report* (Washington, D.C.) 29, no. 37 (16 September 1985): 147.
13. *Near East Report* 29, no.34 (26 August 1985): 135; 29, no. 37 (16 September 1985): 148.
14. *Los Angeles Times*, 4 October 1985.
15. *Daily Telegraph* (London), 3 October 1985; *Israel and Palestine* (Paris), September 1986.
16. Sylvia Raphael, letter to the author, dated 18 February 1986.
17. The *Daily Telegraph* piece reporting Raphael's assassination in Cyprus was reprinted in the November–December 1985 issue of *Palestine Perspectives*, a magazine published by the PLO's information office in Washington, D.C. John Bulloch, the article's author, retracted the story about Raphael's death in a letter to the author dated 21 April 1986. Another retraction was published in the October–November 1986 issue of *Israel and Palestine* (Paris), under the heading "A Disinformation Attempt." A further confirmation that Raphael was not one of the victims at Larnaca was contained in a 28 February 1986 letter written by Dag Christensen, a reporter for *Time* magazine based in Oslo and the co-author of *Hit Team*, (London: Futura Publications Ltd., 1976) a book which details Raphael's role in the Mossad squad assigned to avenge the massacre of Israeli athletes at the Munich Olympics.
18. *Los Angeles Times*, 5 October 1985.
19. Ibid., 3 October 1985.
20. Ibid., 5 October 1985.
21. *The Jerusalem Post International Edition*, 21 February 1987.
22. Ibid., 6 October 1985.
23. *U.S. News & World Report*, 14 October 1985, 27.
24. *Los Angeles Times*, 2 October 1985.
25. *Los Angeles Times*, 4 October 1985.
26. Alan Hart, *Arafat* (London: Sidgwick & Jackson, 1985), 339.

27. Lewis, "Israel: The Peres Era And Its Legacy" *Foreign Affairs* 65, no. 3 (1986): 599–600.

28. Harvey Sicherman, interview with author.

29. *Near East Report* 29, no. 44 (4 November 1985): 176.

30. Hirsh Goodman, "Hussein's Predicament," *The New Republic*, 26 August 1985, 19.

31. *Los Angeles Times*, 2 October 1984.

32. Richard L. Armitage, "The Strategic Value of Arming Hussein," *The New York Times*, 2 October 1985.

33. Hirsh Goodman, "The Shorter Wick," *The New Republic*, 18 November 1985, 22.

34. *The New York Times*, 19 July 1985.

35. Ibid.

36. *Near East Report* 29, no. 33 (19 August 1985): 131; Lally Weymouth, "Israel's Dilemma," *The New Republic*, 26 August 1985, 22.

37. Hart, *Arafat*, 154.

38. *The Holy Bible*, Gen. 8:11.

39. Hart, *Arafat*, 239–240.

40. Shabtai Teveth, *Ben-Gurion and the Palestinian Arabs* (Oxford: Oxford University Press, 1985), 83.

41. Sheila Ryan and Muhammad Hallaj, *Palestine Is, But Not In Jordan* (Belmont: AAUG Press, 1983), 14.

42. Y. Porath, *The Emergence of the Palestinian-Arab National Movement*, vol. 1, 1918–1929 (London: Frank Cass, 1974), 105, cited in Ryan and Hallaj, *Palestine Is, But Not In Jordan*, 14–15.

43. Hart, *Arafat*, 238–239.

44. Weymouth, "Israel's Dilemma," 21.

45. *The New York Times*, 26 October 1985.

46. Peres, *David's Sling*, 259.

47. Ibid, 261.

48. Weymouth, "Israel's Dilemma," 22.

49. Frantz Fanon, *The Wretched of the Earth* (New York: Grove Press, 1979), 94.

50. Ibid., 147.

51. *Los Angeles Times*, 20, 22 April 1987.

52. *The New York Times*, 21 April 1987.

53. Jon Kimche, "Algiers: PLO's Road to Ruin," *The Jerusalem Post International Edition*, 4 July 1987, 15.

54. Ibid.

55. *Los Angeles Times*, 26 April 1987.

56. *Los Angeles Times*, 24 April 1987.

57. *Los Angeles Times*, 22 April 1987.

58. Interview with author; the Sharon aide requested anonymity. On a similar tour of the West Bank conducted by a Palestinian leader, Israeli security measures were condemned for their repressive effects upon the local Arab population.

25   The U. S. Shadow in Lebanon

1. Karim Pakradouni, *Stillborn Peace* (Beirut: Fiches du Monde Arabe, 1985), 76.

2. Rabinovich, *The War For Lebanon*, 166; Zeev Schiff, "The Green Light," *Foreign Policy* (Washington, D.C.) 50 (Spring 1983): 76; Wadi D. Haddad, *Lebanon* (New York: Praeger Publishers, 1985), 74.

3. Pakradouni, *Stillborn Peace*, 216.

4. Ibid., 204.

5. Randall, *Going All The Way*, 235.

6. William B. Quandt, *Camp David* (Washington D.C.: The Brookings Institution, 1985), 268.

7. Ibid.

8. Emile Khoury (a pseudonym), interview with author—with members of his family still living in Lebanon and the civil war far from over, Khoury requested anonymity.

9. Nicholas Veliotes, interview with author.

10. Abdallah Bouhabib, interview with author.

11. Alfred Maady, interview with author.

12. Pakradouni, *Stillborn Peace*, 221.

13. Robert Farah, executive director, Lebanese Information and Research Center (Washington, D.C.), interview with author; Richard Straus, editor, *Middle East Policy Survey* (Washington, D.C.), interview with author.

14. William Quandt, interview with author.

15. Pakradouni, *Stillborn Peace*, 96.

16. Alexander M. Haig, Jr., *Caveat* (New York: Macmillan Publishing Company, 1984), 319.

17. Laqueur and Rubin, *The Israel-Arab Reader*, "Defense Minister Ariel Sharon: Israel's Security," 635.

18. Ibid., 637.

19. Harvey Sicherman, interview with author. His thinking reflects the views of at least Haig, if not the Reagan administration in general. In a letter to the author dated 25 July 1985, Haig wrote that Sicherman "is fully conversant with the issues during my period as Secretary of State and you can rely on his insights."

20. Rabinovich, *The War For Lebanon*, 115–116.

21. Raymond Tanter, interview with author.

22. Abdallah Bouhabib, interview with author.

23. Robert Basil, interview with author.

24. William Clark, interview with author.

25. "The Foreign Policy Implications of Arms Sales to Iran and the Contra Connection," *Hearings Before The Committee On Foreign Affairs House Of Representatives*, Ninety-Ninth Congress, Second Session, 8 December 1986 (Washington, D.C.: U.S. Government Printing Office, 1986), testimony of Robert C. McFarlane, former Assistant to the President for National Security Affairs, 105, 147.

26. *Arms Sales*, AEI Forum 56, 9 September 1981 (Washington D.C.: American Enterprise Institute, 1982), 1.

27. Interview with author; the source requested anonymity.

28. Pakradouni, *Stillborn Peace*, 221.

29. Uri Dan, *Blood Libel* (New York: Simon and Schuster, 1987), 63.

30. *The New York Times*, 4 August 1981.

31. Geoffrey Kemp, interview with author.

32. Nicholas Veliotes, interview with author.

33. *Report of the DOD Commission on Beirut International Airport Terrorist Act, October 23, 1983* (Washington, D.C.: U.S. Government Printing Office, 1984), 20 December 1983, 24.

34. Interview with author; the source requested anonymity.

35. Interview with author; the source requested anonymity.

36. Interview with author; the source requested anonymity.

37. Wadi Haddad, interview with author.

38. Haddad, *Lebanon*, 80.

39. *International Documents on Palestine*, (Washington D.C.: Institute for Palestine Studies Research and Document Staff, 1981), translated from the Arabic text, *al-Amal* (Beirut), 22 August 1981.

40. Interview with author; the source requested anonymity.

41. Silver, *Begin*, 224–225.; Ze'ev Schiff and Ehud Ya'arri, *Israel's Lebanon War* (New York: Simon and Schuster, 1984), 103–106, 301.

42. Haig, *Caveat*, 326–327, 335; Harvey Sicherman, "Europe's Role in the Middle East," *ORBIS* (Winter 1985): 818; *Los Angeles Times*, 25 May 1985.

43. Schiff, "The Green Light," 81, 85.

44. Silver, *Begin*, 226.

45. Bashir Gemayel (Antilyas, Lebanon: 29 November 1981), broadcast live in Arabic by the Beirut Voice of Lebanon, monitored and translated by the *U.S. National Technical Information Service*, Middle East and North Africa Daily Report, 30 November 1981, G4.

46. Ibid., page G5.

47. Senator Edward M. Kennedy, press release, 19 June 1981, address before the American Lebanese League, Arlington, Virginia.

48. Ibid.

49. George E. Irani, *The Papacy and the Middle East* (Notre Dame: University of Notre Dame Press, 1986), 125.

50. Robert Kupperman, interview with author.

51. Charles Waterman, interview with author.

52. Interviews with author; the sources requested anonymity.

53. Richard A. Gabriel, *Operation Peace For Galilee*, 131.

54. *The Commission Of Inquiry Into The Events At The Refugee Camps In Beirut*, 7.

55. *The New York Times*, 21 September 1982.

56. *Time*, 4 October 1982, 17.

57. Dan, *Blood Libel*, 145.

58. *Congressional Record—Senate*, Senate Subcommittee On Foreign Relations Of Senate Appropriations Committee (Washington, D.C.: 5 May 1986), Statement by Robert A. Basil—Policy American Lebanese League, 17 April 1986, S 5306.

59. Interview with author; the source requested anonymity.

60. Charles Waterman, interview with author.

26   The Kissinger Ban

1. Kissinger, *Years of Upheaval*, 626.

2. Hermann Eilts, interview with author.

3. Kissinger, *Years of Upheaval*, 503, 626–629.

4. *The Wall Street Journal*, 10 February 1983.

5. Hirst, *The Gun and the Olive Branch*, 318–319.

6. Vernon A. Walters, *Silent Missions* (New York: Doubleday & Company, 1978), 618.

7. *The Wall Street Journal*, 10 February 1983.

8. Fahmy, *Negotiating for Peace in the Middle East*, 166.

9. Ibid., 166–167.

10. Cobban, *The Palestine Liberation Organisation*, 67.

11. Davis and Decter, *Myths and Facts 1981*, 210.

12. Ibid., 211.

13. Kissinger, *Years of Upheaval*, 1037.

14. Randall, *Going All The Way*, 182.

15. Cobban, *The Palestine Liberation Organisation*, 237.

16. Harold Vocke, *The Lebanese War* (New York: St. Martin's Press, 1978) , 62.

17. *The Wall Street Journal*, 10 February 1983.

18. *The New York Times*, 18 August 1979.

19. Cobban, *The Palestine Liberation Organisation*, 237.

20. Ibid.

21. Hermann Eilts, interview with author.

22. Harvey Sicherman, interview with author.

23. Donald McHenry, interview with author.

24. Alfred Atherton, interview with author.

25. "Interview With Harold Saunders," *American-Arab Affairs* (Washington) 15, (Winter 1985–86): 16.

26. Joseph Sisco, interview with author.

27   Dealing the PLO In

1. Hermann Eilts, interview with author.

2. Mr. Morgan (a pseudonym), interview with author.

3. Hermann Eilts, interview with author.

4. Hamdi Fuad, interview with author.

5. Harvey Sicherman, interview with author.

6. *The New York Times*, 20 April 1983; Charles Waterman, interview with author; Raymond Tanter, interview with author.

7. Shamir and Herzog's intelligence connections are a matter of public record.

8. Randall, *Going All The Way*, 223–224; also, *Israel & Palestine* (March–April 1985).

9. "Background Information on Israeli Trade Mission, Teheran," Secret CIA Memorandum, SRF Memo #177, dated 21 June 1977—the document was seized inside the American embassy in Teheran following its takeover by Islamic militants in 1979, published in *Counterspy* (Washington, D.C) 6, no. 3 (May–June 1982): 55; also, *Israel and Palestine* (March–April 1985), for a referral to Lubrani's Mossad links.

10. "Israel: Foreign Intelligence and Security Services," Central Intelligence Agency, March 1979, Secret, NOFORN-Not Releasable to Foreign Nationals, NOCONTRACT-Not Releasable to Contractors or Contractor / Consultants, ORCON-Dissemination and Extraction of Information Controlled by Originator, published in *Counterspy* (May–June 1982): 38–39.

11. *The Washington Times*, 17 February 1985.

12. Smith, *Carlos: Portrait of a Terrorist*, 54

13. Dobson and Payne, *The Carlos Complex*, 21.

14. Y.M. Primakov, *Anatomy of the Middle East Conflict* (Moscow: NAUKA Publishing House, 1979), 144.

15. Hart, *Arafat*, 399.

16. Stansfield Turner, *Secrecy and Democracy* (New York: Harper & Row, 1985), 161.

17. Stansfield Turner, interview with author.

18. Turner, *Secrecy and Democracy*, 161.

19. Lawrence Silberman, interview with author.

20. Interview with author; the source requested anonymity.

21. Schiff, *Israel's Lebanon War*, 288.

22. Pakradouni, *Stillborn Peace*, 255.

23. William Quandt, interview with author.

24. "President Ronald Reagan's Peace Proposal," *The Quest for Peace* (U.S. Government Printing Office: Department of State Publication 9373, 1984), 112–113.

25. Philip Stoddard, interview with author.

26. Landrum Bolling, interview with author.

27. "The PLO/Israeli Dialogue," *Events* (Beirut), 11 February 1977, 10–11.

28. *Los Angeles Times*, 20 February 1984; *The New York Times*, 20 February 1984.

29. Pakradouni, *Stillborn Peace*, 255.

30. *Israel & Palestine* (Paris) (October–November 1983).

31. Letter to the author, dated 16 April 1985; the source requested anonymity.

32. Herzog, *The Arab-Israeli Wars*, 165–166.

33. James M. Ennes, Jr., *Assault On The Liberty* (New York: Random House, 1979), 210–212.

34. Ibid., Foreword by Thomas H. Moorer, Admiral, U.S. Navy (Ret.).

35. Letter to the author, dated 16 April 1985; the source requested anonymity.

36. Interview with author; the source requested anonymity.

37. *Los Angeles Times*, 26 May 1986.

38. *The New York Times*, 8 December 1986; Derk Kinnane Roelofsma, "Hafez al-Assad: Lion of Syria," *Insight* (Washington, D.C.), 23 September 1985, 8.

39. Haig, *Caveat*, 334.

40. Steven L. Spiegel, *The Other Arab-Israeli Conflict* (Chicago: University of Chicago Press, 1985), 418–419.

41. Fawaz Turki, interview with author.

42. *Nightline* (Washington, D.C.), ABC News transcript, Show #312, 20 July 1982, 7–8.

43. *The New York Times*, 23 February 1984.

28   Conspiracy at the Top

1. Katz, *The Hollow Peace*, 81.

2. Fahmy, *Negotiating for Peace in the Middle East*, 31.

3. Hermann Eilts, interview with author.

4. Lawrence Eagleburger, interview with author.

5. *The New York Times*, 7 October 1986.

6. *The New York Times*, 25 October 1986.

7. Interview with author; the source requested anonymity.

8. *Los Angeles Times*, 25 October 1986.

9. Ibid.

10. *The Washington Times*, 10 November 1986.

11. *The New York Times*, 25 October 1986.

12. *Los Angeles Times*, 27 November 1986.

13. *Los Angeles Times*, 28 November 1986.

29   The Hundred Years War

1. Abd El Moniem Said, interview with author.

2. Hamdi Fuad, interview with author.

3. Herman Eilts, interview with author.

4. Herbert C. Kelman, "Overcoming the Psychological Barrier: An Analysis of the Egyptian Israeli Peace Process," in Samual P. Huntington and Joseph S. Nye, Jr., *Global Dilemmas* (Cambridge: Harvard University Center for International Affairs, 1985), 218.

5. *Los Angeles Times*, 2 December 1984.

6. Mukhtar at Baqaa Palestinian refugee camp, Amman, Jordan, interview with author.

7. "The Geneva Conference," *The Quest for Peace* (U.S. Government Printing Office: Department of State Publication 9373, 1984), p. 45.

Bibliography

Abu-Lughod, I., and B. Abu-Laban, eds. *Settler Regimes in Africa and the Arab World*. Wilmette, Illinois: Medina University Press International, 1972.

Antonius, George. *The Arab Awakening*. Beirut: Khayat's College Book Cooperative, 1955.

Avineri, Shlomo. *The Roots of Modern Zionism*. New York: Basic Books, 1981.

Avnery, Uri. *Israel Without Zionists*. New York: Macmillan, 1970.

Ball, George W. *Error and Betrayal in Lebanon*. Washington, D.C.: Foundation for Middle East Peace, 1984.

Bar-Zohar, Michael, and Eitan Haber. *The Quest for the Red Prince*. London: Weidenfeld & Nicolson, 1983.

Becker, Jillian. *The PLO: The Rise and Fall of the Palestine Liberation Organization*. London: Weidenfeld & Nicolson, 1984.

Begin, Menachem. *The Revolt*. New York: Dell Publishing Co., 1978.

Behbehani, S. H. *China's Foreign Policy in the Arab World 1955–1975: Three Case Studies*. London: Kegan Paul International Ltd., 1981.

Ben-Gurion, David. *Israel: A Personal History*. New York: Herzl Press, 1972.

Benziman, Uzi. *Sharon: An Israeli Caesar*. Tel Aviv: Adama Books, 1985.

Blanch, Lesley. *The Sabres of Paradise*. New York: Viking Press, 1960.

Burrell, R. Michael, and Abbas R. Kelidar. *Egypt: The Dilemmas of a Nation—1970–1977*. Beverly Hills: Sage Publications, 1977.

Camus, Albert. *Resistance, Rebellion, and Death*. New York: The Modern Library, 1960.

Carter, Jimmy. *The Blood of Abraham*. Boston: Houghton Mifflin Co., 1985.

Chamieh, Jebran, ed. *Record of the Arab World*. Vol. 1 and 2. Beirut: The Research and Publishing House, 1972.

Chapman, Robert D. *The Crimson Web Of Terror*. Boulder, Colo.: Paladin Press, 1980.

Clarke, Thurston. *By Blood and Fire*. London: Arrow Books, 1982.

Cobban, Helena. *The Palestinian Liberation Organisation*. Cambridge: Cambridge University Press, 1984.

Collins, Larry, and Dominque Lapierre. *O Jerusalem!* New York: Pocket Books, 1972.

Cooley, John. *Libyan Sandstorm*. New York: Holt, Rinehart and Winston, 1982.

Copeland, Miles. *The Game of Nations*. New York: Simon & Schuster, 1969.

Crosbie, Sylvia Kowitt. *A Tacit Alliance: France and Israel from Suez to the Six-Day War*. Princeton: Princeton University Press, 1974.

Dan, Uri. *Blood Libel*. New York: Simon & Schuster, 1987.

———. *The Face of Terror*. New York: Leisure Books, 1978.

Darwish, Mahmoud. *The Music of Human Flesh*. Washington, D.C.: Three Continents Press, 1980.

Davis, Leonard J., and Moshe Decter. *Myths and Facts 1982*. Washington, D.C.: American Israel Public Affairs Committee, 1982.

Dawood, N. J., tran. *The Koran*. New York: Penguin Books, 1980.

Dayan, Moshe. *Breakthrough*. New York: Alfred A. Knopf, 1981.

———. *Story of My Life*. New York: William Morrow & Co., 1976.

Derogy, Jacques, and Hesi Carmel. *The Untold History of Israel*. New York: Grove Press, 1979.

Dobson, Christopher. *Black September: Its Short, Violent History*. New York: Macmillan, 1974.

Dobson, Christopher, and Ronald Payne. *The Carlos Complex*. London: Coronet Books, 1977.

Eidelberg, Paul. *Sadat's Strategy*. Dollard des Ormeaux, Quebec: Dawn Books, 1979.

Elon, Amos. *Flight into Egypt*. New York: Pinnacle Books, 1981.

Emerson, Steven. *The American House of Saud*. New York: Franklin Watts, 1985.

Ennes, James M. *Assault on the Liberty*. New York: Random House, 1979.

Eveland, Wilbur Crane. *Ropes of Sand*. New York: W. W. Norton, 1980.

Fahmy, Ismail. *Negotiating for Peace in the Middle East*. Baltimore: Johns Hopkins University Press, 1983.

Fanon, Frantz. *The Wretched of the Earth*. New York: Grove Press, 1979.

Gabriel, Richard. *Operation Peace for Galilee*. New York: Hill and Wang, 1984.

Golan, Matti. *The Secret Conversations of Henry Kissinger*. New York: Bantam Books, 1976.

Hadawi, Sami. *Bitter Harvest*. Delmar, N.Y.: Caravan Books, 1979.

Haddad, Wadi D. *Lebanon*. New York: Praeger, 1985.

Haig, Alexander M. *Caveat*. New York: Macmillan, 1984.

Halsell, Grace. *Journey to Jerusalem*. New York: Macmillan, 1981.

Hart, Alan. *Arafat*. London: Sidgwick & Jackson, 1985.

Hecht, Ben. *A Guide for the Bedevilled*. New York: Charles Scribner's Sons, 1944.

Heikal, Mohamed. *Autumn of Fury*. New York: Random House, 1983.

———. *The Road to Ramadan*. New York: Quadrangle Books, 1975.

Herzl, Theodor. *The Jewish State*. London: H. Pordes, 1972.

Herzog, Chaim. *The Arab-Israeli Wars*. New York: Random House, Vintage Books, 1984.

Hirst, David. *The Gun and the Olive Branch*. London: Futura Publications Ltd., 1977.

Horne, Alistair. *A Savage War of Peace: Algeria 1954–1962*. New York: Penguin Books, 1979.

Hussaini, Hatem, ed. *Toward Peace In Palestine*. Washington, D.C.: Palestine Information Office, 1975.

Irani, George E. *The Papacy and the Middle East*. Notre Dame, Ind.: University of Notre Dame Press, 1986.

Israeli, Raphael, ed. *PLO in Lebanon: Selected Documents*. London: Weidenfeld & Nicolson, 1983.

Iyad, Abu. *My Home, My Land*. New York: Times Books, 1981.

Jabotinsky, Vladimir. *A Pocket Edition of Several Stories Mostly Reactionary*. Tel Aviv: Jabotinsky Institute in Israel, 1984.

Jansen, Michael. *The Battle of Beirut*. Boston: South End Press, 1983.

Joumblatt, Kamal. *I Speak for Lebanon*. London: Zed Press, 1982.

Jureidini, Paul A., and William E. Hazen. *The Palestinian Movement in Politics*. Lexington, Mass.: D.C. Heath & Co., Lexington Books, 1976.

Kanafani, Ghassan. *Men in the Sun*. Washington, D.C.: Three Continents Press, 1978.

Katz, Shmuel. *The Hollow Peace*. Jerusalem: Dvir and The Jerusalem Post, 1981.

Kepel, Gilles. *Muslim Extremism in Egypt*. Berkeley: University of California Press, 1985.

Khaled, Leila. *My People Shall Live*. Toronto: NC Press, 1973.

Khalidi, Rashid. *Under Siege: PLO Decisionmaking During the 1982 War*. New York: Columbia University Press, 1986.

Kissinger, Henry. *White House Years*. Boston: Little, Brown & Co., 1979.

———. *Years of Upheaval*. Boston: Little, Brown & Co., 1982.

Knightley, Philip, and Colin Simpson. *The Secret Lives of Lawrence of Arabia*. New York: McGraw-Hill, 1970.

Laffin, John. *The Dagger of Islam*. London: Sphere Books Ltd., 1979.

Laqueur, Walter, and Barry Rubin, eds. *The Israel-Arab Reader*. New York: Penguin Books, 1984.

Lewis, Bernard. *Semites and Anti-Semites*. New York: W. W. Norton, 1986.

Lilienthal, Alfred. *The Zionist Connection II: What Price Peace?* New Brunswick, N.J.: North American, 1982.

Lotz, Wolfgang. *The Champagne Spy*. London: Vallentine, Mitchell, 1972.

Lumer, Hyman, ed. *Lenin on the Jewish Question*. New York: International Publishers, 1974.

Mackey, Bruce Douglas. ''The Circassians in Jordan.'' Master's Thesis, Naval Postgraduate School, Monterey, Calif., 1979, distributed by University Microfilms International, Ann Arbor, Michigan.

Marighella, Carlos. *Minimanual of the Urban Guerrilla*. Boulder, Colo.: Paladin Press, 1978.

Meir, Golda. *My Life*. New York: Dell, 1975.

Melman, Yossi. *The Master Terrorist*. New York: Adama Books, 1986.

Meyer, Lawrence. *Israel Now*. New York: Delacorte Press, 1982.

Miller, Aaron David. *The PLO and the Politics of Survival*. New York: Praeger, 1983.

Neff, Donald. *Warriors for Jerusalem*. New York: Simon & Schuster, Linden Press, 1984.

Nixon, Richard. *RN*. New York: Grosset and Dunlap, 1978.

Oz, Amos. *In the Land of Israel*. New York: Random House, Vintage Books, 1984.

Pakradouni, Karim. *Stillborn Peace*. Beirut: Fiches du Monde Arabe, 1985.

Parry, Albert, editor. *Terrorism: From Robespierre to Arafat*. New York: Vanguard Press, 1976.

Peres, Shimon. *David's Sling*. London: Weidenfeld & Nicolson, 1970.

Plume, Christian, and Pierre Demaret. *Target: De Gaulle*. London: Corgi Books, 1976.

Pomeroy, William J. *Guerrilla Warfare and Marxism*. New York: International Publishers, New World Paperbacks, 1968.

Porath, Y. *The Emergence of the Palestinian-Arab National Movement*, Vol. 1, 1918–1929. London: Frank Cass & Co., 1974.

Primakov, Y. M. *Anatomy of the Middle East Conflict*. Moscow: Nauka Publishing House, 1979.

al Qathafi, Muammar. *The Green Book*. Tripoli: Public Establishment for Publishing, Advertising and Distribution, n.d.

Quandt, William B. *Camp David*. Washington D.C.: The Brookings Institution, 1985.

The Quest for Peace. U.S. Government Printing Office: Department of State Publication 9373, 1984.

Rabinovich, Itamar. *The War For Lebanon*. Ithaca, N.Y.: Cornell University Press, 1985.

Randall, Jonathan. *Going All The Way: Christian Warlords, Israeli Adventurers, and the War in Lebanon*. New York: Random House, Vintage Books, 1984.

el-Rayyes, Riad, and Dunia Nahas. *Guerrillas for Palestine*. New York: St. Martin's Press, 1976.

Rokach, Livia. *Israel's Sacred Terrorism*. Belmont, Mass: Assn. Arab-American Univ. Grads. (AAUG), 1980.

Ryan, Sheila, and Muhammad Hallaj. *Palestine Is, But Not in Jordan*. Belmont, Mass.: AAUG, 1983.

Saba, Michael. *The Armageddon Network*. Brattleboro, Vermont: Amana Books, 1984.

el-Sadat, Anwar. *In Search of Identity: An Autobiography*. New York: Harper & Row, 1979.

———. *Those I Have Known*. New York: Continuum Publishing Co., 1984.

Said, Edward W. *Covering Islam*. New York: Random House, Pantheon Books, 1981.

Sanders, Ronald. *The High Walls Of Jerusalem*. New York: Holt, Rinehart and Winston, 1983.

Saunders, Harold H. *The Other Walls*. Washington, D.C.: American Enterprise Institute for Public Policy Research, 1985.

Sayigh, Rosemary. *Palestinians: From Peasants to Revolutionaries*. London: Zed Press, 1979.

Schiff, Zeev, and Ehud Yaarri. *Israel's Lebanon War*. New York: Simon & Schuster, 1984.

Schiff, Zeev, and Raphael Rothstein. *Fedayeen*. New York: David McKay Co., 1972.

Schleifer, Abdullah. *The Fall of Jerusalem*. New York: Monthly Review Press, 1972.

Shami, Seteney Khalid. "Ethnicity and Leadership: The Circassians in Jordan." Ph.D. thesis, University of California, Berkeley, 1982, published on demand by University Microfilms International, Ann Arbor, Michigan.

Shavitt, Matti. *On the Wings of Eagles*. Tel Aviv: Olive Books, 1972.

Shurdom, Jamal. *King Hussein and the Palestinians—Jordan's Civil War 1970* (Miami: University of Miami, Graduate School for International Studies, 1978, unpublished).

Silver, Eric. *Begin*. New York: Random House, 1984.

Smith, Colin. *Carlos: Portrait of a Terrorist*. New York: Holt, Rinehart and Winston, 1976.

Snow, Peter. *Hussein*. New York: Robert B. Luce, Inc., 1972.

Spiegel, Steven L. *The Other Arab-Israeli Conflict*. Chicago: The University of Chicago Press, 1985.

Sterling, Claire. *The Terror Network*. New York: Holt, Rinehart and Winston, 1981.

Stetler, Russell, ed. *Palestine—The Arab-Israeli Conflict*. San Francisco: Ramparts Press, 1972.

Steven, Stewart. *The Spymasters of Israel*. New York: Macmillan, 1980.

Tawil, Raymonda Hawa. *My Home, My Prison*. New York: Holt, Rinehart and Winston, 1979.

Teveth, Shabtai. *Ben-Gurion and the Palestinian Arabs*. Oxford: Oxford University Press, 1985.

Timerman, Jacobo. *The Longest War*. New York: Alfred A. Knopf, 1982.

Tinnin, David. *Hit Team*. London: Futura Publications Ltd., 1976.

Turki, Fawaz. *The Disinherited*. New York: Monthly Review Press, 1974.

———. *Tel Zaatar Was the Hill of Thyme*. Washington, D.C.: Palestine Review Press, 1981.

Turner, Stansfield. *Secrecy and Democracy*. New York: Harper & Row, 1985.

Vocke, Harold. *The Lebanese War*. New York: St. Martin's Press, 1978.

Walters, Vernon A. *Silent Missions*. New York: Doubleday & Co., 1978.

Weizman, Ezer. *The Battle for Peace*. New York: Bantam Books, 1981.

Yaroslavtsev, Igor. *Zionism Stands Accused*. Moscow: Progress Publishers, 1985.

Yodfat, Aryeh, and Yuval Arnon-Ohanna. *PLO Strategy and Tactics*. London: Croom Helm, 1981.

Articles and Transcripts

Allen, Richard. "Qaddafi: Can He Be Neutralized?" Interviewed by Ted Koppel on ABC News *Nightline*. Transcript: Show 912, 20 November 1984. Washington, D.C.; American Broadcasting Co., 1984.

Armitage, Richard L. "The Strategic Value of Arming Hussein." *The New York Times*, 2 October 1985.

Arms Sales. AEI Forum 56, 9 September 1981. Washington D.C.: American Enterprise Institute, 1982.

Aulas, Marie-Christine. "Sadat's Egypt: A Balance Sheet." *MERIP Reports* 12, no. 6 (July–August 1982).

Eppel, Dov. "Arab League Fiasco." *New Outlook* (April 1960).

Fallaci, Oriana. "'We Want a War Like the Vietnam War'—Interview with George Habash." *Life*, 12 June 1970.

Fletcher, Elaine Ruth. "The Circassians: a cohesive, loyal community." *The Jerusalem Post International Edition*, 23 May 1987.

Franklin, Shai. "Keeping the Balance." *Near East Report* (Washington, D.C.) 31, no. 26 (29 June 1987): 104.

Gemayel, Bashir. A live broadcast in Arabic by the Beirut Voice of Lebanon. Antilyas, Lebanon; 29 November 1981, monitored and translated by the *U.S. National Technical Information Service*, Middle East and North Africa Daily Report, 30 November 1981.

Goodman, Hirsh. "Hussein's Predicament." *The New Republic*, 26 August 1985.

Goodman, Hirsh. "The Shorter Wick." *The New Republic*, 18 November 1985.

el-Guindi, Fadwa. "The Killing of Sadat and After, a Current Assessment of Egypt's Islamic Movement." *Middle East Insight*. (Washington, D.C.) 2, no. 5 (January / February 1983).

Harris, Lillian Craig. "China's Relations With The PLO." *Journal of Palestine Studies* (Autumn 1977).

Hersh, Seymour M. "Target Qaddafi." *The New York Times Magazine*, 22 February 1987.

Hussaini, Hatem. "PLO Future—Saudi-Syrian Plan." Interviewed by Sam Donaldson on ABC News *Nightline*. Transcript: Show 312, 20 July 1982. Washington, D.C.: American Broadcasting Co., 1982.

Ibrahim, Saad Eddin. "Egypt's Islamic Militants." *MERIP Reports* 12, no. 2 (February 1982)

Jombolet. "The Legend of Caucasus." *Circassian Star* 3, no. 5 (1980) 38–39.

Karpat, K. H. "Ottoman Immigration, Politics and Settlement in Palestine." In Abu-Lughod, I., and B. Abu-Laban, *Settler Regimes in Africa and the Arab World*. Wilmette, Illinois; The Medina University Press International, 1972.

Kelman, Herbert C. "Overcoming the Psychological Barrier: An Analysis of the Egyptian-Israeli Peace Process." In Huntington, Samuel P., and Joseph S. Nye, eds., *Global Dilemmas*. Cambridge: Harvard University Center for International Affairs, 1985.

Kelman, Herbert C. "Talk With Arafat." *Foreign Policy* 49 (Winter 1982–83).

Kennedy, Senator Edward M. Press release—address before the American Lebanese League. Arlington, Virginia; 19 June 1981.

Kimche, Jon. "Algiers: PLO's Road to Ruin." *The Jerusaelm Post International Edition*, 4 July 1987, 15.

Klein, Yossi. "Journeys into the New Israel." *The Village Voice* 27, no. 43 (26 October 1982).

Lewis, Samuel W. "Israel: The Peres Era And Its Legacy," *Foreign Affairs* 65, no. 3. (1986).

Moorer, Thomas H. Admiral, U.S. Navy (Ret.). Quoted in Ennes, James M., *Assault on The Liberty*. New York: Random House, 1979.

Natho, Kadir I. Comments on the Thesis "The Circassians In Jordan." 1980. Forwarded to the author by Bruce Mackey in a letter dated 30 August 1985.

———. "Editor's Note." *Circassian Star* 3, no. 5 (1980) 7–8.

Palestine Refugees Today. "The Camps." No. 112 (October 1985).

Perlmutter, Amos. "Unilateral Withdrawal: Israel's Security Option." *Foreign Affairs* 64, no. 1 (Fall 1985).

Possony, Stefan T., and Francis L. Bouchey. "Moscow's Support of International Terrorism." *The Ukrainian Quarterly* 34, no. 4 (Winter 1978).

Report of the DOD Commission on Beirut International Airport Terrorist Act, October 23, 1983. Washington, D.C.; U.S. Government Printing Office, 1984.

Riebenfeld, Paul. "The Integrity of Palestine." *Midstream* (August–September 1975).

Roelofsma, Derk Kinnane. "Hafez al-Assad: Lion of Syria." *Insight* (23 September 1985).

Saunders, Harold. "Interview With Harold Saunders." *American-Arab Affairs*, nos. 15, 16 (Winter 1985–86).

Schiff, Zeev. "The Green Light." *Foreign Policy*, no. 50. (Spring 1983).

Shultz, George P. *Terrorism: The Challenge to the Democracies*. Washington, D.C.; Jonathan Institute, 24 June 1984. Address delivered to the Jonathan Institute's Second Conference on Terrorism.

Shurdom, Jamal A. *What About Circassians' Human Rights* and *An Open Letter to the Circassian People*. Paramus, N.J. Dr. Jamal A. Shurdom—Fulbright Scholar-in-Residence at the Bergen Community College Center for International Studies, Professor, University of Jordan, Amman, 1986.

Sicherman, Harvey. "Europe's Role in the Middle East." *ORBIS* (Winter 1985).

Sirhan, Bassam. "Palestinian Refugee Camp Life in Lebanon." *Journal of Palestine Studies* (Winter 1975).

The Commission of Inquiry into the Events at the Refugee Camps in Beirut. Authorized translation. Israeli Government publication, 1983.

Tlas, Mustafa. *The Matzoh of Zion.* Translated excerpts. Los Angeles: Simon Wiesenthal Center, 1986.

UNRWA: A Survey of United Nations Assistance to Palestine Refugees. New York: United Nations, 1972.

U.S. Congress. House. Committee on Foreign Affairs. Hearings on the Foreign Policy Implications of Arms Sales to Iran and the Contra Connection. 99th Cong., 2d sess., 1986.

U.S. Congress. Senate. Subcommittee on Foreign Relations of Senate Appropriations Committee. Report prepared by Robert A. Basil. 5 May 1986.

Weightman, George. "The Circassians." *Middle East Forum* 37, no. 10. (December 1961).

Weymouth, Lally. "Israel's Dilemma." *The New Republic*, 26 August 1985.

Zak, Moshe. "Israeli-Jordanian Negotiations." *The Washington Quarterly* (Winter 1985).

Zion, Sidney, and Uri Dan. "The Untold Story of the Mideast Talks." *The New York Times Magazine*, 21 January 1979.

Newspapers, Magazines, Journals, Reference Books, Newsletters, and Pamphlets

Action and Reaction. Weekly newspaper on Arab affairs. (New York) 1981–82.

Arab Report and Record. (London) 1972, 1974.

Beirut Times. Newspaper issued three times a month. (Los Angeles) 1986–87.

CounterSpy. (Washington, D.C.) 1980–82.

Events. Magazine on Middle Eastern affairs. (Beirut) 1977.

Foreign Intelligence Literary Scene. (Washington, D.C.) 1982–86.

Health for Palestine Refugees. UNRWA (United Nations Relief and Works Agency) Report. Beirut: United Nations, 1972.

International Documents on Palestine. Beirut: Institute for Palestine Studies, 1970 and Washington D.C.: Institute for Palestine Studies Research and Document Staff, 1981.

Israel and Palestine. (Paris) 1981–86.

Jewish Frontier. (New York) 1982.

Lebanon News. (Washington, D.C.) 1981–1982.

The Link. Newsletter on Middle Eastern affairs. (New York) 1981–86.

MERIP Reports. (Washington, D.C.) 1982–86.

Middle East Perspective. (Washington, D.C.) 1981–85.

Near East Report. (Washington, D.C.) 1982–87.

New Outlook. (Tel Aviv) 1982–86.

The Other Israel. (Tel Aviv) 1983–86.

Palestine (also issued under *Palestine Perspectives*). (Washington, D.C.) 1980–87.

PFLP Bulletin. (Beirut and Damscus) 1979–83.

Policy Focus. (Washington, D.C.) 1986–87.

Security Affairs. (Washington, D.C.) 1985–86.

Index

ISRAEL UNDERCOVER

was composed in 10 on 12 Times Roman on a Linotron 202
by E/F Typographic Lab;
printed by sheet-fed offset on 50-pound, acid-free Booktext Natural,
Smyth sewn and bound over 88-point binder's boards in Joanna Arrestox B,
with dust jackets printed in two colors
by BookCrafters;
designed by Will Underwood;
and published by

SYRACUSE UNIVERSITY PRESS
SYRACUSE, NEW YORK 13244-5160